Sustainability for a Warming Planet

SUSTAINABILITY
for a WARMING PLANET

Humberto **Llavador**

John E. **Roemer**

Joaquim **Silvestre**

Harvard University Press

Cambridge, Massachusetts
London, England
2015

Printed in the United States of America
First printing

Library of Congress Cataloging-in-Publication Data

Llavador, Humberto.
Sustainability for a warming planet / Humberto Llavador, John E. Roemer, and Joaquim Silvestre.
pages cm
Includes bibliographical references and index.
ISBN 978-0-674-74409-7 (hardcover : alk. paper) 1. Climate change mitigation. 2. Greenhouse gas mitigation. 3. Carbon sequestration. I. Roemer, John E. II. Silvestre, Joaquim. III. Title.
QC903.L53 2015
363.738'747—dc23 2014041195

for Pau
for Sara and Andrea
for Jordi
and their generation

Contents

Preface

We began work on the questions we address in this book when all three authors were at the University of California, Davis, before the year 2000. Thus, the gestation period for this work has been a long one. Indeed, when we began working on these issues, we did not conceive of the negative environmental externality produced by economic activity as global warming but as other kinds of environmental degradation. This is somewhat embarrassing to report, but it also indicates how the consciousness of climate change has grown in the economics profession over the past fifteen years. Indeed, it was Gus Speth, then dean of the School of Forestry at Yale University, who encouraged us to change our focus to climate change. Although we probably would have caught on eventually, we are grateful to Gus for his intervention.

This brief biography also shows how prescient William Nordhaus was, to begin working on climate change over three decades ago. It was not until 1988 that James Hansen published the critical paper (Hansen et al. 1988) establishing that global warming, not cooling, was the important trend, yet Nordhaus (1976) wrote a paper on carbon dioxide and climate change a decade earlier. We recount this fact because, as the reader will see, we have disagreements with Nordhaus's analysis. We wish, however, to put these into perspective. Our disagreements with him are of the second order: of the first order, we are deep appreciators of his work, which has done more than that of any other economist to bring the challenge of climate change into the arena of public debate.

There are many others whom we wish to thank for their advice and help. Gavin Schmidt of the Goddard Space Institute, at Columbia University, explained some of the science of climate change to us. That having been said, we do not discuss that science in this book, but take it off the shelf as needed. We have made no contributions to this area and shall not pretend to have done so: readers wishing to learn the science should do so from authoritative sources. We learned techniques from Herbert Scarf for solving infinite-dimensional optimization problems that we have used throughout the book. We also consulted Roger Howe about mathematical issues upon occasion. We had fruitful discussions with Donald Brown and Larry Samuelson about mathematical issues as well. Larry Karp read an earlier version of Chapter 6 and alerted us to what turned out to be a serious mistake. Petr Gocev prevented us from misconstruing a quotation from Henry Sidgwick, and Roberto Veneziani read earlier versions of Chapters 1 and 2 and provided valuable comments. Two referees for Harvard University Press provided helpful comments and suggestions. We would also like to thank the many people who provided research assistantship over the years, in particular Luca Gambetti, Michael Schreibweis, Gabriel Zucker, Pablo Fleiss, Zeynep Uyar, and Thomas Stoerk.

We have presented parts of this work at conferences and seminars over the years, in North America, Latin America, Europe, and Asia; we did not keep notes on those events and must simply thank those who gave us suggestions and comments in a collective and anonymous way. One of those comments, however, stands out, and that was Klaus Nehring's suggestion for generalizing the 'sustainabilitarian' objective function in a way that injects a concern with the length of lifetime of the human species. This turns out to be an essential idea in Chapter 6. Robert Keohane added a useful idea at a seminar, for which he is acknowledged in Chapter 5.

Some of the material in this book has been informed by earlier discussions presented in the following publications:

H. Llavador, J. Roemer, and J. Silvestre. 2010. "Intergenerational justice when future worlds are uncertain." *Journal of Mathematical Economics* 46: 728–761.

———. 2011. "A dynamic analysis of human welfare in a warming planet." *Journal of Public Economics* 95: 1607–1620.

———. 2013. "Should we sustain? And if so, sustain what? Consumption or the quality of life?" in R. Fouquet, *Handbook of Energy and Climate Change*, Cheltenham UK: Edward Elgar.

———. 2014. "North-South convergence and the allocation of CO_2 emissions." *Climatic Change*. DOI: 10.1007/s10584-014-1227-8.

J. Roemer. 2011. "The ethics of intergenerational distribution in a warming planet." *Environmental and Resource Economics* 48: 363–390.

Sustainability for a Warming Planet

Introduction

Perhaps the single word that best summarizes the ethos of those who are concerned with climate change and its effects, instigated by carbon emissions since the advent of the Industrial Revolution, is sustainability. It is therefore remarkable that sustainability appears to be of tangential concern in some of the most prominent work of economists who have concerned themselves with this "greatest of all externalities," in the words of the *Stern Review* (Stern 2007), that is, with man-made global warming. The word does not appear in the index of either *A Question of Balance* (2008) or *The Climate Casino* (2013), the most recent books by William Nordhaus, one of the most prominent economists who study global warming. *The Economics of Climate Change: The Stern Review* does refer to sustainability, but this is perhaps an exception. There is an older tradition in economic theory concerned with sustainability: notably, Solow (1974, 1993) proposed what can be thought of as the intellectual ancestor of this book. We will try to explain this disjuncture between the common (although not universal) practice of economists and popular expression and concern.

Solow (1993, 168) proposed a conception of sustainability and linked it to an ethical view. He wrote, "I will assume that a sustainable path for the national economy is one that allows every future generation the option of being as well off as its predecessors. The duty imposed by sustainability is to bequeath to posterity not any particular thing . . . but rather to endow them with whatever it takes to achieve a standard of living at least as good as our own and to look after their next generation similarly."

Two points in this quotation are noteworthy: first, Solow's concern is with sustaining a standard of living, not particular physical or natural assets; second, the conception is unidirectional in time, in that it is said that we must guarantee to future generations at least as good a living standard as we have. We follow Solow regarding the first point, but we extend his unidirectionality with respect to time into bidirectionality. We add that we, the present generation, also have a *right* to be as well off as future generations. Does this view preclude economic growth? We will argue that it does not.

Our attempt, in this book, is to bridge the gap between the concerns of billions of people to put our species' behavior on a sustainable path and economic theory. We propose a formal definition and economic model of sustainability and compute what sustainable paths of economic activity look like. We attempt to answer the questions: Is it possible to sustain human life indefinitely at a *decent* quality level, which means, among other things, limiting carbon emissions so as to control global temperature and climate? Is it possible to do so and to allow the developing world to reach the income levels of the rich world? If so, how would we have to change our economic practices in order to carry out an optimal plan? How much growth would have to be sacrificed?

We define several versions of sustainability in our study. None of them, perhaps, is as radical as the version many environmentalists would advocate—what's called strong sustainability, which means to preserve the flora and fauna of the earth, just as they are, or would be, without human interference. Our approach is anthropocentric and follows Solow: we define a *purely sustainable practice* as one that will maintain human welfare, of all generations now and into the indefinite future, at the highest possible base level or greater, as far as we can tell. We attempt to compute what that base level would be, on the path that maximizes it, subject to many assumptions about how the economy works—in particular, how technological change will respond to investments we make in knowledge creation and how the skills of workers will respond to education.

Pure sustainability, as some readers will recognize, can be phrased in a way that is familiar to those who are acquainted with John Rawls's theory of justice. It requires us to find the path that maximizes the welfare level that can be enjoyed by all generations into the future. In particular, it maximizes the welfare of the least well-off generation. (We abstract, initially, from differences of welfare *within* a generation of people and consider only the average welfare level of each generation in order to focus attention on the problem of *intergenerational equity*. Later, in Chapter 5, we introduce a concern for welfare differences across regions of the world at each generation.) It will transpire that the optimal sustainable path—the one that *guarantees* to all generations who live the highest possible level of welfare—actually *equalizes* the levels of welfare that each generation will experience. No generation would have a welfare level higher than any other in the problem's solution! There would be, on this path, no economic growth, where that growth is conceived of as a growth in welfare over time.

This fact may strike some—or many—as undesirable, perhaps sufficiently so to recommend scuttling this approach to sustainability. It is therefore important to explain why this 'no growth' result occurs. In our model of economic activity, there are a number of ways (four, to be precise) that each generation passes down important resources to the next generation: the education of its children; investment in research and knowledge, which lasts into the next generation; preservation of the biosphere; and investment to replace depreciated capital stock and perhaps augment it. These four activities all require sacrifices by early generations for later ones. Let us imagine, to keep the story simple, that there are only two generations: the first generation contains adults and children, and the second generation contains just adults who matured from those children. Suppose we want to maximize the level of welfare that both generations (of adults) can enjoy, and suppose the solution to the problem were one in which the welfare of Generation 2, u_2, were greater than u_1. So, the largest level of welfare that could be guaranteed to both generations is, by hypothesis, u_1. Now this can't be the correct solution: for have the first generation pass down fewer resources (say, by educating its youth a little less) and keep those resources for itself (adults in Generation 1 teach less and instead manufacture more consumer goods for themselves). This will increase u_1 a little bit and reduce u_2 a little bit, showing that the original solution did not, indeed, maximize the level of welfare that could be guaranteed to all generations. It is this argument, in the much more complicated model that we construct, that shows that on the optimal pure-sustainable path, all generations must enjoy the same level of welfare.

Indeed, we say that each generation has a *right* to insist that this 'maximin' path be chosen. Why? Because we view the date at which a person is born to be a matter of luck—a circumstance beyond his or her control—and we think it is *wrong* that persons be forced to bear the consequences of unchosen luck, if that can be avoided. John Rawls gave exactly this motivation for supporting his 'difference principle': that, in his words, circumstances that are *morally arbitrary* should not affect the conditions of persons. In Rawlsian parlance, we would say that the date at which a person is born is morally arbitrary, and this means that concerns of intergenerational equity require that human society set itself the task of guaranteeing to all who ever live the highest possible level of welfare that can be so guaranteed. At least, this is the *first step* in our argument.

There is, however, a catch. Persons do not have to enforce their rights. They may choose not to enforce this particular right if, for example, they would *prefer* that those who populate future generations be better off than they. We believe that this preference is, indeed, held by most people. Not only would most of us like our children to be better off than we are, but that kind of altruism toward future beings extends beyond our own line of descendants. Perhaps this is because we value human development as a good: we see how much better our lives are than those who lived in the past, and we are willing to sacrifice, up to a point, so that those who live in the future can be better off than we are. Perhaps we desire that humans accomplish great things—learn about the origin of the universe, find a cure for cancer—and these discoveries can only happen if we educate future generations more than we were educated. We do not attempt to test this conjecture but assume that it is so. This motivates our second definition of sustainability, which is to *sustain growth*. Growth sustainability (say, at 25% per generation) means to find that path of economic activity that maximizes the welfare of the present generation, subject to guaranteeing that welfare grows at least at 25% per generation, forever after.

But how do we find the right growth rate? Is it 25% or 50%? According to what we've said, this depends on how much each generation *would like* to sacrifice to enable future humans to enjoy greater welfare than they. We do not try to answer this empirical question, but what we do is compute paths of sustainable growth for several (we think reasonable) growth rates. For instance, a growth rate of welfare of 1% per annum means a growth rate of welfare between generations, each of which is postulated to be active for twenty-five years in our model, of 28.2%, while a growth rate of 2% per annum engenders a generational growth rate of 64.1%.

Pure sustainability and growth sustainability are the main, but not the only, concepts that we employ in this book. Suppose that we calculate the optimal path that sustains a 28.2% generational growth in welfare, forever. Clearly, the first generation will be worse off than it would have been on the pure-sustainable path (where the growth rate of welfare is 0% per generation) because it must invest a little more and consume a little less than it would on the pure-sustainable path. How much worse off would its members be? Very little, it turns out: the sacrifice in welfare that the first generation must sustain in order to potentiate welfare growth of 28.2% per generation forever is less than 1% of its welfare on the pure-sustainable path (see Chapter 3). Indeed, all generations except the first one turn out to be better off on the 28.2% growth path than on the pure-sustainable path. (In other words, only the first generation has to 'sacrifice,' compared to the benchmark of pure sustainability, to guarantee 1% per annum growth indefinitely.) However, at each date the current generation would be better off still if it were to enforce its right to insist on the pure-sustainable path *from that date onward*. We are, however, assuming that *each* generation desires to render future generations better off than they and so the growth path will be voluntarily sustained indefinitely.

How do we measure welfare? We take human welfare, or utility, to be a function of four inputs: material consumption; leisure time multiplied by a factor reflecting one's educational level; the stock of human knowledge, to date; and the quality of the biosphere, which is postulated to decrease as the atmospheric carbon concentration increases. The first two inputs are private goods, and the last two are public goods. We break with economic tradition in two ways: in valuing a person's leisure time by his or her educational level and in including the stock of human knowledge in the utility function. We believe that education increases the diversity of uses of leisure time, and the ability to do many different things with one's leisure increases welfare. We resist the neoclassical tradition in economic theory of viewing education as simply instrumental, as a means to increase future earning power. Likewise, neoclassical economics treats knowledge creation as an activity that is undertaken by a society to increase material wealth and welfare. But this is clearly not the entire story: much of our social investment in the creation of new knowledge (as opposed to educating young people about existing knowledge) is motivated by our *desire to know*. (Think of the $5 billion Hadron collider at the European Organization for Nuclear Research [CERN]. It would be provincial to attempt to justify this investment only on the basis of future inventions that small-particle physics will engender.) This applies not only to the arts and literature, which clearly elevate the human condition, but to mathematics and science as well.

Our utility function, however, does not include a concern for future generations—which, as we've said, we also believe people have. So, it's not intended to capture everything about what's valuable to people but rather what we might call their personal condition, their self-interested welfare. It is a version of the standard of living to which Solow refers. We attempt to address the altruism that people direct to future generations through the concept of growth sustainability, as we explained above.

What we've described so far is how we define sustainability in a model with certainty. However, uncertainty is an essential part of the climate-change problem; we will describe how we modify the model to include uncertainty.

Having explained, briefly, our ethics and the economic approach it leads to, we now briefly explain what most economists who study climate change do. They do not study paths of economic activity that sustain human welfare in either of the two senses that we have defined. Instead, they compute paths that maximize a weighted *sum* of generational utilities, into the distant future, where the weight put on the utility of each future generation declines geometrically (i.e., by a fixed factor at each generation). This is called a *discounted-utilitarian objective*.

There are a number of possible justifications for being interested in the path of economic activity that maximizes a discounted sum of generational utilities, as we explain in Chapter 1. The main ones are the following: Until John Rawls's work, utilitarianism—the view that justice consists in maximizing the sum of utilities of all people in society—was the ruling philosophical view, developed by Jeremy Bentham, John Stuart Mill, and

Henry Sidgwick, among other philosophers in the nineteenth century. Applied to a society that lives over many generations, utilitarianism would say to maximize the sum of utilities of all generations. Let us, for the moment, assume that the horizon is finite—we are concerned with the next five hundred generations only—and that the population is of unchanging size over time. Then the unvarnished utilitarian would seek the path of resource allocation that maximizes the total utility that these five hundred generations enjoy. The major criticism of utilitarianism, leveled not only by Rawls but many others, is that it is indifferent to interpersonal (in this case, intergenerational) inequality. Its sole concern is to maximize the *total* utility experienced, and the allocation of that utility among the generations is entirely subservient to this end. With a two-generation society, a utility profile of (99, 1) would be preferred to a profile of (49, 49), because 100 is bigger than 98.

One might be tempted to respond to this example with the claim that humans exhibit diminishing marginal utility (in resource consumption). But by hypothesis, the numbers given in the above example are *utilities*, not *resource levels*. *Whatever* resource levels give rise to these two possible utility distributions, as long as they are both feasible, are irrelevant: the utilitarian must prefer a utility distribution of (99, 1) to one of (49, 49).

One might also be tempted to respond to this example by saying that each generation should be assumed to have the same utility function (i.e., the same technique for converting resources into welfare). A 'utility monster' is an individual who converts resources into utility especially effectively and so a utilitarian must assign to her the lion's share of resources. However, even if we assume that every generation possesses the same utility function, the problem of the utility monster can arise easily in an intertemporal context because of technological change. Let's assume that technological change occurs over time, as indeed it has since the Industrial Revolution. Then to maximize total utility over five hundred generations, it might be that we should devote a lot of resources to technological innovation in the early generations, leaving these folks very little to consume, so that later generations have a wonderful level of technology, which can convert resources very efficiently into human welfare. Even though every generation may have the same utility function over consumption goods, resources will be able to produce consumption goods in much greater abundance in the future, because of technological innovation, than at present. Technological change makes later generations into utility monsters.[1]

To deal with this problem (and another one, discussed next), one can *discount* the utility of future generations—that is, make it count for less, the farther out in time it is experienced. It should be clear this is an *ad hoc* solution to the problem. In particular, one would have to tailor the discount factor to the rate of technological change. There is no clear, general, ethical instruction as to what it should be. Of course, if technological change is endogenous (as it is in reality—i.e., the investment in research and development is part of the optimization problem), the choice of discount rate is even murkier. The problem is with utilitarianism, and that is addressed by recognizing it as a poor ethical doctrine, especially in situations in which utility monsters can occur, as with intertemporal optimization and technological change.

There is a second problem with utilitarianism in intertemporal economic analysis. Now, however, we assume an infinite time horizon: although humans will eventually disappear, we do not know when this will occur; therefore, there is a strong argument for postulating a possibly infinite time horizon. (We do this throughout the book.) Again, technological progress generates a problem but now of a different sort. It turns out that in most economic models there are many paths (which extend into the infinite future) upon which total utility is *infinite*. Utilitarianism does not tell us how to choose among these. There are two ways of escaping this problem. The first way recognizes that the human species will not exist forever. Suppose we model this by saying that there is a fixed probability π that each generation, conditional upon its coming into being, will be the last one. We call this probability the (*generational*) *hazard rate*. If there is a utilitarian social planner or an Ethical Observer who wishes to maximize the sum of utilities of all those generations that, in the event, exist, subject to the stochastic process described, it turns out that it (or he or she) should maximize the discounted sum of generational utilities (over an infinite

[1] It is not that the individual who converts resources very efficiently into welfare is a monster *per se*: it is that following a utilitarian ethic converts this person into a monster who monopolizes the resource endowment.

future span) where the utility of Generation t is discounted (or multiplied) by the factor $(1-\pi)^{t-1}$. (See Section 1.2.2, third justification.) This is the first escape from the problem of infinite sums. If the factor $1-\pi$ is small enough, then the problem of maximizing the infinite *discounted* sum of utilities, over time, will have a unique, finite solution.

The second way of evading the problem of divergent total utility is to make an analogy with *individual* utility. It is not unreasonable to model a *person's* utility as the discounted sum of his annual utilities over his lifetime. Why might a person discount his future utilities? Because of impatience. From *today's viewpoint*, a 'util' today is more valuable than a util experienced in ten years' time—perhaps because of impatience or a 'defective telescopic faculty' or perhaps, entirely legitimately, because there is a chance the individual may not be around in ten years and so he rationally discounts that future utility. Now some economists move—we think inexcusably—from the reasonable model of a person as someone who maximizes the discounted sum of his or her utilities over periods of life to the unreasonable conclusion that society should maximize the discounted sum of utilities of future generations—as if those generations were simply phases of the life of one infinitely lived being. This is the second way of 'justifying' an intergenerational ethic that maximizes the discounted sum of generational utilities.

While the first solution to the problem of the infinitude of the utilitarian sum descends from the philosophical view of utilitarianism, augmented with the uncertainty represented by the hazard rate, the second derives from an analogy between a human species living for many generations and an 'infinitely lived consumer.' The first solution is the one taken in the *Stern Review;* the second is, essentially, that one taken by William Nordhaus. Stern and Nordhaus have sharp differences in approach, which follow from the different justifications they employ for the 'discounted-utilitarian' approach. We discuss these in detail in Chapters 1 and 4. Essentially, in terms of the mathematics, their different justifications lead to employing different discount factors to apply to the utility of future generations. Stern's discount factor is a version of the '$1-\pi$' that we have described above, and Nordhaus calibrates his discount factor to the rate of impatience of present-day consumers, as estimated from observed market interest rates. Stern's discount factor—the number by which he multiplies the utility of the tth generation—is larger than Nordhaus's, which means he gives more weight to future generations in his objective function than does Nordhaus.

We, however, disagree with both of these justifications for taking the objective to be a discounted-utilitarian one: with Stern because we are not utilitarians (we are *sustainabilitarians*) and with Nordhaus because we reject the analogy between an impatient infinitely lived consumer and an indefinitely long sequence of generations of a human society. In particular, Stern's approach is still vulnerable to the 'utility monster' problem because he chooses a discount factor close to one. We present our opposition to utilitarianism as a good theory of intergenerational justice in Chapter 1.

It may seem surprising that *so many* economists who work on climate change use the discounted-utilitarian model: and indeed, probably most of them follow Nordhaus's lead rather than Stern's. We give citations in Chapter 1 that demonstrate that the justifications for doing so are as lacking in philosophical substance as we have just indicated.

In sum, there are essentially three reasons for adopting a discounted sum of generational utilities as the social objective function:

(1) Because future generations will be better off than we are, we should penalize them by discounting their utility in the social objective.
(2) If the Ethical Observer is a utilitarian but understands that the number of generations that exist is a stochastic event, then she should discount future utilities by a discount factor related to the probability of extinction.
(3) Since many consumers discount their own future utilities due to impatience, it is therefore rational that society should discount the utilities of those who exist later in time.

We reject (1) as entirely *ad hoc* and (3) because the analogy between the consumer who lives many years and a society of different generations does not hold water. We find (2) to be philosophically consistent, but we reject it because we reject utilitarianism as a philosophy due to its indifference toward inequality.

As sustainabilitarians, we also recognize the necessity of discounting because of the uncertainty of the human species' lifetime. But discounting with sustainabilitarianism leads to very different results than with utilitarianism, as the reader will learn.

The core of our analysis, presented in Chapter 3 (the world as a single region) and Chapter 5 (two regions, North and South), involves theory and calibration. It postulates the four above-mentioned intergenerational links (education, knowledge, physical capital, and the quality of the biosphere) and includes the education level and the state of knowledge in a person's quality of life, welfare, or utility function. Our computational approach is inspired by turnpike theory. We prove a turnpike theorem in the simpler, theoretical model of Chapter 2, which has a preliminary character and establishes a link with the familiar Ramsey model, widely used in growth theory. The first-order condition of the Ramsey model (see the Chapter 1 Appendix) yields the Ramsey equation, frequently used by climate-change economists as a calibration tool (Chapter 4).

The traditional Ramsey model has only one intergenerational link (physical capital), whereas our Chapter 2 model adds education. It contains two sectors of production: one sector, to be thought of as manufacturing, produces the only physical 'commodity,' which is used for consumption and investment, and the other sector is education. Manufacturing uses inputs of capital and skilled labor to produce its output, and the education sector uses only the labor of teachers as an input, to produce educated children, who become the next generation's skilled adult workers. As is customary in growth theory, we abstract away from intragenerational issues in that we assume that each generation consists of a single household (one adult, one child). The society's problem, at each date, is to partition the adult's skilled labor endowment among three uses—manufacturing, teaching, and leisure—and to allocate the output of manufacturing between adult consumption and capital investment. (One may either view children as not consuming at all or view the adult's consumption as household consumption. The child's utility, however, is not modeled.) Adults derive utility from two sources: consumption and their educated leisure time. Some may argue that it's a bit inconsistent to value leisure time by one's educational level, since there is no opera or soccer to choose between in this simple world, but all models take shortcuts.

The economy begins, at date zero, with an endowment consisting of adult skilled-teaching labor and a physical capital stock: call these two values x_0^e (for the stock of labor at date zero in the education sector) and S_0^k (for the stock of physical capital at date zero). Given this endowment vector, there is a set of *feasible paths* that specify all the details of economic activity in every generation, forever. Such a path specifies how each generation's adult allocates her time among the three activities (manufacturing, teaching, and leisure) and how it allocates the produced good between immediate consumption and investment to augment the capital stock. Each generation passes on to the next a stock of capital and education, embodied in its (young) adults. In this simple model, there is no knowledge creation, no technological change, no emissions, and no climate change. Nevertheless, the insights we garner from it will apply to the central models, with climate-relevant parts, of Chapters 3 and 5.

Among these paths, the problem is to choose the best sustainable one. In the pure-sustainable variant, optimization means to find the path that maximizes the highest utility that can be guaranteed to every generation. In the growth-sustainable variant, one finds the path that maximizes the first generation's utility, subject to guaranteeing some exogenously specified growth rate of utility per generation, forever.

As we said, in the pure-sustainable variant, on the optimal path, utility is held to a constant for all generations—there is no growth. The first major result is what is called a turnpike theorem, which makes two assertions. First: if the endowment vector (x_0^e, S_0^k) lies on a certain ray in the (x^e, S^k) plane, then the optimal solution to the pure-sustainability problem is a *stationary state*—that is, all economic variables are constant over time. The skill of the labor force is exactly reproduced at every generation, capital is maintained at exactly S_0^k forever, and consumption and the allocation of labor are unchanging over all time. Second: if the endowment vector is not on this special ray, then the optimal solution converges to one of the stationary states. Because, typically, convergence occurs quite rapidly, the turnpike theorem tells us that we get a good picture of what the optimal path of economic activity looks like by understanding what the stationary states look like.[2]

A turnpike theorem also holds for the growth-sustainable variant. There is a ray (which depends on the exogenous growth rate) such that, if the date-zero endowment vector lies on it, then the optimal solution to the problem

[2] Figure 2.1 in Chapter 2 provides an illustration of the turnpike theorem.

is a *balanced growth path*, which means that every economic variable grows at the specified growth rate, forever. If the date-zero endowment vector does not lie on this ray, then the optimal path converges to one of the balanced growth paths.

Let us observe that we can conceptually separate the set of *feasible paths of economic activity* from the *objective function* of the optimization program. For example, the set of feasible paths is the same for both the pure- and growth-sustainable models. It's just that the *optimal* path depends upon the particular objective function chosen. In particular, we can also maximize a discounted-utilitarian objective on the same set of feasible paths of our simple model. We characterize how small the discount factor must be in order for *that* program to have a solution. There turns out to be an exact formula for computing this discount factor, which depends (it so happens) on how productive the educational technology is. We can think of the productivity of the educational technology as being the inverse of the number of hours per year an adult has to spend in educating her child so that the child acquires the same level of skill as she. (There is no genetic variation here between adults and children.) Equivalently, one can think of educational productivity as the student-teacher ratio in a society in which teachers exactly reproduce the skill level of the adult generation in their children. This productivity is represented by the parameter ξ in the model, which, for the US economy, has a value of about 41.[3] It turns out that the discounted-utilitarian program in the simple model converges (i.e., possesses a solution and does not diverge to infinity) exactly when the discount factor is less than $1/\xi$. Suppose we take the discount factor to be $1-\pi$, where π is the per-generation 'hazard rate' of species extinction. Then the discounted-utilitarian objective will diverge when $1-\pi > \frac{1}{\xi} \simeq 0.024$, which means when $\pi < 0.976$. Of course, any reasonable generational hazard rate is far less than 97.6%, and the discounted-utilitarian objective diverges for the model of Chapter 2, given these parameter values.

[3] Roughly speaking, today's cohort of teachers can reproduce their own level of education or skill in today's generation of children with an average class size of forty-one. If class sizes are on average smaller (as they are), then today's teacher cohort will produce children whose average level of skill is greater than that of the adult cohort.

For a while (meaning until Chapter 6), we treat the probability of catastrophe as fixed—some small number, denoted π, that each generation will be the final one, assuming that the species has not already disappeared. This approach to uncertainty is taken, as well, in the *Stern Review*: indeed, Stern takes the catastrophic probability to be 0.1% per annum, which compounds to 2.47% for each twenty-five-year generation ($\pi = 0.0247$). We believe Stern's choice of per annum hazard rate is far too large. The human species has been around for about 100,000 years, or four thousand generations. Suppose the hazard rate has been constant over this period (perhaps until recently). What would that hazard rate have to have been in order that our species should have survived until now with a probability of one-half? It is easy to compute that the generational hazard rate would have been 0.00017 = 0.017%![4] We believe Stern's hazard rate is too large by two orders of magnitude (0.0247/.00017 = 145). If Stern's generational hazard rate of 2.47% were correct, the probability that the human species would have survived four thousand generations is 3.57×10^{-44}—we would not be here today.

Taking the catastrophic probability as exogenous and fixed is a shortcut to a more satisfactory approach, which would model the probability of catastrophe as a function of global emissions that raise carbon concentration, which has climatological consequences that increase the probability that the species will disappear. But endogenizing that probability, as just described, renders the analysis more subtle and will not be attempted until Chapter 6.

Given this uncertainty, with a constant, exogenous hazard rate, what is the appropriate objective to maximize? For a utilitarian or a sustainabilitarian? We return to the Ethical Observer, who represents the intergenerational ethical view. Suppose she is a utilitarian. Then, we say, she wants to maximize the sum of utility levels of all generations that, in the event, exist. The probability that any generation, T, will be the last one, is $\pi(1-\pi)^{T-1}$. Thus, if an infinite path of economic activities is chosen that generates the infinite path of utilities $(u_1, u_2, \ldots.)$, she calculates the *expected value* of her objective function, which is: π times u_1 plus $\pi(1-\pi)$ times $(u_1 + u_2)$ plus

[4] If $(1-\pi)^{4000} = 0.5$, then $\pi = 0.00017$.

$\pi(1-\pi)^2$ times $(u_1+u_2+u_3)$ and so on, forever. The generic element in this sum is the probability that Generation T is the last one multiplied by the total utility experienced in the world in those T generations. This sum can be shown (Section 1.2.2) to equal the usual *discounted-utilitarian sum*, with a discount factor of $1-\pi$: that is, it reduces to the sum $\sum_{t=1}^{\infty}\pi(1-\pi)^{t-1}u_t$. So, as we've noted, for the model of Chapter 2, the discounted utilitarian-objective diverges for any reasonable value of π.

Now suppose the Ethical Observer is a sustainabilitarian. The same reasoning shows that her expected value, on a path, is equal to π times u_1 plus $\pi(1-\pi)$ times the minimum of u_1 and u_2 plus $\pi(1-\pi)^2$ times the minimum of u_1, u_2, and u_3, and so on, forever.

The computation of the optimal solution to the program of the discounting sustainabilitarian might be a difficult undertaking, but we prove a 'simplification theorem,' which asserts the following. If π is sufficiently small, then the solution to the *undiscounted* pure-sustainabilitarian problem is identical to the solution of the *discounted* pure-sustainabilitarian problem. How small does π have to be? Exactly the value for which the *discounted-utilitarian* program just diverges with the discount factor $1-\pi$! Therefore, because we have characterized the exact value of the discount factor that causes the discounted-utilitarian program to diverge, we know how small π has to be for the premise of the simplification theorem to hold. In particular, that premise holds as long as $\pi<0.976$.

The simplification theorem says that, if π is small enough, then the sustainabilitarian *does not have to discount*. This doesn't mean that *conceptually* she does not have to discount—indeed she does, because future generations might not exist, and this must be taken into account. It says, rather, that *computationally*, discounting is not necessary. Discounting turns out not to matter for the result. This is very different from the situation for the utilitarian Ethical Observer, in which discounting is vital—for the optimal solution to the discounted-utilitarian program depends upon the exact value of the discount factor. We attempt to give, in Chapter 2, some intuition for why the simplification theorem holds. The key lies in the high productivity of the education sector—that the adult generation need devote only a very small fraction of its time to reproduce, in its children, the same level of skill as it possesses.

Chapter 3 builds, calibrates, and solves our full intergenerational model, with emissions, climate change, and technological innovation. The economy now has three sectors: manufacturing and education, as in the simple model, and in addition, a knowledge sector, which employs workers to produce knowledge. Knowledge is conceived of as art, literature, science, mathematics, technological innovation, and so on. It is produced, in our actual economy, mainly by researchers in universities and research institutes and in the research divisions of firms. The knowledge and education sectors are different: educators implant existing knowledge in the heads of students, and researchers discover new knowledge but do not teach. (In calibrating the model to actual economies, we must allocate the time of university professors between their research and teaching functions.)

In addition, we now introduce carbon emissions, which are produced by the manufacturing sector. These emissions increase the concentration of carbon in the atmosphere. The concentration of carbon is a public bad, which enters into the economy in two ways. First, it directly diminishes human welfare and second, it enters negatively into the production function of the manufactured commodity. It is harder to produce goods when climate events occur.[5]

Figure I.1 provides a summary of how the economy works. Human welfare now results from five inputs: consumption of commodities, leisure valued at its level of education, the stock of human knowledge, and biospheric quality, which is represented (negatively) by the stock of atmospheric carbon. We have explained above why we consider knowledge a generator of human welfare. There are, as we said, three production sectors. Commodity production now uses as inputs skilled labor, capital, and knowledge, and it is adversely affected by the public bad of carbon concentration. Production produces both emissions and output, an aggregate of all commodities.[6] The knowledge input accounts for technological progress in commodity production. There are now four intergenerational transfers: a stock of capital,

[5] In particular, this may be so for agriculture, although some argue that a moderate increase in global temperature will increase global agricultural production.

[6] Formally, emissions are modeled as a production *input*. The more emissions are allowed, the more of the commodity can be produced, so mathematically, emissions can be viewed as an input in production. Compare with Section 4.3.2.

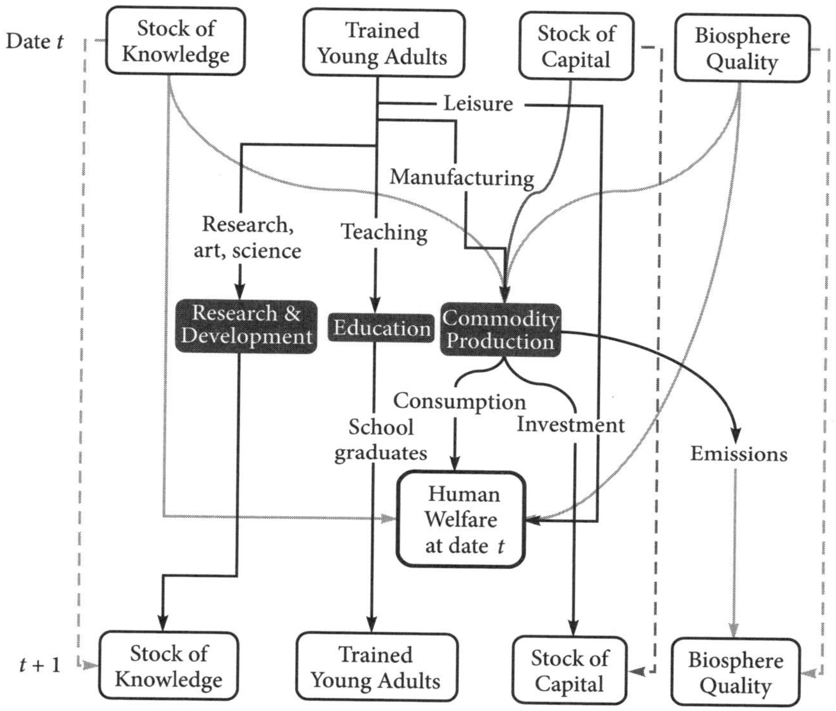

Figure I.1. A flowchart of economic activity from one generation to the next.

skill embodied in young adults, a stock of knowledge, and a stock of biospheric quality (the non-carbon-polluted atmosphere).

The economy begins with a vector of endowments with four components: a stock of capital, educated teachers, a stock of knowledge, and a level of biospheric quality (or, a stock of 'clean' atmosphere). Given these, one can generate the set of feasible paths of economic activity, and along each path, there will be an associated sequence of utilities for all generations.

As before, one can choose a variety of objective functions—in particular, those of pure sustainability, those of growth sustainability, or those of discounted utilitarianism.

We now assume that the main theoretical results concerning the simple model of Chapter 2 are true, as well, of the full models of Chapters 3 and 5. In particular, we assume that turnpike theorems hold. Indeed, we prove the first part of the turnpike theorem for the model of Chapter 3—namely, that if the endowment vector lies on a particular ray in four-space, then the optimal solution to the pure-sustainability program (or growth-sustainability program) is a stationary state (respectively, a balanced growth path). We *assume* that the second part of the turnpike theorem carries over—namely, that if the initial endowment vector does not lie on the ray, then the optimal solution to the program converges to a stationary state (or balanced growth path).

Chapter 3 calibrates the parameters of the model to an actual economy—namely, the US economy. It would be ideal to calibrate the model to the world economy; however, that would introduce large inaccuracies due to the unreliability or nonavailability of data. For the United States, we can be quite confident that the data are reliable. Calibrating the model means attaching numbers to the parameters in the three production functions, to the arguments of the utility function, and to how carbon emissions generate changes in atmospheric carbon concentration. Our calibration methods are explained in Appendix A: Calibration. They follow standard calibration practice and sometimes use data from the *Stern Review* and from Nordhaus (2013, 2008a, 2008b).

Having calibrated the model, we are ready to compute optimal solutions for the programs with the pure- and growth-sustainability objective functions. We take date zero to be 2010, so the endowment vector with which the economy starts is the vector of endowments of the US economy in 2010. The adult in the first generation of the model lives from 2011 to 2035.

A full specification of the optimization problem would require that we optimize over the path of carbon emissions as well as over all other economic variables. This would require estimating the functions that relate emissions to atmospheric carbon concentration, carbon concentration to global temperature, and global temperature to human welfare. The first of these functions is relatively well known; there is a great deal of debate about the second one, and about the third one, we can only make educated guesses. A full *integrated assessment model* (IAM) contains these three equations as well as all the equations we have specified. We have elected not to construct a full IAM because we believe the uncertainties in the specification of the second and third processes are so great. (However, in Chapter 6, we do construct a highly stylized integrated assessment model in order to make some ballpark calculations of how to respond to uncertainty.)

We adopt, instead, a *pis aller*. We constrain carbon concentration to follow a path that converges to a concentration of carbon below 450 parts per million (ppm) in seventy-five years (three generations of our model).[7] Since our model is of the US economy, we therefore constrain the emissions of the manufacturing sector in the model to be a certain fraction of emissions that are globally consistent with staying on the chosen path of carbon concentration. We compute two scenarios: one in which the United States continues to emit 17% of global emissions (its share of total emissions in 2010) and a second in which the United States emits roughly its per capita share of global emissions. Subject to each of these constraints, we solve the sustainability optimization programs (pure, and for various growth rates). Features of the optimal paths are presented in Chapter 3.

We will not rehearse the results here, as their verbal discussion in Section 3.11 provides a nontechnical summary. We do, however, indicate some of their main features. On the pure-sustainable path, human welfare, which is constant, is higher than it was in the base year (2010). Thus, following a sustainable path, which radically reduces carbon emissions over seventy-five years, is technologically feasible, without reduction in human welfare. Indeed, even growth is feasible, at least at moderate growth rates, while respecting the constraint imposed on carbon emissions. This is so for both scenarios—even when the US economy is restricted to emitting only *its per capita share* of global emissions! One might suspect that this is accomplished by radically changing our 'consumption bundle' away from commodities to enjoying more leisure with higher education: for recall, it is only commodity production in the model that generates greenhouse gas (GHG) emissions. This is not so: commodity consumption is in fact higher on the pure-sustainable path than it was in 2010 and becomes much higher on the growth-sustainable paths. And leisure time does not rise above its present levels on the optimal paths—in fact, it falls a little (although its value increases because educational levels increase). Indeed, this may be one of the surprises of addressing global warming: on the optimal path,

[7] The path is constructed from the Representative Concentration Pathway RCP2.6 and is described in Section 3.4.2. The RCP2.6 is representative of precautionary scenarios with very low GHG concentration levels and provides an expected temperature change below 2°C.

we do *not* continue to reduce the length of the working year or working life, as has occurred, dramatically, over the last century.[8]

Now there is, indeed, some change in the consumption bundle, but the main feature of the optimal paths is a sharply increased investment in the creation of knowledge: the fraction of labor engaged in the knowledge industry doubles compared to the benchmark year. Recall that the stock of knowledge is an input into human welfare. The other effect of this new knowledge is to induce technological progress that enables the economy to produce commodities with a much lower emissions/output ratio. A skeptic might question this part of our model: is it realistic to assume that knowledge investments will enable us to reduce the emissions/output ratio as sharply as the model predicts? We must answer by referring to our calibration of the production function, which uses the historical effect of knowledge on that ratio. Indeed, we might conjecture that in the future, research and development (R&D) will have an even stronger impact on the emissions/output ratio than it has in the last fifty years because R&D will focus on reducing that ratio. After all, the urgency of reducing emissions has only become apparent in recent years. Therefore, we do not view paths of feasible output and emissions that our model claims are feasible as reflecting a particularly rosy view.

There are several technical issues that the analysis in Chapter 3 addresses. Paramount among these is how to compute the optimal solution to the pure- and growth-sustainable programs. Consider, for example, the former optimization program. The problem exists because the vector of aggregate endowments at date zero (2010), with which the economy begins, does not lie on the ray from which the optimal solution is a stationary state, a ray that we can compute precisely and analytically. We know the optimal solution will converge to a stationary state, so the endowment vector will converge to a point on that ray, but which point? We solve this problem by an approximation technique that forces convergence in two generations. The technique gives us a very close approximation to the actual optimal path.

---

[8] In 2012 German workers labored 1400 hours per year on average, which amortizes to 28 hours per week for a 50-week year. In 1900 the average work week was 60 hours, or about 3000 hours per annum.

One of the main lessons of Chapter 3 is that, considering only the US economy, the problem of sustainability is solvable, as far as the laws of economics are concerned. It is pretty clear that there are no technological barriers to finding a sustainable path. The real issue is political: Will our society be able to agree on the changes needed to implement a sustainable path? Will we be able to muzzle the energy firms that see their profitability tied to the exploitation of fossil fuels? Will American consumers see the necessity of paying much higher fuel taxes in order to reduce the consumption of fossil fuels? In Chapter 5 we complicate the political problem by addressing the issue of global sustainability, but we do not, in this book, study the political and psychological issues that must be raised. Our task here is to present an economic and philosophical argument.

Section 3.9 carries out an experiment in which we ask: what would the optimal path look like if we chose to sustain *consumption* rather than *utility*? Both Stern and Nordhaus view utility as consisting only of commodity consumption. Some may view this as a useful simplifying move, but we have argued that it is important to include education, knowledge, and the quality of the biosphere in the generational utility function because this engenders the possibility of substituting from commodity consumption to these other goods in order to maintain welfare. In this section, we compare the pure-sustainability problem for *consumption only* with our optimal path for sustaining utility that we have computed.

The results are fairly dramatic. Unsurprisingly, the steady-state consumption when only consumption is sustained is somewhat higher than when utility is sustained: about 16% higher. However, both education and knowledge are much higher when utility is sustained: education is 385% times as much in the utility-sustaining program as in the consumption-sustaining program, and knowledge is 224% times as large. If we compute *utility* at the steady state of the consumption maximizing program, it is only 44% of the utility at the steady state of the other program, achieving a mere 60.3% of the utility level in the 2010 reference year before the end of the century. In other words, a fairly small sacrifice in consumption enables a very large increase in education and knowledge creation. We believe these results underscore the importance of defining utility in an encompassing way.

Before introducing the issue of global cooperation to control carbon emissions, we proceed to Chapter 4, which looks more carefully at the approaches that economists William Nordhaus and Nicholas Stern have taken to climate-change analysis. Nordhaus's objective function appears to be an amalgam of a social-welfare function and a utility function for an infinitely lived consumer. Indeed, we present three interpretations of his objective function (Table 4.1) and argue that none of them is satisfactory, given our philosophical premise that the current generation has no right to impose its own time rate of discount upon the social objective. This is embodied in Nordhaus's choice of discount rate, of 0.015 per annum, which is calibrated from market interest rates, reflecting the degree of impatience of current savers and investors. Nordhaus's discount rate is associated with an annual *discount factor* of $\frac{1}{1+0.015} = 0.9852$. Consequently, he discounts the utility of people living one hundred years from now by a factor of $0.9852^{100} = 0.2256$; that is, their utility counts only 23% as much as today's generation's utility in the social calculus. We claim that this move cannot be justified by an appeal to an impartial Ethical Observer. One consequence of Nordhaus's parameterization of the model is that relatively mild reductions of GHG emissions are recommended in the short run; significant reductions only occur in the late part of this century. The projected temperature increases associated with Nordhaus's DICE 2013 model are considerably more than 2°C by 2100.

The *Stern Review* does not undertake a full optimization exercise, as Nordhaus (2013, 2008a, 2008b) does, but carries out a cost-benefit analysis for a small sample of emission paths. Basically, it argues that a particular alternative emissions path dominates the 'business-as-usual' (BAU) path in the sense that the benefits of adopting it are greater than the costs of doing so. An alternative path to the benchmark BAU path is recommended if and only if the present discounted value of differences in consumption between the two paths over the generations is positive. But what discount factor does Stern use? His discount factor equals $1-\pi = 0.999$ per annum, where the value $\pi = 0.001$ is his choice for the annual probability that a catastrophe will annihilate the human species. Thus, Stern discounts the utility of people one hundred years from now by a factor of $0.999^{100} = 0.9048$: their utility counts about 90% as much as the current generation's utility in the social calculus. As we've said, we find Stern's analysis to be philosophically consistent with a utilitarian theory of justice. It is, for that reason, impartial, unlike Nordhaus's analysis, but we nevertheless do not agree with Stern because we dissent from his utilitarianism. And as we've said, we find Stern's discount rate to be too large by two orders of magnitude (so his discount factor is *too small*).

We review, in Chapter 4, the criticisms that Nordhaus and Martin Weitzman have raised against the *Stern Review*. The best face we can put on Nordhaus's defense of his approach is that it would be politically a non-starter to propose discount rates of future generations' utilities that are far out of line with the discount rates that today's savers exhibit, as deduced from market interest rates. (It is the so-called Ramsey equation, which we discuss in Chapters 1 and 4, that links consumers' subjective discount rates to market interest rates.) The defense, in other words, is one of practical politics. Nordhaus writes, "The time discount rate should be chosen along with the consumption elasticity so that the model *generates a path that resembles the actual real interest rate* [our italics—LRS]." Why must it resemble actual interest rates? Presumably because, did it not, it would be impossible, or extremely difficult, to induce consumers to alter their savings' behavior to fit the recommended path.

We believe climate-change economists must be clear on whether the analysis they are proposing is one based on ethical principles—that is, motivated by considerations of intergenerational (and intragenerational) justice—or one motivated by practical political considerations. There is surely need for both, but one must honestly distinguish between them. Stern's approach is clearly of the former type: it is based upon a utilitarian view of justice combined with a simple approach to uncertainty. As we've just said, Nordhaus's approach, of deducing the discount rate from actual, observed interest rates, which reflect rates of impatience of today's investors and savers, might be justified by a pragmatic, political aim. It might be pretty hard to induce citizens in a democracy to undertake behaviors that reflect very different attitudes toward future generations than their current behavior evidently exhibits. But Nordhaus does not make this argument. He maintains that his approach is purely objective and flows from sensible economic principles.

We believe that, at this point in the analysis, it is wiser to follow our ethics to see where they lead us. Our own approach, at least up until this point in the book, is unabashedly ethical. We do not claim that any rational person *must* be a sustainabilitarian or a growth sustainabilitarian.

We believe that many people will agree that they are one of these ethical types once they understand our definitions. But we cannot say it is crazy to be a utilitarian or to adopt some other conception of intergenerational justice.

We pursue the ethical approach because we believe that if a strong ethical argument can be made for limiting GHG emissions, that will in itself provide a strong rationale for changing patterns of behavior. The argument cannot be strengthened by building in constraints, at the beginning of the analysis, based on market behaviors that developed during a period when global warming was not an issue. In the end, compromises with ideal policies will be inevitable, based upon political realities, but the goalposts should be set prior to that point so that we know at what we should be aiming.

We conclude Chapter 4 by examining an attack that Nordhaus makes on those who, like Stern, apply much smaller discount rates than he. Nordhaus proposes a thought experiment in which scientists learn that a 'wrinkle' in the climate system will cause damages equal to 0.1% of net consumption per year starting in two hundred years and forever after. He points out that, with Stern's discount rate, we should be willing to pay 56% of one year's world consumption today to remove the wrinkle—about $30 trillion, approximately one-half of today's global gross domestic product (GDP), to fix this tiny problem in the distant future. As this strikes Nordhaus as absurd, it must follow that Stern's discount rate is far too low. We show that Nordhaus's example is misconceived, as it fails to anticipate that the proper response to the discovery of the climate wrinkle is an *optimal* response, not the poor response that Nordhaus proposes. We show that, *contra* Nordhaus, if the climate wrinkle were discovered, the *correct* response would be to reduce the consumption of the present and future generations up to when the climate wrinkle occurs by *something less than* 0.1%, in order to increase investments, which would reduce the damages to the people living two hundred years from now when the climate wrinkle occurs. Indeed, assuming that the original proposed path (before the wrinkle was discovered) was an *optimal* path, there is *no* path that will restore aggregate social welfare to what it would have been without the climate wrinkle.

Chapter 5 culminates our analysis by extending the model of Chapter 3 to a world with two regions. A new, *intragenerational* question arises: how should the burden of reducing GHG emissions be allocated between the developing world (the South) and the developed world (the North)? In other words, we add the problem of intragenerational welfare to the intergenerational issues studied in Chapter 3. To keep the analysis as simple as possible, we envisage a South that looks like China (i.e., that has the vector of aggregate endowments of present-day China) and a North that looks like the United States. Formally, the model now consists of an indefinitely long sequence of generations, where each generation consists of a set of identical households of the Chinese type and a set of identical households of the US type, where the numbers of these households are given by UN population estimates of the developing and developed world over the next fifty years. We assume that global population is unchanging after 2060.

Each region's economy is summarized by the relationships illustrated in Figure I.1, with two changes. First, it is assumed that knowledge diffuses from the region that possesses more knowledge to the region with less knowledge. The knowledge accruing to the South at Generation t is equal to the knowledge it has produced, plus the knowledge that has diffused to it from the North (assuming the North continues to be the region with a higher knowledge endowment). Second, each region can transfer commodities to the other. For example, it is conceivable that the North would specialize in the production of knowledge, the South would specialize in commodity production, and the South would export commodities to the North.

We exogenously adopt the same path of world emissions and concentrations as in Chapter 3, which, it will be recalled, provides an expected temperature increase above the preindustrial level of less than 2°C. The central question of Chapter 5 is: how should the global emissions allowance be allocated between the regions at each generation, and what are the optimal regional paths of production, consumption, education, and investment in knowledge?

We advocate policies that will lead to eventual convergence in the levels of welfare per capita in the various regions: this follows from our general egalitarian principle. But we do not have an ethical instruction concerning what the date of convergence should be. Here, we propose a political solution, that is, a particular solution to the bargaining problem that is taking place in the sequence of ongoing Conference of the Parties (COP) meetings that are concerned with resolving the issue of fairly sharing the burden of reducing GHG emissions.[9]

Many writers have proposed ethical solutions that are based upon a conception of the carbon budget that each nation has a right to claim. These claims are often deduced by assuming that, from some starting date in the past, each nation had a right to emit a total amount of carbon proportional to its population. If that date is taken, for example, to be 1990, then one would compute the amount of global GHG emissions that are acceptable from 1990 on, allocate those emissions to nations in proportion to their 1990 populations, and subtract from that endowment the emissions each nation has produced since 1990, to give the remaining budgets. Whatever the ethical merits of these proposals, we believe they are politically unrealistic, and so we search for a solution to which we think all parties could agree.

Our proposal is based on Thomas Schelling's focal-point approach to bargaining (Schelling 1960; Colman 2006). Often, Schelling says, there is a clear focal point in a bargaining problem, and this emerges as the agreement. We propose that there is such a focal point in the climate-change bargaining problem, and it concerns the date at which the developing world will catch up to the developed world in terms of welfare per capita or, more simply, GDP per capita. Our proposal is summarized as 'preserving the date of convergence.'

In our model, as we said, the world has two regions, a South like China and a North like the United States. Suppose that it were common knowledge that, absent the problem of climate change, the South would converge to the North in welfare or GDP per capita in seventy-five years. This is actually not a crazy estimate: we compute in Chapter 5 that, given a predictable decrease in China's rate of growth, a date of convergence of 2085 is a reasonable guess. Our claim is that any solution to the bargaining problem must preserve that date of convergence: preservation of that date is the focal point.

The argument is, as we said, political. Suppose the US negotiators were to propose an allocation of emissions' burdens whose consequence were

[9] The Conference of the Parties (COP) meetings are annual meetings of the parties in the United Nations Framework Convention on Climate Change (UNFCC).

that convergence would occur in one hundred years. The South would argue that that was unacceptable: why should the date of convergence be postponed for twenty-five years from what it would have been under BAU? Impartiality requires that the date of convergence be no farther than seventy-five years away. Conversely, suppose the Chinese negotiators were to propose an allocation of burdens whose consequence was convergence in fifty years: the North would never accept this, arguing that the date of convergence should not be advanced by twenty-five years. The only agreement that will not be rejected by one side or the other is to allocate the emissions' burden so that the date of convergence remains at seventy-five years.

The assumption that must be justified is that *maintaining the date of convergence is a focal point*. We do not have proof that this is so. We propose that it may be so. In fact, proposing this may help make it so. It is not only that the governments necessarily treat the date of convergence as of great political moment, although they might, but that the governments may believe that the date of convergence is highly salient to their polities, and a proposal that maintains that date is one that can be sold to the respective citizenries. More pessimistically, we can say that a proposal that entails a delay or an advance in the date of convergence will surely be vociferously objected to by one region's polity and so the *only* possibility for a solution is one that maintains the date of convergence.

The next step is to relax the assumption that the date of convergence is known by all. There is a fairly simple way of maintaining the date of convergence, even if we do not know what it is, as long as we can predict, fairly accurately, rates of growth in the near future, under various proposed schemes of burden sharing. The *growth factor* of an economy is one plus its growth rate. If growth rates are altered in two regions, but the *ratio of their growth factors* remains unchanged, then the ratio of their GDPs per capita will remain what it would have been without the alterations. For example, suppose that, under BAU, the Chinese growth rate would be 5% and the US growth rate would be 2% during the next year. The ratio of the growth factors is $1.05/1.02 = 1.0294$. This implies that the ratio of China's GDP per capita to the US's GDP per capita a year from now will be 1.0294 times what it is today. Now suppose China reduces its growth rate to 4% this year and the United States reduces its growth rate to 1.103%. One may compute that the ratio of growth factors, 1.04/1.0103, remains at 1.0294. This implies that the *ratio* of GDPs per capita will remain at what it would have been in the original scenario. If ratios of growth factors are invariant, then the date of convergence—which is the date at which the ratio of Chinese GDP per capita to US GDP per capita is unity—will remain unchanged.

We propose that the major regions of the world negotiate around the focal point of allocating emissions rights so as to maintain the ratios of their growth factors as invariants. If this proposal is followed, it will not reduce negotiations to a triviality—there will still be much to truck and barter about as regions argue about what their BAU growth factors would be and what the effects on growth factors would be of restricting GHG emissions. But the problem would be reduced to one whose solution international teams of economists could eventually agree upon. It would be reduced from a huge political problem to a rather technical one of economic computation.

This proposal motivates what we do in Chapter 5. We take the back-of-the-envelope estimate to be true that, under BAU, China and the United States would converge in seventy-five years—that is, in three generations of our model—and we ask: how should the global budget of carbon emissions, specified so that carbon concentration follows our path that converges to a level below 450 ppm, be allocated in each generation over the next seventy-five years, *in an optimal fashion*, so as to maintain that date of convergence of the *welfare levels per capita* in the two regions? We compute the solution to this problem.

We refer the reader to Chapter 5 for the details and state here what is perhaps the most important conclusion. We show that on the optimal sustainable path, the North's utility grows at about 1% per annum over the next seventy-five years, and the South's utility, after growing at 1% per annum during the first twenty-five years, grows at an average of 3.27% per annum in the fifty following years, catching up with the North in 2085.[10] Indeed, there are no feasible paths—that is, ones that obey all our constraints plus

[10] Some readers may be startled by the relatively low growth of the South's utility during the first twenty-five years. This result derives from the aggregation at the generational level and our choice largely to increase the utility of Generation 2 in the South at the expense of a small sacrifice in the utility of its Generation 1. Section A5.3 in Chapter 5 presents an alternative transition path.

the constraint of maintaining the date of convergence—at which the North can grow noticeably faster than 1% per annum on average.

There is both an optimistic and a pessimistic slant to this conclusion. The optimistic slant is that it is possible for the South to catch up to the North in seventy-five years *and* for the North to continue growing, while holding carbon concentration to an ultimate level below 450 ppm. Indeed, the South need not delay its catch-up date to the North because of the climate-change problem. This, we believe, is very good news. The global South need not give up on its goal of reaching the high standard of living of the global North. The pessimistic slant is that Northern citizens will have to accept a reduction of growth rates to about 1% per annum. And, similarly, the South (in particular, China) will have to accept a reduction in its growth rate that is considerable. This will be a major challenge for the politicians in both regions. US politicians will claim they cannot convince their citizens to settle for this slowdown, and the Chinese leadership apparently views its continuation in power as dependent upon continuing the high rates of growth that have characterized the last thirty years. Again, we believe the challenging issues are ones of politics, not of economic feasibility.

To summarize Chapter 5, we claim that the climate-change bargaining problem cannot be solved unless it is admitted that the issues of economic growth and the allocation of rights to emit are *solved together*. They are inextricably intertwined, and it is hopelessly naïve to suppose that one problem can be addressed in isolation from the other. Governments currently take the posture that their own economic decisions are not on the bargaining table, but if this posture is maintained, there is no solution to the challenge that faces us, and we must prepare to live on an increasingly hot planet, with all that that entails. We can only hope that presenting our analysis as clearly as possible will induce the relevant parties to cooperate with each other.

Chapter 6 explores, within simple theoretical models in the spirit of Chapter 2, two departures from the assumption, maintained until now and inherited from the *Stern Review*, that the probability of catastrophe at each generation, or hazard rate, (1) is exogenous, and (2) produces the extinction of the human species.

First (Section 6.2), we propose, more sensibly, that the probability of catastrophe is not appropriately conceived as that of a meteor colliding with Earth but rather as that of a climate-induced catastrophe, following from allowing an imprudently high concentration of atmospheric carbon to evolve. The assumption that the hazard rate is independent of our choices concerning GHG emissions is a poor one: adopting it is akin to looking for the lost jewel under the street lamp because that's where one can see the pavement.

The reason that researchers have assumed an exogenous hazard rate is that it immensely simplifies the calculation of optimal paths. In Chapter 6 we propose a *hazard function* that relates atmospheric carbon concentration to the hazard rate at a point in time. We do not know how to estimate the hazard function with any precision, nor do we think anybody does, at present. Nevertheless, it turns out that we are able to deduce some characteristics of the optimal path, which flow from characteristics of the hazard function, a parametric form that we assume for the sake of argument. Formally speaking, Section 6.2 works with a very simple IAM, which contains the laws of motion of the economy; the relationship between economic variables and carbon concentration; and the relationship between carbon concentration and human welfare, as captured in the probability of a climate-induced catastrophe.

It is now important to observe that the pure-sustainabilitarian Ethical Observer places *no value* on the length of time that the human species exists. A human society that lasts for one date, where the single generation has a utility of 100, is indifferent, for this Ethical Observer, to a society that lasts for a thousand generations, where each generation's household enjoys a utility of 100. When the length of the species' lifetime was exogenous, this was of no import, because economic decisions had no impact upon the expected tenure of the species, but now that that tenure will be a result of the path chosen, the Ethical Observer's indifference to its length is of paramount importance.

Consequently, in Section 6.2, we adopt a new objective function, which could be called 'sustainabilitarian with a concern for species lifetime.' The von Neumann–Morgenstern (vNM) utility the Ethical Observer derives from a world that lasts for T generations is now assumed to be $T \min\{u_1, \ldots, u_T\}$. Thus, the Ethical Observer cares not only about the sustained *level* of utility but also about the sustained *length of time* of utility. The expected utility of this Ethical Observer is the sum of the vNM utilities she would have should the species end at any date along a proposed path, weighted by the probabilities that those events occur, where the probabilities themselves are endogenous to the choice of path.

We take a simple form for the hazard function, which relates atmospheric carbon concentration to the probability of catastrophe; we assume that the probability of the species becoming extinct at any date is a weakly increasing function of the atmospheric carbon concentration at that date. This function is assumed to be constant (nonincreasing) until a certain level of carbon concentration is reached—perhaps the level of 350 ppm. But after this critical level is reached, the probability begins increasing at an increasing rate. We show, by simulation, that if the rate of increase of the hazard function is sufficiently rapid, then the optimal path requires maintaining a carbon concentration very close to the critical level, which we take to be 350 ppm.

In particular, we compute the following: Suppose that we take the hazard rate per generation in the preindustrial era to have been 0.00017, or 0.017% per generation, as we proposed earlier. Now suppose that a doubling of concentration from 350 ppm to 700 ppm would double the hazard rate. Then our simulations show that the optimal path must maintain a concentration close to 350 ppm for a large interval of values of the key parameter in the hazard function.

Now we must append to this conclusion the usual caveats: the model is simple, and we have made assumptions about the functional form of the hazard function that may be wrong. Nevertheless, we believe that the simulations present an argument that should not be ignored.

The penultimate section, Section 6.3, introduces a second conceptualization of catastrophe. Instead of its being conceived of as the disappearance of the species, we now take catastrophe to be the occurrence of a tipping point, above which human life continues to exist but in a compromised state. We model this by assuming that the production function takes a beating at the tipping point: it becomes much more difficult to produce commodities, but human generations continue to exist at a diminished level of existence. Under this supposition, we calculate the optimal path of resource allocation. However, we assume in this section that the hazard rate is exogenous. Introducing one complication in the model is enough, at least for now. We model the sustainabilitarian Ethical Observer, in this case, as desiring to maximize the minimum *expected utility* over all generations, where each generation faces a lottery, *ex ante*, of living before or after the stochastic tipping point is reached. It turns out, perhaps unsurprisingly, that early generations should save to help generations that live after the tipping point occurs, and the greater the probability of that occurrence, the more the early generations should save. On the optimal path, every generation has the same expected utility, and so the sustainabilitarian ethic, once again, produces intergenerational equality. It would, of course, be possible to study, as well, paths that enable a constant growth rate in expected utility, analogous to our earlier growth-sustainability analysis.

The Conclusion summarizes our main conclusions.

CHAPTER ONE

Sustainability and Discounted Utilitarianism

1.1. The General Sustainability Problem

We assume there is a society that will potentially survive for an infinite number of generations. In Section 1.3, we will introduce uncertainty with respect to the date of the last generation of the human species. We abstractly represent this society as a sequence of representative households, one for each generation. The set of feasible streams of utility, or utility possibilities set, for this infinitely lived society is denoted U, whose generic element is written $u=(u_1, u_2, \ldots)$ where u_t is the utility of the household at Generation (or date) t. Defining the set U requires knowing the laws of motion of the economy, how the economy affects climate, and how economic goods and climate produce utility for humans. We take an anthropocentric view in this book, in that it is only the utility of humans with which we are concerned. We do not necessarily believe this is the correct ethical stance, but our task, here, will be the limited one of advocating an approach to climate change in which we take the (perhaps parochial) view that nature is only valuable insofar as it impacts upon human welfare.

We define the *pure-sustainability problem* as:

$$\begin{aligned} &\max \Lambda \\ &\text{subject to: } u_t \geq \Lambda, \quad t = 1, 2, \ldots \\ &\quad u \in U. \end{aligned} \tag{1.1}$$

In words, maximize the level of utility that can be sustained forever. This is equivalent to the more standard 'maximin' formulation:

$$\max_{u \in U} \min_{1 \le t < \infty} u_t. \tag{1.2}$$

(The mathematically more precise statement would replace 'min' in (1.2) with 'inf.') There is a temptation to call (1.1) a Rawlsian formulation, but in fact, Rawls did not advocate 'the difference principle,' or maximin, for intertemporal societies, so we will respect his view by refraining from calling (1.1) a Rawlsian objective.[1]

It is noteworthy that as long as the set U is derived from an economic problem, and if utility is bounded below (conventionally by zero), there will always be a solution to (1.1). This is because, given finite resources for the first generation, there is an upper bound on u_1—call it $\bar{u}_1^*$—and hence the problem is necessarily bounded, and a solution exists. (That is, it must be that $0 \le \Lambda \le \bar{u}_1^*$.)

In Chapter 3 we will introduce the economic environment in which we study climate change, and this will entail defining a specific set U. It will turn out that the solution of (1.1) for that problem has the property that:

$$\bar{u}_t^* = \Lambda, \quad t = 1, 2, \ldots; \tag{1.3}$$

that is, utility is constant forever on the optimal path.[2] Some will rebel against this result, and we agree, it is not necessarily appealing. We therefore introduce a second concept called *growth sustainability*. Consider a given growth rate $\rho \ge 0$. The problem of ρ-*sustainability* is:

[1] See the reference to Solow (1974) in Section 1.4.

[2] This is not the case for all conceivable utility possibilities sets U. If each generation creates public goods for their own benefit that pass on to future generations, the solution to may entail increasing utilities. Note that this phenomenon has nothing to do with the Rawlsian source of unequal utilities at the maximin solution, which is the necessity of paying incentives to productive individuals. For a thorough discussion of when the solution to entails increasing utilities, see Silvestre (2002).

$$\max \Lambda$$

subject to:

$$u_t \geq (1+\rho)^{t-1}\,\Lambda, \quad t = 1, 2, \ldots,$$

$$u \in U, \tag{1.4}$$

that is, find that path that maximizes the utility of the first generation, subject to guaranteeing that utility grows at a rate of at least ρ per generation, forever. For ρ sufficiently small and positive, (1.4) will often have a solution. As a maximin problem, we can write (1.4) as:

$$\max_{u \in U} \min_{1 \leq t < \infty} \frac{u_t}{(1+\rho)^{t-1}}. \tag{1.5}$$

If $\rho > 0$, then the early generation(s) will have lower utility in the solution to (1.4) than in the solution to (1.1): the early generation(s) will have to save more to enable future growth.

We offer the following ethical argument for the attractiveness of taking ρ-sustainability as the approach to climate change. First, we believe that the date at which a person is born is arbitrary from the moral point of view. Therefore, each generation in the future has a right to as much utility as every other generation in the future. (As we note, this view was endorsed by Ramsey 1928; Sidgwick 1907; among many others.) The restriction to future generations is appended because nothing can be done about the past. This leads to the view that the correct solution to the problem of intergenerational social welfare is the path in *U* that equalizes all utilities at the highest possible level. However, this path may be Pareto dominated, and so we pass (as did Rawls) from the highest-equal-utility path to the maximin path, that is, the solution of (1.1). In point of fact, as we noted, for the problem of climate change, as we model it, these two paths are the same. Thus, *according to rights*, each generation can insist on enforcing the solution to (1.1).

However, generations do not have to enforce their rights. And if, as we believe, persons value *human development*, in the sense of the growth of human welfare over the long run, then they may well agree *not* to enforce their right to be as well off as all future generations but to allow growth in utility, even though that reduces their own welfare. Intuitively, if all generations feel this way, this leads to program (1.4).

There is a more rigorous justification of (1.4). Let us interpret u_t as the *standard of living* of Generation t, and let us use the notation V_t for the *all-things-considered welfare* of Generation t. The difference between V_t and u_t is that the latter involves only the consumption items of Generation t, while the former includes their concern for human development as well. Suppose that V_t has the following form:

$$V_t = (u_t)^{\zeta}(V_{t+1})^{1-\zeta}, \quad \text{some } 0 < \zeta < 1; \tag{1.6}$$

that is, people care about their own standard of living and the next generation's overall welfare. Note that we can calculate the value of V_1 only by knowing the entire path $u = (u_1, u_2, \ldots)$ because

$$\begin{aligned} V_1 &= u_1^{\zeta} V_2^{1-\zeta} = u_1^{\zeta} u_2^{(1-\zeta)\zeta} V_3^{(1-\zeta)^2} = u_1^{\zeta} u_2^{(1-\zeta)\zeta} u_3^{(1-\zeta)^2\zeta} V_4^{(1-\zeta)^3} \\ &= \cdots = \left(\prod_{t=1}^{\infty} u_t^{(1-\zeta)^{t-1}} \right)^{\zeta}. \end{aligned} \tag{1.7}$$

We can then ask, what is the path that maximizes V_1, the all-things-considered welfare of the first generation? We will prove in Chapter 2 that, for a simple economic model, the solution to this problem is the utility path that solves (1.4) with a specific value of ρ determined by ζ and a parameter of the economy. This result gives a precise microfoundation to the claim that if each generation possesses the all-things-considered utility function V_t, then solving (1.4) is the correct approach, where we have an auxiliary argument to set the value of ρ. (Of course, this assumes that generations do not place such a high value on human development that no solution to (1.4) exists.)

To review, our argument for advocating the solution to (1.4) as the right ethical approach to climate change has three steps: (1) each generation has a right to as much welfare as every other generation because it is a matter of luck when one is born, (2) this recommends program (1.1). But humans value human development (apart from caring about the welfare of their own children), and this means that each generation may agree to not enforce its right but to permit growth, which recommends program (1.4) for some value ρ. (3) We present one way of computing the value of ρ, given formulation (1.6) as the way of modeling how humans weigh their own standard of living against human development in the future.

We will, further, relate step (1) of our argument to an important current in contemporary political philosophy. The term *brute luck* refers to the outcome of a gamble against which the individual had no possibility to insure: an involuntary, uninsurable lottery. *Option luck* refers to the outcomes of gambles that persons choose to take. The terms were introduced by the political philosopher Ronald Dworkin (1981). The philosophical view, which was first stated imprecisely by Rawls (1971), then precisely by Dworkin (1981), and developed since then by a school known as the luck egalitarians (which includes, as well, Arneson 1989; Cohen 1989; among others) is that it is morally illegitimate to benefit compared to others by virtue of brute luck. The principal application of this principle is that no one has the right to special benefit by virtue of the luck of the birth lottery.[3] Clearly, the principle calls for a good deal of redistribution, for it only recognizes as legitimate those benefits that accrue to persons due to 'autonomous effort.' Our position advocating pure sustainability as the baseline is an application of this principle, since the date of a person's birth is a matter of brute luck.[4]

We note that if program (1.4) possesses a feasible path for a given ρ, then there is a solution to (1.4): the argument is the same as was given earlier with regard to (1.1).

We must emphasize an important point concerning our argument. In step (3) we have moved from maximizing an intergenerational social-welfare function to maximizing the all-things-considered utility of the first generation. We do not believe that *in general* it is correct to say that the welfare of future generations should depend upon how much the present generation wants them to have. *Every generation has a right to as much welfare as every other*, independently of what each generation would *like* future generations to enjoy. Thus, the move from step (1) to step (2) in our argument is *one-sided*: each generation may choose not to enforce its right to be as

[3] For a review of this chapter in modern political philosophy, see Roemer (2009).
[4] The main opposing position, that persons can legitimately benefit by virtue of brute luck, is expounded by Nozick (1974).

well off as future generations, but it may not choose to render future generations worse off than they would have been at the solution of (1.1). *Given* that each generation would like future generations to be better off than they, it is up to them (the early generations) to decide how much better off those in the future can be because it is making a gift to the future, where the no-gift baseline is pure sustainability. This point will become important in the discussion to follow.

We think there are two major ways of disagreeing with our recommendation to adopt (1.4) as the right ethical approach to climate change. The first is to argue that (1.1) is not the correct baseline formulation: it is not true that every generation has a right to as much utility as every other generation. One reason this might be so is because technology develops over time, which means that opportunities for higher welfare are available to later generations that were unavailable to earlier ones, and it would be spiteful if early generations did not allow later generations to take advantage of technological change. A counterargument to this justification is that whether or not technology develops over time is *endogenous* to the solution of the intergenerational welfare problem. If we adopt formulation (1.1), technology will *not* develop over time: typically, the solution will be a stationary state. So it is circular to object to (1.1) on the grounds that technology develops over time.

A second objection is that the abstraction of representing each generation by a single household or agent obscures the important fact of intragenerational inequality. Is it really right to favor growth of the standard of living for future generations at the expense, perhaps, of the very poor today? Of course, given our representative-agent model, this question cannot be posed. But in reality, if a generation decides to sacrifice some of its welfare for future generations, it should surely be at the expense of the rich, not the poor. Nevertheless, even the very poor may favor human development. People may feel quite differently about increasing the welfare of future generations, at some expense to themselves, versus increasing the welfare of their contemporaries, who are much better off than they, at some expense to themselves.[5]

---

[5] We cannot pursue this issue further here, although we do not claim to have definitively justified growth. Some (e.g., Dyson 2008) argue that global injustice

1.2. Utilitarianism and Discounted Utilitarianism

Utilitarianism is the view that the proper problem to solve is:

$$\max \sum_{t=1}^{\infty} u_t$$
$$\text{subject to } u \in U. \tag{1.8}$$

Immediately, there is an issue: for many specifications of the economic environment, the sum of utilities is unbounded and so (1.8) has no solution. This ceases to be a problem if future utilities are sufficiently discounted, as in the *discounted-utilitarian* problem:

$$\max \sum_{t=1}^{\infty} \varphi^{t-1} u_t$$
$$\text{subject to } u \in U, \tag{1.9}$$

where the *discount factor* φ is a fixed number in the interval (0, 1). If φ is sufficiently small, a solution to (1.9) will generally exist. The discount factor is related to the *discount rate* δ by the equation $\varphi = \dfrac{1}{1+\delta}$.

The objective (1.9) is the one most often adopted by climate-change researchers: for example, Nordhaus (2008a), Weitzman (2007), the *Stern Review* (Stern 2007), and Dasgupta (2005). One can say, more generally, that using the discounted-utilitarian objective is an almost ubiquitous practice among macroeconomists and policy economists who work on intergenerational problems.

We will argue that neither utilitarianism nor discounted utilitarianism are appealing intergenerational ethics.

---

today is a more pressing problem than climate change. Presumably, cheap, coal-fired electricity is the best way of increasing the welfare of China's agricultural poor, and this conflicts with solving the climate-change problem, at least for now. Dyson is an optimist with regard to solving the climate-change problem at a later date. In Chapter 5 we explicitly put intragenerational inequality into our model by including two representative households, at each date, one from the developing world and the other from the developed world.

1.2.1. Utilitarianism

In modern times it is Rawls (1971) who laid siege to utilitarianism and convinced a large fraction of the philosophical community to reject it in favor of a kind of egalitarianism. The principal argument against utilitarianism is that it is oblivious to inequality: in a two-person society, a distribution of utility (1, 99) is socially indifferent to the distribution (50, 50). Put somewhat more generally, utilitarianism ignores the boundaries between persons, viewing society as a vessel with compartments (people) into which utility is poured, with no concern for the relative level of utility in its different compartments. It is perhaps puzzling that our field of thought, modern economic theory, which is so sensitive to individuals and individuality, would adopt utilitarianism as an ethical view.[6]

One example of utilitarianism's indifference to inequality is when there exist individuals called 'utility monsters,' who process resources into utility much more efficiently than other people. Consider the simple example with two persons with utility functions $\tilde{u}^1(x)=x, \tilde{u}^2(x)=2x$. If there is a fixed amount of the x resource to be divided between them, a utilitarian would give everything to person two. However, this critique does not apparently apply to utilitarianism as it is used in climate-change analysis because it is always assumed that the utility function of the representative agents is the same for all generations.

Nevertheless, it is clear that a version of the utility monster can occur even when every generation's utility function is the same. Suppose there is exogenous technical progress. Then a unit of productive resource can produce much more utility the later in time it is used because the technology will be that much more developed. Without sufficient discounting, utilitarianism could lead to allocating a fixed resource entirely to the last generation in an economy with a finite horizon. For example, suppose the universal utility function is $u(c)=c$, the technology is $f_t(x)=b^t x$ at date t,

[6] Some might object that this is a mischaracterization: many economic theorists deny the possibility of interpersonal utility comparisons and so believe the utilitarian social-welfare function is incoherent. More generally, if one accepts the premises of Arrow's impossibility theorem, and if utilities are interpersonally noncomparable, there is no coherent social-welfare function, except to identify social welfare with the utility of a single individual (the so-called 'dictatorships').

where $h > 1$, and the total amount of the exhaustible x resource is 1. If the society lasts for T generations, the utilitarian problem is:

$$\max \sum_{t=1}^{T} h^t x_t$$
$$\text{subject to: } \sum_{1}^{T} x_t \leq 1,$$
$$x_t \geq 0 \; t \geqq 1. \tag{1.10}$$

The solution is $x_T = 1$, $x_t = 0$ for all $t < T$. Of course, the example is unrealistic, but how do we know that in an economy with more bells and whistles but with rapid technological change possible, something like this might not occur, with a utilitarian objective? Indeed, Mirrlees (1967) carries out the exercise of maximizing a utilitarian (undiscounted) social-welfare function for a parameterization of the actual economy and comes up with the result that 50% of output of the first generation should be invested, so the utility-monster argument is far from academic.

Henry Sidgwick was an influential philosopher and leading utilitarian, and it is revealing to review his discussion of utilitarianism. Sidgwick (1907) writes that it is always correct to choose that social alternative that maximizes total utility, or the total excess of pleasure over pain. With regard to variable population size, he considers whether the appropriate rule is to choose that size that maximizes average utility or total utility and expressly advocates in favor of total utility. Thus, he would advocate increasing the population size until the point at which every individual considered his life barely worth living, assuming that that choice would maximize total utility. (This example has often been considered to illustrate the undesirability of utilitarianism: see Parfit 1984; Blackorby et al. 2005.) Suppose, however, we have a case in which there are several ways of allocating utility across persons, all of which give the same total. Then Sidgwick (1907, 417) opts for equality:

> In all such cases, therefore, it becomes practically important to ask whether any mode of distributing a given quantum of happiness is better than any other. Now the Utilitarian formula seems to supply no answer to this question: at least we have to supplement the principle of seeking the greatest happiness on the whole by some principle of

> Just or Right distribution of this happiness. The principle which most Utilitarians have either tacitly or expressly adopted is that of pure equality—as given in Bentham's formula, 'everybody to count for one, and nobody for more than one.' And this principle seems the only one which does not need a special justification; for, as we saw, it must be reasonable to treat any one man in the same way as any other, if there be no reason apparent for treating him differently.

Thus, Sidgwick's complete preference order is lexicographic: first, choose the social alternatives that maximize total utility, and then, among them, choose the one that is most equal across persons. Clearly, this preference order is discontinuous.

Sidgwick (1907, 414) has something interesting to say about discounting in the intergenerational problem: "It seems, however, clear that the time at which a man exists cannot affect the value of his happiness from a universal point of view; and that the interests of posterity must concern a Utilitarian as much as those of his contemporaries, except in so far as the effect of his actions on posterity—and even the existence of human beings to be affected—must necessarily be more uncertain."

Here Sidgwick seems, first, to say that there can be no reason to discount utilities of future generations; the last part of the citation opens the door, however, to discounting because of the uncertainty of the existence of future generations. While we are not persuaded by Sidgwick's utilitarianism, we believe his position on intertemporal discounting is sound.

Apart from the nineteenth-century advocacy of utilitarianism, axiomatic characterizations of the utilitarian social-welfare function emerged in the literature spawned by the Arrow impossibility theorem. Arrow's theorem assumed that only the *preferences* of individuals over possible social alternatives were known. If, however, it is assumed that *utility functions* of individuals are known and that these utility functions possess certain properties of measurability and interpersonal comparability, then there do, generally, exist admissible social preference orderings other than the dictatorships—that is, orderings that satisfy the other Arrovian axioms. D'Aspremont and Gevers (1977) proved that if it is assumed that utility functions are cardinally measurable and unit comparable, then, along with the other Arrovian axioms, the unique acceptable social ordering of alternatives is the utilitarian ordering. Maskin (1978) showed that an even stronger restriction on measurability—cardinal full comparability—combined with several other apparently benign axioms—characterizes the utilitarian ordering. For a discussion of this literature, see Roemer (1996, chapters 1 and 4).

These particular theorems do not apply to the problem of intergenerational social welfare as we are formulating it because they postulate societies with a finite number of individuals. Indeed, utilitarianism does not generally define a social-preference order in our infinite-horizon environment because it is not possible to compare two countable streams of utility if their sums are both infinite. Moreover, axioms that may appear benign can have powerful consequences. Maskin's theorem, for example, assumes an axiom called the 'elimination of the influence of indifferent individuals (*EL*).' This axiom eliminates maximin (pure sustainability) as a social ordering—in other words, absent this axiom, both utilitarianism and maximin would be acceptable social orderings according to the remaining axioms of Maskin's theorem. To eliminate one of these contenders because it fails to satisfy an axiom of doubtful philosophical provenance is unconvincing.[7]

The upshot is that we do not find the above characterizations of utilitarianism as the unique acceptable social ordering to be compelling.

1.2.2. Discounted Utilitarianism

We believe that, in practice, many economists work with a discounted-utilitarian objective function because it transforms a problem that is

[7] Consider two profiles of utility numbers, associated with two social alternatives—for example, in a society with two people, the alternative x generates utilities (10, 5), and the alternative y generates utilities (12, 5). The axiom *EL* states that because the second person is 'indifferent' between the two alternatives, the ordering of these alternatives should depend only on the first person's opinion—according to whom x is strictly preferred. Maximin violates this axiom because it ranks x and y as indifferent. Suppose, then, we proceed to refine maximin to leximin, which does rank x as strictly preferred. Leximin, however, is eliminated by another of Maskin's axioms—that the social ordering should be continuous. Together, then, continuity and *EL* eliminate two important egalitarian contenders from consideration. Perhaps, instead, this argument should make us question the attractiveness of these two axioms.

often unbounded into one that has a solution. It is difficult to find a satisfying justification for this move. Indeed, the problem appears in Ramsey's (1928) classical paper, the first to use a discounted-utilitarian objective in an intertemporal setting. Ramsey (1928) writes: "One point should perhaps be emphasized more particularly; it is assumed that we do not discount later enjoyments in comparison with earlier ones, a practice which is ethically indefensible, and arises merely from a weakness of the imagination; we shall, however, in Section 2, include a rate of discount in some of our investigations."

Ramsey honestly admits that there is no ethical basis for discounting but probably introduced the discount factor later in his paper in order to deal with the unboundedness of problem (1.8); it is unfortunate that his ethical caveat has largely been ignored.

We will review three prominent justifications by economists for using a discounted-utilitarian formulation, presenting our critique of each of them.

First Justification for Discounting Utilities: Future Generations as Utility Monsters

Perhaps the most widely held justification for discounting future utilities is the claim that future generations will be richer than the present generation and so their utility should be discounted in order to reduce intergenerational inequality from what it would have been with undiscounted utilitarianism. In other words, discounting is introduced in order to deal with utility monsters, where future generations could become such monsters, due to technological change. The argument can be seen in Figure 1.1, which presents a two-generation world, with a utility possibilities set U for the two generations, that is asymmetrical in a way that reflects rapid technological progress. The utilitarian solution (where the slope of the social indifference curve is -1) is more unequal than the discounted-utilitarian solution, which increases the absolute value of the slope and moves the solution closer to intergenerational equality.

This justification is expressed by Dasgupta (2008, 145) as follows:

> There are two reasons why it may be reasonable [to discount future consumption at a positive rate]. First, an additional unit of consump-

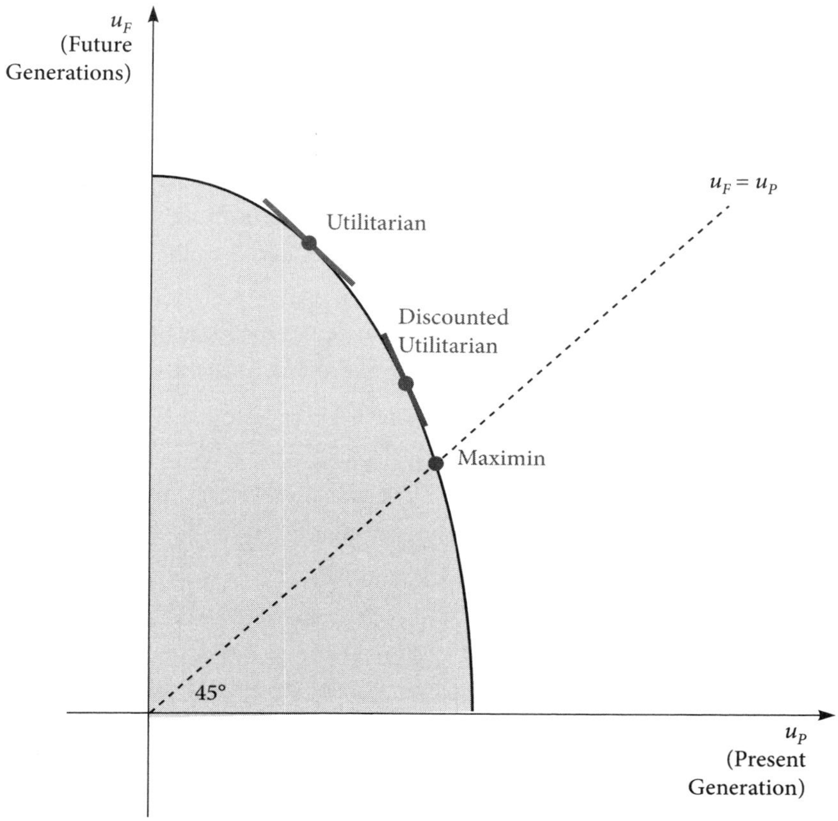

Figure 1.1. The utility possibilities set for a two-generation world with rapid technological progress.

tion tomorrow would be of less value than an additional unit of consumption today *if society is impatient to enjoy that additional unit now* [our italics—LRS]. Therefore, impatience is a reason for discounting future costs and benefits at a positive rate. Second, considerations of justice and equality demand that consumption should be evenly spread across the generations. So, if future generations are likely to be richer than us, there is a case for valuing an extra unit of their consumption less than an extra unit of our consumption, other things being equal. Rising consumption provides a second justification for discounting future consumption costs and benefits at a positive rate.

The first reason for discounted utilitarianism Dasgupta offers here is simply based on confusion, for it can only make sense if 'society' is interpreted as a single generation. 'Society' in our problem is a sequence of generations of persons. In the world imagined by the model, there is no issue of intragenerational impatience because each generation lasts a single period. The second reason offered is the desire to reduce intergenerational inequality that, as we've said, is probably quite broadly adhered to among economists.

The main problem with this justification of discounting is that the desirable discount factor depends upon the shape of the utility possibilities set. Suppose the utility possibilities set were to look like the one in Figure 1.2.

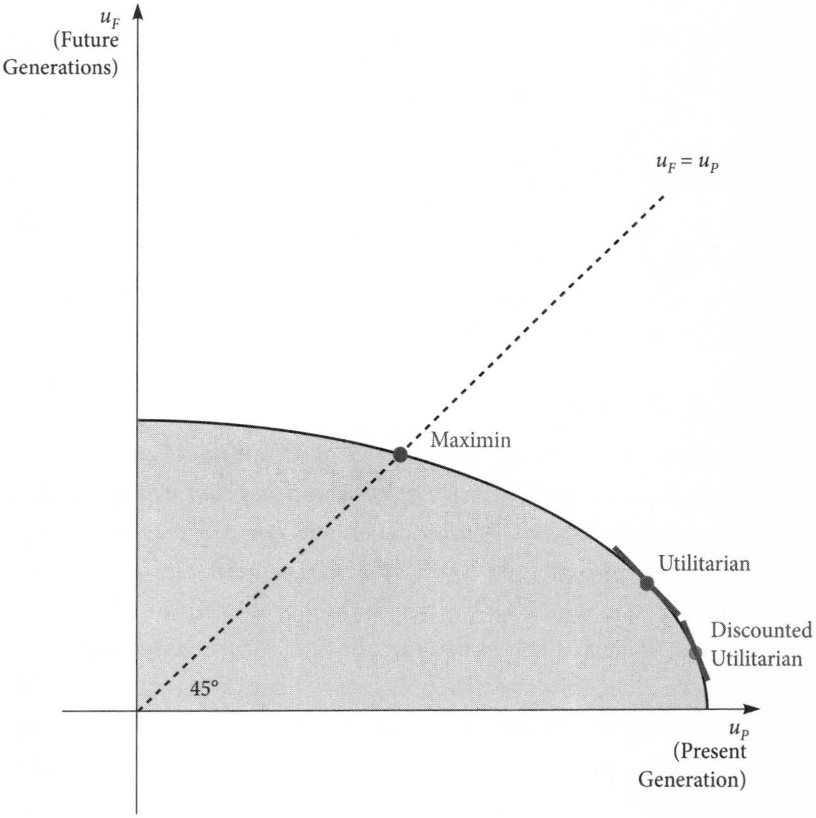

Figure 1.2. The utility possibilities set for a two-generation world when there is technological regress.

Then the Ethical Observer (or social planner) interested in reducing intergenerational inequality would have to *augment* the utility of the future generation with a coefficient greater than 1 in order to induce more intergenerational equality than utilitarianism.

The generic problem with justifying discounting future utilities is that it makes the social objective depend upon the particular economic environment that characterizes the problem: in general, the structure of the utility possibility set U. We believe this puts the cart before the horse. Our ethics should be stated prior to knowledge of what the exact structure of the economic problem is: the ethics are embodied in the objective function to be maximized, and the economic structure is embodied in the constraints defining the feasible set.

There is an additional problem with Dasgupta's justification. How can we assume, as he states, that "future generations are likely to be richer than us?" Whether or not that turns out to be so depends upon how much earlier generations invest—which is *endogenous* to the problem we are trying to solve.

Second Justification for Discounting Utilities: The Long-Lived Agent

Economists often imagine the existence of a long- (usually infinitely) lived agent, where date t is interpreted as the tth period of this agent's life, whose utility over consumption paths is given by

$$\tilde{U}(c_1, c_2, \ldots) = \sum_{t=1}^{\infty} \left(\frac{1}{1+\delta} \right)^{t-1} \tilde{u}(c_t), \tag{1.11}$$

with $\tilde{u}$ interpreted as her single-period utility function. In this case, δ is identified with the rate of impatience or time preference. The identification of the problem of the long-lived agent with the problem of a society of different people that lasts for an infinite number of generations is offered as the justification of employing (1.9) as the objective for climate-change analysis. The obvious objection to this justification is that how much one weights the utility of future generations should not depend upon the rate of impatience of the generation living today—or indeed, on the rate of time discount of *any* generation. Our position is that each generation *does* have the right to decide whether or not to procreate—there is no duty to produce future human beings—but once those future beings exist, they have rights—in particular, the right to enjoy as much utility as every other generation. If the consequence of solving (1.9) where φ is calibrated using the observed time rate of discount δ of the present generation is that later generations have lower utility than earlier ones, then the recommendation is illegitimate, for it violates the aforementioned rights of future generations.

We can again find a defense of this approach from Dasgupta (2005), who writes:

> An individual's lifetime well-being is an aggregate of the flow of well-being she experiences, while intergenerational well-being is an aggregate of the lifetime well-beings of all who appear on the scene. It is doubtful that the two aggregates have the same functional form. On the other hand, I know of no evidence that suggests we would be way off the mark in assuming they do have the same form. As a matter of practical ethics, *it helps enormously* [our italics—LRS] to approximate by not distinguishing the functional form of someone's well-being through time from that of intergenerational well-being.

The second sentence in this citation shows recognition of the issue we are raising, but then Dasgupta decides to ignore it.

The most important evidence, however, that the infinitely lived-agent justification is being used for justifying discounted utilitarianism in climate-change work is the use of the Ramsey equation to calibrate the parameter δ. To explain this, we must first introduce the Ramsey problem. Ramsey (1928) was the first economist to formalize the problem of the infinitely lived agent, as we wrote earlier. His formulation in modern notation is as follows:

$$\max \sum_{t=1}^{\infty} \left(\frac{1}{1+\delta} \right)^{t-1} \tilde{u}(c_t)$$

subject to, for $t \geq 1$:

$$\tilde{u}(c_t) = \frac{c_t^{\,1-\eta}}{1-\eta},$$

$$c_t + i_t \leq F(S_{t-1}),$$

$$S_t \leq (1-d)S_{t-1} + i_t. \tag{1.12}$$

The first constraint defines the per-period utility function $\tilde{u}$; the second constraint is the feasibility condition for the case where the labor force is constant over time, and F is a production function with capital (S) as its only argument; and the third constraint is the law of motion of the capital stock. Ramsey proved that the solution to (1.12) is given by a first-order condition:

$$F'(S_t) - d = \delta + \eta \frac{c_{t+1} - c_t}{c_t}, \tag{1.13}$$

where $F'(S)$ is the marginal product of capital. In a competitive market economy, the real interest rate, r_t, will equal $F'(S_t) - d$, and $\frac{c_{t+1} - c_t}{c_t}$ is the growth rate of consumption at date t, denoted g_t. Thus, (1.13) may be written:

$$r_t = \delta + \eta g_t, \tag{1.14}$$

which is known as the *Ramsey equation*.[8] Now the procedure of Nordhaus and Weitzman is to choose a value of η (which can be interpreted as incorporating an ethical attitude toward intergenerational inequality—see Sections 4.3.3–6) to *observe* r_t and g_t from market data and to thereby deduce the value of δ from (1.14). They then define the discount factor used in their climate-change analysis by $\varphi = 1/(1+\delta)$. Hence, the discount on future utilities is computed as the discount present-day consumers place on *their own* future utility, as reflected by the real market equilibrium and assuming consumers are solving program (1.12).

Now indeed, the procedure these researchers use is not purely that of the long-lived agent, because they choose η to reflect an ethical view about inequality (Nordhaus has used $\eta = 2$ and $\eta = 1.45$, and Weitzman and Stern use $\eta = 1$) rather than calibrating it from observed consumer behavior. But the reliance on the Ramsey equation to calibrate the discount factor is taking the rate of impatience of present-day consumers as the proper way to discount utilities of future generations, and that is, as we have argued, illegitimate.

[8] Condition (1.14) is only approximate because the Ramsey problem has here been written in discrete time. In the continuous-time version of the problem, the Ramsey equation is precise. See the Chapter 1 Appendix for details. See also Section 4.4.2.

We mention a counterargument that those advocating the long-lived-consumer approach to climate change could make against what we have said. They might say, "You (LRS) are being unimaginative in characterizing the parameter δ in the objective of (1.12) as a rate of impatience. Interest rates we see in the market (which we use in our application of the Ramsey equation) reflect the attitudes of present consumer/savers toward future generations, and so we are really calibrating a social-welfare function where the discount factor on future utilities is derived from the attitude of the present generation toward the welfare of their descendants." We are skeptical that this claim about what the real interest rate reflects is empirically correct.[9] Among other reasons, the public-good aspect of benefiting future generations may prevent market behavior from reflecting preferences on the future welfare of mankind.[10] But even granting that it were empirically correct, the welfare of future generations, as we have said, should not depend on how much the present generation wants to save for them. As we have emphasized, this view as a *general principle* is unacceptable. This does not contradict our stated position that if each generation wants to make a gift to the future, rendering future generations *better* off than they would have been on the pure-sustainability path, they may decide how much to give.

Let us note that the long-lived-agent justification of the discounted-utilitarian formulation, if taken literally, in fact has nothing to do with utilitarianism as a political philosophy. There is simply an assumption that a long-lived agent has an intertemporal utility function of a certain, additive form. However, in moving from the interpretation of the objective as the representation of the preferences of a single individual to one of a society, that objective must acquire the status of a social-welfare function. Why take the social-welfare function to have exactly this form? As Dasgupta suggests, it could be just a convenience. Somewhat less prag-

---

[9] See Schneider et al. (2012) and the references in their footnote 3 for the empirical evidence on the importance of life-cycle considerations and the relative unimportance of the bequest motive in explained observed investment by households.

[10] Karp (2013) analyzes how the intragenerational free-rider problem and the degree of altruism toward future generations interact in the determination of equilibrium outcomes.

matically, one could appeal to the first justification for discounting utilities stated above that derives from a desire to moderate the inequality of a purely utilitarian formulation. Using the Ramsey equation suggests that a more 'objective' approach is being taken to decide on the weights of the utilities of future generations—but as we have seen, the measurement of the discount factor via observing actual interest and growth rates is inadmissible from an ethical viewpoint.

Third Justification for Discounting Utilities: The Uncertain Lifetime of the Human Species

Suppose there is a probability $0<\pi<1$ that each generation, should the species have lasted until it arrives, will be the final generation. Then the probability that generation T will be the last generation is $\Pi_T = (1-\pi)^{T-1}\pi$. Suppose there is an Ethical Observer who is a utilitarian: her objective is to maximize the total utility of those generations that exist. When she chooses a path $u \in U$, she is in fact choosing an uncertain prospect or lottery because of the uncertain length of the species' lifetime. We suppose this Ethical Observer has von Neumann–Morgenstern (vNM) preferences over lotteries, and her vNM utility function, defined on the event that the species lasts exactly T periods, is:

$$W^{util}(u,T) = \sum_{t=1}^{T} u_t. \qquad (1.15)$$

Equation (1.15) says she is a utilitarian. Her expected-utility maximization problem is therefore:

$$\max \sum_{T=1}^{\infty} \Pi_T W^{util}(u,T)$$
$$\text{subject to } u \in U. \qquad (1.16)$$

We can expand the objective in (1.16) as follows:

$$\pi u_1 + \pi(1-\pi)(u_1+u_2) + \pi(1-\pi)^2(u_1+u_2+u_3) + \cdots$$
$$= \pi\left[\frac{u_1}{\pi} + \frac{(1-\pi)u_2}{\pi} + \frac{(1-\pi)^2 u_3}{\pi} + \cdots\right] = \sum_{t=1}^{\infty} \varphi^{t-1} u_t, \qquad (1.17)$$

where $\varphi = 1-\pi$. Thus, (1.16) reduces to (1.9).

It must be emphasized that this justification for using the discounted-utilitarian objective in climate-change analysis is completely different from the 'long-lived-agent' justification. It is based on the supposition of an Ethical Observer who is utilitarian and is maximizing her utility under uncertainty. The main exponent of this approach is the *Stern Review*.

1.2.3. Further Discussion

In Section 4.4.3 we show how the different discount factors adopted in the second and third justifications for discounting utilities have massive implications for policy recommendations. Nevertheless, as we have argued, the difference in these discount factors is derivative of choosing different *models*. It is unfortunate that the critiques of Stern by Nordhaus and Weitzman in the literature have focused on the proper size of the discount factor (see Nordhaus 2007; Weitzman 2007). This has derailed the debate from the real question: it really concerns whether the better *model* is that of the long-lived agent or the utilitarian Ethical Observer.

In the argument between Stern, on the one hand, and Nordhaus and Weitzman, on the other, we side with Stern because his use of the discounted-utilitarian objective is philosophically cogent, while the long-lived-consumer analogy fails, we believe, from the beginning. We do not, however, fully endorse Stern because we are not utilitarians: we are sustainabilitarians. We believe the Ethical-Observer argument is legitimate, although we would substitute a sustainabilitarian Ethical Observer for a utilitarian one, as we will in fact do.

We defend our approach of growth sustainability against utilitarianism due to its indifference to inequality. We have argued that its indifference to inequality activates the possibility of utility monsters, who take all the resources, and that in models of intergenerational welfare, a version of the utility-monster problem may occur because of the feasibility of rapid technological progress. We have further argued that amending utilitarianism by discounting is, under the utility-monster justification, *ad hoc*, as it makes the social ethic depend on the feasible set U or, as in the long-lived-agent justification, makes the weights on the utility of future generations depend upon the time rate of impatience of the present generation.

However, we must point out that growth sustainability is certainly not the unique way to implement the view we have advocated in Section 1.1. Indeed, any path in U that is intertemporally consistent, which the present generation chooses *and* which each generation prefers to the pure-sustainability path (the solution to (1.1)) because of their desire for human development, is ethically acceptable according to our argument. We have given a justification of ρ-sustainability based upon the particular formulation of (1.6).

Before proceeding, we should mention axiomatic justifications of discounted utilitarianism. Two of the earliest of these are due to Koopmans (1960) and Diamond (1965). Koopmans proved that if a complete preference order on sets of infinite consumption streams satisfies certain axioms, including continuity, then it must be representable by a utility function of the form (1.11) for *some* choice of $\tilde{u}$ and δ. None of the practitioners of climate change, of whom we know, and who use discounted utilitarianism, justify their approach with reference to Koopmans's theorem. And there is good reason not to: the premises of the theorem are numerous and do not have any clear ethical justification. Moreover, the theorem is silent on the size of the discount rate, which is, as we have explained, at the heart of contemporary controversies.

We do not believe that the axiomatic characterizations of discounted utilitarianism that exist are definitive, in the sense of providing convincing ethical arguments for discounted utilitarianism, and we will make this point with reference to Diamond's theorem, as it is simpler to discuss than Koopmans's. Diamond (1965) proved that if, on a large domain of infinite streams of utility $u=(u_1, u_2, \ldots)$, a preference order obeys *completeness*, *monotonicity*, and *continuity*, then it must obey *social impatience*. Monotonicity states that if u and u' are two paths such that for all t, $u_t \geq u'_t$ and for some t the inequality is strict, then u is socially preferred to u'. Social impatience says that if $u=(u_1, u_2, \ldots, u_t, \ldots)$, $u'=(u_t, u_2, \ldots, u_1, \ldots)$ and $u_t > u_1$, then u' is socially preferred to u. (That is, if two streams differ only in that a later, larger utility is permuted with an earlier, smaller one, then the stream is preferred that has the larger utility appearing earlier in time.) Social impatience is not equivalent to discounted utilitarianism; it is a generalization of the idea of discounting. Notice that completeness eliminates (undiscounted) utilitarianism, monotonicity eliminates 'maximin,' and continuity eliminates 'leximin.'

Consider the preference order and call it $\succsim_\rho$ that is being maximized in program (1.4); it is given by

$$u \succsim_\rho u' \Leftrightarrow \inf_t \frac{u_t}{(1+\rho)^{t-1}} \geq \inf_t \frac{u'_t}{(1+\rho)^{t-1}}.$$

This preference order does not satisfy social impatience. (Let $\rho = 0$, $u = (1, 3, 3^2, 3^3, \ldots, 3^{t-1}, \ldots)$, $u' = (3, 1, 3^2, 3^3, \ldots, 3^{t-1}, \ldots)$; social impatience would then require that $u' \succ_\rho u$, whereas u is in fact indifferent to u'.) The preference order $\succsim_\rho$ is continuous and complete; it violates monotonicity. But is this a reason to reject it? It will turn out that the solution path of (1.4)—when we specify, in Chapter 3, the set of admissible paths U for our problem—is unique. Moreover, it will be the case that there are *no* paths in U that dominate the solution path in the sense of monotonicity. (For if there were, it is easy to show we could find a path with a higher value of Λ than the value on the solution path.) So the nonmonotonicity of $\succsim_\rho$ is immaterial. To this, one might object that, in reality, we often cannot implement the optimal solution to a program but must be satisfied, as policy makers, with evaluating second-best alternatives, and to do so, one needs an entire preference order, not just the best element in a feasible set. But if this practical consideration were true, it would very likely be the case that the set of available alternatives would be small, and it is highly unlikely that the nonmonotonicity of $\succsim_\rho$ would matter because we would not be forced to consider two alternatives that can be ranked by the monotonicity axiom but share the same minimum value. In short, the Diamond theorem can alternatively be stated as follows: the domain axiom, continuity, completeness, monotonicity, and social *patience* (the negation of social impatience) are inconsistent (i.e., there's an impossibility theorem). From this fact, why should we choose to relax the axiom of social patience to get a 'possibility'? Is it so obviously less compelling than the other four axioms? Evidently, Sidgwick, Ramsey, and many others would not have thought so.

1.3. Sustainability and Uncertainty

In this section we apply the Ethical-Observer approach to the sustainabilitarian social-welfare function. As before we assume that there is an exogenous probability $0<\pi<1$ that each generation will be the last one, if it comes into existence. The vNM utility function of the sustainabilitarian Ethical Observer, defined on the event that the species lasts exactly T dates, evaluated at the infinite utility stream u, is:

$$W^{sus}(u,T)=\min_{1\le t\le T} u_t. \tag{1.18}$$

Hence, maximizing the Observer's expected utility means:

$$\max_{u\in U}\sum_{T=1}^{\infty}\Pi_T W^{sus}(u,T). \tag{1.19}$$

Program (1.19) looks difficult because it is nondifferentiable due to the appearance of the 'min' operator in the definition of W^{sus}. Fortunately, one can demonstrate quite easily (see Chapter 2) that for the sets U that we work with, the solution to (1.19) entails that:

$$u_1\ge u_2\ge\cdots\ge u_t\cdots. \tag{1.20}$$

Consequently, at the solution path u, one has, for all T, $W^{sus}(u,T)=u_T$. It follows, from what we argued in the third justification for discounting utilities in Section 1.2, that (1.19) can be rewritten:

$$\max\sum_{t=1}^{\infty}(1-\pi)^{t-1}u_t$$

subject to:

$$u_t\ge u_{t+1},\quad t=1,2,\ldots$$

$$u\in U. \tag{1.21}$$

In other words, the sustainabilitarian Ethical Observer, because of the nature of the economic environment, in fact solves a discounted-utilitarian problem, *with the additional constraint that the utility path be nonincreasing*!

There is immediately a striking corollary to this fact. Suppose the solution of the discounted-utilitarian problem (1.9) with $\varphi = 1 - \pi$ has the property that utilities are nonincreasing with time. *Then this is also the solution to program* (1.21), since the additional set of inequality constraints is true on this path. Thus, it is possible that these two apparently very different social objectives (utilitarianism and sustainabilitarianism) may recommend identical paths. Naturally, it will interest us, in what follows, to see whether this turns out to be the case.

Defining the sustainabilitarian vNM utility function as W^{sus} exposes an unattractive feature of pure sustainability when uncertainty enters the picture, as we have modeled it: the sustainabilitarian Ethical Observer would prefer a world that lasts for two dates, with utilities (1, 1), to a world that lasts for one thousand dates, with utilities (1, 1, 1, . . . , 1, 0.99). In other words, the sustainabilitarian puts no value on the *length* of time that the species survives. Klaus Nehring has suggested that we use instead a sustainabilitarian with a vNM utility function

$$W(u, T) = T \min_{1 \le t \le T} u_t \tag{1.22}$$

to address this problem. More generally, we will study in Sections 2.4 and 6.2 vNM social-welfare functions of the form:

$$W^{\beta}(u, T) = (1 - \beta + \beta T) \min_{1 \le t \le T} u_t \tag{1.23}$$

for $\beta \in [0, 1]$. The adaptation to ρ-sustainability is:

$$W^{\beta,\rho}(u, T) = (1 - \beta + \beta T) \min_{1 \le t \le T} \frac{u_t}{(1+\rho)^{t-1}}. \tag{1.24}$$

We remark that utilitarianism also encounters problems when the population size varies. Perhaps the first of these was that Bentham's 'greatest happiness for the greatest number' formulation of utilitarianism is incoherent. More recently, Parfit's (1984) 'repugnant conclusion' relies on the preference of utilitarianism for a world with a large number of persons, all of whom have lives only barely worth living, to a world with fewer people whose lives are well worth living. It can also prefer a world with a single person who is hugely well off to a world with many people whose lives are well worth living.

1.4. Sustainability in the Economics Literature

Once more, our ethical intergenerational criterion is sustainability rather than utilitarianism. We have argued that utilitarianism, whether discounted or undiscounted, lacks a foundation as solid as the principle of the moral arbitrariness of the date of a person's birth, on which we base our sustainabilitarian criterion. It is moreover the case that the sustainabilitarian ethic is more generally accepted outside of the economics profession than that based on utilitarianism. The present section reviews the literature on the issue of sustainable processes in the macroeconomics of growth.

The study of sustainability originated in the analysis of the sustainable yields, or harvests, of renewable resources, such as fisheries, often developed by biologists and involving a large empirical component (see, e.g., Gordon 1954; Scott 1955; Clark 1990). A main outcome of this work is the characterization of the *maximal sustainable yield* (MSY) of the resource, based on the biological laws of motion. The 'sustainability' of the MSY-type solutions must be understood as an attribute of the steady state because the yield is less than maximal during the transition from the initial conditions to the steady state. If we postulate that a different generation lives at each date, then the earlier generations may well consume less than the later ones.

The same observation applies to the Solow-Swan model of neoclassical growth (Solow 1956; Swan 1956), which, contrary to the MSY literature, is often worded in terms of different generations. The emphasis continues to be on the best steady state, now characterized by the *golden rule* (which corresponds to the MSY of the renewable resource literature): in Phelps's (1961, 642) words: "Each generation invests on behalf of the future generations that share of income that . . . it would have had past generations invest on behalf of it." Again, consumption may be less than maximal during the transition from the initial conditions to the steady state.

Solow (1974) applied the maximin principle to intergenerational equity. As is well known, Rawls himself (1971, sec. 44) was reluctant to do so, but Solow (1974, 30) decided to be "*plus Rawlsien que le Rawls.*" Solow's (1974) model has both an exhaustible natural resource and produced capital: a single produced good is the only argument in the utility function. In order to maintain equal, maximal utility across all generations, the depletion of the nonrenewable resource has to be compensated by the investment in produced capital. Solow's objective was in fact utility sustainability, even though he did not use the word. It is worth quoting from his 1974 article at some length:

> Recently the whole utilitarian approach to social choice has come under fundamental attack by John Rawls. One particular view advanced by Rawls concerns me here. He argues, in effect, that inequality in the distribution of wealth or utility is justified only if it is a necessary condition for improvement in the position of the poorest individual or individuals. In other words, if social welfare, W, is to be written as a function of individual utilities $u_1, \ldots, u_n$, then Rawls argues for the particular function $W = \min\{u_1, \ldots, u_n\}$ so that maximizing social welfare amounts to maximizing the smallest u_i. This welfare function is sensitive only to gains and losses of utility by the poorest person. (29)
>
> In this article I am going to be *plus Rawlsien que le Rawls*: I shall explore the consequences of a straightforward application of the max-min principle to the intergenerational problem of optimal capital accumulation. It will turn out to have both advantages and disadvantages as an ethical principle in this context. The disadvantages are primarily those that led Rawls to shy away from it, though I shall be able to characterize them in more detail. The main advantage is that the max-min principle gives in some respects more sensible precepts than the standard additive-welfare approach. (30)

Hartwick (1977) showed that Solow's (1974) paths for produced capital and for the depletion of the exhaustible resource could be characterized by a Hotelling-type rule (translated as the equality between the marginal product of the extracted amount and the marginal product of the produced capital) together with what is now known as the *Hartwick rule*:

$$\begin{array}{c}\text{INVESTMENT}\\ \text{IN PRODUCED}\\ \text{CAPITAL}\end{array} = \begin{array}{c}\text{MARGINAL PRODUCT}\\ \text{OF EXTRACTED}\\ \text{AMOUNT}\end{array} \times \begin{array}{c}\text{THE}\\ \text{EXTRACTED}\\ \text{AMOUNT}\end{array}$$

The Hartwick rule can be paraphrased as

INVESTMENT IN PRODUCED CAPITAL	=	RENTS OBTAINED BY EXTRACTION;

that is,

NET INVESTMENT IN PRODUCED CAPITAL	=	VALUE OF NET DEPLETION OF THE EXHAUSTIBLE RESOURCE

or

SUM OF NET INVESTMENT IN ALL FORMS CAPITAL	=	0.

A simple argument shows that the Hotelling rule and the Hartwick rule together imply stationary consumption in a continuous-time model. Let $S^k(t)$ denote the stock of produced capital at date t, $m(t)$ be the flow of extraction of the exhaustible resource, $\tilde{f}(S^k, m)$ represent the production function, and $c(t)$ denote consumption. Postulate the law of motion of produced capital:

$$\frac{dS^k}{dt} = \tilde{f}(S^k, m) - c,$$

and define

$$\textit{Hotelling rule: } \frac{\partial \tilde{f}}{\partial S^k} = \frac{\frac{d}{dt}\left(\frac{\partial \tilde{f}}{\partial m}\right)}{\frac{\partial \tilde{f}}{\partial m}};$$

$$\textit{Hartwick rule: } \frac{dS^k}{dt} = \frac{\partial \tilde{f}}{\partial m} m.$$

Then differentiation, with respect to time, of the law of motion of capital yields

$$\frac{d^2S^k}{dt^2} = \frac{\partial \tilde{f}}{\partial S^k}\frac{dS^k}{dt} + \frac{\partial \tilde{f}}{\partial m}\frac{dm}{dt} - \frac{dc}{dt}, \tag{1.25}$$

whereas that of the Hartwick rule yields

$$\frac{d^2S^k}{dt^2}=\frac{d}{dt}\left(\frac{\partial\tilde{f}}{\partial m}\right)m+\frac{\partial\tilde{f}}{\partial m}\frac{dm}{dt}=\frac{\partial\tilde{f}}{\partial S^k}\frac{\partial\tilde{f}}{\partial m}m+\frac{\partial\tilde{f}}{\partial m}\frac{dm}{dt} \quad \text{[by Hotelling rule]}$$

$$=\frac{\partial\tilde{f}}{\partial S^k}\frac{dS^k}{dt}+\frac{\partial\tilde{f}}{\partial m}\frac{dm}{dt}, \quad \text{[by Hartwick rule]}$$

which, together with (1.25) implies that $dc/dt=0$.

The Hartwick rule, in its interpretation "SUM OF NET INVESTMENTS IN ALL FORMS OF CAPITAL = 0," pervades the subsequent sustainability literature. The *Club of Rome Report* (Meadows et al. 1972) and the *Report of the United Nations Conference on the Human Environment*, Stockholm, 1972 (see the United Nations Environment Programme [UNEP], http://www.unep.org, in which the term "sustainable development" appears) expressed an increasing concern about the negative effects of economic activity on the welfare of future generations. This motivated the call for sustainability understood in the oft-quoted terms of the *Brundlandt Report*: "Sustainable development is development that meets the needs of the present generation without compromising the ability of future generations to meet its own needs" (World Commission on Environment and Development 1987).[11]

The Solow-Hartwick theory has a legitimate claim to the title of sustainability and is a precursor of the theory in this book because it focuses on maintaining human quality of life forever. Granted, it defines utility as equal to consumption, but natural environments can easily be added as arguments. The resulting extension of the Solow-Hartwick model to a world where environmental stocks enter the utility function is often called *weak sustainability* (Cabeza Gutés 1996; Neumayer 2010, 21).

The sustainability approach emphasizes sustaining the "capacity for utility" rather than "utility" itself (Neumayer 2010, 8). The distinction, to some extent semantic, entails the notion that *maintaining capital is an end in itself*. *Weak* and *strong* sustainability then interpret "maintaining capital" in different ways. Weak sustainability stays closer to the Hartwick rule,

[11] See also United Nations Department of Economic and Social Affairs, Rio Summit 1992, Earth Summit Agenda 21, http://www.un.org/esa/dsd/agenda21/res_agenda21_00.shtml.

defined as the nonnegativity of the sum of investments in all kinds of capital, including human, natural, renewable, and exhaustible. Strong sustainability emphasizes the lack of substitutability among various forms of capital and advocates maintaining the physical stocks of some forms of natural capital.

Any attempt at aggregating the changes in various forms of capital faces the challenge of pricing them. Market prices are patently inadequate, given the severity of the noninternalized negative environmental externalities (see, e.g., Stern 2008). The sustainability literature often attempts, with little justification, to derive prices from optimization problems where the objective function is the sum of discounted utilities (see, e.g., Neumayer 2010, sec. 5.1.1). The inconsistency of this approach should be evident from our earlier discussion: for a sustainabilitarian, prices must be derived from an optimization problem whose objective is a sustainabilitarian one.

Conventional gross-domestic-product (GDP)-type measures combine consumption and investment. Weak sustainability indicators such as the Genuine Savings (GS) Index (or 'genuine investment,' compiled by the World Bank on a country-by-country basis) aim at correcting the shortcomings of their investment component. The desire to simultaneously correct for the shortcomings of both the investment and consumption components leads to measures such as the Index of Sustainable Economic Welfare (ISEW), also known as the Genuine Progress Indicator (GPI), the evolution of which has been computed and compared to that of the GDP per capita for a variety of countries; see Neumayer (2010, sec. 5.2).

Strong sustainability postulates the nonsubstitutability between natural and produced capital, hence departing from neoclassical economic analysis in a deeper way than does weak sustainability (Neumayer 1999, 2010; Gerlagh and van der Zwaan 2002). While the latter (or the Solow-Hartwick model) aims at preserving an aggregate of the stocks of produced and natural capital, strong sustainability advocates bequeathing to future generations either an aggregate of stocks of natural capital or, better yet, physical stocks of various forms of natural capital. The approach is less precise than weak sustainability and does not deal with future paths of the economic variables, nor does it make an appeal to optimization.

Neumayer (2010, chapter 6) offers detailed arguments and discusses various quantitative indicators of strong sustainability.

In conclusion, our conception of sustainability is similar in spirit to that of Solow (1974) in that it concerns the sustainability of utility rather than particular indices of capital. But as will become evident in Chapter 3, we share with the just-discussed sustainability literature an attention to environmental stocks because, we argue, they affect human welfare directly in a way that traditional capital stocks do not.

1.5. Summary

We have defined an anthropocentric concept of sustainability and have argued that it is an ethically attractive approach to the problem of intergenerational welfare analysis and, in particular, climate change. The fundamental ethical postulate is that the date at which a person is born is a matter of luck (or, in Rawlsian parlance, arbitrary from the moral viewpoint) and that no person deserves to benefit by virtue of luck. This is a *postulate*, not something we claim to be able to prove. One either finds it appealing, or not. Quotations from Ramsey and Sidgwick indicate they assent to this postulate.

We have contrasted the sustainabilitarian approach that we will take in this book with the main competitor on offer, discounted utilitarianism. We have argued that there are several justifications for discounted utilitarianism in the climate-change literature, and have expressed our disagreements with these justifications.

We think that the community of climate-change economists has for practical purposes taken the discounted-utilitarian formulation as a premise and then concerned itself with coming up with reasonable formulations of what the discount rate *and the utility function* should be. But there is no good reason to restrict ourselves to this additive formulation of social welfare and doing so leads to an approach that is to a certain extent *ad hoc*.

APPENDIX 1. THE RAMSEY PROBLEM

In this appendix, we deduce the first-order conditions for the solution of the Ramsey problem (proposition A1.1). We then prove a turnpike theorem for the Ramsey model, which states that the optimal solution converges to a stationary state (proposition A1.2).

The Ramsey program in discrete time is:

$$\max \sum_{t=1}^{\infty}\left(\frac{1}{1+\delta}\right)^{t-1}\frac{c_t^{1-\eta}}{1-\eta},$$

subject to:

$$\begin{aligned}&(a_t)\ F(S_{t-1}) \geq c_t + i_t, && t=1,2,\ldots,\\ &(b_t)\ i_t + (1-d)S_{t-1} \geq S_t, && t=1,2,\ldots,\end{aligned} \tag{A1.1}$$

where S_t is the capital stock at date t, c_t is consumption, and i_t is investment. The time rate of discount is δ. The initial condition is a capital stock $S_0 > 0$. It is assumed that the labor force is one unit at each date and that F is a strictly concave, increasing, differentiable production function, with $F(0) = 0$, defining output of the single commodity as a function of capital, holding constant one unit of labor supplied.

Consider the infinite set of time-dated equations, for $t = 1, 2, \ldots,$

$$F(S_{t-1}) = c_t + i_t, \tag{A1.2}$$

$$S_t = (1-d)\, S_{t-1} + i_t, \tag{A1.3}$$

$$\left(\frac{c_{t+1}}{c_t}\right)^{\eta}(1+\delta) = (1+F'(S_t)-d). \tag{A1.4}$$

Call a path $\{(c_t, i_t, S_t), t = 1, 2, \ldots\}$ which satisfies (A1.2)–(A1.4) for all t for a given S_0 *admissible at* S_0.

Proposition A1.1. *Let* (c_t, i_t, S_t) *be an admissible path at* S_0. *Then it is the unique solution to* (A1.1). *Conversely, suppose the path* $\{(c_t, i_t, S_t), t=1, 2, \ldots\}$ *is strictly positive and is the solution to* (A1.1). *Then it is admissible.*

Proof:

1. We prove the first statement. Let $(\tilde{c},\tilde{i},\tilde{S})$ be any other feasible path. Since the set of feasible paths is a convex set, for any $\varepsilon \in [0, 1]$, the path $((1-\varepsilon)c_t + \varepsilon\tilde{c}_t, (1-\varepsilon)i_t + \varepsilon\tilde{i}_t, (1-\varepsilon)S_t + \varepsilon\tilde{S}_t)$ is a feasible path; we will denote this path $(c_t+\varepsilon\Delta c_t, i_t+\varepsilon\Delta i_t, S_t+\varepsilon\Delta S_t)$ where $\Delta z \equiv \tilde{z} - z$ for $z = c, i, S$. Now define the Lagrangian function of a single variable:

$$\mathfrak{L}(\varepsilon)=\sum_{t=1}^{\infty}\left(\frac{1}{1+\delta}\right)^{t-1}\left(\frac{[c_t+\varepsilon\Delta c_t]^{1-\eta}}{1-\eta}\right)+\sum_{1}^{\infty}a_t(F(S_{t-1}+\varepsilon\Delta S_{t-1})$$
$$-(c_t+\varepsilon\Delta c_t+(i_t+\varepsilon\Delta i_t)))+\sum_{1}^{\infty}b_t((i_t+\varepsilon\Delta i_t)$$
$$+(1-d)(S_{t-1}+\varepsilon\Delta S_{t-1})-(S_t+\varepsilon\Delta S_t)), \tag{A1.5}$$

where a_t and b_t are nonnegative numbers to be specified presently.

2. Note that $\mathfrak{L}$ is a concave function, that $\mathfrak{L}(0)=\sum_{1}^{\infty}\left(\frac{1}{1+\delta}\right)^{t-1}\left(\frac{c_t^{1-\eta}}{1-\eta}\right)$, since by hypothesis, all the constraints are binding on this path, and so the second and third terms in the definition of $\mathfrak{L}$ vanish at $\varepsilon = 0$. Note that $\mathfrak{L}(1)$ is the value of the objective at the path $(\tilde{c},\tilde{i},\tilde{S})$ plus some nonnegative terms. The second and third terms are nonnegative by feasibility of the path $(c+\varepsilon\Delta c, i+\varepsilon\Delta i, S+\varepsilon\Delta S)$ and the postulated nonnegativity of a_t and b_t. If we can appropriately choose numbers a_t and b_t and show that $\mathfrak{L}$ is maximized at zero on the interval [0, 1], it will follow that $\mathfrak{L}(0) \geq \mathfrak{L}(1)$ and therefore that (c, i, S) has an objective value at least as large as the objective value of $(\tilde{c},\tilde{i},\tilde{S})$. Hence it is an optimal path.

3. Let us compute what $\mathfrak{L}'(0)$ would be, assuming it is well-defined. We have:

$$\mathcal{L}'(0) = \sum_{1}^{\infty} \left(\frac{1}{1+\delta} \right)^{t-1} c_t^{-\eta} \, \Delta c_t$$

$$+ \sum_{1}^{\infty} a_t (F'(S_{t-1}) \, \Delta S_{t-1} - \Delta c_t - \Delta i_t)$$

$$+ \sum_{1}^{\infty} b_t (\Delta i_t + (1-d) \, \Delta S_{t-1} - \Delta S_t). \tag{A1.6}$$

Gather together like terms. The coefficient of Δc_t is $\left(\frac{1}{1+\delta} \right)^{t-1} c_t^{-\eta} - a_t$, the coefficient of Δi_t is $-a_t + b_t$; the coefficient of ΔS_t is $a_{t+1} F'(S_t) - b_t + (1-d) b_{t+1}$. Now define

$$a_t = \left(\frac{1}{1+\delta} \right)^{t-1} c_t^{-\eta},$$

$$b_t = a_t, \tag{A1.7}$$

and note that all the Δc_t and Δi_t terms on the right-hand side of (A1.6) vanish. For the ΔS_t terms to vanish as well, we require

$$\frac{a_{t+1}}{a_t} = \frac{1}{1 - d + F'(S_t)}. \tag{A1.8}$$

It is easily checked that (A1.8) is equivalent to (A1.4). Therefore $\mathcal{L}'(0) = 0$, and so $\mathcal{L}(\cdot)$, being a concave function, is maximized at zero.

4. This proves the first claim, if the function $\mathcal{L}$ is well-defined. It suffices to show that for any feasible path $(\hat{c}, \hat{i}, \hat{S})$ the second term in the definition of $\mathcal{L}$ converges. We show this in lemma A1.1 below.

5. We now prove the converse. Since the given path is by hypothesis optimal, constraints (A1.2) and (A1.3) must bind, as stated, for all t; for if not, then some value c_t could be increased, without reducing consumption at any other date, thus increasing the value of the program's objective. Thus we need only show that (A1.4) holds on the path.

6. For any $t \geq 1$, create an amended path as follows: define

$$\hat{i}_t = i_t - \varepsilon, \text{ for some } \varepsilon \text{ small in absolute value,}$$

$$\hat{c}_t = c_t + \varepsilon,$$

$$\hat{S}_t = S_t - \varepsilon,$$

$$\hat{i}_{t+1} = i_{t+1} + (1-d)\varepsilon,$$

$$\hat{c}_{t+1} = F(S_t - \varepsilon) - i_{t+1} - (1-d)\varepsilon. \tag{A1.9}$$

Since the postulated solution is strictly positive, the 'hat' values can be defined and will be positive for all ε sufficiently close to zero, for any given t. Check that the amended solution is still feasible and note that the only consumption values that are changed are for dates t and $t+1$. Nothing is changed before date t or after date $t+1$. Since the original solution was optimal, it follows that the expression $(\hat{c}_t(\varepsilon)^{1-\eta} + (1/(1+\delta))\hat{c}_{t+1}(\varepsilon)^{1-\eta})/(1-\eta)$ must be maximized at $\varepsilon = 0$, for otherwise, by substituting the amended values into the path at dates t and $t+1$ for some ε near zero, we could increase the value of the program's objective. But this means that

$$\left.\frac{d}{d\varepsilon}\right|_{\varepsilon=0} \frac{\hat{c}_t(\varepsilon)^{1-\eta} + \dfrac{1}{1+\delta}\hat{c}_{t+1}(\varepsilon)^{1-\eta}}{1-\eta} = 0, \tag{A1.10}$$

which in turn means

$$c_t^{-\eta} + \left(\frac{1}{1+\delta}\right) c_{t+1}^{-\eta}(-F'(S_t) - (1-d)) = 0, \tag{A1.11}$$

which can be rewritten as condition (A1.4). The argument holds for all t, and hence the optimal path is admissible.

7. Uniqueness of the optimal solution follows from strict concavity of the objective function. First note that the values of consumption must be unique, and from this it follows that the entire path must be unique. ∎

The method of proof of this proposition, via constructing the function $\mathfrak{L}$, we call the *Lagrangian method*, since it is a Lagrangian function. We will use this method throughout the book. Because our problems typically possess an infinite number of binding constraints, it must always be noted that the Lagrangian function is well-defined—that is, that once the Lagrangian multipliers have been solved for, the various infinite series in the definition of $\mathfrak{L}$ converge for any feasible point. We will often skip this step in the proofs, except when its verification is not straightforward. Lemma A1.1 verifies this claim for the Lagrangian function of the above proposition.

How does condition (A1.4) relate to the Ramsey equation? Define:

$$\frac{c_{t+1}}{c_t} = 1 + g_t,$$

$$r_t = F'(S_t) - d, \tag{A1.12}$$

where the notation comes from the fact g_t is the growth rate of consumption from date t to date $t+1$, and the interest rate in a competitive economy is equal to the marginal product of capital minus the rate of depreciation. Then (A1.4) can be written:

$$(1+\delta)(1+g_t)^{\eta} = 1 + r_t. \tag{A1.13}$$

Taking the logarithm of this equation:

$$\ln(1+\delta) + \eta \ln(1+g_t) = \ln(1+r_t). \tag{A1.14}$$

Now suppose that δ is small, and g_t and r_t are small for large t. Using the fact that for small x, $\ln(1+x) \approx x$, we can write (A1.14) as:

$$\delta + \eta g_t = r_t, \tag{A1.15}$$

which is the Ramsey equation.

In fact, it can be shown that if the Inada conditions hold:

$$\lim_{S\to 0} F'(S) = \infty, \quad \lim_{S\to\infty} F'(S) = 0,$$

then there exists an optimal solution to the Ramsey program for any $S_0 > 0$, and the solution converges to a stationary state. The stationary state can be computed by substituting $S_t = S^*$ for all t, $c_t = c^*$ for all t into equations (A1.2)–(A1.4), giving:

$$i^* = dS^*, \quad \delta + d = F'(S^*), \quad c^* = F(S^*) - dS^*.$$

The Inada conditions and the strict concavity of F guarantee a solution (c^*, i^*, S^*) to these equations, and this solution, being admissible at S^*, is the optimal solution for the initial condition $S_0 = S^*$, by the proposition. Since (as we prove following) the optimal solution for any S_0 converges to this stationary state, it follows that g_t does indeed approach zero and r_t approaches δ. So if δ is small, the Ramsey equation approximately holds for large t.[12]

An interesting fact follows from this analysis. Note that, given S_0 and c_1 all the other values (c_t, i_t, S_t) are determined, iteratively, by the equations (A1.2)–(A1.4). Since there exists a unique admissible path (because there exists a unique optimal path to the Ramsey program), it follows that, given S_0, there is a unique choice of c_1 that then determines the admissible path. In other words, if we begin with the wrong value for c_1 and then try to define the admissible path iteratively, we will at some date be unable to continue: some value on the path will become negative.

For the model written in continuous time, the Ramsey equation is precisely correct on the optimal path because the approximation that allowed us to deduce (A1.15) from (A1.14) becomes precisely true as the time interval goes to zero.

We next state and prove a turnpike theorem for the Ramsey problem.

► **Proposition A1.2.** *Assume that* $\eta > 0$ *and F satisfies the Inada conditions. Let* (c_t, i_t, S_t) *be the optimal solution to the Ramsey problem, with an initial capital stock of* $S_0 > 0$. *Define* (c^*, S^*, i^*) *by*:

$$F'(S^*) = d + \delta, \quad i^* = dS^*, \quad c^* = F(S^*) - dS^*.$$

Then $\lim\limits_{t \to \infty} c_t = c^*$, $\lim\limits_{S_t \to \infty} = S^*$.

[12] In an amended Ramsey model with exogenous neutral technical progress, the growth rate g is positive on the balanced-growth path.

Note, first, S^* exists because F is concave and satisfies the Inada conditions, and that $c^* > 0$ by the concavity of F.

▶ **Remark.** From the turnpike theorem, it follows that the growth rate of consumption eventually becomes small, and $F'(S_t) - d = r_t$ approaches δ. So if δ is small, then the condition for deriving (A1.15) from (A1.14) indeed holds for large t, justifying the Ramsey equation.

▶ **Proof of Proposition A1.2.**

1. Define the function $\Xi : \Re^2_+ \to \Re^2$ by $\Xi(x, y) = (xg(y), (1-d)y + F(y) - xg(y))$ where $g(y) = \left(\frac{F'(y)+1-d}{1+\delta}\right)^{1/\eta}$. Define a partial order $\succsim$ on $\Re^2$ as follows:

$$(x, y) \succsim (w, z) \Leftrightarrow x \geq w \text{ and } y \leq z.$$

Check that Ξ is weakly monotone increasing with respect to $\succsim$: that is,

$$(x, y) \succsim (w, z) \Leftrightarrow \Xi(x, y) \succsim \Xi(w, z).$$

This follows from the monotonicity and concavity of F.

2. Note that we can write the characterizing equations of the Ramsey solution (A1.2)–(A1.4) as:

$$S_{t+1} = (1-d)S_t + F(S_t) - c_{t+1},$$

$$c_{t+1} = c_t g(S_t),$$

and so it follows that, along the solution path, $\Xi(c_t, S_t) = (c_{t+1}, S_{t+1})$.

3. Check from the definition (step 1) that Ξ has precisely two fixed points (0, 0) and (c^*, S^*) (To be precise, Ξ is undefined when $y = 0$.)

4. Suppose on the optimal path there is a T such that $\Xi(c_T, S_T) \succsim (c_T, S_T)$. Then, applying Ξ iteratively, we deduce by the $\succsim$-monotonicity of Ξ that $(c_T, S_T) \precsim (c_{T+1}, S_{T+1}) \precsim \cdots (c_t, S_t) \precsim \cdots$ for all $t \geq T$. Hence $\{S_t\}$ is a monotone decreasing sequence and

converges to a limit $\underline{S} \geq 0$. Likewise, $\{c_t\}$ is a monotone increasing sequence and must be bounded, since S_t approaches a finite value, and so $\{c_t\} \to \bar{c}$. It follows that $\Xi(\bar{c}, \underline{S}) = (\bar{c}, \underline{S})$ and hence either $(\bar{c}, \underline{S}) = (0, 0)$ or $(\bar{c}, \underline{S}) = (c^*, S^*)$.

5. The same conclusion follows if there is a date T at which $\Xi(c_T, S_T) \precsim (c_T, S_T)$.
6. For our optimal path, there are three possibilities: either $S_1 < S^*$ or $S_1 = S^*$ or $S_1 > S^*$. We will assume the first case holds here. The other two cases can be dealt with in similar manner. Suppose it were the case that $\Xi(c_1, S_1) \succsim (c_1, S_1)$. Then by the argument of step 4, (c_t, S_t) converges to one of the fixed points of Ξ. But it cannot converge to (c^*, S^*) since $\{S_t\}$ is a weakly decreasing sequence (by step 4) and $S_1 < S^*$. Hence $(c_t, S_t) \to (0, 0)$. But since $\{c_t\}$ is a weakly increasing sequence, this implies that for all t, $c_t = 0$. Therefore the value of the Ramsey problem is zero, which is false.
7. It therefore follows that $\Xi(c_1, S_1) \not\succsim (c_1, S_1)$. However, since $S_1 < S^*$, check that $g(S_1) > 1$ and so $c_2 > c_1$ by step 2. It therefore follows that $S_2 > S_1$ because otherwise $\Xi(c_1, S_1) \succsim (c_1, S_1)$.
8. We now claim that $S_2 \leq S^*$. For suppose not, and $S_2 > S^*$. Then $g(S_2) < 1$ and so $c_3 < c_2$ (step 2). Therefore we must have $S_3 < S_2$. For if $S_3 \geq S_2$, then $\Xi(c_2, S_2) \precsim (c_2, S_2)$ and the argument of steps 4 and 5 show that (c_t, S_t) approaches a limit point, which leads to a contradiction. Hence, the claim of this step is true.
9. Repeated application of this argument shows that:

   $$(c_1, S_1) < (c_2, S_2) < \cdots < (c_t, S_t) < \cdots$$

   and $S_t \leq S^*$ for all t. Consequently, the sequence $\{c_t, S_t\}$ is bounded and approaches a limit point $(\bar{c}, \bar{S})$. By definition, this limit point is a fixed point of Ξ and therefore it must be (c^*, S^*).
10. This proves the proposition for the case $S_1 < S^*$. The other two cases have similar proofs. ■

Finally, we return to show that the function $\mathfrak{L}$ in the proof of proposition A1.1 is well-defined and hence differentiable.

▶ **Lemma A1.1.** *For any feasible path for the Ramsey problem* $(\hat{c}, \hat{i}, \hat{S})$, *where the optimal solution is* (c_t, i_t, S_t), *the series*

$$\sum\left(\frac{1}{1+\delta}\right)^{t-1} c_t^{-\eta}(F(\hat{S}_{t-1})-\hat{c}_t-\hat{i}_t) \text{ converges.}$$

Note that the proof below does not use the direction of proposition A1.1 for which this lemma is required.

▶ **Proof:**

1. From proposition A1.2, we know that $c_t \to c^*$, so it suffices to show that $F(\hat{S}_{t-1})-\hat{c}_t-\hat{i}_t$ must eventually grow at a factor less than $(1+\delta)$. For this, it suffices to show $F(S_t)$ must eventually grow at a factor less than $(1+\delta)$.
2. Consider the feasible path along which $c_t \equiv 0$; this is the path along which S_t grows as fast as possible. We have $S_t = (1-d)S_{t-1} + F(S_{t-1})$ along this path. Define the function $\Upsilon(x) = (1-d)x + F(x)$: Υ is concave, strictly monotone increasing, and possesses exactly two fixed points: zero and $\bar{S}^*$ where $F(\bar{S}^*) = d\bar{S}^*$. Note that $\Upsilon(S_{t-1}) = S_t$.
3. We claim that for any $S_0 > 0$, the path $\{S_t\}$ converges to $\bar{S}^*$. Suppose $S_{t-1} < \bar{S}^*$. Then $S_{t-1} < S_t < \bar{S}^*$. To verify the first inequality, we need to show that $(1-d)S_{t-1} + F(S_{t-1}) > S_{t-1}$, which is equivalent to $F(S_{t-1}) > dS_{t-1}$, true by the strict concavity of F (the graph of F on the interval $[0, \bar{S}^*]$ lies entirely above the chord connecting $(0, 0)$ to $(\bar{S}^*, F(\bar{S}^*))$. The second inequality follows because $\Upsilon(\bar{S}^*) = \bar{S}^*$ and Υ is strictly monotone increasing. Therefore, if $S_0 < \bar{S}^*$, then the sequence $\{S_t\}$ is strictly monotone increasing and bounded above by $\bar{S}^*$. Since its limit point is a fixed point of Υ, it must be $\bar{S}^*$.
4. A similar argument shows that if $S_0 > \bar{S}^*$, then $\{S_t\}$ is a strictly monotone decreasing sequence converging to $\bar{S}^*$.
5. Hence the growth rate of $\{S_t\}$ approaches zero. Therefore the growth rate of capital for any feasible path cannot approach any positive number in the limit, which proves the lemma. ■

CHAPTER TWO

An Introductory Model with Education and Skilled Labor

2.1. Introduction

This chapter develops an introductory, purely theoretical model that provides important results for our core contribution, which is presented in Chapter 3 and Chapter 5 and is obtained by the optimization of a calibrated model with economic and environmental variables.

In particular, with this chapter we attain the following objectives:

First, we prove a turnpike theorem that underpins the optimization method of Chapters 3 and 5.

Second, we prove a simplification theorem that will extend the applicability of our results in Chapters 3 and 5 to sustainability with uncertainty.

Third, we provide the justification (microfoundations) for growth sustainability promised in Section 1.1 earlier.

Fourth, we introduce and motivate our modeling of the role of education.

The introductory model of this chapter has two sectors, one that produces the consumable-investible commodity and the other that educates youth. In addition, utility will now be a function of commodity consumption and *skilled leisure*; that is, the amount of the individual's leisure time multiplied by her skill level, acquired through education. Thus, the skilled labor-leisure endowment of the adult will have three uses: as labor in commodity production, as teaching labor (educating the young), and as leisure. Note that child-rearing can be thought of as one component of educating the young. This role of education will be maintained in our full-fledged models of Chapters 3 and 5, which, in addition, will tackle the climate issue by incorporating greenhouse gas (GHG) emissions and concentrations.

The justification for studying the model of the present chapter is that it is simpler than our full model with climate change and allows us to deduce important facts about optimal paths with a sustainabilitarian objective function, as well as to deduce relationships between sustainabilitarian and discounted-utilitarianian optimal paths.

This chapter is the most theoretically difficult in the book. Readers may skip the details and still understand the remaining chapters. We do, however, suggest that readers do at least read the verbal summary of the turnpike and simplification theorems (in sections 2.2 and 2.5), as these results play an important role in the following chapters.

2.2. The Model and Its Turnpike Theorem

The initial endowment is an ordered pair $(x_0^e, S_0^k) \in \Re_{++}^2$, where x_0^e is the endowment of labor-leisure in efficiency units of the adult at Generation 0 that was devoted to educating the young, and S_0^k is the capital stock at date zero. At each date, labor-leisure will be partitioned into a vector (x_t^e, x_t^c, x_t^l) where x_t^e is the labor in efficiency units employed in the education sector, x_t^c is the labor in efficiency units employed in commodity production, and x_t^l is leisure in efficiency units. We denote the total labor-leisure endowment of Generation t by $x_t := x_t^e + x_t^c + x_t^l$. The problem of sustaining growth at rate ρ, when there is no uncertainty ($\pi = 0$), and so the discount factor ($\varphi = 1 - \pi$) is 1, is denoted $\rho - SUS[1, x_0^e, S_0^k]$ and is given by:[1]

[1]Thus, to be more general, $\rho - SUS[\varphi, x_0^e, S_0^k]$ is the program of sustaining growth at rate ρ, discounted by the discount factor φ as in equation (1.19), where $\Pi_T = \varphi^{T-1}\pi$.

$$\max \Lambda$$

subject to, for all $t \geqq 1$:

$$(P1) \quad c_t^{\alpha}(x_t^l)^{1-\alpha} \geq (1+\rho)^{t-1}\Lambda,$$

$$(P2) \quad \xi x_{t-1}^e \geq x_t^e + x_t^c + x_t^l \equiv x_t,$$

$$(P3) \quad (S_t^k)^{\theta}(x_t^c)^{1-\theta} \geq c_t + i_t,$$

$$(P4) \quad (1-d)S_{t-1}^k + i_t \geq S_t^k. \tag{2.1}$$

We also use the notation $\hat{u}$ for the Cobb-Douglas utility function of (P1) and $\hat{f}$ for the production function of (P2); the parameters are $(\alpha, \theta, d) \in (0, 1)^3$, $\xi > 1$ and $\rho \geq -1$. (Thus, negative growth is possible.) Commodity production, teaching, and utility all use educated labor (leisure). The education sector (P2) is purely labor intensive: the efficiency units of the child's labor-leisure endowment after education are proportional to the efficiency units devoted to teaching (at date $t-1$). The parameter ξ may be thought of as the student-teacher ratio in a stationary state, in which the skill level is not changing across generations.

The assumption that requires justification is that utility is a function of consumption and *educated* leisure. In standard economics, education is only instrumental for producing skills, which earn higher wages and therefore allow more commodity consumption. But we believe that education is an end in itself, and our choice of utility function models that. Indeed, the simplest justification is that the more educated a person is, the more uses are available for her leisure time, and this, *ceteris paribus*, should increase utility. We quote Wolf (2007): "The ends people desire are, instead, what makes the means they employ valuable. Ends should always come above the means people use. The question in education is whether it, too, can be an end in itself and not merely a means to some other end—a better job, a more attractive mate or even, that holiest of contemporary grails, a more productive economy."

The answer has to be yes. The search for understanding is as much a defining characteristic of humanity as is the search for beauty. It is, indeed, far more of a defining characteristic than the search for food or for a mate. Anybody who denies its intrinsic value also denies what makes us most fully human. In Piketty's (2014, 308) words: "In all human societies, health and education have an intrinsic value: the ability to enjoy years of good health, like the ability to acquire knowledge and culture, is one of the fundamental purposes of civilization."

One reason we believe it is important to introduce education as an end in itself—aside from the fact that we believe it is a realistic assumption—is that, when we consider the problem of climate change, it will be important to consider the option of moderating commodity consumption and substituting other goods that generate utility and produce fewer carbon emissions than commodity production. Education is such a good.

It is interesting to recall Keynes's (1930) essay "Economic Possibilities for Our Grandchildren," in which he speculates about economic development, at least in what he calls the "progressive" countries, in a century's time. He predicted, more or less correctly, that the standard of living would increase by between four- and eight-fold, which took some foresight, writing after the 1929 crash. His other prediction, however, was off the mark: he believed that the "progressive" countries would solve the problem of economic scarcity that has plagued mankind since its beginning, the workweek would be reduced to about fifteen hours, and the new challenge would be how to use leisure time: "Thus for the first time since his creation man will be faced with his real, his permanent problem—how to use his freedom from pressing economic cares, how to occupy leisure, which science and compound interest will have won for him, to live wisely and agreeably well."

Alas, Keynes has not yet been borne out. But because we are, here, thinking about resource allocation over a long future, it seems prudent to design a model in which education amends the value of leisure time for people. Probably, we should go further and consider the fact that education also makes work more interesting, but we have not implemented this in the model.

The *pure-sustainability model* is $0-SUS[1, x_0^e, S_0^k]$, when the growth rate ρ of utility is stipulated to be zero.

We assume throughout that $\xi > 1$, so that the educational technology is productive.

The following theorem is one of the main results for this model.

▶ **Theorem 2.1.** Turnpike Theorem. *Let* $\xi > 1$.

1. *There is a ray* $\Gamma \in \Re^2_+$ *such that, if* $(x^e_0, S^k_0) \in \Gamma$, *then the solution path to the pure-sustainability program* $0 - SUS[1, x^e_0, S^k_0]$ *is stationary.*
2. *If* $(x^e_0, S^k_0) \notin \Gamma$, *then along the solution path the sequence* $((x^e_1, S^k_1), (x^e_2, S^k_2), \ldots)$ *converges to a point on* Γ.
3. *Along the solution path, all constraints hold with equality (in particular, utility is constant over t).*
4. *The solution to* $0 - SUS[1, x^e_0, S^k_0]$ *is unique.*

▶ **Proof:** Chapter 2 Appendix.

The turnpike theorem is illustrated in Figure 2.1: the solution path determined by initial conditions off ray Γ has constant utility, and it has the property that, along this path, the sequence converges to a point in Γ.

The turnpike theorem says that, in the long run (and, indeed, convergence might occur fairly rapidly), we can view the optimal path as being stationary in all the variables, and therefore we get a good picture of what the economy will be like by focusing on the stationary path. It is often convenient to postulate that the economy begins at an endowment vector on the ray Γ, and so the path is stationary from the very beginning.

We will use the turnpike theorem to compute optimal paths in our full-fledged model of Chapter 3. In that model, we begin off the stationary ray. We can, however, compute this ray, and so our optimization strategy consists in requiring the path to converge to the ray in a small number of dates—thus reducing a problem with an infinite number of periods to one with a small finite number of periods—and then verifying that the value of the (finite) program does not change much if we increase the date at which convergence is required to occur.

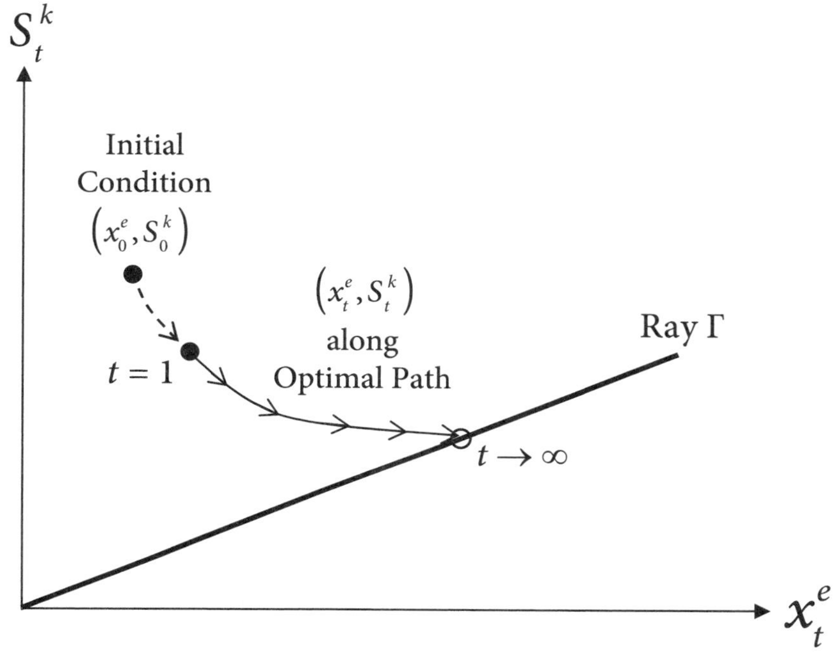

Figure 2.1. Convergence to ray Γ.

2.3. Justification of Growth Sustainability

To review the discussion of Chapter 1, we said that every generation has a right to at least as much utility as any other, and this engenders the solution to pure sustainability ($0 - SUS[1, x_0^e, S_0^k]$) as the benchmark. Nevertheless, generations need not enforce their right—they may choose to render future generations better off than they are (but not worse off). We suggested growth sustainability as a natural alternative but did not derive what the growth rate should be. Intuitively, the growth rate ρ should be derived from a specification of how much each generation values *human development*, meaning an increasing standard of living for generations in the future.

We propose to specify preferences as follows. Interpret the Cobb-Douglas utility function $\hat{u}$ of Section 2.2 as the *standard of living* of Generation t, while their *all-encompassing utility* V_t is given by equation (1.7). Let us consider the program that maximizes V_1, which can be written:

$$\max \sum_{1}^{\infty} (1-\zeta)^{t-1} \ln u_t$$

subject to, for all $t \geqq 1$:

$$(\nu_t) \quad (S_t^k)^{\theta}(x_t^c)^{1-\theta} \geq c_t + i_t,$$

$$(\rho_t) \quad i_t + (1-d)S_{t-1}^k \geq S_t^k,$$

$$(\lambda_t) \quad \xi x_{t-1}^e \geq x_t^e + x_t^c + x_t^l,$$

$$(\mu_t) \quad c_t^{\alpha}(x_t^l)^{1-\alpha} \geq u_t, \tag{2.2}$$

where dual variables are written in parentheses before each constraint. We have the following:

► **Theorem 2.2.** *If* $(1-\zeta)\xi > 1$, *then there exists a unique positive number* S_0 *such that, if the initial endowment vector lies on the ray in* $\Re_+^2$ *containing* $(1, S_0)$, *then the optimal solution to* (2.2) *is a steady-state growth path with positive growth rate* $\rho = (1-\zeta)\xi - 1$.

► **Proof:** Chapter 2 Appendix.

The next task is to study the relationship between the solution to program (2.2) and the solution to $\rho - SUS[1, x_0^e, S_0^k]$. The answer is given by the next result.

► **Theorem 2.3.** *Let* $\rho = (1-\zeta)\xi - 1$. *If the initial endowment vector lies on the ray defined by* $(1, S_0)$ *of theorem* 2.2, *then the optimal solution to* $\rho - SUS[1, x_0^e, S_0^k]$ *is identical to the solution to program* (2.2).

► **Proof:** Chapter 2 Appendix.

Theorems 2.2 and 2.3 provide microfoundations for our claim that 'growth sustainability,' as we have defined it, is an ethically attractive objective. In particular, the solution of $\rho - SUS[1, x_0^e, S_0^k]$ is ethically superior to pure sustainability, as long as $\rho > 0$, and as long as all generations share the all-encompassing utility function V, because if each generation desires to relax its claim to being as well off as future generations, it should be allowed to do so. The value of ξ that we estimate in Chapter 3 is approximately 40, and so for values of ζ not too far from 1, surely $\rho = (1-\zeta)\xi - 1 > 0$, and therefore the conclusion of theorem 2.2 holds.

Theorems 2.2 and 2.3 only give a rigorous justification for growth sustainability when the initial endowment vector lies on the ray specified in the theorems. We assume convergence for program (2.2) and for $\rho - SUS[1, x_0^e, S_0^k]$; so although their solutions from an arbitrary initial vector (x_0^e, S_0^k) may not be identical, they will converge to the same path.[2]

For what values of ρ does a solution to $\rho - SUS[1, x_0^e, S_0^k]$ exist? The next theorem tells us exactly when a balanced growth path exists and is optimal for $\rho - SUS[1, x_0^e, S_0^k]$.

▶ **Definition.** A *balanced growth path at rate* ρ is a path satisfying the first three time-dated constraints of program (2.2) with equality such that:

$$S_t^k = (1+\rho)^t S_0^k, \quad x_t^e = (1+\rho)^t x_0^e, \quad \text{for all } t \geq 0,$$

$$z_t = (1+\rho)^{t-1} z_1 \quad \text{for all variables } z \in \{x^c, x^l, i, c\} \quad \text{for all } t \geq 1.$$

▶ **Theorem 2.4.** *Let* $x_0^e = 1$. *Given any growth rate* $0 \leq \rho < \xi - 1$, *there exists a value* $S_0^k(\rho) > 0$ *such that the solution to* $\rho - SUS[1, 1, S_0^k(\rho)]$ *exists and is a balanced growth path at rate* ρ. *Conversely, if* $\rho \geq \xi - 1$, *there are no feasible solutions to* $\rho - SUS[1, 1, S]$ *for any* $S > 0$.

▶ **Proof:** Chapter 2 Appendix.

Theorem 2.4 asserts that the critical value of the growth *factor* is ξ. *Thus, the extent of growth is determined by the productivity of the educational sector.* This highlights a critical difference between the model of this chapter and the classical Ramsey model, where there is no path that can sustain positive growth forever. Only by inserting exogenous technical change into the Ramsey model can one sustain growth. Therefore, the insertion of education into our model marks a fundamental contrast with the Ramsey model without technical change.

We denote the ray defined by the vector $(1, S_0^k(\rho))$ by $\Gamma(\rho) \in \Re_+^2$. Since the set of feasible paths of the $0 - SUS[1, x_0^e, S_0^k]$ program is a convex cone, we may multiply an initial endowment vector by any positive constant and

---

[2] We say "we assume" this convergence, because the turnpike theorem 2.1 was only proved for the case of zero growth (pure sustainability). The generalization to growth sustainability should be straightforward.

generate an optimal solution by multiplying the initial optimal solution by that constant.

2.4. The Discounted-Utilitarian Program

For a discount factor $\varphi \leq 1$, we denote by $DU[\varphi, x_0^e, S_0^k]$ the *discounted-utilitarian program* associated with the model we are studying. It is:

$$\max \sum_{t=1}^{\infty} \varphi^{t-1}\, \hat{u}(c_t, x_t^l)$$

subject to:

$$(1-d)S_{t-1}^k + i_t \geq S_t^k, \quad t = 1, 2, \ldots$$

$$\hat{f}(S_t^k, x_t^c) \geq c_t + i_t, \quad t = 1, 2, \ldots$$

$$\xi x_{t-1}^e \geq x_t^e + x_t^c + x_t^l, \quad t = 1, 2, \ldots \tag{2.3}$$

Next, we characterize the convergence properties of $DU[\varphi, x_0^e, S_0^k]$.

► **Theorem 2.5.**

A. *If* $\varphi\xi > 1$, *then* $DU[\varphi, x_0^e, S_0^k]$ *diverges for all* $(x_0^e, S_0^k) \in \Re_{++}^2$.

B. *If* $\varphi\xi < 1$, *then* $DU[\varphi, x_0^e, S_0^k]$ *converges for all* $(x_0^e, S_0^k) \in \Re_{++}^2$.

► **Proof:** Chapter 2 Appendix.

As noted, we compute a parameterization in Chapter 3 and estimate that $\xi \approx 40$; therefore, the discount factor would have to be very small for the *DU* program to converge, approximately less than 0.02! Note that this is the discount *factor*, not the discount rate. For the discount factors that economists typically use, *DU* diverges in the present model. In contrast, the pure-sustainability program always has a solution, and we have noted that for growth rates less than $\xi - 1$, the growth sustainability program has a solution as well.[3]

[3] If $\xi \approx 40$, then solutions to the pure-sustainability program exist for growth rates less than 39, which means 3900% generational growth! Of course, the higher the growth rate to be sustained, the lower the utilities of the early generations.

Discounted utilitarians have attempted to deal with divergence of the DU objective by introducing partial orders on paths that diverge according to the DU objective; these are often called *overtaking criteria.* A recent proposal along these lines is that from Basu and Mitra (2007). The utility path $(\bar{\bar{u}}_1, \bar{\bar{u}}_2, \ldots)$ is said to be *at least as good as the utility path* $(\bar{u}_1, \bar{u}_2, \ldots)$ *according to the overtaking criterion* if there exists a T such that $\sum_{t=1}^{T-1} \varphi^{t-1}\bar{\bar{u}}_t \geq \sum_{t=1}^{T-1} \varphi^{t-1}\bar{u}_t$ and $t \geq T \Rightarrow \bar{\bar{u}}_t \geq \bar{u}_t$. This defines a preorder (i.e., an incomplete order) on feasible paths when a program diverges. The overtaking criterion says that there is a date T such that the sum of discounted utilities up to date T is greater on path A than on path B, and for $t > T$, each generation's utility is greater on path A than on path B.

The proof of theorem 2.4 showed that balanced growth paths exist for the education and capital economy as long as $\rho < \xi - 1$. The condition for divergence of such a path in program DU is $\varphi[1+\rho] \geq 1$. This condition surely holds when ρ is close to $\xi - 1$ because $\varphi[1+(\xi-1)] = \varphi\xi > 1$.

Let $(\bar{u}_1, \bar{u}_2, \ldots)$ and $(\bar{\bar{u}}_1, \bar{\bar{u}}_2, \ldots)$ be two feasible balanced-growth paths for a given initial endowment (x_0^e, S_0^k) that grow at rates ρ_1 and ρ_2, respectively, where $\rho_2 > \rho_1$. It is easy to see that $(\bar{\bar{u}}_1, \bar{\bar{u}}_2, \ldots)$ is better than the utility path $(\bar{u}_1, \bar{u}_2, \ldots)$ according to the overtaking criterion. But it is also the case that utility will be smaller for some early date(s) on the preferred path. (To grow forever faster requires making early sacrifices.) This is interesting, because discounted utilitarianism is usually associated with implying that the *later* generations sustain low utility. *This, however, is only the case when the DU program converges.* Indeed, as the proof of theorem 2.4 shows, as the growth rate ρ approaches its unattainable supremum $(\xi - 1)$ (and these high-growth-rate paths are the most desirable paths according to the overtaking criterion), the utility of the first generation approaches zero. We do not take this unpleasant feature to be a criticism of the overtaking criterion as such; rather, it is a criticism of discounted utilitarianism. As we noted in Chapter 1, the central unattractive feature of utilitarianism is its lack of concern for intertemporal inequality.

As the growth rate approaches $\xi - 1$, the utility of Generation 1 approaches zero. Indeed, the utilities of the first T generations approach zero, for any T, as the growth rate approaches $\xi - 1$. So high growth rates, although feasible, are not desirable, as they force the early generations to starve.

What does the solution of the *DU* program look like when it converges? The next theorem says that, if the initial capital-labor ratio is sufficiently large, then the solution of *DU* is a balanced growth path with *negative* growth, so that utility converges to zero.

For an initial condition (x_0^e, S_0^k), define the capital-labor ratio $C_0 = S_0^k / x_0^e$. Define the following variables for all $t \geq 1$:

$$E := [\varphi\xi]^{1/(\alpha\theta)}[1-d],$$

$$\tilde{x}_t^c := E^{t-1}\frac{[\xi - E]\alpha[1-\theta]}{1-\alpha\theta}, \quad \tilde{x}_t^l := E^{t-1}\frac{[\xi - E][1-\alpha]}{1-\alpha\theta}, \quad \tilde{x}_t^e = E^{t-1},$$

$$\tilde{c}_t := \left[[1-d]^{\theta} E^{1-\theta}\right]^{t-1}[C_0]^{\theta}\,[\tilde{x}_1^c]^{1-\theta}\,[1-d]^{\theta}, \quad \tilde{S}_t^k := [1-d]^t\, S_0^k, \quad \tilde{i}_t = 0.$$

▶ **Theorem 2.6.** *Suppose that* $\varphi\xi < 1$ *and that* $C_0 \geq C^*$, *where* C^* *is the root of the equation:*

$$1-\theta\left[\frac{\tilde{x}_1^c}{[1-d]C}\right]^{1-\theta} = \frac{\tilde{c}_1}{\tilde{x}_1^l}[\varphi\xi]^{1/(\alpha\theta)}\frac{\theta[1-\alpha]}{\sigma[1-\alpha\theta]}. \tag{2.4}$$

Then the solution to $DU[\varphi, 1, C_0]$ *is given by the balanced negative growth path, with growth factor* $E < 1$, *defined above.*

▶ **Proof:** Chapter 2 Appendix.

Theorem 2.6 says that if the initial 'capital-labor' ratio is sufficiently large, and the discount factor is small enough so that the *DU* program converges, then utility in fact converges to zero on the optimal path. (We put capital-labor in scare quotes, because C is actually the ratio of date-zero capital to date-zero labor in the education sector.)

What does the solution of the *DU* program look like when $C_0 < C^*$ and the program converges? The solution will not be the nicely behaved geometric-decay solution of theorem 2.6. We compute an example.

▶ **Example 2.7.** Let $(\alpha, \theta, d, \xi, \varphi) = (0.66, 0.25, 0.1, 1.1, 0.9)$ and $(x_0^e, S_0^k) = (1, 0.15)$. Note $\varphi\xi < 1$. Then $C^* = 0.186198$ and so $C_0 = 0.15 < C^*$. The solution to $DU[\varphi, 1, S_0^k]$ is given by $(c_1, x_1^l, x_1^c, x_1^e, i_1, S_1^k) = (0.192294,$

0.0482943, 0.870989, 0.154375, 0.0746361, 0.114795). We have $C_1 = 0.1979 > C^*$ and the variables from date two onward are given by theorem 2.6. In particular, $u_1 = 0.1138$ and $u_2 = 0.1169 > u_1$. The utilities from date two onward decay geometrically (theorem 2.6).

▶ **Proof:** Chapter 2 Appendix.

Based on example 2.7, we may conjecture what the general solution of $DU[\varphi, x_0^e, S_0^k]$ looks like when the program converges and when $S_0^k / x_0^e < C^*$. There will be a sequence of numbers $\tilde{C} > C^* > C_1 > C_2 > \cdots > 0$ where C^* is given in theorem 2.6; if $C_T > C_0 > C_{T+1}$, the first T dates will have $i_t > 0$, and at date $T+1$, the capital-labor ratio will be C_{T+1}, at which point the geometric-decay solution of theorem 2.6 takes over.

2.5. Sustainability with Uncertainty in the Capital-Education Model

We return to the model of sustainability with uncertainty that we introduced in Section 1.3. We will call an Ethical Observer with the vNM utility function $W^{\beta,\rho}$ of equation (1.24) a *time-weighted sustainabilitarian* (TWS). In this section, we study the solution of the TWS's program for the model of this chapter, namely:

▶ **Program** $\rho - SUS^{\beta}[\varphi, x_0^e, S_0^k]$

$$\max\left(u_1 + \varphi[1+\beta]\min\left\{u_1, \frac{u_2}{1+\rho}\right\}\right.$$
$$\left. + \varphi^2[1+2\beta]\min\left\{u_1, \frac{u_2}{1+\rho}, \frac{u_3}{(1+\rho)^2}\right\} + \cdots\right)$$

subject to:

$$(1-d)\,S_{t-1}^k + i_t \geq S_t^k, \quad t \geq 1,$$

$$\hat{f}(S_t^k, x_t^c) \geq c_t + i_t, \quad t \geq 1,$$

$$\xi x_{t-1}^e \geq x_t^e + x_t^c + x_t^l, \quad t \geq 1,$$

$$c_t^{\alpha}(x_t^l)^{1-\alpha} \geq u_t, \quad t \geq 1, \tag{2.5}$$

given the initial endowment (x_0^e, S_0^k), where $\varphi = 1 - \pi$ and ρ is the desired growth rate. This is the program that a ρ-sustainabilitarian must solve if she discounts future utilities because there is probability π that each generation, should it come into being, will be the last generation.

▶ **Proposition 2.8.**

A. *For any sequence of nonnegative numbers* $(u_1, u_2, \ldots) \in \Re_+^\infty$, *and any* $0 \le \varphi < 1$, *and any* $0 \le \beta \le 1$, $\sum_{t=1}^{\infty} \varphi^{t-1}(1 + (t-1)\beta) \min\{u_1, \ldots, u_t\}$ *converges.*

B. *At any solution to program* (2.5), *the utilities at all dates are positive.*

C. *If* $(u_1, u_2, \ldots)$ *are the utilities associated with a solution to* (2.5), *then for all* t, $(1+\rho)u_t \ge u_{t+1}$.

▶ **Proof:** Chapter 2 Appendix.

Part C of proposition 2.8 is the analog of the fact that, in the zero-growth program, utilities must be weakly monotone decreasing on the optimal path. Recall, it is this property that allowed us to simplify the objective function of the program to the discounted-utilitarian objective, by inserting the inequalities '$u_t \ge u_{t+1}$' in the set of constraints. We can perform a similar trick for program (2.5), by virtue of part C of proposition 2.8.

We now state the second main result of this chapter (the first one being the turnpike theorem).

▶ **Theorem 2.9.** **Simplification Theorem.** *Let* $(x_0^e, S_0^k) \in \Gamma(\rho)$. *If* $\varphi\xi \ge 1 + \rho$, *then for any* $\beta \in [0, 1]$, *any solution to the discounted, time-weighted growth-sustainabilitarian program* $\rho - SUS^\beta[\varphi, x_0^e, S_0^k]$ *(i.e., to program* (2.5)) *is a solution to the growth-sustainabilitarian program* $\rho - SUS^0[1, x_0^e, S_0^k]$. *The solution exists and is unique (independent of* β).

▶ **Proof:** Chapter 2 Appendix.

The simplification theorem asserts that, if the growth factor is not too large ($\varphi\xi \ge 1 + \rho$), then a TWS who discounts future utilities because of the possibility of species extinction can simplify her computation of the optimal path in two ways: first, she can ignore the discount factor (i.e., set it equal to one) and second, she can also ignore the time weight (and set $\beta=0$)! Therefore, the theorem justifies a substantial computational simplification. Conceptually, it is surprising that neither time-weighting nor discounting impose *any extra restriction* on the sustainabilitarian Ethical Observer *if the economy is sufficiently productive* (i.e., if ξ is 'large').

In particular, consider the case $\rho=0$. Then theorem 2.9, in conjunction with theorem 2.5, tells us that if the DU program diverges, then the solution to the *discounted-SUS* program is the same as the solution to the *undiscounted-SUS* program. This is a result that has no counterpart in the discounted-utilitarian problem. It tells us, surprisingly, that often discounting does not matter for the sustainabilitarian Ethical Observer, even though she is fully aware that account must be taken of the fact that future generations are less likely to exist because of the exogenous probability of species extinction.

It is worthwhile to give an intuitive explanation of the fact that discounting is superfluous, even when $\varphi<1$. Take the case when $\beta=0=\rho$. By proposition 2.8C, we can write program (2.5) as:

$$\max \sum_{t=1}^{\infty} \varphi^{t-1} u_t$$

subject to:

$$\begin{aligned}
&(1-d)S^k_{t-1} + i_t \geq S^k_t, \quad t \geq 1,\\
&\hat{f}(S^k_t, x^c_t) \geq c_t + i_t, \quad t \geq 1,\\
&\xi x^e_{t-1} \geq x^e_t + x^c_t + x^l_t, \quad t \geq 1,\\
&c^{\alpha}_t (x^l_t)^{1-\alpha} \geq u_t, \quad t \geq 1,\\
&u_t \geq u_{t+1}, \quad t \geq 1.
\end{aligned} \tag{2.6}$$

As we noted in Chapter 1, because the utilities at the optimal solution of the discounted-*SUS* program are monotone decreasing, the discounted-*SUS* program becomes the *DU* program *with additional constraints requiring utilities to be decreasing* (see program (1.21) and the discussion that precedes it). Now if the *DU* program diverges (i.e., when $\varphi\xi>1$), it is likely that there are utility paths giving an infinite value to that program that are strictly monotone increasing (for we know there must be unbounded paths of utility). This suggests that the optimal solution to program (2.6) has $u_t = u_{t+1}$ for all t: that is, the economy is so powerful that in the solution to (2.6), the last set of time-dated constraints are all binding. But in this case, program (2.6) becomes, simply, a program to maximize a constant times the sustainable value of utility, that is, $0 - SUS^0[1, x_0^e, S_0^k]$.

In our theory, we take $\varphi = 1 - \pi$ where π is the probability that any given generation is the last one. (See the third justification for discounting utilities in Section 1.2.2.) Therefore, as long as $1 - \pi \geq \frac{1+\rho}{\xi}$, theorem 2.9 tells us that we do not need to discount the $\rho - SUS^\beta[\varphi, x_0^e, S_0^k]$ program to find the optimal solution under uncertainty—at least for initial endowments on the balanced-growth ray.

As we have said, if we calibrated the model of this chapter to an actual modern economy, for reasonably small growth rates, we believe that we would be in the case $(1-\pi)\xi > 1 + \rho$, and hence, theorem 2.9 tells us that the growth-sustainability problem with uncertainty reduces to the growth-sustainability problem with certainty. Nevertheless, it may be interesting to compare the solutions of the sustainabilitarian program and the discounted-utilitarian program when the latter *converges*. In the case when the solution of the *DU* program displays strictly decreasing utility over time (see theorem 2.6), we know that this is also the solution to program $0 - SUS^0[\varphi, x_0^e, S_0^k]$ because the two programs are identical except for the constraints in the latter that require utility to be weakly monotone decreasing with time, and those constraints are nonbinding in this case.

This is not, however, the case in example 2.7, and it is interesting to compute the solution to the discounted pure-sustainability program $(0 - SUS^0[\varphi, x_0^e, S_0^k])$ in this case. We will simply present the result in Table 2.1.

Table 2.1. Utilities at the optimal solutions of the *DU* and *SUS* programs for example 2.7.

	$u[1]$	$u[2]$	$u[t], t>2$
$DU[0.9, 1, 0.15]$	0.1138	0.1169	geometric decay
$0 - SUS^0[0.9, 1, 0.15]$	0.1152	0.1152	geometric decay

In addition, the ratio of the utilities on the two solution paths is constant at 1.015 for all dates $t \geq 2$. Here, then, the discounted utilitarian gives higher utility to all distant generations than the pure sustainabilitarian.

2.6. Summary

We have argued that, given the important role of human capital in growth, it is important to include an education sector in the standard growth model. Moreover, we argue that education not only plays a role in commodity production, in which it improves the skill level of labor, but also plays a role as a direct input into utility. We model this by viewing utility as a function of commodity consumption and educated leisure (i.e., leisure in efficiency units). Indeed, it may be, in reality, just as important to view utility as depending upon the *kind* of labor one performs, where labor is more pleasurable or less onerous the more highly educated is the worker. Nevertheless, we have not modeled this view.

It turns out that the possibility of balanced growth depends upon the productivity in the education sector: it must be the case that a teacher, if she works full time, can impart her level of skill to more than one student. (Or, to stick to the representative- household interpretation, the adult can impart her level of skill to the child by allocating to teaching only part of her labor time.) Empirically, we estimate that this productivity is quite high: an average teacher in the US economy, who works full time, can impart her level of skill to about forty students. It is this educational productivity that gives rise to the existence of paths, in our economy, that can sustain growth forever.

We proved a turnpike theorem for the pure-sustainability model, showing that from any initial endowment vector, the optimal sustainable path converges to a stationary state. This means we can get a quick picture of optimal resource allocation in the economy by looking at the optimal stationary states. Due to the constant-returns nature of the model, the initial endowment vectors that yield optimal stationary paths from the very beginning all lie on a ray in $\Re^2_+$. The optimal paths are identical except for a scale factor.

In Chapter 1 we proceeded to justify our claim, that growth sustainability is an attractive amendment to pure sustainability if individuals possess an all-encompassing utility function of a certain form, by showing that the solution of the maximization of the all-encompassing utility of Generation 1 is the same as the solution of the growth- sustainability problem, where we gave a formula for the desirable growth rate depending upon the parameter in the all-encompassing utility function. From a technical viewpoint, each generation can feasibly desire sustainable growth because of the productivity of the education sector, which permits sustainable growth.

Perhaps the most interesting result in this chapter asserts that if the discounted-*utilitarian* program for the model under consideration and for a given discount factor diverges, then the discounted *pure-sustainabilitarian* program has the same solution as the *un*discounted-sustainabilitarian program (theorem 2.9). (This remains true if we generalize from the sustainabilitarian formulation to the time-weighted-sustainabilitarian formulation.) In this case, then, the sustainabilitarian can ignore the discount factor. There is a generalization to the growth-sustainabilitarian program. It bears repeating that although discounting is *conceptually* necessary if there is uncertainty concerning the length of species lifetime, it is *computationally* unnecessary, assuming that the premises of theorem 2.9 hold.

We studied the discounted-utilitarian program when it converges—which, we argued, is not likely to be the case, given realistic values of the parameters. When it does converge, in some cases, it has the same solution as the analogous discounted-sustainabilitarian program. In other cases, the two solutions are different.

The purpose of this chapter has been to build some intuition for the idea of growth sustainabilitarianism and its relationship to discounted utilitarianism. The model, however, ignores our central concern—the relationship between commodity production, carbon emissions, and climate change. We introduce these issues next.

APPENDIX 2. PROOFS

A2.1. Proof of Theorem 2.1

The Program

The program we study is:

► **Program** $0-SUS[1, x_0^e, S_0^k]$

$$\max \Lambda \quad \text{subject to:}$$

$$\text{(P1)} \quad c_t^{\alpha}(x_t^l)^{1-\alpha} \geq \Lambda, \qquad t \geq 1,$$

$$\text{(P2)} \quad \xi x_{t-1}^e \geq x_t^e + x_t^l + x_t^c, \qquad t \geq 1,$$

$$\text{(P3)} \quad (S_t^k)^{\theta}(x_t^c)^{1-\theta} \geq c_t + i_t, \qquad t \geq 1,$$

$$\text{(P4)} \quad (1-d)S_{t-1}^k + i_t \geq S_t^k, \qquad t \geq 1.$$

In what follows, we frequently denote the utility function by $\hat{u}$ and the production function by $\hat{f}$.

The *value function* of the program maps the initial endowment into the value Λ at the solution; thus we write $V(x_0^e, S_0^k) = \Lambda$.

Define $E^{\Lambda} = \{(x_0^e, S_0^k) | V(x_0^e, S_0^k) = \Lambda\}$. This is the set of initial endowments that generate the same value for the program.

We define a *feasible path* as a set of sequences $\{x_t^e\}_{t=0,1,2...}, \{S_t^k\}_{t=0,1,2...}$ and all other variables beginning at $t=1$, such that inequalities (P2), (P3), and (P4) hold. Denote the set of feasible paths by P.

Denote the set of feasible paths beginning at a given initial vector (x_0^e, S_0^k) by $P(x_0^e, S_0^k)$.

► **Proposition A2.1.** *The set P is a closed convex cone. The set $P(x_0^e, S_0^k)$ is closed and convex.*

► **Proposition A2.2.** *At any solution to program $0-SUS[1, x_0^e, S_0^k]$, all the constraints* (P1)–(P4) *bind at all dates. The solution is unique.*

▶ **Proof:**

1. It is obvious that (P2)–(P4) bind. What requires proof is that $\hat{u}(c_t, x_t^l) = \Lambda$ for all t. We first prove this is the case for $t=1$. Suppose, to the contrary, that at an optimal solution, $\hat{u}(c_1, x_1^l) > \Lambda$. Reduce x_1^l by ε and increase each of x_1^e and x_1^c by $\varepsilon/2$ so that $\hat{u}(c_1, x_1^l - \varepsilon) \equiv \Lambda' > \Lambda$. Now define $(\hat{i}_1, \hat{S}_1^k)$ to be the simultaneous solution of the two equations:

$$c_1 + \hat{i}_1 = \hat{f}\,(\hat{S}_1^k, x_1^c + \frac{\varepsilon}{2}),$$
$$(1-d)S_0^k + \hat{i}_1 = \hat{S}_1^k.$$

Obviously, $\hat{S}_1^k > S_1^k$; therefore $(\hat{S}_1^k, x_1^e + \varepsilon/2) > (S_1^k, x_1^e)$. It follows that, with this altered vector of endowments, $(\hat{S}_1^k, x_1^e + \varepsilon/2)$, the value of the program beginning at date two is greater than Λ, since the value function is strictly increasing. Let the value of the program, beginning at date two, be $\Lambda^* > \Lambda$. We have now produced a feasible path where for all t, $\hat{u}(\hat{c}_t, \hat{x}_t^l) \geq \min(\Lambda', \Lambda^*) > \Lambda$. This contradiction proves that $\hat{u}(c_1, x_1^l) = \Lambda$.

2. Assume now that in any optimal solution, for $1 \leq t < T$, $\hat{u}(c_t, x_t^l) = \Lambda$, but there is an optimal solution for which $\hat{u}(c_T, x_T^l) > \Lambda$. Reduce x_{T-1}^e by ε/ξ and increase x_{T-1}^l by the same amount, increasing utility at date $T-1$, which is now greater than Λ. This decreases x_T by ε, and let this decrease be implemented by decreasing x_T^l by ε; ε may be chosen small enough that utility at date T is still greater than Λ. We have now produced an optimal path for the program for which $\hat{u}(c_{T-1}, x_{T-1}^l) > \Lambda$, which contradicts the induction hypothesis. This proves that for all t, $u[t] = \Lambda$.

3. We next show that the solution is unique. Any two solutions must have the same values of $\{c_t, x_t^l\}$: for if not, take any nontrivial convex combination of the two solutions, producing another optimal solution for which the constraints (P1) do not bind; this contradicts what has been proved above. In like manner, the values $\{S_t^k, x_t^c\}$ must be the same in the two solutions, since otherwise a

convex combination of them would produce an optimal solution in which the constraints (P3) do not bind. But if the dated capital stocks are identical in the two solutions, so must be the dated investments. Since the values $\{x_t^c, x_t^l\}$ are identical in the two solutions, we see, by iteration, that the values of $\{x_t^e\}$ are also identical. This proves the claim. ■

Proposition A2.3.

A. *Let* $(\tilde{x}_0^e, \tilde{S}_0^k) > (x_0^e, S_0^k)$. *Then* $V(\tilde{x}_0^e, \tilde{S}_0^k) > V(x_0^e, S_0^k)$.

B. *Along the optimal path beginning at* (x_0^e, S_0^k), *there is no* T *such that* $(x_T^e, S_T^k) > (x_0^e, S_0^k)$.

C. *Let* $\{(x_{0j}^e, S_{0j}^k) \in E^\kappa\}$ *be an infinite sequence of points in* E^κ, *some fixed* κ, *such that* $x_{0j}^e \to \infty$. *Then* $S_{0j}^k \to 0$.

Proof:

A. If $(\tilde{x}_0^e, \tilde{S}_0^k) > (x_0^e, S_0^k)$, then there is a positive number δ^* such that $(x_T^e, S_T^k) > (1+\delta^*)(x_0^e, S_0^k)$. Since P is a cone, and the utility of Generation t is homogenous of degree one in its arguments, it follows immediately that $V(\tilde{x}_0^e, \tilde{S}_0^k) > (1+\delta^*)V(x_0^e, S_0^k)$.

B. Suppose that there is a T such that $(x_T^e, S_T^k) > (x_0^e, S_0^k)$. Let the value of the program be κ. By part A, the value of the subprogram *that begins at date* T is strictly greater than κ. This contradicts the fact that the constraints (P1) are binding for all t.

C. Suppose the premise were false; then there is a subsequence $S_{0j}^k \to S > 0$, for some S. We can choose a number $\hat{S} > S$ and a number $\hat{x}$ such that $V(\hat{x}, \hat{S}) = \hat{\kappa} > \kappa$. Because $x_{0j}^e \to \infty$, we can also choose an index j such that the program beginning with the endowments (x_{0j}^e, S_{0j}^k) possesses a feasible path that, at its first date, has three properties:

i. $S_1^k > \hat{S}$,

ii. $x_1^e > \hat{x}$,

iii. $c_1^\alpha (x_1^l)^{1-\alpha} > \hat{\kappa}$.

(This is obvious from examining the technology.) It therefore follows that $V(x_1^e, S_1^k) > \hat{\kappa}$: invoke part A of this proposition. But this is a contradiction, because $V(x_{0j}^e, S_{0j}^k) = \kappa < \hat{\kappa}$.

Since all the constraints of program *SUS* bind, we can write down the Kuhn-Tucker conditions for this concave program. It turns out that these conditions imply only three new pieces of information, which are:

$$\text{(D1)}\ \frac{x_t^l}{c_t} = \frac{1-\alpha}{\alpha(1-\theta)} \frac{x_t^c}{c_t + i_t} \text{ for all } t \geq 1;$$

$$\text{(D2)}\ \frac{x_{t+1}^l}{c_{t+1}} = \frac{x_t^l}{c_t} \frac{\xi}{1-d} \left(1 - \frac{\theta(c_t + i_t)}{S_t^k}\right), \quad t \geq 1.$$

$$\text{(D3)}\ \sum_t \left(\frac{1}{\xi}\right)^t x_t^l \text{ converges.}$$

The other Kuhn-Tucker conditions just define the various Lagrangian multipliers, which are all nonnegative.[1]

It follows that: *a feasible path and a number* Λ *for which all the primal constraints bind at all t, and for which* (D1), (D2) *and* (D3) *hold, is an optimal solution.* ■

The Stationary Ray

We ask: is there a ray of initial endowments in $\Re_+^2$ for which the optimal solution is *stationary*, that is, for which all variables are constant over time? We study this by writing down the primal constraints and equations (D1) and (D2) for a hypothetical stationary ray and see what they imply. Indeed, we can solve them: there is a unique such ray for the initial condition. The ray passes through the following point.[2]

---

[1] We remind the reader that the Kuhn-Tucker conditions for this infinite program are derived by constructing the Lagrangian function, as in the proof of proposition A1.1.

[2] This is actually the point that characterizes the ray when the production function is $\hat{f}(S, x^c) = kS^\theta (x^c)^{1-\theta}$. We have included the parameter k as it will be useful to have later. x^{c^*} is the value of x^c on the ray.

$$x_0^e = 1,\ S_0^k = \left(\frac{k\xi\theta}{\xi + d - 1}\right)^{\frac{1}{1-\theta}} x^{c^*},$$

$$\text{where } x^{c^*} = \frac{(\xi - 1)\alpha(1-\theta)(\xi + d - 1)}{\alpha(1-\theta)(\xi + d - 1) + (1-\alpha)(\xi + d - 1 - \xi d\theta)}.$$

Indeed, we can compute the values of all the variables on this ray. Call these the *stationary state values.* Of course they are defined up to a multiplicative constant. Let us denote this ray by Γ.

The Turnpike Theorem

► **Proposition A2.4.** *From any initial vector* (x_0^e, S_0^k), *the optimal solution to* $0 - SUS[1, x_0^e, S_0^k]$ *converges to a point on* Γ.

In the following, given any two variables a_t and b_t, we use the notation for ratios: $a_t/b_t = (a/b)_t$.

The proof proceeds in the following steps.

► **Lemma.** *Suppose, in the optimal solution, the limit of the sequence* $\{(x^l/c)_{t=1,2,\ldots}\}$ *exists and is finite. Then the solution converges to the stationary state values.*

► **Proof:**

1. Denote the limit of the sequence $\{(x^l/c)_{t=1,2,\ldots}\}$ by $\bar{\lambda}$. We first argue that $\bar{\lambda} \neq 0$. If $\bar{\lambda} = 0$, then $\lim\,(c/x^l)_t = \infty$. By (D1), $\lim\left(\frac{x^c}{c+i}\right)_t = 0$, and so $\lim\,(x^c/S^k)_t = 0$, by invoking (P3). Now $\frac{\theta(c_t + i_t)}{S_t^k} = \theta\left(\frac{x_t^c}{S_t^k}\right)^{1-\theta}$, so $\lim \frac{\theta(c_t + i_t)}{S_t^k} = 0$, which means, by (D2), that $\frac{(c/x^l)_{t+1}}{(c/x^l)_t} \to \frac{1-d}{\xi} < 1$, because $\xi > 1$. It is therefore impossible that $\lim\,(c/x^l)_t = \infty$. Therefore $\bar{\lambda} > 0$.

2. By (P1), $x_t^l(c_t/x_t^l)^\alpha = \Lambda$ for all t. Therefore $\lim x_t^l = \Lambda\bar{\lambda}^\alpha$ and so $\lim c_t = \Lambda\bar{\lambda}^{\alpha-1}$. From (D2), it also follows that $\frac{\xi}{1-d}\lim\left(1 - \frac{\theta(c_t + i_t)}{S_t^k}\right) = 1$; therefore $\lim\left(\frac{c+i}{S^k}\right)_t$ has the value of the ratio of $(c+i)/S^k$ in the stationary state. Therefore $\lim\,(x^c/S^k)_t$ has the same value as the ratio of those variables in the stationary

state. By (D1) it now follows that $\overline{\lambda}$ is also the ratio of x^l/c in the stationary state.

3. Suppose that there were a subsequence of $\{S_t^k\}$ that diverged to infinity. Since $\lim(x^c/S^k)_t$ is finite, it follows that the same subsequence of $\{x_t^c\}$ diverges to infinity. It follows from (P2) that the same subsequence of $\{x_t^e\}$ diverges to infinity. In particular, there exists a T such that $(x_T^e, S_T^k) > (x_0^e, S_0^k)$. But this contradicts part B of proposition A2.3. Therefore the sequence $\{S_t^k\}$ is bounded. It immediately follows that the sequence $\{x_t^c\}$ is bounded, since $\lim\,(x^c/S^k)_t$ exists and is finite; and since $\lim\left(\frac{c+i}{S^k}\right)_t$ also exists and is finite, the sequence $\{i_t\}$ is bounded.

Thus all the sequences of variables, except possibly for $\{x_t^e\}$, are bounded. Therefore we can choose a single subsequence of all the variables (except possibly of $\{x_t^e\}$), which *converges* to values $(\overline{S}^k, \overline{x}^c, \overline{i})$, and we have already shown that $\{x_t^l\}$, $\{c_t\}$ converge to values $\overline{x}^l$ and $\overline{c}$. Furthermore, we know that $\{S_t^k\}$ converges to a positive number, because $\lim\left(\frac{\theta(c_t+i_t)}{S_t^k}\right)$ has the value of the same ratio in the stationary state and $\{c_t\}$ converges to a positive number.

It now follows, by invoking proposition A2.3, part C, that $\{x_t^e\}$ does not diverge to infinity—since $(x_t^e, S_t^k) \in E^\wedge$ for all t. So there is a subsequence of the original sequence such that *all* variables converge.

We proceed to show that this subsequence of variables converges to stationary-state values. Denote the limits:

$$\overline{\lambda}_1 = \lim \frac{c_t + i_t}{x_t^c} = \lim \frac{\overline{c} + i_t}{x_t^c}, \tag{A2.1}$$

$$\overline{\lambda}_2 = \lim\left(\frac{S^k}{x^c}\right)_t. \tag{A2.2}$$

We have shown that $\overline{\lambda}_1$ and $\overline{\lambda}_2$ are the values of the corresponding ratios in the stationary state. Now from (P3) we have:

$$x_t^c \overline{\lambda}_2^\theta - i_t \to \overline{c}.$$

Note that equations (A2.1) and (A2.2) comprise two simultaneous equations, in the limit, for the limits of the variables x^c and i. Hence, the sequences $\{x_t^c\}$ and $\{i_t\}$ must converge, and to stationary-state values, since these same two equations hold for the stationary-state variables. We therefore have, by (A2.2), that $\{S_t^k\}$ also converges to the appropriate stationary-state value. Likewise with $\{x_t^e\}$.

Finally, indeed the *whole* sequence of variables converges to the same stationary state: for if not, there would be another limit point approached simultaneously by some other subsequence of the variables, to a stationary state. But since the stationary ray is unique, the limit of (x_t^e, S_t^k) must also be on the ray Γ. However, we cannot have two subsequences approaching different points on the ray: that would violate proposition A2.3, part B. ■

▶ Proof of Proposition A2.4.[3]

1. On the optimal path, the sequence $\{(x^l/c)_{t=1,2,...}\}$ does not diverge to infinity.

   Suppose it did diverge to infinity. Then from (D1), the sequence $\frac{x_t^c}{c_t + i_t}$ diverges to infinity also. But, invoking (P3), $\frac{x_t^c}{c_t + i_t} = \left(\frac{x_t^c}{S_t^k}\right)^{\theta}$, and so $\frac{x_t^c}{S_t^k} \to \infty$. Now $\frac{\theta(c_t + i_t)}{S_t^k} = \theta\left(\frac{x_t^c}{S_t^k}\right)^{1-\theta}$ and so it follows that $\frac{\theta(c_t + i_t)}{S_t^k}$ diverges to infinity. But this contradicts (D2), for it would mean that eventually the ratio $\frac{x_t^l}{c_t}$ is negative.

2. Hence, it follows that on the optimal path, the sequence $\{(x^l/c)_{t=1,2,...}\}$ has a (finite) limit point. If the sequence $\{(x^l/c)_{t=1,2,...}\}$ indeed converges to this limit point, then the theorem is proved, by the lemma.

3. Thus, the remainder of the proof will show that the limit point of the sequence $\{(x^l/c)_{t=1,2,...}\}$ is unique, and hence it is the limit of the sequence.

---

[3] We thank Cong Huang, who collaborated on this proof.

By exploiting equations (D1) and (P3), we can rewrite (D2) as follows:

$$\text{(D2*)}\quad \left(\frac{x^l}{c}\right)_{t+1} = \left(\frac{x^l}{c}\right)_t \frac{\xi}{1-d}\left(1-\theta\left(\frac{\alpha(1-\theta)}{1-\alpha}\right)^{\frac{1-\theta}{\theta}}\left(\frac{x^l}{c}\right)_t^{\frac{1-\theta}{\theta}}\right).$$

It will be convenient to define the function: $f^*(x) = ax(1-bx^r)$, where $a = \frac{\xi}{1-d}$, $b = \theta\left(\frac{\alpha(1-\theta)}{1-\alpha}\right)^{\frac{1-\theta}{\theta}}$, and $r = (1-\theta)/\theta$. Thus (D2*) says that

$$f^*\left(\frac{x_t^c}{c_t}\right) = \frac{x_{t+1}^c}{c_{t+1}} \text{ for all } t.$$

Compute that $\frac{d^2 f^*}{dx^2} = -rab(1+r)x^{r-1}$, and so f^* is a concave function on $\Re_+$. Let A^* be the value of the ratio x^l/c in the stationary state. Then we have: $f^*(A^*) = A^*$ and $f^*(0) = 0$. The first claim follows since the equation (D2*) holds, of course, at the stationary state as well.

Finally, note that another root of f^* is given by $x^* = (1/b)^{1/r}$. Concavity implies that f^* has only the two fixed points 0 and A^*.

Because $\{(x^l/c)_{t=1,2,\ldots}\}$ is bounded, it possesses a lim inf and a lim sup. For convenience, denote $y_t = (x^l/c)_t$, and define

$$\Phi := \liminf y_t, \quad \Phi^* := \limsup y_t.$$

Since $f^*(y_t) = y_{t+1}$, we have $\inf f^*(y_t) = \Phi$, and by continuity of f^*, $\inf f^*(y_t) = f^*(\inf y_t) = f^*(\Phi) = \Phi$, so Φ is a fixed point of f^*. In like manner, Φ^* is a fixed point of f^*.

If we can establish that $\Phi \neq 0$, then we must have $\Phi = A^* = \Phi^*$, and hence the limit of $\{y_t\}$ exists. But this is established by an argument that mimics step 1 of the proof of the lemma, as follows.

If $\Phi = 0$ then, by (D1), $\liminf\left(\frac{x^c}{c+i}\right)_t = 0$, and so lim inf $(x^c/S^k)_t = 0$, by invoking (P3). Now $\frac{\theta(c_t+i_t)}{S_t^k} = \theta\left(\frac{x_t^c}{S_t^k}\right)^{1-\theta}$, so

$\liminf \frac{\theta(c_t + i_t)}{S_t^k} = 0$, which means, by (D2), that $\liminf \frac{y_{t+1}}{y_t} = \frac{\xi}{1-d} > 1$, because $\xi > 1$. But this immediately implies that $\liminf y_t > 0$, a contradiction. Therefore, $\Phi \neq 0$, and proposition A2.4 is proved. ■

The proof of theorem 2.1, the turnpike theorem, follows from the previous discussion, in particular from propositions A2.2 and A2.4.

A2.2. Proof of Theorem 2.2

The Kuhn-Tucker conditions for program (2.2) are:

$$(\partial i_t) \quad \nu_t = \rho_t,$$

$$(\partial u_t) \quad \mu_t = \frac{(1-\zeta)^{t-1}}{u_t},$$

$$(\partial s_t) \quad \rho_t \left(1 - \frac{\theta y_t}{S_t}\right) = (1-d)\rho_{t+1},$$

$$(\partial c_t) \quad \rho_t = \mu_t \frac{\alpha u_t}{c_t},$$

$$(\partial x_t^e) \quad \lambda_t = \left(\frac{1}{\xi}\right)^{t-1} \lambda_1,$$

$$(\partial x_t^c) \quad \lambda_t = \rho_t \frac{(1-\theta) y_t}{x_t^c},$$

$$(\partial x_t^l) \quad \lambda_t = \mu_t \frac{(1-\alpha) u_t}{x_t^l}.$$

Let us now look for a solution exhibiting steady-state growth for some growth rate ρ. This will characterize a ray in $\Re_+^2$ such that if the initial endowment lies on the ray, the ρ-steady-state growth path will be the optimal solution to program (2.2). We solve as follows. Normalize by setting $x_0^e = 1$. First, we have the three primal constraints (here, the variables c, i, etc., are c_1, i_1, etc.), and one of the variables is the unknown ρ.

$$\hat{f}(S_0(1+\rho), x_c) = c+i, \tag{A2.3}$$

$$i+(1-d)S_0 = (1+\rho)S_0, \tag{A2.4}$$

$$\xi-(1+\rho) = x^c + x^l. \tag{A2.5}$$

Now observing the Kuhn-Tucker constraints shows immediately that λ_t, ρ_t, and μ_t all grow at the same rate, and so:

$$\mu_t = \left(\frac{1}{\xi}\right)^{t-1}\mu_1, \quad \rho_t = \left(\frac{1}{\xi}\right)^{t-1}\rho_1.$$

We can write the (∂s) constraint as:

$$\rho_t = \left(\left(\frac{1}{1-d}\right)\left(1-\frac{\theta y}{(1+\rho)S_0}\right)\right)^{t-1}\rho_1, \quad \text{where } y = c+i,$$

from which it follows that:

$$\frac{1}{\xi} = \left(\frac{1}{1-d}\right)\left(1-\frac{\theta y}{(1+\rho)S_0}\right). \tag{A2.6}$$

Now the (∂u) constraint can be written:

$$(1-\zeta)^{t-1} = \mu_1\left(\frac{1}{\xi}\right)^{t-1}\bar{u}(1+\rho)^{t-1},$$

from which two things follow, namely:

$$(1+\rho) = (1-\zeta)\xi \tag{A2.7}$$

and $\bar{u}\mu_1 = 1$. Now the (∂c) constraint says:

$$\rho_1 = \frac{\alpha\mu_1\bar{u}}{c} = \frac{\alpha}{c}.$$

Equating the right-hand sides of the (∂x^c) and (∂x^l) constraints gives:

$$(1-\alpha)\frac{\bar{u}\mu_1}{x^l} = (1-\theta)\frac{y}{x^c}\frac{\alpha}{c} \quad \text{or}$$

$$(1-\alpha)\frac{c}{x^l} = (1-\theta)\frac{y}{x^c}\alpha. \tag{A2.8}$$

(The reader can compute that (A2.8) means MRS = MRT at each date.) The six equations (A2.3)–(A2.8) are equations in the six unknowns S_0, c, i, x^c, x^l, ρ. Obviously, ρ is directly determined by equation (A2.7) and is positive because $(1-\zeta)\xi > 1$. We proceed to show that the remaining five equations have a unique positive solution (c, i, x^c, x^l, S_0).

Equation (A2.6) can be written:

$$\left(\frac{1-(1-d)/\xi}{\theta}\right) = \frac{\hat{f}((1+\rho)S_0, x^c)}{(1+\rho)S_0} = \left(\frac{x^c}{(1+\rho)S_0}\right)^{1-\theta},$$

or $x^c = k(1+\rho)S_0$ where $k := \left(\frac{1-(1-d)/\xi}{\theta}\right)^{1/(1-\theta)}$; note that $k > 0$ since $\xi > 1$.

Equations (A2.7) and (A2.5) give us $x^c + x^l = \xi\zeta$ and equation (A2.4) gives us $i = (d+\rho)S_0$. Therefore we need only solve the four equations:

$$\hat{f}(S_0(1+\rho), x^c) = c + (d+\rho)S_0, \tag{A2.9}$$

$$\xi\zeta = x^c + x^l, \tag{A2.10}$$

$$x^c = k(1+\rho)S_0, \tag{A2.11}$$

$$\frac{x^l}{x^c} = \frac{(1-\alpha)}{\alpha(1-\theta)}\frac{c}{y}, \tag{A2.12}$$

for (c, x^c, x^l, S_0), which are the equivalent to (A2.3), (A2.5), (A2.6), and (A2.8), respectively. Solving (A2.10) and (A2.12) simultaneously gives:

$$x^c = \frac{\alpha\xi\zeta(1-\theta)}{\alpha(1-\theta) + (1-\alpha)\dfrac{c}{y}}. \tag{A2.13}$$

Note that from (A2.9) and (A2.11), $\hat{f}((1+\rho)S_0, x^c) = k^{1-\theta}(1+\rho)S_0$ and so we can solve (A2.9) for:

$$c = (k^{1-\theta}(1+\rho) - (d+\rho))\,S_0,$$

or $c = \hat{k}S_0$ where $\hat{k}$ is the coefficient in the last equation.

We must verify that $\hat{k} > 0$, or $k^{1-\theta} > \dfrac{d+\rho}{1+\rho}$. Expanding this inequality and manipulating shows it is equivalent to the statement

$$(1-\zeta)\xi > (1-d)\left(1-\frac{\zeta}{1-\theta}\right),$$

which is true because the left-hand side is greater than one by the premise, and the right-hand side is less than one.

We can now write (A2.13) as:

$$x^c = \frac{\alpha\xi\zeta(1-\theta)}{\alpha(1-\theta)+(1-\alpha)\dfrac{\hat{k}}{k^{1-\theta}(1+\rho)}}.$$

For this to give a positive value for x^l, we must have $x^c < \xi\zeta$. This follows immediately from the last expression.

Finally, we solve for S_0 from the equation (A2.11), which can be written $S_0 = \dfrac{x^c}{k(1+\rho)}$. ■

A2.3. Proof of Theorem 2.3

As in the proof of theorem 2.2, our strategy is to ask whether there is a ray such that, if the initial endowment vector lies on the ray, then the solution to $\rho - SUS[\varphi, 1, S_0^k]$ is a steady-state path at growing at rate ρ. Analysis of the Kuhn-Tucker conditions for $\rho - SUS[\varphi, 1, S_0^k]$ yields the following five equations:

$$\hat{f}(S_0(1+\rho), x_c) = c + i, \tag{A2.14}$$

$$i + (1-d)S_0 = (1+\rho)S_0, \tag{A2.15}$$

$$\xi - (1+\rho) = x^c + x^l, \tag{A2.16}$$

$$\frac{1}{\xi} = \left(\left(\frac{1}{1-d}\right)\left(1-\frac{\theta y}{(1+\rho)S_0}\right)\right), \tag{A2.17}$$

$$(1-\alpha)\frac{c}{x^l} = (1-\theta)\frac{y}{x^c}\alpha \quad \text{(i.e., MRS = MRT)}. \tag{A2.18}$$

These equations are identical to their corresponding equations ((A2.3), (A2.5), (A2.6), and (A2.8)) in the proof of theorem 2.2 derived from program (2.2) and of course, equation (A2.7) of that proof is true here, because it is taken as the definition of the growth factor $1+\rho$. This proves the theorem. ■

A2.4. Proof of Theorem 2.4

1. We write program $\rho - SUS[1, 1, S_0^k]$ with its dual variables indicated:

$$\max \Lambda \quad \text{subject to, for all } t \geqq 1:$$

$$(P1) \quad c_t^{\alpha}(x_t^l)^{1-\alpha} \geq (1+\rho)^{t-1}\Lambda, \quad (r_t)$$

$$(P2) \quad \xi x_{t-1}^e \geq x_t^e + x_t^c + x_t^l \ , \quad (d_t)$$

$$(P3) \quad (S_t^k)^{\theta}(x_t^c)^{1-\theta} \geq c_t + i_t, \quad (a_t)$$

$$(P4) \quad (1-d)S_{t-1}^k + i_t \geq S_t^k \ . \quad (b_t)$$

The Kuhn-Tucker conditions are:

$$(\partial\Lambda): \quad 1 = \sum_1^{\infty} r_t(1+\rho)^{t-1},$$

$$(\partial c_t): \quad r_t u_1[t] = a_t,$$

$$(\partial x_t^l): \quad r_t u_2[t] = d_t,$$

$$(\partial x_t^e): \quad \xi d_{t+1} = d_t,$$

$$(\partial x_t^c): \quad a_t f_2[t] = d_t,$$

$$(\partial S_t^k): \quad a_t f_1[t] + (1-d)b_{t+1} = b_t,$$

$$(\partial i_t): \quad a_t = b_t,$$

where the first and second partial derivatives of the functions $\hat{u}$ and $\hat{f}$ at date t are denoted by $u_j[t], f_j[t], j=1, 2$. In addition, let all the primal constraints hold with equality. We shall attempt to solve all these equations for a balanced growth path.

On such a path, $u_j[t] = u_j[1]$ and $f_j[t] = f_j[1]$ for $j=1, 2$ and $t \geq 1$. The primal and dual equations yield the following substantive relations on a balanced growth path for the economic variables:

$$i_1 = (\rho + d)S_0^k, \tag{A2.19}$$

$$\xi - (1+\rho) = x_1^c + x_1^l, \tag{A2.20}$$

$$f_2[1] = \frac{u_2[1]}{u_1[1]}, \tag{A2.21}$$

$$\xi = \frac{1-d}{1-f_1[1]}, \tag{A2.22}$$

$$f((1+\rho)\,S_0^k, x_1^c) = c_1 + i_1. \tag{A2.23}$$

The other dual constraints simply define nonnegative dual variables in terms of the primal variables, with one exception: we must verify that the series in the ($\partial\Lambda$) constraint converges. Thus, given ρ, if we can solve the five equations (A2.19)–(A2.23) for $(S_0^k, x_1^c, x_1^l, c_1, i_1)$ and the series in ($\partial\Lambda$) converges, then the balanced growth path at rate ρ defined by these values, along with the associated dual variables, solves the Kuhn-Tucker constraints. Assuming the convergence conditions for the Lagrangian function $\mathfrak{L}$ hold, which we will comment upon below, and since *SUS* is a concave program, the theorem will be demonstrated.

2. From the dual Kuhn-Tucker conditions, we deduce that $r_t = \frac{d_1}{u_2[1]}\left(\frac{1}{\xi}\right)^{t-1}$. Consequently the series in the ($\partial\Lambda$) Kuhn-Tucker condition defines a value for d_1 if and only if $\frac{1+\rho}{\xi} < 1$. This is true because by hypothesis, $\rho < \xi - 1$.
3. Thus, it remains to solve the five equations (A2.19)–(A2.23). Specializing to the Cobb-Douglas specification, we rewrite the five equations as follows.

$$i_1 = (\rho + d)S_0^k, \tag{A2.24}$$

$$\xi - (1+\rho) = x_1^c + x_1^l, \tag{A2.25}$$

$$(1-\theta)\left(\frac{(1+\rho)\,S_0^k}{x_1^c}\right)^{\theta} = \frac{(1-\alpha)c_1}{\alpha\, x_1^l}, \tag{A2.26}$$

$$\theta\left(\frac{x_1^c}{(1+\rho)S_0^k}\right)^{1-\theta}=\frac{\xi-(1-d)}{\xi},\tag{A2.27}$$

$$((1+\rho)S_0^k)^{\theta}(x_1^c)^{1-\theta}=c_1+(\rho+d)S_0^k.\tag{A2.28}$$

4. Now denote $X=\frac{x_1^c}{S_0^k}$, $Y=\frac{c_1}{x_1^l}$. Solve (A2.27) and (A2.28) for X and Y:

$$X=(1+\rho)\left(\frac{\xi-(1-d)}{\theta\xi}\right)^{1/(1-\theta)},$$

$$Y=\frac{\alpha(1-\theta)}{1-\alpha}\left(\frac{\xi-(1-d)}{\theta\xi}\right)^{-\theta/(1-\theta)}.$$

Next, divide equation (A2.28) through by S_0^k, giving:

$$\frac{c_1}{S_0^k}=(1+\rho)^{\theta}X^{1-\theta}-(\rho+d).\tag{A2.29}$$

which generates a *necessary condition*:

$$(1+\rho)^{\theta}X^{1-\theta}>(\rho+d).\tag{A2.30}$$

Now, noting that, $XY=\frac{c_1}{S_0^k}\frac{x_1^c}{x_1^l}$, and using (A2.29), we have:

$$Z\frac{x_1^c}{x_1^l}=XY,\text{ where } Z\equiv(1+\rho)^{\theta}X^{1-\theta}-(\rho+d),$$

or $x_1^c=\frac{x_1^l XY}{Z}$. Using (A2.25) and substituting this value for x_1^c, we can solve for x_1^l:

$$x_1^l=\frac{Z}{Z+XY}(\xi-(1+\rho)).$$

Consequently $x_1^c=\frac{XY}{XY+Z}(\xi-(1+\rho))$. Thus both x_1^c and x_1^l are positive numbers. We can now use the equations to solve quickly for positive values of S_0^k, i_1 and c_1.

5. We now verify (A2.30). Define the function $Q(\rho):=(1+\rho)\,\frac{\xi-(1-d)}{\theta\xi}-(\rho+d)$. Check that $Q(0)>0$ if and

only if $\xi > \frac{1-d}{1-\theta d}$; but this is true because $\xi > 1$. Check that $Q(\xi-1) = (\xi-(1-d))\frac{1-\theta}{\theta} > 0$. Since Q is linear, it follows that $Q(\rho) > 0$ on the interval $[0, \xi-1]$, demonstrating (A2.30).

6. We finally remark that all the convergence conditions for the Lagrangian function hold because each sequence of dual variables (e.g., $(a_1, a_2, \ldots)$) converges to zero geometrically. This proves the first direction of the theorem.

7. To prove the converse, let $\rho = \xi - 1$. On a balanced growth path, we therefore require $x_1^e = (1+\rho)x_0^e = \xi x_0^e$, which implies that $x_1^c = x_1^l = 0$. So no balanced growth path can be supported at the rate $\rho = \xi - 1$. It is obvious, *a fortiori*, that no such path exists for $\rho > \xi - 1$. ■

A2.5. Proof of Theorem 2.5

Proof of Part A

1. Let $x_0^e = 1$. We claim that for any small $\varepsilon > 0$, we can find positive numbers C and i such that:

$$i = (\xi - \varepsilon + d - 1)C,$$

$$i = \hat{f}((\xi-\varepsilon)C, \varepsilon).$$

By plotting the graphs of these two functions in (C, i) space, we can observe that they intersect at the origin and at some positive value of i—using the Cobb-Douglas form of $\hat{f}$.

2. Let $\varepsilon < (\xi\varphi - 1)/\varphi$, and let C be chosen to satisfy the equations in step 1, thus defining investment at date one when

$$x_1^c = \varepsilon, \quad x_1^e = \xi - \varepsilon, \quad c_1 = 0 = x_1^l.$$

Note from step 1 that we may take $S_1^k = (\xi - \varepsilon)C$. Let $V(x_0^e, S_0^k)$ be the value of program $DU[\varphi, x_0^e, S_0^k]$, if it converges. Then we must have, by consideration of the choice of date-one values above, $V(1, C) \geq 0 + (\xi - \varepsilon)\varphi\, V(1, C)$. But $(\xi - \varepsilon)\varphi > \xi\varphi - (\xi\varphi - 1) = 1$, implying that the last equation stated cannot hold, and hence program *DU* must diverge beginning with endowment (1, *C*).

3. It immediately follows that program *DU* diverges for $\hat{C} > C$. (Just throw away some capital at date one and reduce the capital-labor ratio to *C*.) Moreover, the program must diverge for $0 < \hat{C} < C$ as well (at date one, invest very little in education, thus increasing the capital-labor ratio at date two to a value $S_1^k / x_1^e \geq C$).

Proof of Part B

1. Let $x_0^e = 1$. The largest possible investment that can be made at date one if $S_0^k = C$ is given by $I(C)$, defined by the equation:

$$\hat{f}((1-d)C + I(C), \xi) = I(C),$$

because $x_1^e \leq \xi$. Define C^* such that:

$$\frac{\hat{f}((1-d), \xi / C^*)}{\xi - (1-d)} = 1 - \hat{f}_1((1-d)C^*, \xi),$$

where $\hat{f}_1(S, x) = \frac{\partial \hat{f}}{\partial S}(S, x)$. A monotonicity argument, invoking the intermediate value theorem, shows that C^* exists and is unique.

Let $m = \hat{f}_1((1-d)C^*, \xi)$ and note that $0 < m < 1$.

2. The graph of the function $z(i) = \hat{f}((1-d)C^* + i, \xi)$ lies everywhere on or below the graph of the function $y(i) = \hat{f}((1-d)C^*, \xi) + mi$ and $y(0) = z(0)$ (by the concavity of $\hat{f}$). The second graph meets the 45° ray in (i, y) space at the point $i = \frac{\hat{f}((1-d)C^*, \xi)}{1-m}$. Therefore:

$$I(C^*) \leq \frac{\hat{f}((1-d)C^*, \xi)}{1-m}.$$

3. Hence, beginning at $S_0^k = C^*$:

$$S_1^k \leq (1-d)C^* + I(C^*) \leq (1-d)C^* + \frac{f((1-d)C^*, \xi)}{(1-m)}$$
$$\leq (1-d)C^* + C^*(\xi - (1-d)) = \xi C^*.$$

Therefore:

$$\hat{u}(c_1, x_1^l) \le \hat{u}(\hat{f}(S_1^k, \xi), \xi) \le \hat{u}(\hat{f}(\xi C^*, \xi), \xi) \le \xi M,$$

where $M \equiv \hat{u}(\hat{f}(C^*, 1), 1)$.

4. For any number $\gamma > 1$, we have:

$$\hat{f}((1-d)\gamma C^* + \gamma I(C^*), \xi) < \hat{f}((1-d)\gamma C^* + \gamma I(C^*), \gamma \xi) = \gamma I(C^*).$$

Consider the function $\hat{\Gamma}(x) = x - \hat{f}((1-d)\gamma C^* + x, \xi)$; note that $\hat{\Gamma}'(x) > 0$ (since $m < 1$). We have (from the above) that $\hat{\Gamma}(\gamma I(C^*)) > 0$, and by definition, $\hat{\Gamma}(I(\gamma C^*)) = 0$. It follows that $I(\gamma C^*) < \gamma I(C^*)$.

5. Now compute that

$$\begin{aligned} S_2^k &\le (1-d)S_1^k + I(S_1^k) \le (1-d)\xi C^* + I(\xi C^*) \\ &\le (1-d)\xi C^* + \xi I(C^*) = \xi((1-d)C^* + I(C^*)) \le \xi^2 C^*, \end{aligned}$$

which follows by invoking the definition of $I(\cdot)$ and steps 3 and 4.

By induction we have $S_t^k \le \xi^t C^*$. But $x_t^c \le \xi^t$ and $x_t^l \le \xi^t$ as well, and so $\hat{u}(c_t, x_t^l) \le \hat{u}(\hat{f}(S_t^k, \xi^t), \xi^t) \le \xi^t M$. It follows that $\sum \varphi^{t-1} u_t \le \xi \sum (\varphi \xi)^{t-1} M < \infty$.

6. Now suppose that $C > C^*$; let $C = \gamma C^*$, $\gamma > 1$. Then beginning at $S_0^k = C$:

$$\begin{aligned} S_1^k &\le (1-d)C + I(C) = (1-d)\gamma C^* + I(\gamma C^*) \\ &< \gamma((1-d)C^* + I(C^*)) \text{ [by Step 4]} \\ &\le \gamma \xi C^* = \xi C. \end{aligned}$$

And so $\hat{u}(c_t, x_t^l) \le \hat{u}(\hat{f}(S_t^k, \xi^t), \xi^t) \le \xi^t \hat{u}(f(C,1),1)$, and as before:

$$\sum (\varphi \xi)^{t-1} u_t < \infty.$$

7. Therefore *DU* converges for $C \ge C^*$. *A fortiori*, it converges for $C < C^*$, by the free disposal of capital. ■

A2.6. Proof of Theorem 2.6

1. Without loss of generality, we assume that $x_0^e = 1$, and $S_0^k = C_0$. Since the set of feasible paths is a convex cone, the primal variables at the solution of the general problem where $x_0^e \neq 1$ are simply the ones computed here, multiplied by x_0^e.

   We write the $DU[\varphi, 1, C_0]$ program with its dual variables:

$$\max \sum_1^\infty \varphi^{t-1} \hat{u}(c_t, x_t^l) \quad \text{subject to, for all } t \geqq 1:$$

$$\text{(C1):} \quad (1-d)S_{t-1}^k + i_t \geq S_t^k, \quad (a_t)$$

$$\text{(C2):} \quad \hat{f}(S_t^k, x_t^c) \geq c_t + i_t, \quad (b_t)$$

$$\text{(C3):} \quad \xi x_{t-1}^e \geq x_t^e + x_t^l + x_t^c, \quad (d_t)$$

$$\text{(C4):} \quad i_t \geq 0 . \quad (e_t)$$

The Kuhn-Tucker conditions for a solution to this program where all the constraints bind are:

$$\begin{aligned}
&(KT1) && (\partial c_t): && \varphi^{t-1} u_1[t] = b_t, \\
&(KT2) && (\partial x_t^l): && \varphi^{t-1} u_2[t] = d_t, \\
&(KT3) && (\partial x_t^e): && d_t = (1/\xi)^{t-1} d_1, \\
&(KT4) && (\partial x_t^c): && b_t f_2[t] = d_t, \\
&(KT5) && (\partial S_t^k): && (1-d)a_{t+1} = a_t - b_t f_1[t], \\
&(KT6) && (\partial i_t): && a_t = b_t - e_t,
\end{aligned}$$

where all equations hold for $t=1, 2, 3, \ldots$. Again, $u_j[t]$ and $f_j[t]$ are the jth partial derivatives of the utility function ($\hat{u}$) and the production function ($\hat{f}$), for $j=1, 2$.

We will show that there exist nonnegative dual variables such that the proposed path satisfies all the Kuhn-Tucker conditions. All the relevant infinite series converge in the Lagrangian function $\mathfrak{L}$, so that the satisfaction of the Kuhn-Tucker conditions suffices to prove optimality of this infinite program.

2. Our method will be to substitute the values on the proposed solution path into the primal and dual conditions and to show that nonnegative values of all dual variables can be computed. To this end, the educational constraint (C3) gives us:

$$\xi - E = x_1^l + x_1^c, \tag{A2.31}$$

recalling that $x_0^e = 1$.

3. The dual Kuhn-Tucker conditions imply the following:

$$u_2[t] = f_2[t]u_1[t], \tag{A2.32}$$

$$\varphi\xi u_2[t+1] = u_2[t], \tag{A2.33}$$

$$e_t - (1-d)e_{t+1} = (1 - f_1[t])b_t - (1-d)b_{t+1}. \tag{A2.34}$$

The remaining dual conditions simply define (nonnegative) values of the dual variables.

4. Equation (A2.32) says that

$$\frac{1-\alpha}{\alpha}\frac{c_t}{x_t^l} = (1-\theta)\left(\frac{(1-d)^t\sigma_0}{E^{t-1}x_1^c}\right);$$

substituting $\tilde{c}_t$ for c_t allows us to reduce this equation to:

$$\frac{(1-\alpha)x_1^c}{\alpha(1-\theta)} = x_1^l. \tag{A2.35}$$

Equations (A2.34) and (A2.35) comprise two linear equations in (x_1^c, x_1^l), which solve to give

$$x_1^c = \tilde{x}_1^c, \quad x_1^l = \tilde{x}_1^l,$$

as required.

5. We next analyze equation (A2.33), which says:

$$\varphi\xi\left(\frac{c_{t+1}}{x_{t+1}^l}\right)^\alpha\left(\frac{x_t^l}{c_t}\right)^\alpha = 1.$$

Substituting in the values $\tilde{c}_t$ and $\tilde{x}_t^l$ gives us an equation in the variable E:

$$\varphi\xi\left(\frac{1-d}{E}\right)^{\alpha\theta}=1,$$

which solves to give the prescribed value for E. Note that $E<1-d$ since $\varphi\xi<1$.

6. The prescribed values of all primal variables have been verified. The Kuhn-Tucker equations (KT1-3) give us nonnegative solutions for b_t and d_t. It is left only to solve for e_t and to show that for all t, $b_t \geq e_t$, which will give nonnegative values for a_t.

7. Define the new variables:

$$m_t=(1-f_1[t])\,\varphi^{t-1}u_1[t]-(1-d)\,\varphi^t u_1[t+1].$$

We show in this step that there exists a number $\hat{\sigma}$ such that if $\sigma_0 \geq \hat{\sigma}$, then $m_t \geq 0$ for all $t \geq 1$. The desired result is equivalent to:

$$(\forall t\geq 1)\quad 1-\theta\left(\frac{\tilde{x}_1^c E^{t-1}}{\sigma(1-d)^t}\right)^{1-\theta} \overset{?}{\geq} (1-d)\varphi\left(\frac{E}{1-d}\right)^{(1-\alpha)\theta}. \tag{A2.36}$$

Since $\dfrac{E}{1-d}<1$, the left-hand side of (A2.36) is increasing in t; thus we need only verify (A2.36) for $t=1$, which is to say, to verify that:

$$1-\theta\left(\frac{\tilde{x}_1^c}{\sigma(1-d)}\right)^{1-\theta} \overset{?}{\geq} (1-d)\varphi\left(\frac{E}{1-d}\right)^{\theta(1-\alpha)},$$

an inequality that holds for sufficiently large σ if and only if:

$$1>(1-d)\varphi\left(\frac{E}{1-d}\right)^{\theta(1-\alpha)},$$

which is immediately seen to be true from the definition of E.

8. Now note that equation (A2.34) can be written

$$e_t-(1-d)e_{t+1}=m_t,\quad t\geq 1.$$

This system of difference equations yields the following solution:

$$e_T = \frac{e_1}{(1-d)^{T-1}} - \sum_{t=1}^{T-1} m_t(1-d)^{t-T}, \quad T = 2,3,\ldots$$

Now choose $e_1 = \sum_{t=1}^{\infty}(1-d)^{t-1}m_t$. (We note that this series converges.)

To verify that $e_T \geq 0$ for all $T \geq 1$ we must show that

$$T \geq 2 \Rightarrow e_1 \geq \sum_{t=1}^{T-1} m_t(1-d)^{t-1},$$

a fact that follows from the definition of e_1 and the fact that $(m_1, m_2, \ldots)$ is a nonnegative sequence.

9. The final step is to show that $a_t \geq 0$ where $a_t = b_t - e_t$. It suffices to show that for all $T \geq 1$, $(1-d)^{T-1}\, b_T \geq (1-d)^{T-1}\, e_T$, or that:

$$(1-d)^{T-1} b_T \overset{?}{\geq} \sum_{t=T}^{\infty} m_t(1-d)^{t-1}.$$

The right-hand side of this inequality can be shown (with some algebra) to equal

$$((1-d)\varphi)^{T-1}(1-f_1[T])u_1[T] - \sum_{T+1}^{\infty} f_1[t]((1-d)\varphi)^{t-1}u_1[t];$$

since $b_T = \varphi^{T-1}\, u_1[T]$, our desired inequality reduces to

$$((1-d)\varphi)^{T-1}u_1[T] \overset{?}{\geq} ((1-d)\varphi)^{T-1}(1-f_1[T])\, u_1[T] - \text{a positive term},$$

which is surely true. This concludes the demonstration that all the Kuhn-Tucker conditions hold with the dual variables as defined.

10. Finally, we derive the critical value C^*. The infinite-series expression for e_1 can be expanded and reduced (with much algebra) to show that

$$e_1(C_0) = (1-f_1[1])\, u_1[1] - \left(\frac{\tilde{c}_1}{\tilde{x}_1^l}\right)^{\alpha} \frac{\alpha\theta}{C_0}(\varphi\xi)^{\frac{1}{\alpha\theta}} \frac{1-\alpha}{1-\alpha\theta}, \qquad \text{(A2.37)}$$

which we write as a function of the initial capital-labor ratio. The reader should note, from the Kuhn-Tucker conditions (*KT*1-6) in step 1, that the dual variables are functions only of the *marginal* utilities and productivities at the various dates, which are, for the Cobb-Douglas case, functions of *ratios* of the primal variables. Therefore, the dual variables are independent of the scale of the endowment vector (i.e., the value of x_0^e).

The critical value of C_0 is that number C^* for which $e_1(C^*)=0$: for if $e_1(C_0)>0$ then a slight decrease in C_0 will still deliver a positive value of e_1 and all the other e_t. But this would mean that investment remains identically zero on the optimal path. The zero of equation (A2.37) is the solution to the equation in the statement of the theorem, which concludes the proof. ■

A2.7. Proof of Example 2.7

1. We will produce the example by finding an initial endowment vector $(1, S_0^k)$ such that $C_0 < C^*$ and the solution to $DU(\varphi, 1, S_0^k)$ has the following property: on the optimal path, at date one, we have $C_1 = S_1^k / x_1^e > C^*$. For we then know what the optimal path is from date one onward: it is just the path stipulated in theorem 2.6. Our strategy will be to find a value S_0^k where, on the optimal path, we have $u[1] < u[2]$.

We write down the program we wish to solve, where $(1, S_0^k)$ is now an unknown endowment.

▶ **Program** PP^*. $\max \sum_1^\infty \varphi^{t-2} \hat{u}(c_t, x_t^l)$ subject to:

$$
\begin{array}{lll}
(1-d)S_{t-1}^k + i_t \geq S_t^k, & t \geq 1, & (a_t) \\
\hat{f}(S_t^k, x_t^c) \geq c_t + i_t, & t \geq 1, & (b_t) \\
\xi x_{t-1}^e \geq x_t \equiv x_t^e + x_t^l + x_t^c, & t \geq 1, & (d_t) \\
i_t \geq 0, & t \geq 1. & (e_t)
\end{array}
$$

Note that we have factored out φ from the usual statement of the objective function. Of course this makes no difference to the solution. The reason for doing so will become apparent momentarily.

We are searching for a solution such that $C_1 > C^*$, $i_1 > 0$, and it follows (by theorem 2.6) that $i_t = 0$, $t \geq 2$. Hence, all constraints of program PP^* will bind except for the first investment constraint. This gives the following Kuhn-Tucker conditions:

$$
\begin{array}{lll}
(\partial c_t): & \varphi^{t-2} u_1[t] = b_t, & t \geq 1, \\
(\partial x_t^l): & \varphi^{t-2} u_2[t] = a_t, & t \geq 1, \\
(\partial x_t^c): & b_t f_2[t] = d_t, & t \geq 1, \\
(\partial x_t^e): & \xi d_{t+1} = d_t, & t \geq 1, \\
(\partial i_t): & a_1 = b_1, & t \geq 1, \\
 & a_t = b_t - e_t, & \\
(\partial s_t^k): & (1-d) a_{t+1} = a_t - b_t f_1[t], & t \geq 1.
\end{array}
$$

2. In theorem 2.6, we solved the *DU* problem with the normalization $C_0 = S_0^k$, $x_0^e = 1$. Recall from step 10 of the proof of theorem 2.6 that the values of the dual variables of that program are functions *only* of C_0: that is, they depend only on the capital-labor ratio at date zero, not on the scale of the initial endowment vector.

3. Program PP^* beginning at date one (not date zero) is *exactly* the program solved in theorem 2.6. (That is why we factored out φ from the objective.) Since $C_1 > C^*$ in the solution we are looking for, it follows that the dual variables from date one on in program PP^* are exactly the dual variables computed in theorem 2.6, where the initial capital-labor ratio is C_1, and the primal variables from date one are exactly the tilde primal variables of theorem 2.6, multiplied by x_1^e, whatever that turns out to be.

   Denote the dual variables computed in the proof of theorem 2.6 with tildes—$\tilde{a}_t(C)$, $\tilde{b}_t(C)$, etc., where C is the initial capital-labor ratio of that program.

4. We now compute what information is contained in the Kuhn-Tucker constraints for program PP^*. First, we know

that $d_2 = \tilde{d}_1(C_1)$: this follows from the above discussion. But $d_2 = \frac{1}{\xi} d_1 = \varphi^{-1} u_2[1]$ and therefore:

$$u_2[1] = \varphi \xi \tilde{d}_1(C_1). \tag{A2.38}$$

From theorem 2.6, we know that $\tilde{d}_1(C_1) = \tilde{u}_2[1] = (1-\alpha)\left(\frac{\tilde{c}_1(C_1)}{\tilde{x}_1^l(C_1)}\right)^{\alpha}$, and we therefore can write, manipulating equation (A2.38):

$$\frac{c_1}{x_1^l} = (\varphi\xi)^{1/\alpha}\left(\frac{\tilde{c}_1(C_1)}{\tilde{x}_1^l(C_1)}\right), \tag{A2.39}$$

where c_1, x_1^l are the date one values on the optimal path for program *PP**.

Our second equation is

$$\frac{u_2[1]}{u_1[1]} = f_2[1],$$

which comes from the first three Kuhn-Tucker constraints of program *PP**. This gives:

$$\frac{1-\alpha}{\alpha}\frac{c_1}{x_1^l} = (1-\theta)\frac{\hat{f}(S_1^k, x_1^c)}{x_1^c} = (1-\theta)\left(\frac{S_1^k}{x_1^c}\right)^{\theta}. \tag{A2.40}$$

The next three equations simply restate the primal constraints:

$$(1-d)S_0^k + i_1 = S_1^k, \tag{A2.41}$$

$$\xi x_0^e = x_1^e + x_1^l + x_1^c, \tag{A2.42}$$

$$\hat{f}(S_1^k, x_1^c) = c_1 + i_1. \tag{A2.43}$$

The next equation comes from the (∂S_1^k) Kuhn-Tucker condition. As before, we know that $b_2 = \tilde{b}_1(C_1)$ and $e_2 = \tilde{e}_1(C_1)$ and so $a_2 = b_2 - e_2 = \tilde{b}_1(C_1) - \tilde{e}_1(C_1)$. Thus, we may write that Kuhn-Tucker condition as:

$$(1-d)(\tilde{b}_1(C_1) - \tilde{e}_1(C_1)) = \alpha\varphi^{-1}\left(\frac{x_1^l}{c_1}\right)^{1-\alpha}\left(1-\theta\left(\frac{x_1^c}{S_1^k}\right)^{1-\theta}\right). \tag{A2.44}$$

The six equations (A2.39)–(A2.44) comprise six equations in the six unknowns x_1^e, x_1^l, x_1^c, i_1, c_1, S_1^k when the endowment $(1, S_0^k)$ is given. Of course, $C_1 = S_1^k / x_1^e$. We know the expressions for all the tilde variables from theorem 2.6, as functions of C_1.

Indeed, these six equations contain all the new information about the solution to program *PP**—the remaining Kuhn-Tucker conditions simply emulate the solution of the program from date one onward, which we know from theorem 2.6.

We now show how to solve these six equations. Define two new variables:

$$A = \frac{c_1}{x_1^l}, \quad B = \frac{S_1^k}{x_1^c}.$$

Note that equations (A2.39), (A2.40), and (A2.44) are simultaneous equations in the three unknowns A, B, and C_1. Hence, we can solve for these three variables (which we will do in an example following). Now, knowing these three variables, we can write all the information remaining in the six equations as the following system of six linear equations in the six unknowns:

$$S_1^k = C_1 x_1^e,$$

$$(1-d)S_0^k + i_1 = S_1^k,$$

$$x_1^c \hat{f}(B,1) = c_1 + i_1,$$

$$c_1 = A x_1^l,$$

$$\xi = x_1^e + x_1^l + x_1^c,$$

$$S_1^k = B x_1^c.$$

We write these equations in matrix form:

$$\mathbf{M}z = Q,$$

where

$$\mathbf{M}=\begin{pmatrix} 0 & 0 & 0 & -C_1 & 0 & 1 \\ 0 & 0 & 0 & 0 & -1 & 1 \\ -1 & 0 & \hat{f}(B,1) & 0 & -1 & 0 \\ -1 & A & 0 & 0 & 0 & 0 \\ 0 & 1 & 1 & 1 & 0 & 0 \\ 0 & 0 & B & 0 & 0 & -1 \end{pmatrix}, \quad Q=\begin{pmatrix} 0 \\ (1-d)\,S_0^k \\ 0 \\ 0 \\ \xi \\ 0 \end{pmatrix}.$$

(The order of the variables is $(c_1, x_1^l, x_1^c, x_1^e, i_1, S_1^k)$.) Hence, we can compute the solution $z=\mathbf{M}^{-1}Q$. *If we insert an endowment vector* $(1, S_0^k)$ *with* $C_0 < C^*$ *and the solution* Q *generated is a positive vector, and* $\frac{S_1^k}{x_1^e} \geq C^*$, *then we have a solution to PP* of the required form.* For it will immediately follow that all the dual variables are nonnegative, from the Kuhn-Tucker conditions, and so we have produced a path where all the Kuhn-Tucker conditions hold—by again invoking theorem 2.6.

5. A *Mathematica* program (available from the authors) calculates this solution for several numerical values, in particular for those in the example. ■

A2.8. Proof of Proposition 2.8

Part A

For any $(u_1, u_2, \ldots)$, $\min\{u_1, \ldots, u_t\} \geq \min\{u_1, \ldots, u_{t+1}\}$. Therefore

$$\begin{aligned}
&\sum_1^\infty \varphi^{t-1}[1+(t-1)\beta]\min\{u_1, \ldots, u_t\} \\
&\quad \leq u_1 \sum_1^\infty \varphi^{t-1}[1+(t-1)\beta] \\
&\quad = u_1[1+\varphi+\varphi^2+\varphi^3+\cdots \\
&\qquad\quad +\beta\varphi+\beta\varphi^2+\beta\varphi^3+\cdots \\
&\qquad\qquad\quad +\beta\varphi^2+\beta\varphi^3+\cdots \\
&\qquad\qquad\qquad\quad +\beta\varphi^3+\cdots \\
&\qquad\qquad\qquad\qquad\quad +\cdots]
\end{aligned}$$

$$= u_1\left[\frac{1}{1-\varphi}+\beta\left(\frac{\varphi}{1-\varphi}+\frac{\varphi^2}{1-\varphi}+\cdots\right)\right]$$
$$= u_1\left[\frac{1}{1-\varphi}+\frac{\beta}{1-\varphi}\frac{\varphi}{1-\varphi}\right]<\infty.$$

Part B

1. If, at a solution of (2.5), $u[1]=0$, then the value of the program is zero. But this is impossible, since the endowment vector is positive, and hence it is possible to produce a path where utility is positive at date one, and hence the program's value is positive.

2. Suppose there is a solution of (2.5) where $u[t]>0$ for $t=1,\ldots,$ T but $u[T+1]=0$. There are three possibilities: either $c_{T+1}=0$ or $x^l_{T+1}=0$ or $c_{T+1}=0=x^l_{T+1}$. We will treat the case when only $x^l_{T+1}=0$. We can therefore reduce x^l_T by a small ε, increase x^e_T by ε and increase x^l_{T+1} by $\xi\varepsilon$. Denote the gain in utility to Generation $T+1$ by B and the loss in utility to Generation T by A. This change will surely increase the value of the objective of the program as long as $\varphi(1+T\beta)B>(1+(T-1)\beta)A$, that is, as long as $B/A>\frac{1+(T-1)\beta}{1+T\beta}$. Note that $\frac{\partial u[T+1]}{\partial x^l_{T+1}}=\infty$ (so to speak), because $x^l_{T+1}=0$ and $c_{T+1}>0$. Therefore, if ε is sufficiently small, the ratio B/A can be made as large as we please. Therefore, this case cannot occur. In like manner, the other cases mentioned cannot occur. By induction, the claim is proved.

Part C

1. We prove this first for $t=1$. Suppose, to the contrary, that there is an optimal solution to program (2.5) such that $u[1]<\frac{u[2]}{(1+\rho)}$. We shall produce another path on which $\hat{u}[1]<\frac{\hat{u}[2]}{1+\rho}$, $\hat{u}[1]>u[1]$, $\hat{u}[2]<u[2]$, and $\hat{u}[t]=u[t]$ for all $t\geq 3$. This will increase the first two terms in the objective, leaving all other terms either the same or larger, and hence will increase the value of the objective, a contradiction.

2. Note that we can choose a small ε such that the following inequalities hold:

$$0 < \varepsilon < \frac{x_2^l}{\xi}, \quad \varepsilon < x_1^e, \quad \hat{u}(c_1, x_1^l + \varepsilon) < \frac{\hat{u}(c_2, x_2^l - \xi\varepsilon)}{1+\rho}.$$

This is possible since we know, by part B, that all utilities are positive, and hence x_1^e and x_2^l are positive. Now consider the new path with

$$\tilde{x}_1^e = x_1^e - \varepsilon, \; \tilde{x}_1^l = x_1^l + \varepsilon, \; \tilde{x}_2^e = x_2^e - \xi\varepsilon, \; \tilde{x}_2^l = x_2^l - \xi\varepsilon,$$

and all other values the same as the original path. By the three inequalities just stated, this is a feasible path. It is easy to check that the sum of the first two terms of the objective has increased with this amendment, and the other terms in the objective function cannot decrease, a contradiction proving the claim.

3. Now suppose that for every optimal solution to program (2.5) (for fixed values of the parameters), $(1+\rho)u[t] \geq u[t+1]$ for $t \leq T$, but there is a solution for which $(1+\rho)u[T+1] < u[T+2]$. There are two possibilities concerning this solution:

case (i): $(1+\rho)u[T] > u[T+1]$,

case (ii): $(1+\rho)u[T] = u[T+1]$.

We know, since the utilities at all dates are positive (part B), we can amend the path and decrease $u[T+2]$ a small amount while increasing $u[T+1]$ a small amount, while leaving utilities at all other dates unchanged. If case (i) holds, this change will increase at least two terms in the objective, leaving other terms either the same or increased, a contradiction to the optimality of the original path. If case (ii) holds, the amended path increases at least one term in the objective, leaving all other terms at least as large. This contradiction proves the claim. ■

A2.9. Proof of Theorem 2.9

In steps 1 through 5 we prove the theorem for the case $\beta=0$. In the remaining steps, we prove it for $0<\beta\leq 1$.

1. It follows from proposition 2.8C that we may write the $\rho-SUS[\varphi, x_0^e, S_0^e]$ program as follows:

$$\max\sum_1^\infty\left(\frac{\varphi}{1+\rho}\right)^{t-1}u_t$$

subject to, for all $t\geq 1$:

$$\begin{aligned}
&(\nu_t) \quad \hat{f}(S_t^k, x_c^t)\geq c_t+i_t,\\
&(\gamma_t) \quad i_t+(1-d)S_{t-1}^k\geq S_t^k,\\
&(\beta_t) \quad \xi x_{t-1}^e\geq x_t^e+x_t^c+x_t^l,\\
&(\mu_t) \quad c_t^\alpha(x_t^l)^{1-\alpha}\geq u_t,\\
&(\lambda_t) \quad (1+\rho)u_t\geq u_{t+1},
\end{aligned} \tag{A2.45}$$

which is a concave program.[4] Lagrangian multipliers are listed in parentheses.

2. By hypothesis, the endowment vector $(1, S_0^k)$ lies on the ray $\Gamma(\rho)$. In other words, the ρ-steady-state-growth path is the optimal solution to $\rho-SUS[1, 1, S_0^k]$. We must demonstrate this path is also the optimal solution to $\rho-SUS[\varphi, 1, S_0^k]$.

3. We look for a solution at which all constraints in (A2.45) bind. We must find non-negative Lagrangian multipliers such that the following dual first-order conditions hold for all $t\geq 1$:

[4] A maximization program is concave if its objective function is a concave function and its constraint set is a convex set.

$$(\partial u_t)\quad \left(\frac{\varphi}{1+\rho}\right)^{t-1}+(1+\rho)\lambda_t=\lambda_{t-1}+\mu_t,$$

$$(\partial S_t^k)\quad \nu_t\theta\frac{(c+i)}{S^k}+(1-d)\gamma_{t+1}=\gamma_t,$$

$$(\partial c_t)\quad \nu_t=\mu_t\frac{\alpha u}{c},$$

$$(\partial i_t)\quad \gamma_t=\nu_t,$$

$$(\partial x_t^c)\quad \nu_t(1-\theta)\frac{(c+i)}{x^c}=\beta_t,$$

$$(\partial x_t^e)\quad \xi\beta_{t+1}=\beta_t,$$

$$(\partial x_t^l)\quad \mu_t(1-\alpha)\frac{u}{x^l}=\beta_t, \tag{A2.46}$$

where (c, i, x^c, x^l, u) are the first-period values of these variables, the first period values of the endowment variables are $x^e=(1+\rho)$ and $S^k=(1+\rho)S_0^k$, and $\lambda_0\equiv 0$. The primal variables satisfy the equations:

$$\hat{f}((1+\rho)S_0^k, x^c)=c+i\equiv y, \tag{A2.47}$$

$$i+(1-d)S_0^k=(1+\rho)\,S_0^k \quad \text{or} \quad i=(\rho+d)S_0^k, \tag{A2.48}$$

$$\xi-(1+\rho)=x^c+x^l, \tag{A2.49}$$

$$u=c^{\alpha}(x^l)^{1-\alpha}.$$

Along the path, we have $u_{t+1}=(1+\rho)\,u_t$.

Besides the primal equations just displayed, we derive two additional first-order conditions from the dual conditions; these are:

$$\frac{1-\alpha}{\alpha}\frac{c}{x^l}=\frac{(1-\theta)y}{x^c}, \tag{A2.50}$$

$$\xi(1-d)=\left(1-\frac{\theta y}{(1+\rho)S_0^k}\right). \tag{A2.51}$$

(Condition (A2.51) is obtained by noting, from the (∂S_t^k) condition, that $\gamma_t = \gamma_1 \left(\frac{1}{1-d} \left(1 - \frac{\theta y}{(1+\rho)S_0^k} \right) \right)^{-(t-1)}$, and that the growth factor of γ_t must be $\left(\frac{1}{\xi} \right)$.)

The five equations (A2.47)–(A2.51) determine the five values (c, i, x^c, x^l, S_0^k) of the ρ-steady-state growth path, which exist and are positive if $\xi > 1+\rho$ according to theorem 2.4. Equation (A2.50) states that, in each period, the marginal rate of substitution between leisure and output is equal to the marginal rate of transformation between labor and output, obviously an efficiency condition. Equation (A2.51) is the analogue of the Ramsey equation for this model. Note that $\frac{\theta y}{(1+\rho)S_0^k}$ is the marginal product of capital. Note that equations (A2.47)–(A2.51) are identical to equations (A2.24)–(A2.28) in the proof of theorem 2.4.

4. Our task is to find nonnegative Lagrangian multipliers associated with this path, satisfying the dual conditions displayed above, such that the Lagrangian function $\mathfrak{L}$ converges. Note that β_t, γ_t, μ_t must all shrink at the rate $(1/\xi)^{t-1}$, so it is only necessary to define the first-period values of these variables. In turn, these will be defined and positive once we have a value for μ_1, upon which everything therefore hinges.

   We deduce the value of μ_1 as follows. Study the (∂u_t) first-order condition. For $t=1$, it says that $(1+\rho)\lambda_1 = \mu_1 - 1$. By induction, we can compute that these conditions imply that:

$$\text{for all } t \geq 1, \quad (1+\rho)\lambda_T = \mu_1 \left(\sum_{t=0}^{T-1} \left(\frac{1}{1+\rho} \right)^{T-1-t} \left(\frac{1}{\xi} \right)^t \right) - \left(\frac{1}{1+\rho} \right)^{T-1} (1+\varphi+\cdots+\varphi^{T-1}). \quad \text{(A2.52)}$$

We will try a value for μ_1 that renders $\lim \lambda_T = 0$. Note that the term multiplying μ_1 in equation (A2.52) is a geometric series whose multiplicative factor is $\frac{1+\rho}{\xi}$. It follows that we define:

$$\mu_1 := \lim \frac{\left(\frac{1}{1+\rho}\right)^{T-1} \frac{1}{1-\varphi}}{\frac{\left(\frac{1}{1+\rho}\right)^{T-1}}{1-\frac{1+\rho}{\xi}}} = \frac{1}{1-\varphi}\left(1-\frac{1+\rho}{\xi}\right).$$

We have noted that to get $\lambda_1 \geq 0$, we require $\mu_1 \geq 1$, which, for the value just defined, is equivalent to $\varphi\xi \geq 1+\rho$, assured by our premise.

5. The demonstration that $\lambda_t \geq 0$ is *pro forma*. Finally, we must show that the series $\Sigma\lambda_t$ converges for the Lagrangian function $\mathfrak{L}$ to converge. Simply check that the terms $(1+\rho)\lambda_T$, defined in (A2.52), converge to $\left(\frac{1}{1+\rho}\right)^{T-1}\left(\mu_1\left(\frac{\xi}{\xi-(1+\rho)}\right)-\frac{1}{1-\varphi}\right)$, and hence their sum converges. This proves the theorem for the case $\beta = 0$.
6. We now extend the theorem to the case $0 < \beta \leq 1$. The objective function must now be written $\sum_{t=1}^{\infty}\left(\frac{\varphi}{1+\rho}\right)^{t-1}(1+(t-1)\beta)u_t$, which we know converges. Hence, by rearranging terms, we can write:

$$\begin{aligned}
&\sum_{t=1}^{\infty}\left(\frac{\varphi}{1+\rho}\right)^{t-1}(1+(t-1)\beta)\,u_t \\
&= \sum_{t=1}^{\infty}\left(\frac{\varphi}{1+\rho}\right)^{t-1}u_t + \beta\left(\sum_{t=2}^{\infty}\left(\frac{\varphi}{1+\rho}\right)^{t-1}u_t \right.\\
&\left. + \sum_{t=3}^{\infty}\left(\frac{\varphi}{1+\rho}\right)^{t-1}u_t + \cdots\right).
\end{aligned} \tag{A2.53}$$

Contrary to what we wish to prove, assume that there is a solution to the program $\rho - SUS^{\beta}[\varphi, x_0^e, S_0^e]$ that is not the solution to $\rho - SUS^0[1, x_0^e, S_0^k]$. Denote the utilities in the former solution by $u^* = (u_1^*, u_2^*, \ldots.)$ while we denote the solution of $\rho - SUS^0[1, x_0^e, S_0^k]$ by the path $\tilde{u} = (\tilde{u}_1, (1+\rho)\tilde{u}_1, \ldots, (1+\rho)^{t-1}\tilde{u}_1, \ldots)$

because we know the solution to that program is a balanced growth path (here, $\tilde{u}_1$ is the utility of Generation 1 on that path). Then it must be the case that u^*, which is of course feasible for $\rho - SUS^0[1, x_0^e, S_0^k]$, gives a lower value than the optimal solution; that is:

$$\sum_{t=1}^{\infty}\left(\frac{\varphi}{1+\rho}\right)^{t-1} u_t^* < \tilde{u}_1 \frac{1}{1-(\varphi/(1+\rho))}. \tag{A2.54}$$

Now consider the identity (A2.53) evaluated at the path u^*. It follows that the first term on the right-hand side of (A2.53) is less than the first term on the right-hand side of (A2.53) evaluated at the path $\tilde{u}$.

7. Suppose now that the second term on the right-hand side of (A2.53) evaluated at the path u^* were at least as large as the second term on the right-hand side of (A2.53) evaluated at the path $\tilde{u}$. Then, since $\beta > 0$, we would have

$$\sum_{t=2}^{\infty}\left(\frac{\varphi}{1+\rho}\right)^{t-1} u_t^* \geq \tilde{u}_1 \frac{\varphi/(1+\rho)}{1-\varphi/(1+\rho)}. \tag{A2.55}$$

We wish to show this is impossible. There are two cases to consider:

(i) $u_1^* \geq \tilde{u}_1$;

(ii) $u_1^* < \tilde{u}_1$.

In case (i), add the inequality of case (i) to the inequality (A2.55), producing:

$$u_1^* + \sum_{t=2}^{\infty}\left(\frac{\varphi}{1+\rho}\right)^{t-1} u_t^* \geq \tilde{u}_1 + \tilde{u}_1 \frac{\varphi/(1+\rho)}{1-\varphi/(1+\rho)} = \frac{\tilde{u}_1}{1-\varphi/(1+\rho)},$$

which contradicts (A2.54). So case (i) cannot occur. In case (ii), we would have $\frac{u_t^*}{(1+\rho)^{t-1}} \leq u_1^* < \frac{\tilde{u}_1}{(1+\rho)^{t-1}}$ for all $t > 1$, by proposition 2.8C, and hence the path $\tilde{u}$ would dominate the path u^* for the program $\rho - SUS^\beta[\varphi, x_0^e, S_0^k]$, a contradiction to the presumed optimality of u^*. Therefore case (ii) cannot occur, and so we conclude that (A2.55) is impossible, and hence:

$$\sum_{t=2}^{\infty}\left(\frac{\varphi}{1+\rho}\right)^{t-1} u_t^* < \tilde{u}_1 \frac{\varphi/(1+\rho)}{1-\varphi/(1+\rho)}.$$

8. We can proceed by induction and show that each term on the right-hand side of (A2.53) evaluated at the path u^* is less than its value, evaluated at the path $\tilde{u}$. This contradicts the original supposition that the path u^* is not an optimal path for the program $\rho - SUS^0[\varphi, x_0^e, S_0^k]$. Since $\tilde{u}$ is the unique optimal path for this program, the theorem is proved. ■

CHAPTER THREE

Sustainability for a Warming World

3.1. Introduction

This chapter develops, calibrates, and optimizes the full-fledged model by incorporating carbon dioxide (CO_2) emissions and atmospheric concentration, as well as a sector that produces knowledge. We study the problem of intergenerational equity in a world that is constrained to limit greenhouse gas (GHG) emissions in order to keep global temperature at an acceptably low level. We neglect, for the time being, intragenerational issues and postulate a representative person, or household, in each generation. We defer to Chapter 5 the consideration of a world partitioned into North and South.

Our model is dynamic, involving economic and environmental variables. However, we do not specify a physical model of emission-stock interactions but consider instead a particular path for the environmental variables following the Representative Concentration Pathway RCP2.6, which provides an expected temperature change not exceeding the 2°C (van Vuuren, Stehfest et al. 2011), entails low emissions after 2050, and realistically appears to be feasible given the present knowledge of climate dynamics.[1] The economic variables are then endogenous in our optimization program. We develop a computational algorithm based on the turnpike property

[1] See the United Nations Environment Program (UNEP 2011, 7).

proved in Chapter 2 and compute paths of resource allocations that, in a society that consists of a representative agent for each generation beginning with the present, optimize an objective function that sustains growth in human welfare forever for exogenously specified rates of growth, taken to include zero as one possibility.

The analysis of the simple model in Chapter 2 should guide the reader in thinking about the more highly articulated model that we now present. Although we believe it is possible to prove the main theorems (such as the turnpike theorem and the simplification theorem) for the present model, we have not done so.

3.2. Social Objectives

3.2.1. GDP, Consumption, and the Quality of Life

A large segment of economics, particularly in empirical applications, takes as the index of welfare per capita gross domestic product (GDP) or gross national income (GNI, which includes net income generated abroad) or net national income (NNI, which in addition excludes capital depreciation). Each of these GDP-related measures has two main components: consumption and investment. Consumption is related to current welfare, whereas investment is a contribution to capital, a factor for future welfare. The correlation of any GDP-related measure to consumption is necessarily imperfect: a country like Singapore, with a high investment-to-GDP ratio, has levels of consumption substantially lower than other countries with the same GDP per capita. Hence, the two components, consumption and investment, should be separated.

Section 1.4 of Chapter 1 studied the investment component of the GDP-related measure as an appropriate index of the accumulation of the diverse forms of capital. Now we address whether the consumption component of the GDP-related measure is an appropriate index of human welfare or, more generically, ask what is an appropriate index of human welfare?

The shortcomings of the consumption component of a GDP-related measure as a welfare index have been discussed for decades: see the *Sarkozy Report* (Stiglitz et al. 2009) for a recent, comprehensive assessment. The criticisms have spurred three different approaches: (1) the inclusion of additional variables besides consumption in the welfare or utility index, in particular nonmarketed goods or services; (2) the measurement of subjective happiness; and (3) the capabilities approach. We refer to Fleurbaey (2009) and Fleurbaey and Blanchet (2013) for a critical review of (2) and (3), and we focus here on (1).

Population size and the level of inequality have potentially important impacts on mankind's well-being. Some of the existing social-welfare indices explicitly consider inequality (e.g., the Inequality-adjusted Human Development Index (IHDI), by the United Nations Development Programme 2010; Jones and Klenow 2010; and the recommendations in Stiglitz et al. 2009). Population size is on occasion taken into consideration (see, e.g., Nordhaus 2008a; Section 3.5.1), based on the utilitarian idea that an increase in the total number of people with sufficiently high welfare levels is desirable (Blackorby and Donaldson 1984). But climate-change economics often abstracts from population and distributional ethics: we frequently assume that the number of people in a generation is given and ignore inequality by representing each generation by a single agent.

The main variables that have been introduced, besides consumption, in various indices of human welfare are *leisure*, the *environment*, *health*, and *education*: observe that these variables may contribute very differently to carbon emissions. It should be noted that a large segment of the economic-growth literature, as well as of the economic-analysis-of-climate-change literature (e.g., Nordhaus 2008a) does consider improvements in knowledge, education, or the environment, but only insofar as they make possible the production of consumption goods with less labor time or produced capital. We focus, on the other hand, on their role as direct arguments in the utility function or welfare index.

For instance, Nordhaus and Tobin's (1972) Measure of Economic Welfare (MEW) modifies GDP per capita by excluding depreciation and including leisure and nonmarket work, in addition to taking congestion and pollution into account. Labor economics has traditionally considered both consumption and leisure as arguments in the utility function, with leisure interpreted as a broad aggregate of unpaid activities, including home production, the care of children and relatives, and home educational activities, in addition to free time and rest and recreation. (We mentioned, in Chapter 2, that it might be more appropriate to account for child-rearing as part of the labor in the education sector of the economy.) Jones and Klenow (2010) provide a welfare index in which leisure plays an important role in comparing the quality of life across countries.

Environmental economics has emphasized the quality of air and water, as well as the recreational opportunities offered by natural environments. Pollution appears as an argument in Keeler et al. (1972) and, as just noted, in the MEW of Nordhaus and Tobin (1972). The amenity value of the forest was stressed by Hartman (1976) and that of undeveloped ecosystems by Fisher, Krutilla, and Cicchetti (1972) and Barrett (1992).

Health economics has constructed indices of health and longevity by means of defining quality-adjusted life years (QALY) in order to quantify the benefits of medical intervention. Life expectancy is recognized as a major factor in human welfare. As societies become wealthier, extending life becomes increasingly valuable. Hall and Jones (2007) estimate that, in the United States, "a sixty-five year old would give up 82 percent of her consumption . . . to have the health status of a 20 year old."[2] Many recent welfare indices include life expectancy as an argument; see, for example, Jones and Klenow (2010) and the HDI of United Nations Human Development Programme (2013).

Education and the accompanying accumulation of human capital have traditionally been considered production factors, increasing the productivity of the time worked and associated wages (see Freeman 1986). Education increases productivity both in the market and in some areas of home production (Michael 1972, 1973; Leibowitz 1975; Gronau 1986; Ortigueira 1999; Heckman 1976). As a result, highly educated women spend more time in childcare and education but less in meal preparation and doing laundry than their less-educated counterparts (Leibowitz 1975). The literature uses the language of production and output, but as noted by Michael (1973, 307), "A distinguishing characteristic of human capital is that it is embedded in an individual: it therefore accompanies him whenever he goes, not only in

[2] Perhaps surprisingly, life expectancy seems to increase linearly with time. Hall and Jones (2007) estimate that during the last fifty years, life expectancy in the United States has increased by 1.4 months per year. And Oeppen and Vaupel (2002, 1029) report that "female life expectancy in the record-holding country has risen for 160 years at a steady pace of almost 3 months per year."

the labor market, but also in the theater, the voting booth, the kitchen and so forth." Even though the home production literature views education as affecting nonmarket productivity, he continues, "One could alternatively argue, for example, that education affects the household utility function."

We have mentioned the Human Development Index (HDI): it was proposed by the first *United Nations Human Development Report* (United Nations Development Program 1990) and has been updated yearly (see the *United Nations Human Development Report 2013* for the latest issue: the 2010 edition introduced some changes in its composition). It aggregates three dimensions: (1) health, with life expectancy at birth as indicators; (2) education, with mean and expected years of schooling as indicators; and (3) living standards, with GNI per capita as indicators (see, e.g., United Nations Development Programme 2010, fig. 1.1). The more recent Human Development reports, as well as Neumayer (2001), among others, emphasize three dimensions of human welfare acknowledged by the authors of the 1990 HDI but neglected in its definition, namely environmental and climate sustainability, inequality, and human security, rights, and freedoms. The 2011 report introduces an 'inequality adjusted HDI,' which reduces the HDI by a factor reflecting income inequality in the country.

3.2.2. The Utility Function

A large segment of the literature in the economics of climate change postulates an individual or generational utility function with the consumption of a single, produced good as its only argument (sometimes augmented by leisure time): improvements in knowledge, education, and the environment are then important only insofar as they make possible the production of consumption goods with less labor time or capital.

In fact, both the consumption of goods and the availability of natural capital positively affect human welfare. Indeed, the spectacular increase in consumption in developed economies during the last century has undoubtedly provided a major welfare improvement (Johnson 2000). But, in our view, two other factors have also had major impacts. First are the improvements in life expectancy, health status, and infant survival, partly due to the rise in consumption but to a large extent due to medical discoveries and their implementation by the public health system. Second is the improvement in literacy and, more generally, in the amount of education received by the average person, which has enhanced not only the productivity of labor but also her utility: the contribution of leisure to utility increases as leisure time embodies higher levels of human capital; see Ortigueira (1999) and Wolf (2007), as well as Heckman (1976), Oreopoulos and Salvanes (2011) and Michael (1972).[3] Recall the citation from Wolf (2007) in Chapter 2.

Our approach follows the spirit of the Human Development Index. The first argument in the utility function is consumption. But we emphasize other factors as well:

(1) Education, which modifies the value of leisure time to the individual;
(2) Knowledge, in the form of society's stock of culture and science, which directly increases the value of life (in addition to any indirect effects through productivity) via improvements in health and life expectancy and because an understanding of how the world works and an appreciation of culture are intrinsic to human well-being;
(3) An undegraded biosphere, which is valuable to humans for its direct impact, for example, on physical and mental health.[4]

Hence, consumption, educated leisure, the stock of human knowledge, and the quality of the biosphere are arguments in our utility function. In the model of the present chapter, we therefore augment the arguments in the utility function of Chapter 2 to incorporate knowledge and the environment.

We continue to abstract from all conflicts except for the intergenerational one and, accordingly, we postulate in this chapter a representative agent in each generation. We assume that a generation lives for twenty-five years, and we formally postulate the following utility function of Generation t, $t \geq 1$:

$$\hat{u}(c_t, x_t^l, S_t^n, S_t^m) := (c_t)^{\alpha_c}(x_t^l)^{\alpha_l}(S_t^n)^{\alpha_n}(\hat{S}^m - S_t^m)^{\alpha_m}, \tag{3.1}$$

[3] Increases in the human capital of the parents can also improve the quality of their child-rearing services, which can be thought of as either a component of the parents' 'leisure' or a component of the education sector, introduced in Chapter 2.

[4] This is captured in the cost-benefit literature on global warming by the computation of the so-called "noneconomic effects."

where the exponents are positive and normalized such that $\alpha_c+\alpha_l+\alpha_n+\alpha_m=1$, and where c_t and x_t^l are the annual average consumption and leisure (in efficiency units) per capita by Generation t; S_t^n is the stock of knowledge per capita; and S_t^m and $\hat{S}^m$ are the total and 'catastrophic' levels of CO_2 in the atmosphere.[5] (See Appendix A: Calibration for a list of all variables and parameters.)

The presence of the stock of CO_2 in the utility function captures our view that environmental deterioration and the extinction of species are public bads in consumption (and also in production, as it will be evident in the economic constraints, Section 3.4.1).

3.3. Optimization Programs: Sustainable Utility Levels and Sustainable Growth

We are concerned with *human sustainability*, which requires maintaining human welfare, rather than *green sustainability*, which may be defined as keeping the quality of the biosphere constant (see Section 1.4). We have summarized our view in Chapter 1.

Maximizing the utility of the worst-off generation will often require the maximization of the utility of the first generation subject to maintaining that utility for all future generations so that there is no *utility growth* after the first generation.[6] Formally, the optimization program is of the following type.

Pure-Sustainability Optimization Program

$$\max \Lambda \quad \text{subject to } (c_t)^{\alpha_c}(x_t^l)^{\alpha_l}(S_t^n)^{\alpha_n}(\hat{S}^m - S_t^m)^{\alpha_m} \geq \Lambda, \quad t \geq 1, \qquad (3.2)$$

subject to the feasibility conditions given by specific production relations and laws of motion of the stocks and resource constraints and with the initial conditions given by the relevant stock values in the base year.

[5] Acemoglu, Aghion et al. (2012) use a similar approach. In their notation, $S = C_{CO_2,\,disaster} - \max\{C_{CO_2}, 280\}$ represents the quality of the environment, where C_{CO_2} is the atmospheric concentration of carbon dioxide.

[6] If the investments undertaken during the lifetime of the first generation benefit both the first generation and subsequent ones, then conceivably maximizing the utility of the first generation could imply higher welfare for the second generation than for the first one. See Silvestre (2002).

At a solution to the pure-sustainability optimization program, the path of the utility will typically be stationary, and it can be (at least asymptotically) supported by stationary paths in all the arguments of the utility function. We have argued in previous chapters for assuming that a positive rate of growth in the utility of future generations may be preferred.

If we assume that each generation has the all-encompassing utility function V discussed in Section 1.1 and that a positive rate of growth of utility ρ is justified (see theorem 2.3), then the optimization program becomes:

Sustainable-Growth Optimization Program

$$\max \Lambda \quad \text{subject to } (c_t)^{\alpha_c}(x_t^l)^{\alpha_l}(S_t^n)^{\alpha_n}(\hat{S}^m - S_t^m)^{\alpha_m} \geq (1+\rho)^{t-1}\Lambda, \quad t \geq 1,$$

for $\rho \geq 0$ given and subject again to the feasibility and initial conditions.

Note that the pure-sustainability optimization program can be written in this form by letting $\rho = 0$.

At a solution to this program, utility grows at a constant rate, but it is impossible to have steady positive growth of all variables because of the finite capacity $\hat{S}^m$ of the biosphere.

3.4. Feasible Paths

Feasible paths are characterized by economic constraints and by environmental stock-flow relations. We call emissions and concentrations *environmental* variables, whereas the remaining variables are called *economic*.

3.4.1. Economic Constraints

We take the initial condition to be an endowment vector (x_0^e, S_0^k, S_0^n) and adopt the following economic constraints. Recall that $t = 1, 2, \ldots$ is measured in generations (twenty-five years).

- Aggregate production function.

$$f(x_t^c, S_t^k, S_t^n, e_t, S_t^m) := k_1(x_t^c)^{\theta_c}(S_t^k)^{\theta_k}(S_t^n)^{\theta_n}(e_t)^{\theta_e}(S_t^m)^{\theta_m} \quad (3.3)$$
$$\geq c_t + i_t, \quad t \geq 1,$$

with $k_1 > 0$, $\theta_c > 0$, $\theta_k > 0$, $\theta_n > 0$, $\theta_c + \theta_k + \theta_n = 1$, $\theta_e > 0$ and $\theta_m < 0$.

- Law of motion of physical capital.

$$(1-d^k)S_{t-1}^k + k_2 i_t \geq S_t^k, \quad t \geq 1, \quad \text{with } k_2 > 0 \text{ and } d^k \in [0,1].$$

- Law of motion of the stock of knowledge.

$$(1-d^n)S_{t-1}^n + k_3 x_t^n \geq S_t^n, \quad t \geq 1, \quad \text{with } k_3 > 0 \text{ and } d^n \in [0,1].$$

- Allocation of efficiency units of labor.

$$x_t^l + x_t^c + x_t^n + x_t^e = x_t, \quad t \geq 1.$$

- Education production function.

$$\xi\, x_{t-1}^e \geq x_t, \quad t \geq 1, \quad \text{with } \xi > 0.$$

All variables are in per capita terms, with the exception of the level of CO_2 in the atmosphere (S_t^m), a public good acting as a proxy for environmental quality. Notation follows our convention and uses S for stocks and x for labor (in efficiency units), with a super-index indicating the sector to which they belong. Consumption (c_t), leisure (x_t^l), and the stock of knowledge (S_t^n) have already been introduced in Section 3.2.2. S_t^k is the capital stock per capita available to Generation t. The average annual efficiency units of time (labor and leisure) per capita available to Generation t is represented by x_t, while x_t^c, x_t^n, and x_t^e are the efficiency units of labor devoted to the production of output, to the production of knowledge, and to teaching, respectively. Finally, i_t is the average annual investment per capita, and e_t represents the annual emissions of CO_2 from production by Generation t.

The following remarks compare our technology to some common in the growth literature.

▶ **Remark 1.** The labor input in production, x_t^c, is measured in efficiency units of labor, which may be viewed as the number of labor-time units ('hours') multiplied by the amount of human capital embodied in one labor-time unit (as is customary since Uzawa 1965 and Lucas

1988). We assume that $\theta_c + \theta_k + \theta_n = 1$; that is, returns to the economic inputs are constant. This implies decreasing returns to 'capital' when construed to consist of physical and human capital only. But returns to 'capital' are constant if we broaden the notion of capital to also include the stock of knowledge.

▶ **Remark 2.** We assume that the production of new knowledge requires only efficiency labor (dedicated to research and development [R&D], or to 'learning by not doing'), but that knowledge depreciates at a positive rate.

These assumptions are in line with a large segment of the growth literature.

▶ **Remark 3.** Our education production function, $x_t = \xi x^e_{t-1}$, states that the education of a young generation requires only the efficiency labor of the previous generation. If we normalize to unity the total labor-leisure time available to Generation t, then x_t can be interpreted as the amount of human capital per time unit in Generation t. Because our model is generational (t is a generation), instead of being a long-lived consumer (for whom t is just a period, or even an instant, in her life), our education production function cannot be interpreted in exactly the same manner as in many existing models of investment in human capital, which, in addition, are often cast in continuous time. More specifically, our formulation displays the following features: (1) As in Uzawa (1965) and Lucas (1988), we do not include physical capital as an input in the production of education. (2) We interpret the labor input in the production of education as that of teachers, rather than students. This departs from the interpretations by Lucas (1988) and Rebelo (1991), but it agrees with the comments in Uzawa (1965) and Barro and Sala-i-Martin (1999). (3) We see the education of a generation as a social investment, in line with Lucas (1988). Also, we adopt a broad view of educational achievement, which in particular bestows the ability to adapt to new technologies, as emphasized by Goldin and Katz (2008).

▶ **Remark 4.** We have postulated Cobb-Douglas utility and production functions, which implies an elasticity of substitution of one between 'natural' and 'manmade' variables. This type of substitutability is no doubt controversial (Neumayer 2010; Gerlagh and van der Zwaan 2002). But, because we exogenously adopt the values for the environmental stocks and flows (as discussed in Section 3.4.2), the implications of substitutability are less drastic in our analysis than in models that aim at the endogenous determination of both natural and manmade variables.

3.4.2. Environmental Constraints: Emissions and Concentrations

Anthropogenic GHG emissions have caused atmospheric concentrations of CO_2, unprecedented in the last half a million years (see, e.g., Friedlingstein and Salomon 2005). The unparalleled behavior of GHG concentrations has motivated a growing literature that tries to predict the relationship among the paths of emissions, concentrations, and global temperature changes. Following a large segment of literature, we focus on CO_2 emissions and concentrations.[7]

Most of the more recent and detailed physical models have no steady states, in the strict sense, with positive emissions. But if emissions are steady at low-enough levels, then the stock of GHG eventually grows very slowly, experiencing minor increases in a scale of thousands of years. The stocks of GHG are then said to be 'stabilized' even though, strictly speaking, they are not constant in the very long run. Here we assume a constant 'long-term' value of the stock of GHG, where 'constant' is a simplification of 'stabilized' and where the 'long-term' scale refers to a few hundreds, but not thousands, of years.

Because of the complexity of the climate models proposed and the lack of a canonical physical model of the current state of climatology, we shun false precision and do not attempt to specify the set of feasible flow-stock sequences $\{(e_t, S_t^m)\}_{t=1}^{\infty}$. Accordingly, we do not try to compute optimal paths for emissions and the environmental stock. Instead, we adopt a path of CO_2

[7] The long-term effects of non-CO_2 GHG emissions have been addressed by Sarofim et al. (2005).

emissions based on the Representative Concentration Pathway RCP2.6. The RCPs are a new set of consistent projections of the components of radiative forcing extending until 2100 that have been prepared to serve as inputs for climate modeling in the development of new scenarios for the Intergovernmental Panel on Climate Change (IPCC)'s Fifth Assessment Report (AR5).[8] The RCP2.6 pathway (a.k.a. RCP3-PD) provides an expected temperature change not exceeding 2°C and is representative of precautionary scenarios with very low GHG concentration levels. Its radiative forcing level first peaks at 3.1 W/m^2 in the middle of the century and then returns to 2.6 W/m^2 by 2100, thus its name: 'Peak & Decline' (van Vuuren et al. 2007; van Vuuren, Edmonds et al. 2011). Our setting requires constant annual emissions within a generation as well as stabilized emissions and concentration after year 2060. We adapt the emissions in RCP2.6 to these requirements and run them in MAGICC 6.4.[9] Figure 3.1 describes the transformation from RCP2.6 to our path and shows that the latter is a good approximation of the original RCP2.6 with constant emissions after 2060, both in the levels of CO_2 concentration and in temperature change. The values for emissions and concentration in our path are presented in Table 3.1.

Note that this path adopts the simplification of postulating only three levels of emissions and stock, which average over each generation the lifetime paths for emissions while taking as stock those values dated at the end of the life of the generation. The algorithm described in Section 3.5 and the application to the intragenerational conflict (see Chapter 5) motivate our choice of a two-generation interval to reach the target stabilization level.

We calibrate our economic model with US data due to the difficulty of obtaining reliable world data. But our CO_2 emissions paths refer to world emissions. We must therefore allocate emissions to the United States in

[8] The RCPs are described in the 2011 special issue of *Climatic Change*. For a summary see Meinshausen et al. (2011) and van Vuuren, Edmonds, et al. (2011). The data can be obtained from http://www.pik-potsdam.de/~mmalte/rcps.

[9] We keep emissions constant for all GHGs after 2060, except for land-use change emissions, which decline following the original path.

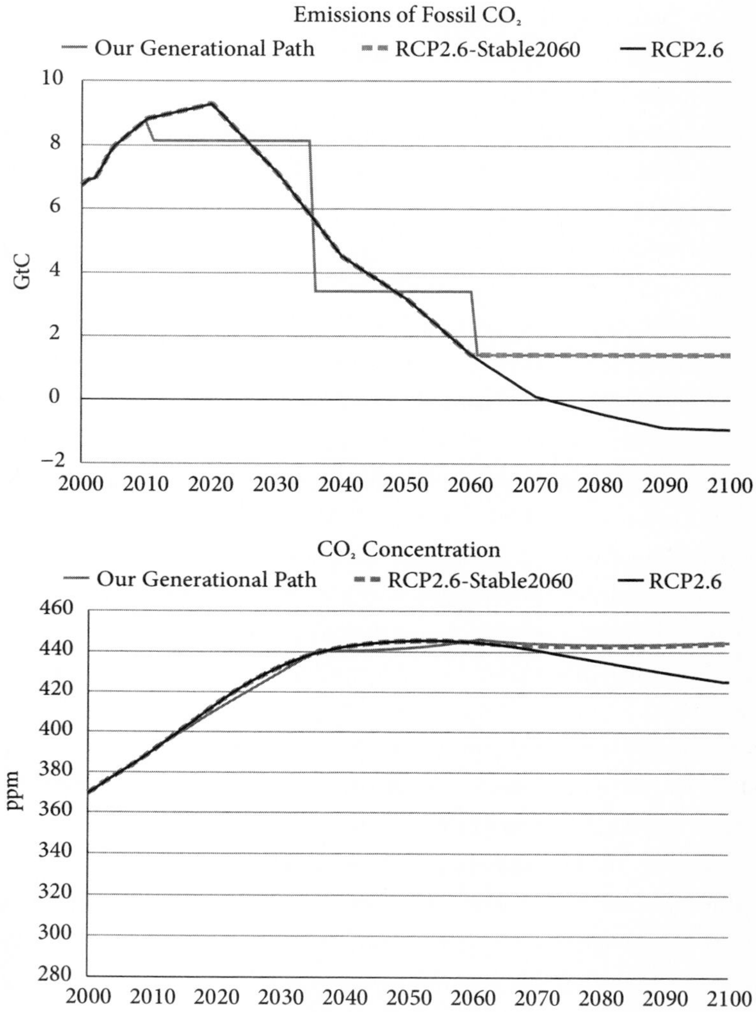

Figure 3.1. Adapting the RCP2.6 to our environment. The final CO_2 emissions path provides a good approximation to the RCP2.6 with constant emissions after 2060. The top graph plots together three emissions paths: the original RCP2.6; the *RCP2.6-stable2060*, which only differs from RCP2.6 by stabilizing emissions after 2060; and the *Generational Path*, which assigns to each generation its average annual emissions according to *RCP2.6-stable2060*. CO_2 concentrations and temperature changes are obtained by running MAGICC 6.4 for each of the three emissions paths.

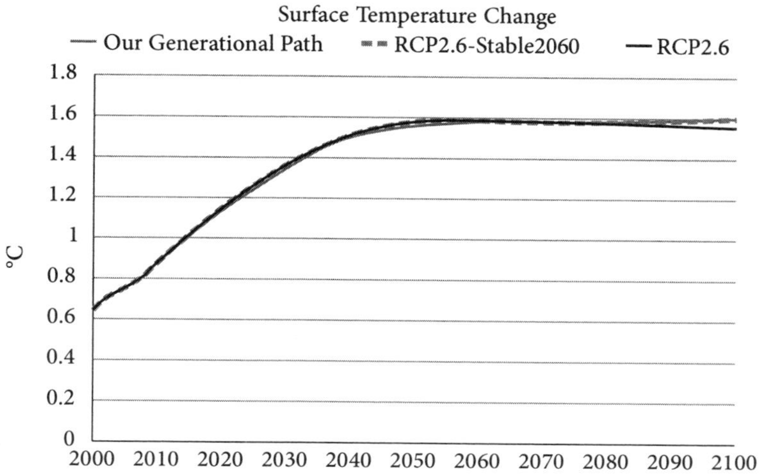

line with the global emissions path that we adopt. To do so, we consider two alternative scenarios.

The first scenario maintains the share of US emissions at its base-year share. The United States accounted for 17% of all energy (fuel and cement) emissions in 2010 (World Resources Institute, 2013). Hence, in our Scenario 1, future US total emissions are given by the 17% of (E_1^W, E_2^W, E^{W^*}). Using the United Nations projections for US population (United Nations, 2013), we obtain the emissions per capita $(e_1, e_2, e^*) = (4.02, 1.36, 0.59)$ (in tC per capita), as displayed in the third column of Table 3.1.

The second scenario assumes that the United States emits its per capita share of global emissions. We use the United Nations projections for world population and compute the emissions per capita along E_1^W, E_2^W, and E^{W^*}, as $(e_1^W, e_2^W, e^{W^*}) = (1.03, 0.34, 0.15)$ (in tC per capita), corresponding to the values in Scenario 2, as displayed in the fourth column of Table 3.1.

These two scenarios represent upper and lower bounds for the welfare of the US representative agent: we conjecture that, even if emission permits were distributed on a per capita basis to the various countries, the United States would end up purchasing rights permits from other countries. Hence, Scenario 2 provides a lower bound on the welfare of the representative US citizen.

Table 3.1. Our postulated paths for the environmental variables.

	World total CO_2 emissions [GtC]	World CO_2 emissions per capita [tC per capita]	US CO_2 emissions per capita. (Scenario 1: $E^{US} = 0.17 \times E^{W}$) [tC per capita]	US CO_2 emissions per capita. (Scenario 2: $e^{US} = e^{W}$) [tC per capita]	CO_2 concentration in the atmosphere [ppm]
Generation 0	$E_0^W = 9.04$	$e_0^W = 1.31$	$e_0^{US} = 4.95$	$e_0^{US} = 4.95$	$S_0^m = 390$
Generation 1	$E_1^W = 8.15$	$e_1^W = 1.03$	$e_1^{US_1} = 4.02$	$e_1^{US_2} = 1.03$	$S_1^m = 439$
Generation 2	$E_2^W = 3.41$	$e_2^W = 0.34$	$e_2^{US_1} = 1.36$	$e_2^{US_2} = 0.34$	$S_2^m = 446$
Gen. t, $t \geq 3$	$E^{W^*} = 1.47$	$e^{W^*} = 0.15$	$e^{US_1^*} = 0.59$	$e_2^{US^*} = 0.15$	$S^{m^*} = 445$

3.5. Computational Strategy and Algorithm

Our computational strategy is based on the ray optimization theorem, in the spirit of the turnpike theorem (2.1) that we proved for the simpler model of Chapter 2. Consider a pair (e^*, S^{m^*}) such that the constant sequence $\{(e^*, S^{m^*})\}_{t=1}^{\infty}$ is an environmentally feasible flow-stock path and the following optimization program:

▶ **Program** $E[\rho, e^*, S^{m^*}]$.

Given (ρ, e^*, S^{m^*}), $\max \Lambda$ subject to:

$$c_t^{\alpha_c}(x_t^l)^{\alpha_l}(S_t^n)^{\alpha_n}(\hat{S}^m - S^{m^*})^{\alpha_m} \geq \Lambda(1+\rho)^{t-1}, \quad t \geq 1,$$

$$k_1(x_t^c)^{\theta_c}(S_t^k)^{\theta_k}(S_t^n)^{\theta_n}(e^*)^{\theta_e}(S^{m^*})^{\theta_m} \geq c_t + i_t, \quad t \geq 1,$$

$$(1-d^k)S_{t-1}^k + k_2 i_t \geq S_t^k, \quad t \geq 1,$$

$$(1-d^n)S_{t-1}^n + k_3 x_t^n \geq S_t^n, \quad t \geq 1,$$

$$x_t^e + x_t^n + x_t^l + x_t^c \equiv x_t, \quad t \geq 1,$$

$$\xi\, x_{t-1}^e \geq x_t, \quad t \geq 1,$$

with initial conditions (x_0^e, S_0^k, S_0^n).

Recall that ρ is the rate of growth of the utility per generation. It will be convenient to denote by g the rate of growth of the economic variables, again per generation.

▶ **Theorem 3.1.** Ray Optimization Theorem. *Assume constant returns to scale in production in the sense that $\theta_c + \theta_k + \theta_n = 1$. Given $(g, e^*, S^{m^*}) \in [0, \xi - 1) \times \Re_{++} \times (0, \hat{S}^m)$, there is a ray $\Gamma(g, e^*, S^{m^*}) := \{(x^e, S^k, S^n) \in \Re_+^3 : (S^k, S^n) = x^e(q^k(g, e^*, S^{m^*}),\ q^n(g))\}$, such that if $(x_0^e, S_0^k, S_0^n) \in \Gamma(g, e^*, S^{m^*})$, $(x_0^e, S_0^k, S_0^n) \neq 0$, then the solution path to program $E[\rho, e^*, S^{m^*}]$ satisfies:*

(i) $(x_t^e, S_t^k, S_t^n) = (1+g)^t(x_0^e, S_0^k, S_0^n)$, $t \geq 1$, *and hence* $(x_t^e, S_t^k, S_t^n) \in \Gamma(g, e^*, S^{m^*})$, $t \geq 0$;

$$c_1 = p^c(g)\cdot q^k(g, e^*, S^{m^*})\cdot x_0^e,$$

$$i_1 = p^i(g)\cdot q^k(g, e^*, S^{m^*})\cdot x_0^e,$$

(ii) $$x_1^l = v^l(g)\cdot q^n(g)\cdot x_0^e,$$

$$x_1^n = v^n(g)\cdot q^n(g)\cdot x_0^e,$$

$$x_1^c = v^c(g)\cdot q^n(g)\cdot x_0^e,$$

where $p^j, j=c, i, q^j, j=k, n,$ and $v^j, j=e, n,$ are coefficients defined in the Chapter 3 Appendix;

(iii) $(c_t, i_t, x_t^l, x_t^n, x_t^c) = (1+g)^{t-1}(c_1, i_1, x_1^l, x_1^n, x_1^c),\ t \geq 1.$

Utility grows at rate ρ, where $1+\rho=(1+g)^{1-\alpha_m}$, and all other variables grow at rate g except for emissions and concentrations, which remain constant at (e^*, S^{m^*}).

▶ **Proof:** Chapter 3 Appendix.

It is important to observe that for $g=\rho=0$, whenever the initial endowments (x_0^e, S_0^k, S_0^n) lie in $\Gamma(0, e^*, S^{m^*})$, the solution to program $E\,[0, e^*, S^{m^*}]$ is stationary over time.

We conjecture that a turnpike theorem analogous to theorem 2.1 is true for program $E[\rho, e^*, S^{m^*}]$ for any g, and so, if we begin with an endowment vector off the ray $\Gamma(g, e^*, S^{m^*})$, then the optimal solution will converge to the ray $\Gamma(g, e^*, S^{m^*})$. Hence, in the long run, the solution will be almost a steady-state path. Motivated by this conjecture, we now construct feasible paths that begin at the actual base-year endowment values (x_0^e, S_0^k, S_0^n) and reach the ray $\Gamma(g, e^*, S^{m^*})$ in two generations, taking as given the values (e_1^{USj}, S_1^m), (e_2^{USj}, S_2^m), and (e^{USj^*}, S^{m^*}) for each one of the two scenarios $j=1, 2$, reported in Table 3.1.[10]

[10] Why two generations? Our optimization program can allow for the convergence to the ray to occur at generations later than Generation 2. Relaxing a constraint cannot hurt, but we have performed the computations for three and four generations, with very little modification of the results. Allowing stocks to converge to the ray in four generations instead of two improves the common utility of all generations by only about one-tenth of 1%. We have also maximized the utility of Gen-

Computationally, we solve program G below for the chosen $(\rho, e_1, S_1^m, e_2, S_2^m, e^*, S^{m*})$.

▶ **Program** G. (3.4)

Given $(\rho, e_1, S_1^m, e_2, S_2^m, e^*, S^{m*})$, max Λ subject to:

$$\left.\begin{array}{l} c_1^{\alpha_c}(x_1^l)^{\alpha_l}(S_1^n)^{\alpha_n}(\hat{S}^m - S_1^m)^{\alpha_m} \geq \Lambda \\ c_2^{\alpha_c}(x_2^l)^{\alpha_l}(S_2^n)^{\alpha_n}(\hat{S}^m - S_2^m)^{\alpha_m} \geq (1+\rho)\Lambda \end{array}\right\} \text{utility growth,}$$

$$\left.\begin{array}{l} k_1(x_1^c)^{\theta_c}(S_1^k)^{\theta_k}(S_1^n)^{\theta_n}(e_1)^{\theta_e}(S_1^m)^{\theta_m} \geq c_1 + i_1 \\ k_1(x_2^c)^{\theta_c}(S_2^k)^{\theta_k}(S_2^n)^{\theta_n}(e_2)^{\theta_e}(S_2^m)^{\theta_m} \geq c_2 + i_2 \end{array}\right\} \text{output production,}$$

$$\left.\begin{array}{l} (1-d^k)S_0^k + k_2 i_1 \geq S_1^k \\ (1-d^k)S_1^k + k_2 i_2 \geq S_2^k \end{array}\right\} \text{physical capital accumulation,}$$

$$\left.\begin{array}{l} (1-d^n)S_0^n + k_3 x_1^n \geq S_1^n \\ (1-d^n)S_1^n + k_3 x_2^n \geq S_2^n \end{array}\right\} \text{knowledge accumulation,}$$

$$\left.\begin{array}{l} \xi x_0^e \geq x_1^e + x_1^n + x_1^l + x_1^c \\ \xi x_1^e \geq x_2^e + x_2^n + x_2^l + x_2^c \end{array}\right\} \text{human capital accumulation, and}$$

$$(x_2^e, S_2^k, S_2^n) \in \Gamma(g, e^*, S^{m*})\} \text{ steady state,}$$

for the initial conditions (x_0^e, S_0^k, S_0^n).

---

eration 1 subject to its stocks reaching the ray. Note that Generation 1's investment in knowledge (which affects the utility of Generation 1 both directly and indirectly through production) and Generation 1's investment in physical capital (which affects the utility of Generation 1 only indirectly through production) create intergenerational public goods. It turns out that, even for a zero-growth target, when Generation 1 maximizes its own utility subject to the stock proportionality dictated by the ray, it invests so heavily as to make the utility of the future generations higher that its own, a feature formally similar to the one discussed in Silvestre (2002).

Using the *NMaximize* function in *Mathematica 8*, we compute the numerical solution paths to program G for our calibrated parameter values. We perform this calculation for three sustained annual growth rates of utility, namely $\hat{\rho} = 0.00$ (no growth), $\hat{\rho} = 0.01$, and $\hat{\rho} = 0.02$, with corresponding rates of growth per generation defined by $\rho = (1+\hat{\rho})^{25} - 1$.[11]

3.6. Calibration

As noted, we draw on US data in order to calibrate the parameters of the utility function, the output and education production functions, and the laws of motion for physical capital and knowledge, as well as the benchmark year-zero values of economic stocks and flows. All the values are found in Appendix A: Calibration, where we also detail our calibration procedures.

3.7. Sustainable Paths

Recall (see Section 3.4.2) that we postulate a path of total world emissions following the RCP2.6 and consider two scenarios: Scenario 1 ($E^{US} = 0.17 \times E^{W}$), in which the United States is responsible for 17% of all emissions (its share of total emissions in 2010); and Scenario 2 ($e^{US} = e^{W}$), in which total emissions are allocated on a per capita basis. The optimizations yield the paths of utility and of the economic variables described in Table 3.2 and illustrated in Figure 3.2. To facilitate interpretation, most values are unit-free relative, rather than absolute, often relative to the reference-year values.

Consider first the pure-sustainability program (3.2). The utility of the first generation jumps to 37.3% (resp. 30.9%) above that of the reference year in the first (resp. second) scenario on US emissions and stays there forever. This fact is illustrated by the horizontal, solid lines in both graphs of Figure 3.2. The utility-growth ratios are presented by the first row for each scenario in Table 3.3. As expected, the lower US emissions

---

[11] Appendix B: *Mathematica* Code, provides a comprehensible version of the program.

Table 3.2. Paths of economic variables for different sustained growth rates.

3.2(a) $\hat{\rho} = 0.00$ (sustainable utility, no growth)

	Utility u_t/u_0	Utility growth u_t/u_{t-1}	Consumption c_t/c_0	Consumption growth c_t/c_{t-1}	Investment i_t/i_0	Stock of capital S_t^k/S_0^k	Stock of knowledge S_t^n/S_0^n
Generation				Scenario 1			
0	1.000	—	1.000	—	1.000	1.000	1.000
1	1.373	1.373	1.454	1.454	3.123	2.889	2.336
2	1.373	1.000	1.331	0.916	2.046	2.368	2.439
3	1.373	1.000	1.257	0.944	2.175	2.368	2.439
4	1.373	1.000	1.257	1.000	2.175	2.368	2.439
Generation				Scenario 2			
0	1.000	—	1.000	—	1.000	1.000	1.000
1	1.309	1.309	1.248	1.248	2.633	2.469	2.333
2	1.309	1.000	1.140	0.914	1.754	2.028	2.446
3	1.309	1.000	1.077	0.944	1.863	2.028	2.446
4	1.309	1.000	1.077	1.000	1.863	2.028	2.446

(continued)

Table 3.2. (continued)

3.2(b) $\hat{\rho} = 0.01$ (1% annual growth)

	Utility u_t/u_0	Utility growth u_t/u_{t-1}	Consumption c_t/c_0	Consumption growth c_t/c_{t-1}	Investment i_t/i_0	Stock of capital S_t^k/S_0^k	Stock of knowledge S_t^n/S_0^n
Generation				Scenario 1			
0	1.00	—	1.000	—	1.000	1.000	1.000
1	1.36	1.36	1.443	1.443	3.097	2.866	2.318
2	1.75	1.28	1.705	1.182	2.893	3.088	3.157
3	2.24	1.28	2.081	1.221	3.889	3.990	4.078
4	2.87	1.28	2.687	1.292	5.024	5.153	5.268
Generation				Scenario 2			
0	1.00	—	1.000	—	1.000	1.000	1.000
1	1.30	1.30	1.239	1.239	2.611	2.450	2.315
2	1.67	1.28	1.460	1.179	2.479	2.646	3.166
3	2.14	1.28	1.782	1.221	3.331	3.417	4.089
4	2.74	1.28	2.302	1.292	4.303	4.414	5.282

3.2(c) $\hat{\rho} = 0.02$ (2% annual growth)

	Utility u_t/u_0	Utility growth u_t/u_{t-1}	Consumption c_t/c_0	Consumption growth c_t/c_{t-1}	Investment i_t/i_0	Stock of capital S_t^k/S_0^k	Stock of knowledge S_t^n/S_0^n
Generation				Scenario 1			
0	1.00	—	1.000	—	1.000	1.000	1.000
1	1.35	1.35	1.429	1.429	3.064	2.838	2.295
2	2.22	1.64	2.173	1.521	3.957	3.995	4.059
3	3.63	1.64	3.419	1.574	6.768	6.649	6.756
4	5.96	1.64	5.691	1.664	11.264	11.066	11.224
Generation				Scenario 2			
0	1.00	—	1.000	—	1.000	1.000	1.000
1	1.29	1.29	1.227	1.227	2.582	2.425	2.292
2	2.11	1.64	1.861	1.517	3.391	3.422	4.070
3	3.47	1.64	2.929	1.574	5.797	5.695	6.773
4	5.69	1.64	4.875	1.664	9.649	9.479	11.274

(a) Scenario 1: $E^{US} = 0.17 \times E^{W}$

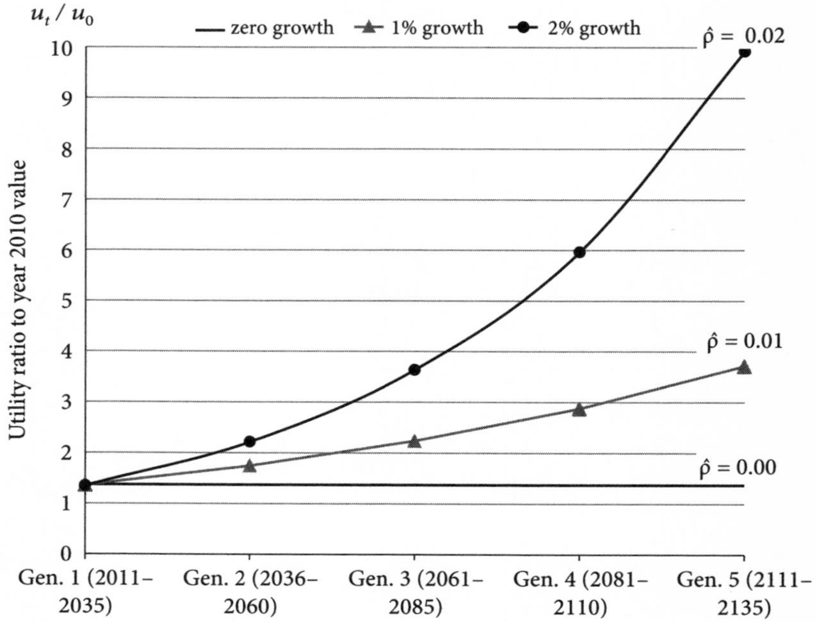

(b) Scenario 2: $e^{US} = e^{W}$

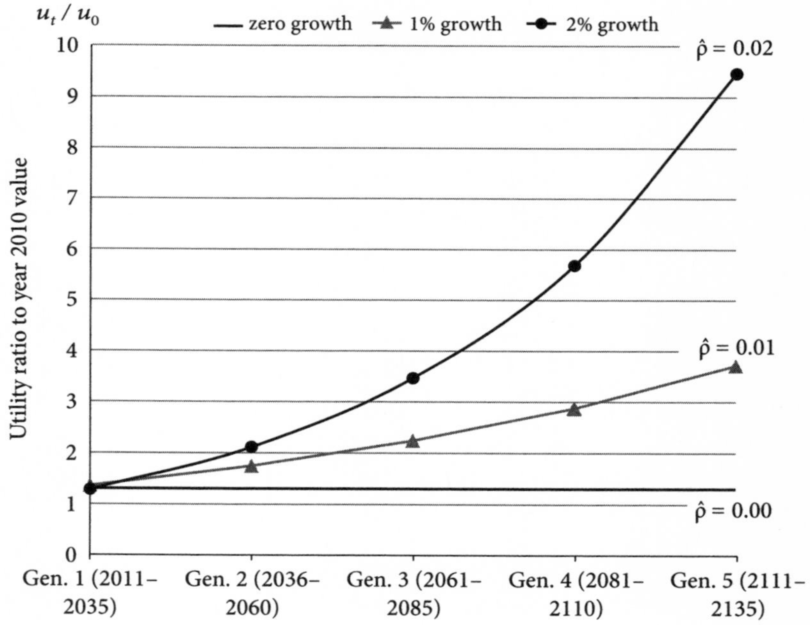

of Scenario 2 yield smaller increases in the utility of the US representative agents.

Utility can be sustained forever at a significantly higher level than the year 2010 reference level: 37.3% higher in Scenario 1 and 30.9% higher in Scenario 2.

A tradeoff between the utility of the first generation and the subsequent growth rates must indeed be expected. But our analysis shows that its magnitude is quite small: Generation 1's sacrifice for the sake of a higher growth rate is tiny for reasonable growth rates.

As Figure 3.2 illustrates, utility paths under the different growth targets stay well above the reference-year level (represented by the horizontal line at value 1). However, it is not possible at the scale of the graph to distinguish among the three values of the utility of the first generation (for annual growth rates of 0%, 1%, and 2%, respectively). Table 3.4 shows the actual values: in order to subsequently sustain a 1% annual growth rate, the utility of the first generation falls by a mere 0.7%, with respect to the no-growth value. In other words, a sustained growth rate of 1% per year can be reached at the cost of a less than 1% reduction of the utility of the first generation relative to the sustainable (no growth) path. Similarly, sustaining a 2% growth rate per year can be reached at the cost of a less than 2% reduction of the utility of the first generation relative to the no-growth path.

Although the values in Table 3.4 were calculated by our computational algorithm, we can show (see Section A3.2 in the Chapter 3 Appendix), using the envelope theorem and knowledge of the shadow prices for program G, that if $\tilde{\Lambda}(\rho)$ is the value of the ρ-sustainable program, then $\tilde{\Lambda}'(0) = -\tilde{\Lambda}(0)/(\xi - 1)$. From this it follows that, to a first-order approximation, $\tilde{\Lambda}(0)/\tilde{\Lambda}(0.28) = 1.00697$, consistent with the estimate in Table 3.4 of a first-generation utility fall of 0.7% if the generational growth rate increases from 0% to 28%, corresponding to an annual 1% growth rate. This agreement provides a check on the precision of our computational algorithm.

Figure 3.2. Paths of utility (generations 1 to 5) for alternative annual growth rates in utility $\hat{\rho}$. All variables grow at a rate slightly higher than $\hat{\rho}$, with the exception of emissions and CO_2 concentrations, which follow the path described in Table 3.1.

Table 3.3. Paths of relative utility for different sustained growth rates.

	Gen. 0 u_0/u_0	Gen. 1 u_1/u_0	Gen. 2 u_2/u_0	Gen. 3 u_3/u_0	Gen. 4 u_4/u_0	Gen. 5 u_5/u_0
			Scenario 1			
$\hat{\rho} = 0.00$: Sustainable, no growth	1.000	1.373	1.373	1.373	1.373	1.373
$\hat{\rho} = 0.01$: 1% annual growth	1.000	1.363	1.748	2.242	2.875	3.713
$\hat{\rho} = 0.02$: 2% annual growth	1.000	1.350	2.215	3.634	5.962	9.923
			Scenario 2			
$\hat{\rho} = 0.00$: Sustainable, no growth	1.000	1.309	1.309	1.309	1.309	1.309
$\hat{\rho} = 0.01$: 1% annual growth	1.000	1.300	1.667	2.137	2.741	3.541
$\hat{\rho} = 0.02$: 2% annual growth	1.000	1.287	2.112	3.456	5.685	9.462

Table 3.4. Paths of relative utility for different sustained growth rates. The tildes denote the solution for the corresponding utility as a function of $\hat{\rho}$.

	Utility of first generation $\tilde{u}_1(\hat{\rho})/u_0$	Sacrifice of first generation $\frac{\tilde{u}_1(0)-\tilde{u}_1(\hat{\rho})}{\tilde{u}_1(0)}$
	Scenario 1	
$\hat{\rho}=0.00$: Sustainable, no growth	1.373	0.000
$\hat{\rho}=0.01$: 1% annual growth	1.363	0.007 = 0.7%
$\hat{\rho}=0.02$: 2% annual growth	1.350	0.017 = 1.7%
	Scenario 2	
$\hat{\rho}=0.00$: Sustainable, no growth	1.309	0.000
$\hat{\rho}=0.01$: 1% annual growth	1.300	0.007 = 0.7%
$\hat{\rho}=0.02$: 2% annual growth	1.287	0.017 = 1.7%

Moderate growth rates can be achieved at the cost of a small reduction in the utility of the first generation, which stays well above the level in the reference year.

How are these utility paths implemented? Labor time is, in the reference year, allocated to the various ends as indicated in the 'Generation 0' rows of Table 3.5, while the rows for generations 1 through 3 indicate how these fractions should be modified in the proposed solutions.

The largest change displayed in Table 3.5 occurs in the fraction of labor allocated to knowledge, which must be about twice the reference-year level. The fraction of time devoted to investment in physical capital must be slightly higher, whereas the fractions of labor time devoted to the production of consumption goods and to leisure are slightly lower.[12]

The most important change required by the implementation of the proposed paths is the doubling of the reference fraction of labor devoted to the creation of knowledge.

Finally, we turn to the implications of increasing the growth rates, evidenced by comparing the rows of Table 3.5. Higher growth rates require

[12] Compare with Jones and Williams (1998), who estimate that the socially optimal investment in R&D is two to four times present investment.

Table 3.5. The allocation of labor for different sustained growth rates.

(a) $\hat{\rho} = 0.00$ (sustainable utility, no growth)

	Labor in efficiency units			Labor as a fraction of total labor-leisure available						
	Total x_t	Education x_t^e	Knowledge x_t^n	Leisure x_t^l	Education x_t^e/x_t	Knowledge x_t^n/x_t	Output x_t^c/x_t	Consumption $\frac{x_t^c}{x_t}\frac{c_t}{c_t+i_t}$	Investment $\frac{x_t^c}{x_t}\frac{i_t}{c_t+i_t}$	Leisure x_t^l/x_t
Generation	Scenario 1									
0	2.171	0.072	0.036	1.448	0.0333	0.0167	0.2831	0.2425	0.0406	0.6670
1	2.995	0.073	0.102	1.937	0.0245	0.0342	0.2945	0.2167	0.0779	0.6467
2	3.044	0.076	0.094	2.023	0.0250	0.0308	0.2798	0.2226	0.0572	0.6644
3	3.149	0.076	0.093	2.081	0.0241	0.0294	0.2855	0.2214	0.0641	0.6609
Generation	Scenario 2									
0	2.171	0.072	0.036	1.448	0.0333	0.0167	0.2831	0.2425	0.2425	0.6670
1	2.995	0.074	0.102	1.940	0.0246	0.0342	0.2936	0.2170	0.2170	0.6477
2	3.052	0.076	0.094	2.028	0.0250	0.0308	0.2798	0.2226	0.2226	0.6644
3	3.158	0.076	0.093	2.087	0.0241	0.0294	0.2855	0.2214	0.2214	0.6609

(b) $\hat{\rho} = 0.01$ (1% annual growth)

	Labor in efficiency units			Labor as a fraction of total labor-leisure available						
	Total x_t	Education x_t^e	Knowledge x_t^n	Leisure x_t^l	Education x_t^e/x_t	Knowledge x_t^n/x_t	Output x_t^c/x_t	Consumption $\frac{x_t^c}{x_t}\frac{c_t}{c_t+i_t}$	Investment $\frac{x_t^c}{x_t}\frac{i_t}{c_t+i_t}$	Leisure x_t^l/x_t
Generation	Scenario 1									
0	2.171	0.072	0.036	1.448	0.0333	0.0167	0.2831	0.2425	0.0406	0.6670
1	2.995	0.096	0.102	1.923	0.0320	0.0339	0.2923	0.2150	0.0772	0.6419
2	3.966	0.128	0.129	2.594	0.0322	0.0324	0.2813	0.2191	0.0622	0.6541
3	5.292	0.165	0.164	3.447	0.0312	0.0311	0.2864	0.2182	0.0682	0.6513
Generation	Scenario 2									
0	2.171	0.072	0.036	1.448	0.0333	0.0167	0.2831	0.2425	0.2425	0.6670
1	2.995	0.096	0.101	1.926	0.0320	0.0339	0.2913	0.2153	0.2153	0.6428
2	3.977	0.128	0.129	2.601	0.0322	0.0324	0.2813	0.2191	0.2191	0.6540
3	5.306	0.165	0.165	3.456	0.0312	0.0311	0.2864	0.2182	0.2182	0.6513

(continued)

Table 3.5. (continued)

(c) $\hat{\rho} = 0.02$ (2% annual growth)

	Labor in efficiency units			Labor as a fraction of total labor-leisure available						
	Total x_t	Education x_t^e	Knowledge x_t^n	Leisure x_t^l	Education x_t^e/x_t	Knowledge x_t^n/x_t	Output x_t^c/x_t	Consumption $\frac{x_t^c}{x_t}\frac{c_t}{c_t+i_t}$	Investment $\frac{x_t^c}{x_t}\frac{i_t}{c_t+i_t}$	Leisure x_t^l/x_t
Generation	Scenario 1									
0	2.171	0.072	0.036	1.448	0.0333	0.0167	0.2831	0.2425	0.0406	0.6670
1	2.995	0.124	0.101	1.904	0.0414	0.0336	0.2893	0.2129	0.0764	0.6357
2	5.144	0.213	0.172	3.311	0.0414	0.0335	0.2813	0.2156	0.0657	0.6437
3	8.834	0.355	0.284	5.667	0.0402	0.0322	0.2861	0.2149	0.0712	0.6415
Generation	Scenario 2									
0	2.171	0.072	0.036	1.448	0.0333	0.0167	0.2831	0.2425	0.2425	0.6670
1	2.995	0.124	0.100	1.907	0.0416	0.0335	0.2883	0.2133	0.2133	0.6366
2	5.158	0.214	0.173	3.320	0.0414	0.0335	0.2814	0.2156	0.2156	0.6437
3	8.857	0.356	0.285	5.682	0.0402	0.0322	0.2861	0.2149	0.2149	0.6415

substantial increases in the fraction of labor devoted to education (of the order of a 30% increase for each additional 1% of annual growth). They also require moderate increases in the fraction of labor devoted to investment in physical capital and in knowledge. These increases are compensated by minor decreases in the fractions of labor devoted to consumption and leisure.

3.8. Discounting

We now contemplate the discounted-sustainabilitarian program associated with program $E[\rho, e^*, S^{m^*}]$, in which we maximize $\sum_{t=1}^{\infty}\left(\frac{1-\pi}{1+\rho}\right)^{t-1} u_t$ and append the constraints:

$$(1+\rho)u_t \geq u_{t-1}, \quad t = 1, 2, \ldots$$

to the set of constraints of program $E[\rho, e^*, S^{m^*}]$. Recall that π is the probability that each generation is the last one, conditional upon its coming into existence. The procedure is exactly the one we followed in moving from program $\rho - SUS^0[1, x_0^e, S_0^k]$ to $\rho - SUS^0[1-\pi, x_0^e, S_0^k]$ in Chapter 2. We conjecture that the analogue of the simplification theorem (2.9) continues to hold for the more complex model of this chapter—that is to say, that the solution of discounted- and undiscounted-sustainabilitarian programs (now with growth) are the same if the discounted-utilitarian program, defined on the same feasible set, diverges. It is therefore of interest to know when the discounted-utilitarian program associated with the set of feasible paths of the present model diverges. To be precise, that discounted-utilitarian program is:

► **Program** $DU[\varphi, e^*, S^{m^*}]$

Given (e^*, S^{m^*}),

$$\text{maximize} \sum_{t=1}^{\infty} \varphi^{t-1} u_t$$

subject to:

$$u_t = c_t^{\alpha_c}(x_t^l)^{\alpha_l}(S_t^n)^{\alpha_n}(\hat{S}^m - S^{m^*})^{\alpha_m}$$

$$k_1(x_t^c)^{\theta_c}(S_t^k)^{\theta_k}(S_t^n)^{\theta_n}(e^*)^{\theta_e}(S^{m^*})^{\theta_m} \geq c_t + i_t, \quad t \geq 1,$$

$$(1-d^k)S_{t-1}^k + k_2 i_t \geq S_t^k, \quad t \geq 1,$$

$$(1-d^n)S_{t-1}^n + k_3 x_t^n \geq S_t^n, \quad t \geq 1,$$

$$x_t^e + x_t^n + x_t^l + x_t^c \equiv x_t, \quad t \geq 1,$$

$$\xi\, x_{t-1}^e \geq x_t, \quad t \geq 1,$$

with initial conditions (x_0^e, S_0^k, S_0^n).

We have:

► **Proposition 3.2.** *Program* $DU[\varphi, e^*, S^{m^*}]$ *diverges if* $\varphi\xi^{1-\alpha_m} > 1$.

► **Proof:** Chapter 3 Appendix.

If the analogue of theorem 2.9 is true for the model $E[1, e^*, S^{m^*}]$, then proposition 3.2 tells us that discounting the program $E[1,e^*,S^{m^*}]$ because of the possibility of human extinction is not necessary as long as $(1-\pi)\xi^{1-\alpha_m} > 1$. Given our calibrated values of $\xi = 41.434$ and $\alpha_m = 0.028$, it follows that we do not need to discount the sustainabilitarian program as long as

$$1 - \pi > 0.027.$$

In other words, the large value of ξ implies that the economy is sufficiently productive so as to make the discounted-utilitarian version of our program diverge even for small values of the discount factor φ, which in turn implies that, unless the probability π of extinction is huge, discounting our program $E[1, e^*, S^{m^*}]$ is unnecessary. According to theorem 2.9, it also follows that for relatively small growth rates, discounting the program $E[\rho, e^*, S^{m^*}]$ is unnecessary. In particular, for the generational growth rate $\rho = 0.28$, the required inequality in the premise of theorem 2.9 holds as long as $1 - \pi > 0.031$.

Readers may be surprised by the implication of proposition 3.2—namely, that the discounted-utilitarian program associated with the set of paths of the model $E[1, e^*, S^{m^*}]$ diverges for any reasonable discount factor—because, in models based on the Ramsey formulation, the discounted-utilitarian program converges for much higher discount factors. For instance, in Nordhaus's (2008a) model, the discounted-utilitarian objective $\sum_{t=1}^{\infty}\varphi^{t-1}\frac{c_t^{1-\eta}}{1-\eta}$ converges when $\varphi \approx 0.98$ and $\eta = 2$.[13] We believe that two differences between our model and that of Nordhaus (2008a), explain this: (1) his choices of a 'large' value for η, to concavify the utility function, and (2), *not* modeling the formation of human capital through education. Our objective function, in contrast, enjoys constant-returns-to-scale; more precisely, if we hold the biospheric term $(\hat{S} - S_t^m)^{\alpha_m}$ fixed, then the returns-to-scale in the other arguments of our utility function are almost constant, since $1 - \alpha_m = 0.972$. Comparable returns-to-scale would be achieved in the Ramsey-Nordhaus objective function with a choice of $\eta = 0.028$. Nordhaus chooses his 'large' value of η for ethical reasons, to moderate intergenerational inequality. We, however, have no need to concavify the utility function in order to constrain intergenerational inequality because our sustainability approach builds in a concern for such inequality. And we see from theorem 2.5 and proposition 3.2 the very important role that the education sector (with parameter ξ) plays in determining whether or not the discounted-utilitarian objective diverges.

3.9. Sustaining Consumption Instead of Utility

As discussed in Section 3.2.1, a large segment of the literature, including Nordhaus (2008a), considers consumption, or GDP per capita, as the only argument in human welfare. We, on the contrary, include education, knowledge, and CO_2 stocks in addition to consumption and leisure, as formalized in (3.1). One may ask: to what extent do our results depend on our formulation of welfare? In order to address this issue, the present section replicates the optimization with no growth but substitutes consumption

---

[13] Nordhaus is not explicitly concerned with the convergence issue because he only considers a finite horizon of six hundred years (Nordhaus 2008a, 208).

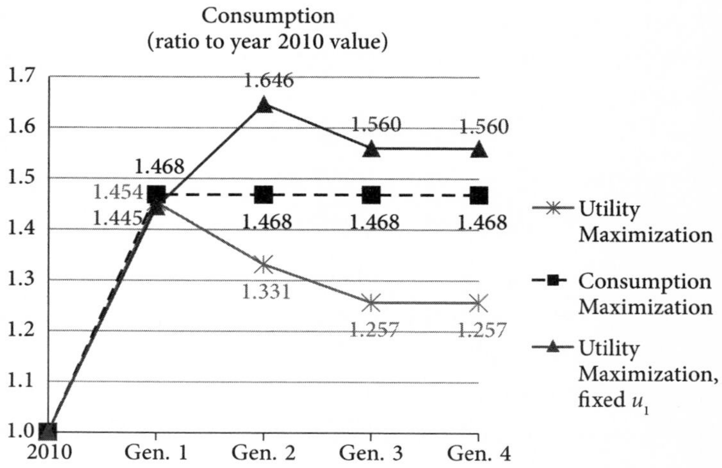

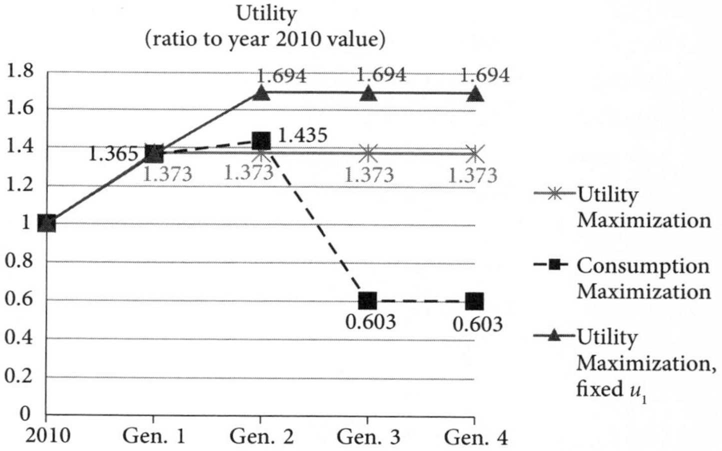

Figure 3.3. Paths of utility, consumption, knowledge, and education for the pure-sustainability program (no growth) under three regimes: (i) maximizing utility; (ii) maximizing consumption; and (iii) maximizing utility while fixing the utility of Generation 1 at the value obtained under the consumption maximization program (36.5% above the reference year).

for utility and assumes that the fraction of the time devoted to leisure is the same as in the solution to the pure-sustainability optimization program of (3.4) above for $\rho = 0$.[14]

[14] We fix leisure at the level given by the solution to the utility maximization program in order to render the results of the two programs comparable, because leisure has no value in the consumption maximization program.

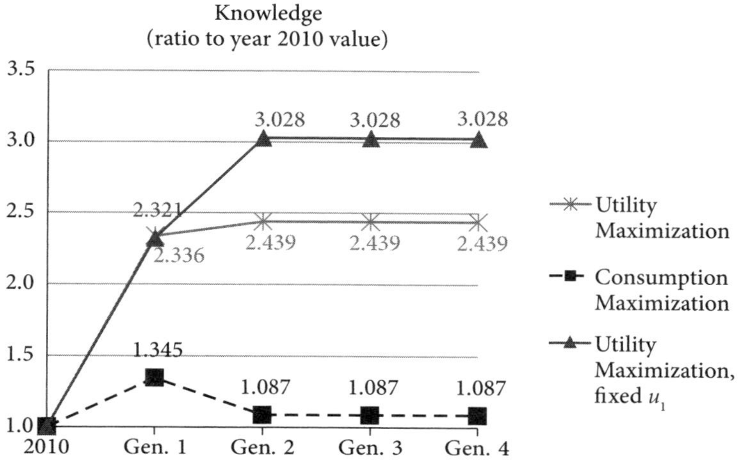

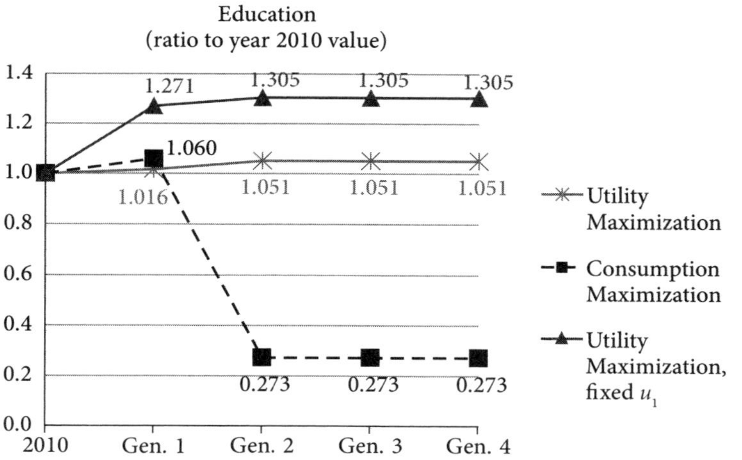

Figure 3.3 compares the solution paths for utility, consumption, knowledge, and education in the two optimization problems: utility maximization (solid lines with star marks) and consumption maximization (dashed lines with square marks; disregard for the moment the lines with triangular marks).

Predictably, consumption is higher and utility is lower when the objective is consumption rather than our extended notion of utility defined in (3.1). But, while consumption is about 16% higher at the steady state, utility is more than 55% lower and even falls below current levels, achieving a mere 60.3% of the utility level in the 2010 reference year before the end of the century. Table 3.6 presents the steady-state values for the two models.

Table 3.6. Utility versus consumption maximization.

	Steady-state values (fraction over year 2010)			
	Utility	Consumption	Stock of knowledge	Efficiency units in education
Utility maximization	1.37	1.26	2.44	1.05
Consumption maximization	0.60	1.47	1.09	0.27

The evolution of stocks and flows along the paths is revealing. The first two generations enjoy similar levels of consumption and utility: utility is 0.5% lower for Generation 1 and 4.5% higher for Generation 2, under consumption maximization, while consumption is 0.9% and 10.2% higher for generations 1 and 2, respectively. However, utility rapidly drops to levels below the 2010 reference year under consumption maximization, while consumption remains around 26% above the reference level when maximizing utility. Remarkably, the notion of welfare has dramatic consequences for the allocation of resources. When the objective is utility instead of consumption, the steady-state stock of knowledge is more than twice as large, and steady-state education is over four times as large.

The comparison reinforces the case for maintaining an extended notion of utility to include more than just consumption. Suppose we are uncertain about the appropriate objective we should adopt: utility or consumption. If we choose utility, we pay a relatively small consumption cost. On the other hand, if we sustain consumption when utility is the appropriate objective, the steady-state level of utility falls considerably.[15]

Finally, observe that maximizing consumption yields a slightly lower utility level for the first generation (36.5% higher than the value in the reference year, compared to a 37.3% in the utility maximization program). We have already seen that small *sacrifices* by the first generation can generate high utility for future generations. (Very small decreases in

[15] In order to clarify the intuition, Section A3.4 of the Chapter 3 Appendix provides a stripped-down model, which derives a similar result, although with less striking numbers, validating the robustness of our findings.

the utility of the first generation endow future generations with more human capital, the growth engine in our economy, allowing for sustained annual growths of 1% and 2% per year; see Figure 3.2.) Hence, we have run the pure-sustainability program (program G for $\rho = 0$; see (3.4)) with a constraint modification that allows for an apples-to-apples comparison with the consumption maximization program, namely, fixing the utility level of the first generation at the value obtained under the consumption maximization program: a value of 7.250, or 37.3% higher than the utility in the reference year. Formally, the constraint for the utility of Generation 1 in program G is modified as follows:

$$c_1^{\alpha_c}(x_1^l)^{\alpha_l}(S_1^n)^{\alpha_n}(\hat{S}^m - S_1^m)^{\alpha_m} \geq 1.373\bar{u}_0 \equiv 7.250.$$

The solution paths are represented by the solid lines with triangular marks in Figure 3.3. Now the differences relative to the consumption-maximizing paths are even more striking, yielding substantially higher values even in consumption levels (except for the first generation, when consumption is very similar).

The comparisons in this section reinforce the case for sustaining growth, as in Section 3.3, a position we maintain in Chapter 5 when introducing intragenerational issues. The first generation may opt for small sacrifices in its levels of utility and consumption, which would sustain much higher levels of consumption, knowledge, education, and hence utility for all future generations.

3.10. Neglecting Emissions and Concentrations

To what extent are our results due to the problem of climate change rather than just the need to sustain welfare or growth? We contemplate a counterfactual world to address this issue.[16] An Ethical Observer mistakenly believes that emissions and concentration are economically irrelevant: concentrations do not affect production or utility, and emissions do not have a role in production. Formally, the 'mistaken' Ethical Observer replaces (3.1) by

---

[16] This exercise was suggested by two referees of Harvard University Press.

$$(c_t)^{\alpha_c}(x_t^l)^{\alpha_l}(S_t^n)^{\alpha_n}$$

and (3.3) by

$$k_1^*(x_t^c)^{\theta_c}(S_t^k)^{\theta_k}(S_t^n)^{\theta_n}.$$

Of course, if both production functions (the correct one with parameter k_1 and the mistaken one with parameter k_1^*) are calibrated with year 2010 data, then

$$k_1^* = k_1(e_{2010})^{\theta_e}(S_{2010}^m)^{\theta_m},$$

so that in fact the mistaken Ethical Observer fixes emissions and concentration at their 2010 levels and incorporates them into the constant k_1^* of the production function. (Evidently, the constant path for the environmental variables $(e_t, S_t^m) = (e_{2010}, S_{2010}^m)$ is infeasible.)

How would the recommendations of the mistaken Ethical Observer deviate from those of the correct one? By comparing the values of variables (knowledge, education, consumption) on the optimal paths of the correct and mistaken ethical observers, both at a 1% annual growth rate, we get a feeling for how much of our investment in knowledge and education is due to the climate problem rather than being explained by climate-neutral growth considerations. Table 3.7 displays some relevant results.[17]

First note that, because the aggregate efficiency units of labor at time t are determined by the investment in education at $t=1$, the first two rows of Table 3.7 show that the mistaken Ethical Observer is devoting too few resources to education, although the gap is not large. The next three rows show that, after $t=1$, she is also devoting too few resources to investment in knowledge, whereas the last two rows show that she recommends too much investment in physical capital, as well as too much consumption, by a substantial margin.

[17] It is irrelevant to compare utilities in the two models, as this would be akin to comparing apples to oranges.

Table 3.7. The effects of neglecting emissions and concentrations at 1% annual growth rate.

	Mistaken EO	Correct EO	Ratio mistaken/ correct
x_2 (Total efficiency units of labor at $t=2$)	3.786	3.966	0.955
x_3 (Total efficiency units of labor at steady state)	4.860	5.292	0.918
S_1^n (Stock of knowledge at $t=1$)	62.572	62.470	1.002
S_2^n (Stock of knowledge at $t=2$)	78.713	85.097	0.925
S_3^n (Stock of knowledge at steady state)	100.943	109.924	0.918
S_3^k (Stock of capital at steady state)	492.573	418.691	1.176
c_3 (Consumption at steady state)	100.313	85.228	1.177

3.11. Summary

In this chapter, we have presented a model of intergenerational resource allocation with emissions and a utility function in which one argument is the atmospheric concentration of carbon. The model builds on the simpler model of Chapter 2: it introduces CO_2 emissions and concentrations and a technology that produces knowledge from skilled labor. The stock of social knowledge has been introduced as an input in the output-production function, modeling endogenous technical progress, and also as an argument in the utility function. Indeed, many researchers model the climate-change problem as one in which human welfare is a function of commodity consumption only and where the skill of labor, knowledge, and CO_2 emissions and concentrations enter only into the commodity-production function (with emissions perhaps entering via emission abatement costs). We, on the contrary, recognize that education, knowledge, and GHG concentrations also have a direct impact on welfare.

Various theorems, proved for the simpler model of Chapter 2, are assumed to possess analogues for the model of this chapter, although we do not prove those analogues. The ray optimization theorem, which is proved, tells us that if the growth rate is sufficiently small, then there exists a ray in endowment space such that, should the vector of initial endowments lie on this ray, the solution to the growth-sustainability optimization program is a steady-state path, where we fix exogenously the path of carbon emissions.

We assumed that the analogue of the turnpike theorem of Chapter 2 holds for this model so that if the initial endowment vector lies off the ray, the optimal solution to the growth-sustainability optimization program converges to this steady-state solution. We used this property in Chapter 3 to compute solutions to its optimization program. In short, using the turnpike property, we are able to replace an optimization program with an infinite number of time-dated constraints with one that has only a small number of constraints, by forcing the solution to converge to the ray described in three dates. Granted, this will give us only an approximation to the true optimal solution, but we showed that the approximation is very good because it does not change significantly if we extend the number of generations in which convergence is mandated. Convergence to ray, in other words, occurs rapidly.

We also assumed that the analogue to the simplification theorem (2.9) in Chapter 2 holds for the model introduced here: that is to say, if the *discounted-utilitarian* program for the model of this chapter diverges, then the solution to the *discounted-sustainabilitarian* program is identical to the solution of the *undiscounted-sustainabilitarian* program. We computed that, assuming this conjecture is true, then for any reasonable assumptions about the size of the probability of extinction π we can ignore discounting in the sustainabilitarian program. It is the high productivity of the economy, as captured in the parameter ξ of the educational production function, that is responsible for this result.

We showed that optimal solutions exist for several growth rates and calculated the cost to the first generation of increasing the sustainable growth rate. That cost appears to be quite low, which further supports our argument in Chapter 1 and Chapter 2 that, if the present generation values human development, it will assent to relaxing its right to be as well off as future generations and will permit growth. Growth sustainability with a positive rate of growth seems to be an attractive approach.

This view becomes reinforced when comparing the results under consumption maximization *versus* utility maximization. The comparison also strengthens the case for sustaining an extended notion of utility, which has dramatic consequences not only for the levels of utility but also for the allocation of resources. We believe our utility function is a better index of welfare than just consumption, and therefore we recommend substantially deeper investment in knowledge and education than would be optimal in models in which these variables only affect productivity.

Some readers may be unhappy with our advocacy of a positive rate of growth of human welfare, which implies, on our optimal paths, a positive rate of growth of consumption, forever. There are two caveats. First, the only natural constraint we have introduced that might inhibit growth is the accumulation of atmospheric carbon. However, other natural constraints with respect to land and water may well apply. If those natural constraints cannot be addressed through technological innovation, then the possibility of permanent growth would be compromised. The second caveat involves the necessity of permitting more rapid growth in the developing world. We have calibrated the model of this chapter to the American economy. Will it be possible for growth to occur at a rate that is politically and ethically required in the global South and still adhere to a path of global emissions that does not produce dangerous climate change? We will address this question in Chapter 5.

APPENDIX 3. PROOFS

A3.1. Proof of Theorem 3.1

The program we study is:

► **Program** $E[\rho, e^*, S^{m^*}]$

$$\max \Lambda \qquad \text{subject to:}$$

$$(a_t^1) \quad c_t^{\alpha_c}(x_t^l)^{\alpha_l}(S_t^n)^{\alpha_n}(\hat{S}^m - S^{m^*})^{\alpha_m} \geq \Lambda(1+\rho)^{t-1}, \quad t \geq 1,$$

$$(a_t^2) \quad k_1(S^{m^*})^{\theta_m}(e^*)^{\theta_e}(x_t^c)^{\theta_c}(S_t^k)^{\theta_k}(S_t^n)^{\theta_n} \geq c_t + i_t, \quad t \geq 1,$$

$$(a_t^3) \quad (1-d^k)S_{t-1}^k + k_2 i_t \geq S_t^k, \quad t \geq 1,$$

$$(a_t^4) \quad (1-d^n)S_{t-1}^n + k_3 x_t^n \geq S_t^n, \quad t \geq 1,$$

$$(a_t^5) \quad \xi x_{t-1}^e \geq x_t^e + x_t^n + x_t^l + x_t^c, \quad t \geq 1, \tag{A3.1}$$

where emissions and concentrations are fixed at levels e^* and S^{m^*}, respectively. The Lagrangian multipliers $(a_t^\#)$ have been written to the left of the constraints

Our problem is to find conditions on the endowment vector (x_0^e, S_0^k, S_0^n) such that the optimal solution to the program is a path of steady growth. At steady-state growth there will be two different growth rates: utility will grow at a rate ρ per generation, while the economic variables $(S_t^k, S_t^n, x_t^l, x_t^c, x_t^n, x_t^e, i_t, c_t)$ will grow at a rate g, with $1+g=(1+\rho)^{1/(\alpha_c+\alpha_l+\alpha_n)}$.

Given the ordered triple (g, e^*, S^{m^*}), there will be a ray $\Gamma(g, e^*, S^{m^*}) \subset \Re_+^3$ such that if the endowment vector $(x_0^e, S_0^n, S_0^k) \in \Gamma(g, e^*, S^{m^*})$ then balanced growth at rate g (and ρ) will occur at the optimal solution to the program. We proceed to determine this ray.

To do so, we first derive the Kuhn-Tucker conditions for the program, which are:

$$(\partial\Lambda)\quad 1-\sum_{t=1}^{\infty} a_t^1(1+\rho)^{t-1}=0,\quad t\geq 1, \tag{A3.2}$$

$$(\partial x_t^e)\quad \xi a_{t+1}^5 - a_t^5 = 0,\quad \text{i. e., } a_t^5=(1/\xi)^{t-1}a_1^5,\quad t\geq 1, \tag{A3.3}$$

$$(\partial x_t^l)\quad \frac{a_t^1\alpha_l\,\Lambda(1+\rho)^{t-1}}{x_t^l}-a_t^5=0,\quad t\geq 1, \tag{A3.4}$$

$$(\partial x_t^n)\quad k_3a_t^4=a_t^5,\quad t\geq 1, \tag{A3.5}$$

$$(\partial x_t^c)\quad \frac{a_t^2\theta_c(c_t+i_t)}{x_t^c}-a_t^5=0,\quad t\geq 1, \tag{A3.6}$$

$$(\partial c_t)\quad a_t^1\frac{\alpha_c\Lambda(1+\rho)^{t-1}}{c_t}-a_t^2=0,\quad t\geq 1, \tag{A3.7}$$

$$(\partial i_t)\quad -a_t^2+k_2a_t^3=0,\quad t\geq 1, \tag{A3.8}$$

$$(\partial S_t^k)\quad \frac{a_t^2\theta_k(c_t+i_t)}{S_t^k}-a_t^3+(1-d^k)a_{t+1}^3=0,\quad t\geq 1, \tag{A3.9}$$

$$(\partial S_t^n)\quad \frac{a_t^1\alpha_n\Lambda(1+\rho)^{t-1}}{S_t^n}+\frac{a_t^2\theta_n(c_t+i_t)}{S_t^n} +(1-d^n)a_{t+1}^4-a_t^4=0,\quad t\geq 1. \tag{A3.10}$$

We now substitute into these equations the variable values on a balanced growth path.

1. (A3.3) and (A3.4) imply that

$$a_t^1=\left(\frac{a_1^5x_1^l}{\alpha_l\Lambda}\right)\left(\frac{1+g}{\xi(1+\rho)}\right)^{t-1}. \tag{A3.11}$$

2. By (A3.2), it follows that $1=\left[\sum_{t=1}^{\infty}\left(\frac{1+g}{\xi}\right)^{t-1}\right]\frac{a_1^5x_1^l}{\alpha_l\Lambda}$. This defines a_1^5 at the solution, and hence a_t^5. Note that a_1^5 will be defined as long as $\xi>1+g$, so that the series converges. It follows that:

$$1=\left(\frac{a_1^5x_1^l}{\alpha_l\Lambda}\right)\frac{\xi}{\xi-(1+g)}. \tag{A3.12}$$

3. (A3.5) defines $a_t^4 = a_t^5/k_3 = (a_1^5/k_3)(1/\xi)^{t-1}$, whereas (A3.6) defines $a_t^2 \geq 0$, and (A3.8) defines $a_t^3 = a_t^2/k_2$. Thus, all the dual variables are defined and nonnegative. This leaves equations (A3.9), (A3.7), and (A3.10), which we now analyze.

4. *Analysis of* (A3.9)

   (A3.6) implies $a_t^2 = \dfrac{a_t^5 x_t^c}{\theta_c(c_t + i_t)}$, so (A3.9) says $\dfrac{a_t^5 x_t^c \theta_k}{\theta_c S_t^k} = \dfrac{a_t^2 - (1-d^k)a_{t+1}^2}{k_2}$. Substituting for a_t^2 and multiplying by θ_c/a_t^5 gives $\dfrac{k_2 x_t^c \theta_k}{S_t^k} = \dfrac{x_t^c}{c_t + i_t} - \dfrac{1-d^k}{\xi}\dfrac{x_{t+1}^c}{c_{t+1} + i_{t+1}}$, which, using the balanced growth property of the path, means $\dfrac{k_2 x_1^c \theta_k}{S_0^k(1+g)} = \dfrac{x_1^c}{c_1 + i_1} - \dfrac{1-d^k}{\xi}\dfrac{x_1^c}{c_1 + i_1}$.

   Multiplying by $\dfrac{1+g}{x_1^c}$, we have:

$$\frac{k_2\theta_k}{S_0^k} = \frac{(1+g)}{c_1 + i_1}\left(1 - \left(\frac{1-d^k}{\xi}\right)\right). \qquad \text{(A3.13)}$$

5. *Analysis of* (A3.7)

   (A3.7) implies $\dfrac{a_t^1 \alpha_c \Lambda (1+\rho)^{t-1}}{c_t} = \dfrac{a_t^5 x_t^c}{\theta_c(c_t + i_t)}$, which may be reduced to the equation:

$$\frac{x_1^l}{\alpha_l} = \frac{c_1 x_1^c}{\alpha_c \theta_c (c_1 + i_1)}. \qquad \text{(A3.14)}$$

6. *Analysis of* (A3.10)

   We express a_t^1, a_t^2, a_t^4 in terms of a_t^5; after some algebraic manipulation, (A3.10) reduces to:

$$\frac{\alpha_n x_1^l}{\alpha_l(1+g)S_0^n} + \frac{\theta_n x_1^c}{\theta_c(1+g)S_0^n} + \frac{1}{k_3}\left(\frac{1-d^n}{\xi} - 1\right) = 0. \qquad \text{(A3.15)}$$

   In sum, we have the three equations (A3.13), (A3.14), and (A3.15). From the primal constraints we have:

$$k_1(1+g)^{\theta_n + \theta_k}(S_0^k)^{\theta_k}(S_0^n)^{\theta_n}(x_1^c)^{\theta_c}(S^{m*})^{\theta_m}(e^*)^{\theta_e} = c_1 + i_1, \qquad \text{(A3.16)}$$

$$x_0^e(\xi-(1+g)) = x_1^n + x_1^c + x_1^l, \tag{A3.17}$$

$$k_2 i_1 = S_0^k(g+d^k), \tag{A3.18}$$

$$k_3 x_1^n = (g+d^n)S_0^n. \tag{A3.19}$$

Define the following expressions:

$$\nu^n(g) = \frac{d^n+g}{k_3},$$

$$p^i(g) = \frac{d^k+g}{k_2},$$

$$p^c(g) = \left(1-\frac{1-d^k}{\xi}\right)\frac{1+g}{k_2\theta_k} - \frac{d^k+g}{k_2},$$

$$\nu^l(g) = \left(1-\frac{1-d^n}{\xi}\right)\frac{\alpha_l}{k_3}\frac{p^c(g)}{\alpha_c\theta_n(p^c(g)+p^i(g))+\alpha_n p^c(g)}(1+g),$$

$$\nu^c(g) = \left(1-\frac{1-d^n}{\xi}\right)\frac{\alpha_c\theta_c}{k_3}\frac{p^c(g)+p^i(g)}{\alpha_c\theta_n(p^c(g)+p^i(g))+\alpha_n p^c(g)}(1+g),$$

$$q^n(g) = \frac{\xi-(1+g)}{\nu^n(g)+\nu^l(g)+\nu^c(g)},$$

and

$$q^k(g,e^*,S^{m^*})$$

$$= \left(\frac{k_1(\nu^c(g))^{\theta_c}}{p^c(g)+p^i(g)}\right)^{\frac{1}{\theta_n+\theta_c}}(1+g)^{\frac{\theta_n+\theta_k}{\theta_n+\theta_c}}q^n(g)(e^*)^{\frac{\theta_e}{\theta_n+\theta_c}}(S^{m^*})^{\frac{\theta_m}{\theta_n+\theta_c}}.$$

Note that these seven functions are all positive. In particular, it is easily checked that $p^c(g) > 0$ for any $g \geq 0$, since $\xi > 1$.

Now from (A3.18) we solve for i_1:

$$i_1 = p^i(g)S_0^k.$$

From (A3.19), we have

$$x_1^n = \nu^n(g)S_0^n.$$

From (A3.13) and the above expression for i_1, we have

$$c_1 = p^c(g)S_0^k.$$

Now view (A3.14) and (A3.15) as a pair of simultaneous linear equations in (x_1^c, x_1^l). Solving them gives

$$(x_1^c, x_1^l) = (\nu^c(g), \nu^l(g))S_0^n.$$

Substituting these values into (A3.17) gives

$$S_0^n = q^n(g)x_0^e.$$

Finally, we obtain

$$S_0^k = q^k(g, e^*, S^{m^*})x_0^e$$

by substituting $S_0^n = q^n(g)x_0^e$ and $x^c = \nu^c(g)q^n(g)x_0^e$ into equation (A3.16) and solving for S_0^k.

Statement (ii) of theorem 3.1 is immediately derived from the above equations. Statement (i) asserts that the endowments grow along the ray $\Gamma(g, e^*, S^{m^*})$ at rate $1+g$, and statement (iii) says that all flow variables exhibit balanced growth. ■

A3.2. How the Value of Program $E(\rho, e^*, S^{m^*})$ Changes at $\rho = 0$ as ρ Increases

Write our program $E(\rho, e^*, S^{m^*})$ schematically as:

$$\max \tilde{\Lambda}(\rho) \quad \text{subject to, for all } t \geqq 1:$$

$$(a_t^1) \quad u(x_t) \geq (1+\rho)^{t-1}\tilde{\Lambda}(\rho),$$

$$(b_t) \quad \bar{F}(x_t) \geq 0,$$

where we represent all the other constraints abstractly by a function $\bar{F}$. Viewing the values of all optimal variables, including the dual variables, as functions of ρ, we have:

Proposition A3.1.

$$\tilde{\Lambda}'(0) = -\frac{\tilde{\Lambda}(0)}{\xi - 1}.$$

Proof:

Write the Lagrangian:

$$\mathfrak{L} = \tilde{\Lambda}(\rho) + \sum_{1}^{\infty} a_t^1(\rho)(u(x_t(\rho)) - (1+\rho)^{t-1}\tilde{\Lambda}(\rho)) + \sum_{1}^{\infty} b_t(\rho)\bar{F}(x_t(\rho)). \quad \text{(A3.20)}$$

Note that the two summations on the right-hand side of (A3.20) are identically zero for all ρ, since all the constraints are binding at the optimum. It follows that

$$\frac{d\mathfrak{L}}{d\rho} = \tilde{\Lambda}'(\rho). \quad \text{(A3.21)}$$

Now calculate

$$\frac{d\mathfrak{L}}{d\rho} = \tilde{\Lambda}'(\rho) + \sum_{t=1}^{\infty} a_t^1(\rho)\left(\nabla u(x_t)\frac{\partial x_t}{\partial \rho} - (1+\rho)^{t-1}\tilde{\Lambda}'(\rho) - (t-1)(1+\rho)^{t-2}\tilde{\Lambda}(\rho)\right) + \sum_{t=1}^{\infty}\frac{\partial a_t^1(\rho)}{\partial \rho}(u(x_t) - (1+\rho)^{t-1}\tilde{\Lambda}(\rho)) + \sum_{1}^{\infty} b_t(\rho)\nabla\bar{F}(x_t)\frac{\partial x_t}{\partial \rho} + \sum_{1}^{\infty} b_t'(\rho)F(x_t). \quad \text{(A3.22)}$$

Now observe that all the terms on the right-hand side of (A3.22), except for the ones listed below, vanish by the Kuhn-Tucker conditions. We are left with:

$$\frac{d\mathfrak{L}}{d\rho} = \tilde{\Lambda}'(\rho) - \sum_{1}^{\infty} a_t^1(\rho)((1+\rho)^{t-1}\tilde{\Lambda}'(\rho) + (t-1)\tilde{\Lambda}(\rho)(1+\rho)^{t-2}). \quad \text{(A3.23)}$$

Now use (A3.21), and evaluate (A3.23) at $\rho = 0$:

$$\tilde{\Lambda}'(0) = \tilde{\Lambda}'(0) - \sum_{1}^{\infty} a_t^1(0)\tilde{\Lambda}'(0) - \sum_{2}^{\infty}(t-1)a_t^1(0)\tilde{\Lambda}(0).$$

Recalling the Kuhn-Tucker condition that $\sum_{t=1}^{\infty} a_t^1(0) = 1$,

$$\tilde{\Lambda}'(0) = -\tilde{\Lambda}(0)\sum_{t=2}^{\infty}(t-1)a_t^1(0). \tag{A3.24}$$

Next, (A3.12) and (A3.11), from the proof of theorem 3.1 in Section A3.1, show that:

$$1 = \frac{a_1^5(0)x_1^l}{\alpha_l \Lambda}\frac{\xi}{\xi-1} \quad \text{and} \quad a_t^1(0) = \frac{a_1^5(0)x_1^l}{\alpha_l \Lambda}\left(\frac{1}{\xi}\right)^{t-1},$$

and therefore:

$$a_t^1(0) = \frac{\xi-1}{\xi}\left(\frac{1}{\xi}\right)^{t-1}.$$

Substituting these values into (A3.24) and summing the infinite series demonstrates the proposition. ■

Thus, $\tilde{\Lambda}'(0) = -\tilde{\Lambda}(0)/(\xi-1) = -0.0247\tilde{\Lambda}(0)$, given our value of $\xi = 41.4341$. For small values of ρ, it follows that:

$$\tilde{\Lambda}(\rho) - \tilde{\Lambda}(0) = -\rho(0.0247)\tilde{\Lambda}(0), \quad \text{or} \quad \tilde{\Lambda}(\rho) = \tilde{\Lambda}(0)(1-0.0247\rho).$$

For $\rho = 0.28$, corresponding to a growth rate of utility of 1% per annum, this implies that:

$$\frac{\tilde{\Lambda}(0)}{\tilde{\Lambda}(0.28)} = 1.00697,$$

as reported in the text, which is in close agreement with our computed optimal paths, that the utility of Generation 1 falls by 0.7% if the generational growth rate is increased from 0 to 0.28.

A3.3. Proof of Proposition 3.2

By theorem 3.1, for any $g < \xi - 1$ there is a ray $\Gamma(g, e^*, S^{m^*})$ such that, from any initial endowment vector on this ray, the balanced growth path where the economic variables grow at rate g is feasible. For any $g < \xi - 1$, we can construct a path that, in a finite number of dates, moves from the given endowment vector (x_0^e, S_0^k, S_0^n) to some point on this ray. We then complete the path by appending the balanced growth path just referred to. Again by theorem 3.1, utility grows by a factor of $1+\rho$ at each date, after the initial section of the path, where $1+\rho=(1+g)^{1-\alpha_m}$. But g may be chosen so that $1+g$ is arbitrarily close to ξ. Hence, the terms of the discounted-utilitarian objective will grow by a factor arbitrarily close to $\varphi\xi^{1-\alpha_m}$: in particular, g can be chosen so that this factor is greater than one, by the premise, which proves the corollary. ■

A3.4. A Stripped-Down Model Comparing Utility Maximization with Consumption Maximization

Consider an economy producing a consumption commodity, using as inputs labor and knowledge (there is no capital good). Utility is a function $c^{\alpha}S^{1-\alpha}$ of consumption (c) and the stock of knowledge (S), and knowledge is produced each period according to a linear production function of labor. Consider the following program:

$$\max \chi c+(1-\chi)c^{\alpha}S^{1-\alpha}$$

subject to:

$$c\le k(x_c)^{\theta}S^{1-\theta}, \tag{A3.25}$$

$$1\ge x_c+x_n, \tag{A3.26}$$

$$S\le k_3x_n, \tag{A3.27}$$

where x_c (resp. x_n) denotes the amount of labor denoted to the production of the consumption good (resp. knowledge), and the weight $\chi\in[0,1]$ is fixed. Constraint (A3.25) is the commodity production function, constraint (A3.26) is the labor constraint, and constraint (A3.27) is the knowledge production function. We may solve the constraints (which will be binding at the solution) and rewrite the program as:

$$\max \chi c+(1-\chi)c^{\alpha}S^{1-\alpha}$$

subject to

$$c\le k\left(1-\frac{S}{k_3}\right)^{\theta}S^{1-\theta}. \tag{A3.28}$$

There are two Kuhn-Tucker conditions characterizing the solution to (A3.28): the first is the constraint in (A3.28), which must be binding, and the second one is the dual constraint that, after some algebra, can be written:

$$\left(1-\frac{S}{k_3}\right)(1-\chi)(1-\alpha)\hat{u}+(\chi c+(1-\chi)\hat{u}\alpha)\left(1-\frac{S}{k_3}-\theta\right)=0, \tag{A3.29}$$

where $\hat{u}\equiv c^{\alpha}S^{1-\alpha}$.

Now let $\chi=1$, and so (A3.28) is maximizing consumption only. Condition (A3.29) reduces to $c(1-S/k_3-\theta)=0$, that is, $\overline{\overline{S}}\equiv k_3(1-\theta)$.

On the other hand, let $\chi=0$; then (A3.28) is maximizing utility, and (A3.29) reduces to $S^{**}\equiv k_3(1-\alpha\theta)$.

It follows that the ratio of optimal knowledge in the utility formulation to optimal knowledge in the consumption-only formulation is

$$\frac{S^{**}}{\overline{\overline{S}}}=\frac{1-\alpha\theta}{1-\theta} \tag{A3.30}$$

If we take (reasonably) $\alpha=2/3$ and $\theta=0.9$, then this ratio is 4, a large number.

The expression for consumption is, from the constraint in (A3.28),

$$c=k\left(1-\frac{S}{k_3}\right)^{\theta}S^{1-\theta}.$$

Hence,

$$\frac{c^{**}}{\overline{\overline{c}}}=\frac{\left(1-\frac{S^{**}}{k_3}\right)^{\theta}(S^{**})^{1-\theta}}{\left(1-\frac{\overline{\overline{S}}}{k_3}\right)^{\theta}\overline{\overline{S}}^{1-\theta}}=\frac{(1-1+\alpha\theta)^{\theta}k_3^{1-\theta}(1-\alpha\theta)^{1-\theta}}{(1-1+\theta)^{\theta}k_3^{1-\theta}(1-\theta)^{1-\theta}}$$

$$=\alpha^{\theta}\left(\frac{1-\alpha\theta}{1-\theta}\right)^{1-\theta}, \tag{A3.31}$$

which for $\alpha=2/3$ and $\theta=0.9$ gives $c^{**}/\overline{\overline{c}}=0.80$.

On the other hand, using (A3.31) and (A3.30), the quotient for the utility levels is

$$\frac{\Lambda^{**}}{\overline{\overline{\Lambda}}} = \left(\frac{c^{**}}{\overline{\overline{c}}}\right)^{\alpha} \left(\frac{S^{**}}{\overline{\overline{S}}}\right)^{1-\alpha} = \alpha^{\alpha\theta} \left(\frac{1-\alpha\theta}{1-\theta}\right)^{(1-\theta)\alpha} \left(\frac{1-\alpha\theta}{1-\theta}\right)^{1-\alpha} = \alpha^{\alpha\theta} \left(\frac{1-\alpha\theta}{1-\theta}\right)^{1-\alpha\theta},$$

which for $\alpha = 2/3$ and $\theta = 0.9$ gives $\Lambda^{**}/\overline{\overline{\Lambda}} = 1.37$.

This computation may provide some understanding for why changing the objective function from 'consumption only' to 'utility' can have a large effect on the production of knowledge and on the utility level but only a rather small reduction in consumption.

CHAPTER FOUR

The "Climate-Change Economics" Literature: Nordhaus and Stern

4.1. Intergenerational Equity versus the Evaluation of Consumption Paths

We pause in the development of our analysis, to be reprised in Chapter 5, and offer a comparative discussion of the literature exemplified by Nordhaus (2008a, 2013) and the *Stern Review* (Stern 2007). Both Nordhaus and Stern characterize their work as "climate-change economics." Their approach differs from ours, not only by the normative criterion, but also by the failure to explicitly analyze the *welfare* of the various generations, even when alluding to intergenerational ethics. They instead evaluate the time paths (by year or by decade) of a macroeconomic variable: commodity consumption or gross domestic product (GDP) per capita.

The formal analyses of Nordhaus (2008a) and the *Stern Review* use an objective function of the type $\sum_{t=1}^{\infty}\varphi^{t-1}u_t$ (see (1.9) in Chapter 1), as in standard macroeconomic models, and accordingly, they both appeal to the Ramsey equation (see the Chapter 1 Appendix), although in different forms and from different theoretical standpoints. Stern is explicitly a discounted utilitarian, who adopts a low discount rate on generational utility, based on an exogenous probability of the extinction of mankind. Nordhaus's normative stance is more obscure, but to the extent that it can be considered discounted utilitarian, he bases the rate at which the utility of future generations is discounted on current marketplace interest rates. This leads to markedly higher discounting than that of Stern.

Their macroeconomic approach also explains the centrality, in their work, of the consumption discount rate, denoted r, which determines the evaluation, in units of present consumption (or current dollars) of one unit of consumption (or of inflation-adjusted dollars) t time units from now; that is, one unit consumed t time units from now is worth $\frac{1}{(1+r)^t}$ units consumed now. (The expression $\frac{1}{1+r}$ is the discount *factor* associated with the *rate* r.)

Both Nordhaus and Stern agree on the seriousness of the problem and upon accepting the consensus of climate science that anthropogenic greenhouse gas (GHG) emissions are a major contributor to global warming. But their policy recommendations are in stark contrast: Nordhaus (2008a, 2013) recommends an optimal policy that does relatively little in the near term and postpones for many decades the implementation of significant reductions in GHG emissions. Stern, on the contrary, emphasizes urgency and calls for immediate action. To a large extent, the conflicting recommendations are due to the different consumption discount rates that they adopt, which depend, in part, on the utility discount rate. Other differences in the estimation of the various cost and benefits also play a role, but by and large the different magnitudes of the consumption discount rate either support, or do not support, early strong action.

Nordhaus (2008a) and the *Stern Review* also differ, importantly, on methodology: Nordhaus is a prominent exponent of the integrated assessment models (IAM) approach, while Stern performs a cost-benefit analysis (CBA).[1] The present chapter discusses these two paradigmatic studies and contrasts them with our sustainability approach.

4.2. The Climate, the Economy, and Policy

Any economic analysis of climate change embodies a more or less detailed view of the effect of GHG emissions on temperature change, of the operation of the economic system, of the effects of temperature changes on the

[1] But it should be noted that the less technical Nordhaus (2013), while based on the integrated assessment model DICE of Nordhaus (2008a, 2008b), casts its arguments in CBA terms. On the other hand, the *Stern Review*'s numerical values of costs and benefits are to a large extent based on the PAGE2002 (Hope 2006), an IAM that, however, does not engage in normative analysis.

economy, and of the channels by which economic policy may affect economic decisions. It also refers, explicitly or implicitly, to human welfare.

Figure 4.1 depicts a simplified scheme of the major interactions. The top four cells illustrate the *climate module*, which embodies the influence of GHG emissions on concentrations (link [1]) and that of concentrations on temperature changes (link [2]) and ocean acidification.

Human welfare is portrayed in the bottom cell of the figure. The intermediate cells represent the *economic module*. Gross output (produced by using inputs such as capital and labor, not explicitly shown in Figure 4.1) is allocated to three uses:

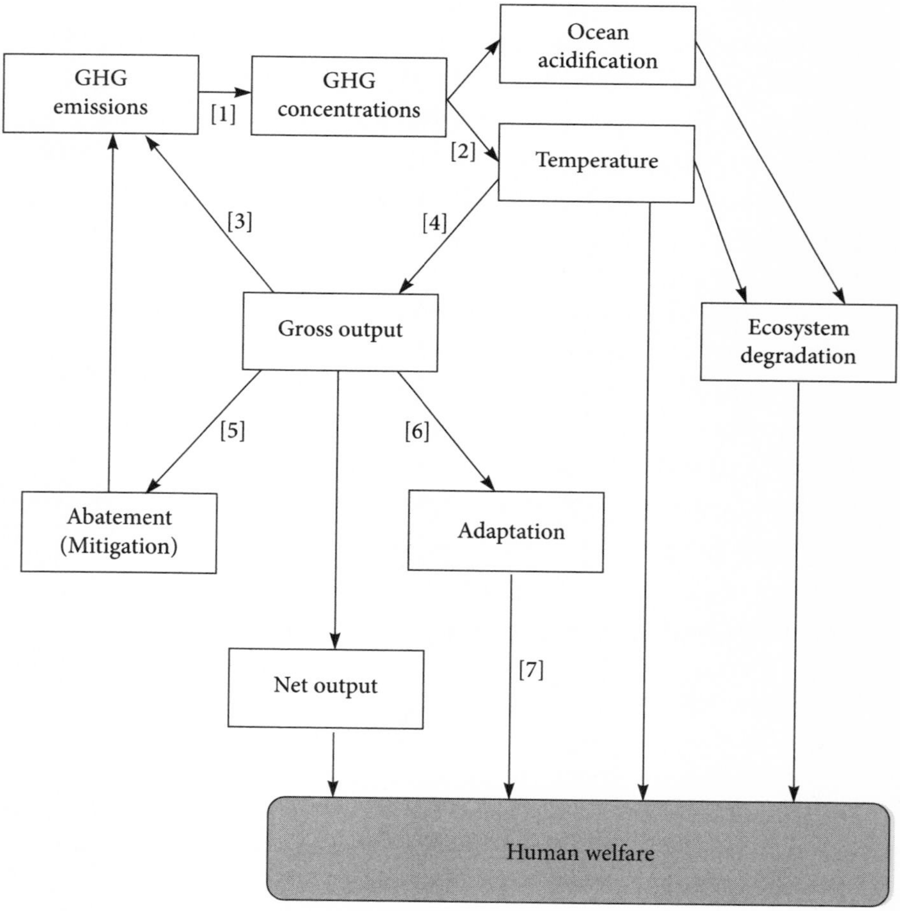

Figure 4.1. Climate-economy interactions.

(1) *net output*, further divided into consumption and investment;
(2) actions aimed at the *adaptation* to the changes in temperature and other environmental factors (link [6]);
(3) actions, usually referred to as *mitigation* or *abatement*, aimed at reducing GHG emissions (link [5]).[2]

As noted in Section 3.4.2, our models (Chapters 3 and 5) lack an explicit climate module. The climate-welfare relations are expressed in a reduced form, via the role of GHG concentrations in welfare and technology and that of emissions in technology.

The climate module interacts with the economic module in two ways: emissions accompany economic activity (link [3]) and temperature changes affect production possibilities, mainly in agriculture ([4]). (Ocean acidification also affects the production of output in the fisheries.) In addition, both temperature increases and the acidification of oceans affect ecosystems by, for example, destroying coral reefs and causing the extinction of species. Finally, consumption and adaptation activities increase human welfare, which is negatively affected by temperature increases and ecosystem degradation.

The connection between economic activity and emissions, depicted as link [3] in Figure 4.1, can be modeled in various ways. Figure 4.1 reflects the common approach in the conventional climate-change economics literature: a reference level of emissions at time t is implicitly or explicitly postulated, say, as a business-as-usual (BAU) or *laissez-faire* path, and an emissions-reduction cost function is estimated.[3]

The emissions-output ratio is a useful summary measure of this connection. Even under *laissez-faire*, this ratio tends to decline as an economy develops, partly through the decreasing weight of emissions-intensive sectors. But active policy is typically needed to further reduce the emissions-output ratio, through regulation or through a policy-imposed carbon price

[2] 'Abatement' is commonly used in the environmental literature, whereas 'mitigation' is popular in climate-change economics. The latter use is somewhat ambiguous since it confounds the reduction of the amounts emitted with the lessening of the effects of climate change, as in adaptation actions.

[3] As indicated in Chapter 3, we take the alternative approach of viewing emissions as a production input. More on this in Section 4.3.2.

(via, for instance, a cap-and-trade system, such as the European Union Emission Trading System [EUETS], or California's cap-and-trade program for GHG emissions, or possibly a carbon tax). Active efforts to reduce the emissions-output ratio, or the volume of emissions, are often referred to as abatement activities. They may include filtering out emissions at the source, switching to cleaner inputs, or adopting green technologies. The costs associated with their implementation, called abatement or mitigation costs, are represented by link [5] in Figure 4.1: a fraction of gross output is diverted to abatement activities.

An increase in mean global temperature causes sea levels to rise and changes ecosystems and precipitation patterns. This directly affects human welfare, in particular through the spread of diseases and the destruction of environmental public goods, as well as indirectly through its effects on production possibilities (link [4]). Adaptation activities, which entail costs that absorb a portion of gross output (link [6]), reduce the ill effects of temperature change (link [7]): they may include resettlement and migration, coastal defense and protection, heating and cooling of buildings, recovery of air and water quality, combating new diseases, and efforts to maintain the diversity of species. Some of these adaptation efforts will be undertaken as a *laissez-faire*, self-interested response to changes in the environment while others will require deliberate policy measures.

Our own work, as presented in the previous chapters, explicitly considers the direct welfare effects of consumption and the state of the biosphere, in addition to the effects of the stock of knowledge and education (as illustrated in Figure I.1). IAMs, on the contrary, usually focus on the effect on consumption, sometimes augmented with 'noneconomic effects,' a proxy for the direct effects of temperature and environmental degradation on human welfare.

4.3. Integrated Assessment Models and the Nordhaus Approach

IAMs formulate, estimate, and calibrate a number of equations dealing with the climate and economic modules and their interaction. In particular, they aim at quantifying the effects on output of emission abatement and GHG concentrations. Nordhaus's (2008a) dynamic integrated model of climate and the economy (DICE) constructs and solves several constrained optimization models, defined by their objective function—specifying what is to be maximized—and by their constraints.

Some constraints are defined by models, borrowed from the scientific literature, of the physical processes involved in climate. Often called general circulation models (GMT), they specify the relations among the top three cells of Figure 4.1. Other constraints are specified by the interactions between the economy and the climate through emissions and temperature changes, and by economic constraints involving the technology and resources.

Nordhaus has been a pioneer of the economic analysis of climate change: see Nordhaus (1977, 1991) for some of his early work. The results of his research, sustained throughout the years and eventually cast in terms of an IAM, are reported in four influential books (Nordhaus 1994; Nordhaus and Boyer 2000; Nordhaus 2008a; Nordhaus 2013) and are frequently updated online (Nordhaus and Sztorc 2013).

4.3.1. The Climate Module

Detailed climate models are offered by Nordhaus and his collaborators: Nordhaus (2008a, 2008b) presents the DICE, and Nordhaus and Boyer (2000) introduce the regional dynamic integrated model of climate and the economy (RICE).[4] These models include a carbon cycle with three reservoirs: atmosphere, surface (or upper oceans), and deep oceans. Concentrations in the atmosphere depend linearly on current emissions and previous concentrations in the atmosphere and on the surface. Concentrations on the surface depend linearly on previous concentrations in all three reservoirs, whereas concentrations in the deep oceans depend linearly on previous concentrations on the surface and in the deep oceans. These relationships generate a lagged response of atmospheric concentrations to GHG emissions, providing link [1] in Figure 4.1.

---

[4] We focus our presentation on the DICE-2007 model (Nordhaus 2008a), which builds on the earlier versions DICE123 (Nordhaus 1994) and DICE-99 (Nordhaus and Boyer 2000). The latest versions (RICE2010 and DICE2013R) retain the main modeling structure of DICE2008 and RICE-99. See section XII in Nordhaus and Sztorc (2013) for a comparison between the different versions.

Atmospheric concentrations are linked to temperature (link [2]) via radiative forcing, a logarithmic function of the ratio of concentrations at time t to the preindustrial level of concentrations (to which the exogenous radiative forcing is added). Radiative forcing then enters a linear model with two lagged temperature variables: those of the atmosphere and the deep ocean. It is often postulated that the increase in global average surface temperature over its preindustrial level, ΔT (in °C) depends on the long-run GHG concentrations, S^e, according to the equation

$$\Delta T = \sigma \frac{\ln(S^e/S_0^e)}{\ln 2},$$

(where S_0^e corresponds to preindustrial levels); that is, the increase in temperature over preindustrial levels caused by doubling the preindustrial amount of GHG is a constant σ, called the *climate sensitivity* parameter. Nordhaus (2008a, 2008b) adopts the value $\sigma = 3$, while Nordhaus and Sztorc slightly lower the value to $\sigma = 2.9$.[5]

4.3.2. The Economic Module

Nordhaus's (2008a, 2008b) economic module has a single final (net) output with production function

$$Q(t) = \Omega(t)[1 - \Lambda(t)]A(t)K(t)^{\gamma} L(t)^{1-\gamma} \tag{4.1}$$

where we reproduce his notation, as follows:

- $Q(t)$ is net output,
- $\Omega(t)$ is the damage rate due to the increase in temperature,
- $\Lambda(t)$ is the rate of abatement cost,[6]
- $A(t)$ is total factor productivity, determined by an exogenous Hicks-neutral path of technological progress,

[5] See Nordhaus (2008b) and the discussion in Nordhaus (2013, 42–43). The calibration in the present book takes the commonly used value $\sigma = 3$; see Section A.7 in Appendix A: Calibration.

[6] Recall that this is Nordhaus's notation. Of course, the symbol Λ has a totally different interpretation in the rest of the present book.

- $K(t)$ is capital input, and
- $L(t)$ is labor input.[7]

A major difference between (4.1) and our production function, given in (3.2), is that productivity growth is exogenous in (4.1), whereas in our formulation it depends on the stock of knowledge (S_t^n in (3.2)), which is endogenously determined by society's choices on the investment of resource in the knowledge sector.

In addition, $L(t)$ of (4.1) roughly corresponds to x_t^c of (3.2), except that the latter embodies human capital endogenously determined by the investment in education.[8]

A main connection between the climate and economic modules is manifest in the effect of temperature on output (link [4]), often referred to as the *damage function*, as well as other direct impacts on human welfare. These effects are poorly understood and cannot be confidently quantified. As Nordhaus (2013, 69) writes in his introduction to chapter 6 of his book: "The focus now shifts from determining geophysical changes to anticipating their impacts on humans and other living systems. This subject might seem easier than the deep physics and chemistry of climate science because it is more familiar to us, but the opposite is true. In reality, this task—projecting impacts—is the most difficult and has the greater uncertainties of all the processes associated with global warming."

Nordhaus's (2008a, 2008b) production function (4.1), represents the damage function by $\Omega(t)$, defined as the reciprocal of a quadratic function of the increase in temperature, ΔT.[9]

[7] The production function in Nordhaus (2008a, 2008b), reported in (4.1), is simpler than its previous version in Nordhaus and Boyer (2000), which has a 'carbon-energy' input. The carbon-energy sector is there modeled by relating the cost of carbon energy to the cumulative use of carbon and by postulating a ratio of carbon-energy to emissions that decreases, exogenously, over time. The DICE2013R version (Nordhaus and Sztorc 2013) simplifies the output function to $Q(t)=[1-\Lambda(t)-\Omega(t)]A(t)K(t)^{\gamma}\,L(t)^{1-\gamma}$, where $\Lambda(t)$ and $\Omega(t)$ are the marginal damage and abatement cost, respectively, in terms of gross output.

[8] On the other hand, $K(t)$ of (4.1) basically corresponds to our S_t^k of (3.2).

[9] As noted, our production function (3.2) has, instead, GHG concentrations, S_t^m, as negatively affecting output.

The other important links between the climate and economic modules concern the relations between output, abatement, and emissions (links [3] and [5]). These links are captured in (4.1) by the *rate of abatement cost*, that Nordhaus denotes $\Lambda(t)$. Nordhaus (2008a, 2008b) defines it as a function of the rate of emissions abatement. More specifically, if we denote by $\overline{e}(t)$ the reference level of emissions (*laissez-faire*, or BAU level, not explicit in Nordhaus) and by $e(t)$ the actual emissions, then Nordhaus (2008a, 2008b) postulates that $\Lambda(t)$ is proportional to $\left[\frac{\overline{e}(t)-e(t)}{\overline{e}(t)}\right]^{2.8}$. It follows, as expected, that output is decreasing in emissions. Our own formulation (3.2) has emissions $e(t)$ (or e_t) as an input with positive productivity in the production of output in a qualitatively similar way, although the mathematical formulation is different.[10]

4.3.3. The Ranking of Paths of Consumption and the Long-Lived Consumer

Nordhaus performs an optimization problem with the constraints defined by the climate and economic models and by their interaction, as described in the two preceding sections. What does he maximize?

The 'Objective Function' in Nordhaus (2008a, 39) states that policy should "optimize the flow of consumption over time." He then adds: "The value or 'utility' of consumption in each period is an iso-elastic function of per capita consumption." Note the quotation marks on utility: it is not the utility of a *consumer* but the utility of *consumption* in a period. In fact, Nordhaus's computations define a period t as a span of ten years—too short to be considered the lifespan of a generation.

More precisely, he describes his objective function as follows: "The world is assumed to have a well-defined set of preferences, represented by a 'social welfare function,' which ranks different paths of consumption" (2008a, 33).

He formally defines the social-welfare function as (2008a, 205):

$$\sum_{t=1}^{T} L_t \frac{1}{1-\eta}(c_t)^{1-\eta} \frac{1}{(1+\delta)^t}, \tag{4.2}$$

[10] For instance, RICE-99 (Nordhaus and Boyer 2000) and ENTICE (Popp 2004, 2006) also incorporate emissions as an input in the production function.

with parameters δ and η, where L_t denotes population in 'period t' and c_t the consumption per capita in period t, $t=1, \ldots, T$.[11]

Letting $L_t=1$, for all t, and except for the finiteness of the horizon T, expression (4.2) is basically the same as the objective function of (1.12), the Ramsey optimization problem analyzed in Chapter 1.[12] It will be recalled that Ramsey has a long-lived consumer, as exemplified by problem (1.12). She has preferences over streams of consumption $\{c_t\}$ represented by the utility function in (1.12) or (4.2). The discount factor $\frac{1}{1+\delta}$ (or the discount rate δ) reflects her *impatience*: a more impatient consumer has a larger δ and attaches less value to a unit of consumption made available to her later in her life. On the other hand, the parameter η can be interpreted as the reciprocal of the consumer's elasticity of intertemporal substitution: as $\eta \to 0$, the consumer preferences display a high degree of substitutability between consumption at different dates, and she exhibits intertemporal complementarity as $\eta \to \infty$.

Thus, Nordhaus's objective function appears to be in line with that of the long-lived consumer model popular in current macroeconomic modeling: the first column of Table 4.1 summarizes this interpretation. But it fits less well with the intergenerational equity problem, which looks at paths of generational welfare. In fact, as we discuss next, Nordhaus's verbal discussion injects intergenerational notions that render an unambiguous interpretation problematical.

4.3.4. A Social-Welfare Function with Inequality Aversion

What is a 'period?' As noted, in Nordhaus's practice a period spans ten years.[13] But, he asserts: "The economic units in the economy are generations or cohorts" (Nordhaus 2008a, 172), and the parameters δ and η affect "the

---

[11] Nordhaus's notation is different from ours: he uses α for our η and ρ for our δ; see Nordhaus (2008a, 205). The optimization is numerically solved with the General Algebraic Modeling System (GAMS) software; see Nordhaus (2008b) and Nordhaus and Sztorc (2013). It is assumed that $\eta > 0$; for $\eta = 1$, $\ln c$ replaces $\frac{1}{1-\eta} c^{1-\eta}$. In addition, as noted, Nordhaus's time horizon is finite.

[12] Of course, Ramsey's constraints only involve consumption, investment, and the accumulation of physical capital, whereas those in the optimization problem proposed by Nordhaus must also include the climate-change constraints.

[13] The time span is further reduced to five years in DICE2013R.

Table 4.1. Three interpretations of Nordhaus's objective function (4.2).

	Interpretation 1: Long-lived consumer, as in Ramsey	Interpretation 2: *SWF* with discounting and inequality aversion	Interpretation 3: Discounted utilitarianism with iso-elastic utility of consumption
Interpretation of Period t	One in the many periods in the consumer's long life.	Generation t, with utility $= c_t$.	Generation t, with utility $= \frac{1}{1-\eta}[c_t]^{1-\eta}$.
Interpretation of c_t	The consumer's consumption in period t.	The consumption of Generation $t =$ utility of Gen. t.	The consumption of Generation t.
Interpretation of $\frac{1}{1-\eta}c^{1-\eta}$	The period subutility of the consumer.	A term in the definition of the *SWF* involving the 'utility' c_t.	The utility of Generation t.
Interpretation of (4.2)	A utility representation of the intertemporal preferences of the consumer.	A two-parameter Bergson-Samuelson *SWF* with time discounting and inequality aversion.	A discounted-utilitarian Bergson-Samuelson *SWF*.
Interpretation of η	Degree of intertemporal complementarity in the consumer's preferences.	Social aversion to inequality of different generations.	The elasticity of the marginal utility of consumption in the utility function of Generation t.
Interpretation of δ	Parameter representing the consumer's impatience.	Social pure-time discount rate.	Rate for the social discounting of the utility of a future generation.
Interpretation of g		Rate of growth of consumption.	
Interpretation of $r := \delta + g\eta$		Consumption discount rate.	

relative importance of different generations" (Nordhaus 2008a, 33). The parameter η represents "the aversion to inequality of different generations" (Nordhaus 2008a, 60). The parameter δ is, in turn, a "pure social time discount rate:" the "discount rate that provides the welfare weights of the utilities of the different generations" (Nordhaus 2008a, 39).

Observe that, under this intergenerational interpretation, if the rates of growth turn out to be negative, then δ and η push in opposite directions, a high δ favoring the earlier generations and a high η favoring the later, less well-off generations. But for positive rates of growth, when the latter generations are better off, as is the case in the paths proposed by Nordhaus (2008a, 2008b; see Section 4.3.8), high values of either δ or η favor the earlier generations.

This suggests an alternative interpretation of (4.2) as a two-parameter social-welfare function. A Bergson-Samuelson social-welfare function (SWF) has as arguments the utilities of the members of society, here the representative consumers of the various generations. Nordhaus's assertions that "the economic units in the economy are generations" and that "the parameter η reflects the aversion to inequality of different generations" suggest that the utility of Generation t is c_t. Disregarding the fact that a Nordhaus period is just ten years, (4.2) would depict a two-parameter Bergson-Samuelson SWF displaying aversion to inequality whenever $\eta > 0$: indeed, the maximin SWF of (1.2) in Chapter 1 could be viewed as a limit case of (4.2), letting $L_t = 1$, $\delta = 0$, $c_t = u_t$ and $\eta \to \infty$. The second column of Table 4.1 summarizes this interpretation for the case where a period t corresponds to one generation, with utility c_t.

4.3.5. Discounted Utilitarianism

Still within the interpretation of t as corresponding to one generation, there is another characterization of (4.2) as a Bergson-Samuelson SWF if we think of $\frac{1}{1-\eta}c^{1-\eta}$ as the generational utility function: this interpretation is supported by Nordhaus's definition of the parameter η as the "elasticity of the marginal utility of consumption."[14] The interpretation of the functions and parameters of (4.2) is then somewhat different: see the third column of Table 4.1.

As discussed in Chapter 1, discounted utilitarianism is popular among economists. It is in particular also adopted by the *Stern Review*, to be discussed in Section 4.4 following.

---

[14] See Nordhaus (2008a, 39, 206). Recall that Nordhaus uses the notation α for our η.

4.3.6. What Is the Correct Interpretation of Nordhaus's Objective Function?

The previous sections have presented three possible interpretations of Nordhaus's objective function (4.2): each of them can be supported by his practice or rhetoric. But which of the three is Nordhaus's true one? Given that the time period is defined as a ten-year span, one is led to believe that Nordhaus's optimization horizon covers several generations, each of them living for several periods. But then none of the three interpretations is really appropriate.

If a generation lives for, say, two periods, is its utility function

$$\frac{1}{1-\eta}c_t^{1-\eta}+\frac{1}{1+\delta}\frac{1}{1-\eta}c_{t+1}^{1-\eta}?$$

And is it discounted by society to

$$\frac{1}{(1+\delta)^t}\left[\frac{1}{1-\eta}(c_t)^{1-\eta}+\frac{1}{1-\eta}(c_{t+1})^{1-\eta}\frac{1}{1+\delta}\right]? \tag{4.3}$$

If so:

(1) Is there a reason why the rate at which that generation discounts its second-period subutility (a positive notion that reflects its degree of impatience) should equal the social-discount rate (a normative notion) at which the utility of that generation must be discounted in the social-welfare function?

(2) Why should the parameter η that represents a consumer's feelings about the complementarity of her consumption among different periods of her life have anything to do with society's aversion to inequality among different generations?[15, 16]

---

[15] In all fairness, Nordhaus shares these problems with a large fraction of the literature on economic growth and the economics of climate change. The parameter η is often subjected to a further equivocation as the coefficient of relative risk aversion in models devoid of uncertainty.

[16] Schneider et al. (2012) discuss this issue in a continuous time, overlapping-generations model.

These difficulties in understanding the parameters η and δ carry over with a vengeance to their calibration, to which we now turn.

4.3.7. Parameter Calibration: The Ramsey Equation and the Consumption Discount Rate

IAMs often appeal to the Ramsey equation in the calibration of the parameters of their objective functions, and Nordhaus's work is no exception.[17] His calibration procedure proceeds as follows.

The starting point is the Ramsey equation, computed in Chapter 1 and given by (1.14), which we can rewrite as

$$\hat{r} = \hat{\delta} + \eta\hat{g}, \tag{4.4}$$

where $\hat{r}$ is the real per year rate of interest on capital and $\hat{g}$ is the per year rate of growth of consumption.[18]

Second, Nordhaus infers $\hat{r}$ from "observed economic outcomes as reflected by interest rates and rates of return on capital" (Nordhaus 2008a, 33–34). Similarly, he infers $\hat{g}$ from observed growth rates.

Third, he chooses $\hat{\delta}$ and η subject to the Ramsey equation, which gives one degree of freedom. In particular, Nordhaus (2008a, 178) takes the values $(\hat{r}, \hat{g}) = (0.055, 0.02)$. Equation (4.4) then holds for any $(\hat{\delta}, \eta)$ pair satisfying $\hat{\delta} = 0.055 - 0.02\eta$, in particular for the values $(\hat{\delta}, \eta) = (0.015, 2)$ chosen by Nordhaus (2008a, 178): see the first row of Table 4.2. (Ignore for the moment the other rows.)[19]

As proved in the Chapter 1 Appendix, (4.4) is the first-order condition of the Ramsey optimization problem for the objective function (4.2) and is subject to the constraints involving consumption, investment, and the accumulation of physical capital. Hence, even when the objective function

---

[17] See, e.g., Weitzman (2007).

[18] Recall that we use a notational caret ^ for per year values, whereas the notation without carets corresponds to values per period, or per generation. In general, if a period lasts for τ years, then $\frac{1}{1+\delta} = \frac{1}{(1+\hat{\delta})^{\tau}}$.

[19] Nordhaus (2008a, 9–11, 108) also refers to an $\hat{r}$ of 0.04 and to a $\hat{g}$ of 0.013. Nordhaus and Boyer (2000) adopted $\hat{\delta} = 0.03$, later reduced to 0.015; see Nordhaus (2008a, 50).

Table 4.2. Applications of the Ramsey equation $\hat{\delta} + \eta\hat{g} = \hat{r}$.

	$\hat{\delta}$ Pure-time discount rate (per year)	η	$\hat{g}$ Consumption growth rate (per year)	$\hat{r}$ Consumption discount rate (per year)
Nordhaus (2008a, 178)	0.015	2	0.02	0.055
Weitzman's (2007) "rule of twos"	0.02	2	0.02	0.06
Weitzman's (2007) "reasonable" ex. 1	0.01	2.5	0.02	0.06
Weitzman's (2007) "reasonable" ex. 2	0.00	3	0.02	0.06
Stern (2007)	0.001	1	0.013	0.014

is the same, the Ramsey problem differs from the optimization problems of IAM models in that the latter include the climate-change constraints, absent from the Ramsey problem. Note that in the first-order condition (4.4), $\hat{\delta}$ and η are parameters, while $\hat{g}$ and $\hat{r}$ are endogenous to the solution of the Ramsey problem.

Nordhaus's calibration procedure might be rationalized as follows:

(1) 'The market' has obtained the observed values of $\hat{r}$ and $\hat{g}$ by solving a Ramsey problem, with parameters $\hat{\delta}$ and η unknown to us.
(2) The Ethical Observer wants to solve the climate-change problem with the same $\hat{\delta}$ and η that the market has used in solving the Ramsey problem.

First note that, in any event, the market observations on $\hat{g}$ and $\hat{r}$, together with the Ramsey equation, give us just a linear link between $\hat{\delta}$ and η. So, even if we wanted to, we cannot infer both: we have to guess one or the other.

Our main objection is to the justification of (2). In reality, the market aggregates investment and savings decisions by various agents, but each of these agents lives at more than one date, thus their individual impatience and intertemporal-substitution preferences must have a role in these decisions. Therefore, as in the discussion leading to the expression (4.3), the observed market outcomes will respond to a mixture of each market participant's preferences on her own future and her feelings about future generations.

But assume, for the sake of the argument, that the observed interest rates (which Nordhaus uses in his Ramsey equation) do reflect the attitudes of present consumers toward future generations. As noted in the second justification for discounting utilities in Section 1.2, we are skeptical that this claim is empirically correct; but even then, the welfare of future generations should not depend on how much the present generation wants to save for them.

In contrast to our position, Nordhaus is adamant in asserting that the views of the present generation on future ones should carry the day: see in particular his critique of the *Stern Review*, discussed in Section 4.4.5. Perhaps his justification, although not precisely stated in his work, is more pragmatic: that it would be foolhardy to impose upon a society discount rates on the utility of future generations that do not approximate the discount rates that actual investors and savers indicate they are using. The planner, our Ethical Observer, would, as it were, be forcing society to behave in a way that is contrary to its observed preferences. Our view, however, is that this justification is too deferential to the parochialism of the current generation. An impartial approach, as we have explained in Chapter 1, recommends otherwise.

4.3.8. Nordhaus's Proposed Paths

The paths for emissions and concentrations proposed as optimal by Nordhaus differ markedly from the ones that we postulate or the ones recommended by the *Stern Review*. In a nutshell, Nordhaus recommends substantially milder reductions of GHG emissions in the short run and postpones until late in the twenty-first century any significant reductions.

For instance, Nordhaus (2008a, 14) proposes as optimal emission-reduction rates, relative to the BAU path: 15% before 2050, 25% by 2050, and 43% by 2100. As a result, temperature increases are allowed to rise to 2.6°C by 2100 and 3.4°C by 2200.

Recent updates of his model, with revised parameters, generate less extreme paths than the optimal paths prescribed by his previous versions. Figure 4.2 compares three paths for CO_2 emissions (4.2(a)), CO_2 concentrations (4.2(b)), and temperature change (4.2(c)). The first path, labeled 'RCP2.6-stable2060,' is the Representative Concentration Pathway RCP2.6, used by the IPCC and similar to the path that we adopt in the present

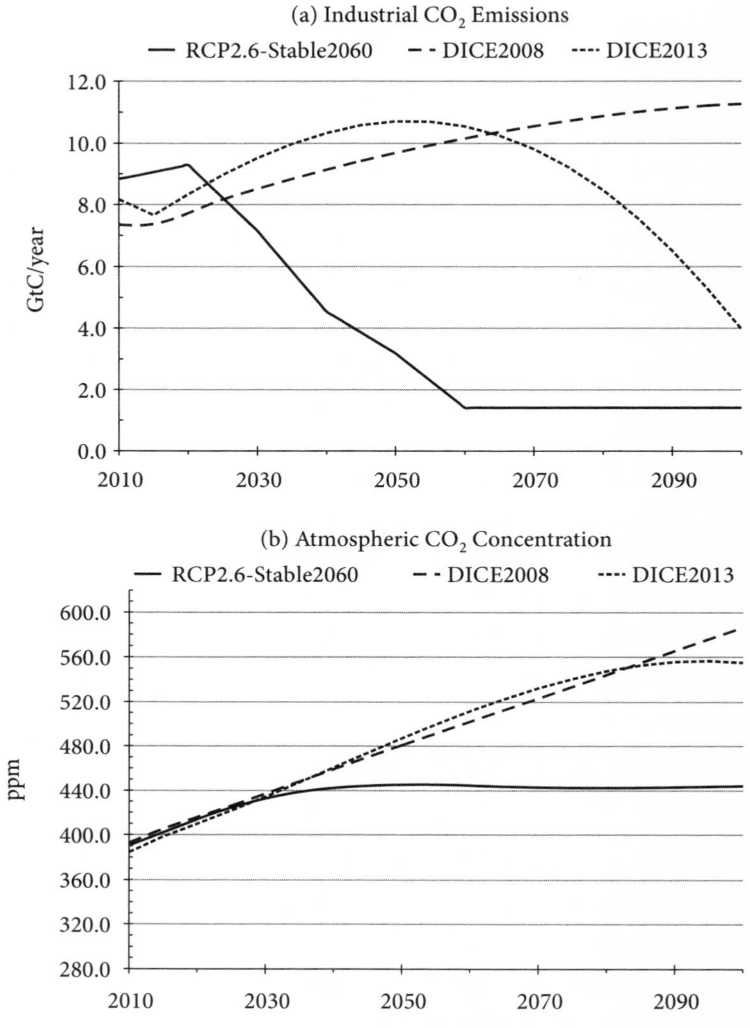

Figure 4.2. Path comparisons. DICE2008: optimal path from Nordhaus (2008a, tables 5.6–5.8). DICE2013: optimal path from DICE-2013 model, beta version of April 22, 2013, developed by William Nordhaus. RCP2.6-Stable2060 reproduces RCP2.6 with constant GHG emissions after 2060 (own elaboration).

book. The two other paths have been proposed by Nordhaus: a recent one, labeled 'DICE2013,' is based on Nordhaus (2013), and an older one, labeled 'DICE2008,' was published in Nordhaus (2008a).

Figure 4.2(a) shows the RPC-proposed path of global emissions, in GtC, as peaking in 2020 and decreasing rapidly to a low level below 2 GtC by

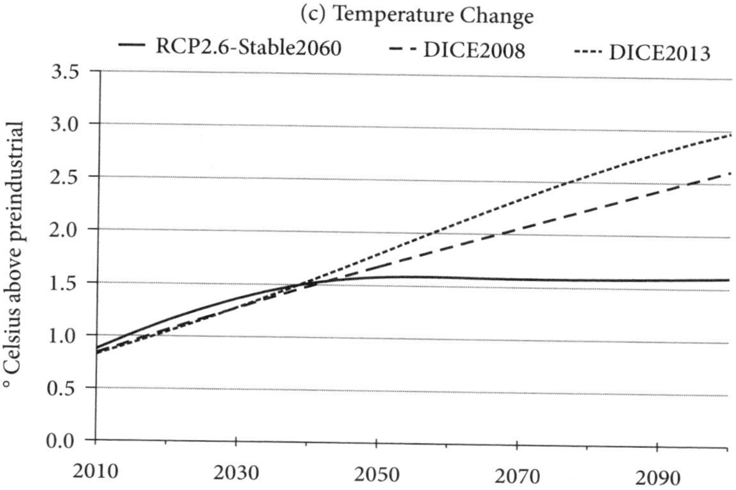

2060. The DICE2008 path does not peak before 2100 while the more recent DICE2013 peaks at over 10 GtC by 2050. Either of Nordhaus's paths leads to a temperature increase above 2.5°C by 2100, with an increasing trend after that.[20]

As noted, Nordhaus's recommendation of postponing serious reductions of GHG emissions until the relatively distant future (contrary to the recommendations of the *Stern Review* and the IPCC) is due, to a large extent, to his choice of a relatively high intertemporal discount rate. But there are other contributing factors due in part to modeling decisions. Technological progress is assumed to be exogenous. There is no need to invest in knowledge in order to develop green technologies: the passage of time by itself will make GHG reductions easier and cheaper in the future than in the present; hence, it is preferable to wait. But this modeling choice is not innocuous, as asserted by Ackerman et al. (2009, 12): "Most IAMs advocate a cautious approach that involves only modest early action to limit emissions with gradually increasing limits over time. Alternative models that endogenize technical change reach different conclusions and frequently recommend more aggressive carbon abatement policies, with results varying according to how the models are specified."

[20] The higher temperature increase under DICE2013 compared to DICE2008, despite the sharp decrease in emissions, responds to the more recent calibration of the climate model in DICE2013.

Second, Nordhaus's choice of functional forms (see Section 4.3.2) and parameter estimation procedures for the costs of emissions abatement and for the damage function may be challenged. As Ackerman et al. (2009, 11) note: "There is a significant degree of subjective judgment involved in the estimation of the value of climate damages; but IAM are completely dependent on the shape of their assumed damage functions." They subsequently refer to the sensitivity analysis of Dietz et al. (2007, 141–146), where it is shown that if a popular quadratic damage function is replaced by one that is cubic, a huge increase in damages occurs.[21]

Of course, the estimation of the benefits of abatement, which are realized in the future, is trickier than that of its costs and is strongly affected by the discount rate and technological progress (Ackerman et al. 2009, 12).

A striking feature of Nordhaus (2008a, 108–109) is that the path of per capita consumption (his only variable in the individual utility function) is virtually identical (at least for the twenty-first century) in the 'optimal' and in the 'baseline' (*laissez-faire*) paths. Yet he (2008a, 82) claims that the value of the objective function at the 'optimal' solution is 3.37 trillions of 2005 US dollars higher than at the baseline solution. We conjecture that this puzzle may be partially explained by population growth, which increases the value of the objective function for a given level of consumption per capita, together with minute differences in consumption per capita. Because of the little difference between the optimal and nonoptimal paths of consumption per capita, we conjecture that his rate of growth in consumption per capita is basically driven by his postulated exogenous growth in total factor productivity.

4.4. The *Stern Review*

4.4.1. Theoretical Model

The *Stern Review* also evaluates flows of consumption, although, contrary to Nordhaus, it does not attempt to solve an optimization program: it is rather a CBA that computes sums of discounted changes in consumption and applies to them the cost-benefit test.

---

[21] This quadratic damage function is not the one in Nordhaus (2008a, 2008b), although both involve the square of the temperature change.

Stern (2007, 51) casts his theoretical model in terms of continuous time and an infinite horizon. Consider a reference consumption stream $\{c(t): t \in [0, \infty)\}$ that grows at rate g, with $c(0)=1$, and a 'small' project that will modify the consumption stream by $\{\Delta c(t): t \in [0, \infty)\}$. Will the introduction of the small project increase the value of the function $\int_0^\infty u(c(t))e^{-\delta t}\,dt$, where δ is now an instantaneous utility, or 'pure time,' discount rate, and $u(c) = \frac{1}{1-\eta}c^{1-\eta}$? Up to a first-order approximation, the change in the value of the function is:

$$\int_0^\infty u'(c(t))\Delta c(t)e^{-\delta t}\,dt = \int_0^\infty c(t)^{-\eta}\Delta c(t)\,e^{-\delta t}\,dt$$
$$= \int_0^\infty (e^{gt})^{-\eta}\Delta c(t)e^{-\delta t}\,dt = \int_0^\infty e^{-(\eta g+\delta)t}\Delta c(t)\,dt.$$

The project $\{\Delta c(t): t \in [0, \infty)\}$ passes the cost-benefit test if $\int_0^\infty e^{-(\eta g+\delta)t}\Delta c(t)\,dt > 0$: that is, if the integral of consumption changes discounted at the instantaneous rate of $r := \eta g + \delta$ is positive.

Note that $\int_0^\infty \frac{1}{1-\eta}c(t)^{1-\eta}e^{-\delta t}\,dt$ is the continuous-time, infinite-horizon counterpart of (4.2) (for $L_t = 1$). But Stern unambiguously interprets it as the social-welfare function of an Ethical Observer who discounts the utility of future generations at the rate δ, as in the last column of Table 4.1.

The definition $r := \eta g + \delta$ is formally identical to the Ramsey equation. Stern uses it to compute $\hat{r}$, the consumption discount rate needed to perform the CBA.

4.4.2. The Ramsey Equation in Optimization and in CBA

In fact, Nordhaus and Stern often use a common language, and both appeal to the Ramsey equation for the calibration of their discount rates. They adopt, however, differing values for these rates, and their methods are quite different: constrained optimization versus the cost-benefit test.

The formal connection between constrained optimization and the cost-benefit method, particularly in the manners in which they obtain the Ramsey equation, can be shown in a simple two-period example. Let there be two periods, or generations, 1 and 2, and a single consumption good, with initial endowments (ω_1, ω_2). Denote consumption in the first period by c_1 and that in the second period by c_2. Postulate the objective function

$$W(c_1, c_2) = \frac{c_1^{1-\eta}}{1-\eta} + \frac{1}{1+\delta}\frac{c_2^{1-\eta}}{1-\eta}, \tag{4.5}$$

formally a simple special case of (4.2), which could well be interpreted as the utility function of a consumer who lives for two periods. But now we view (4.5) as the SWF, involving the welfare levels of two generations and used by an Ethical Observer who discounts the utility of Generation 2 at rate δ.

Consider first the constrained maximization problem. Let there be a social technology, which, when society invests $y_1 \geq 0$ units in period 1, produces $y_2 = \tilde{F}(y_1)$ units in period 2. The Ethical Observer solves the following problem:

▶ Program SDU (Simple Discounted Utilitarian)

$$\max_{(c_1,c_2)} \frac{c_1^{1-\eta}}{1-\eta} + \frac{1}{1+\delta}\frac{c_2^{1-\eta}}{1-\eta} \text{ subject to } c_2 = \omega_2 + \tilde{F}(\omega_1 - c_1),$$

which can be written:

$$\max_{c_1} \frac{c_1^{1-\eta}}{1-\eta} + \frac{1}{1+\delta}\frac{[\omega_2 + \tilde{F}(\omega_1 - c_1)]^{1-\eta}}{1-\eta},$$

with FOC:

$$\frac{1}{1+\delta}\left[\frac{c_2}{c_1}\right]^{-\eta} \tilde{F}'(\omega_1 - c_1) = 1 \tag{4.6}$$

Denoting with asterisks the optimal solution and defining g^* and r^* by $1+g^* := \frac{c_2^*}{c_1^*}$ and $1+r^* := \tilde{F}'(\omega_1 - c_1^*)$, (4.6) can be written

$$1+r^* = (1+\delta)(1+g^*)^{\eta},$$

as in (A1.13) of the Chapter 1 Appendix. As in that appendix, taking logarithms and using the approximation $\ln(1+x) \approx x$ for small x yields the 'Ramsey equation'

$$r^* = \delta + \eta g^*, \tag{4.7}$$

which is the first-order condition for an optimization problem with parameters δ and η, where g^* is endogenous (as is r^*, as long as $\tilde{F}$ is nonlinear).

For the CBA, consider a reference (feasible) consumption path $(\overline{c}_1, \overline{c}_2)$ and a proposed project that spends 1 unit of consumption in period one and yields Δc_2 units of consumption in period two, such that the path $(\overline{c}_1 - 1, \overline{c}_2 + \Delta c_2)$ is feasible. Of course, adopting the project will hurt Generation 1 and benefit Generation 2 relative to $(\overline{c}_1, \overline{c}_2)$. But will it increase the value of W? Up to a first-order approximation, the change in the value of W is

$$-\frac{\partial W}{\partial c_1}(\overline{c}_1, \overline{c}_2) + \frac{\partial W}{\partial c_2}(\overline{c}_1, \overline{c}_2)\Delta c_2 = -\overline{c}_1^{\,-\eta} + \frac{1}{1+\delta}\overline{c}_2^{\,-\eta}\,\Delta c_2. \qquad (4.8)$$

Writing $\overline{g} := \frac{\overline{c}_2}{\overline{c}_1} - 1$, the sign of (4.8) is that of $-1 + \frac{\Delta c_2}{(1+\delta)(1+\overline{g})^{\eta}}$, or writing

$$\overline{r} := (1+\delta)(1+\overline{g})^{\eta} - 1, \qquad (4.9)$$

that of

$$-1 + \frac{\Delta c_2}{1+\overline{r}}; \qquad (4.10)$$

that is, the *project passes the cost-benefit test if the sum of discounted-consumption changes is positive.*

As before, applying to (4.9) the approximation $\ln(1+x) \approx x$, for small x, yields the 'Ramsey equation'

$$\overline{r} \approx \delta + \eta\overline{g}, \qquad (4.11)$$

which here can be interpreted as defining the 'consumption discount rate' $\overline{r}$ in terms of the parameters (δ, η) and the reference growth rate $\overline{g}$.

The main difference between (4.7) and (4.11) (if both are interpreted in annual terms) is that g^* is endogenous in (4.7), obtained from an optimization problem where the technology is described by '$c_2 = \omega_2 + \tilde{F}(\omega_1 - c_1)$,' whereas $\overline{g}$ is exogenous in (4.11). Note that (4.10) assumes that the path $(\overline{c}_1 - 1, \overline{c}_2 + \Delta c_2)$ is feasible, which is an additional assumption even when $\overline{g}$ is chosen to be g^*, as in the solution to problem SDU. Moreover, the possibility of adding the project $(-1, \Delta c_2)$ will modify the technology on which the solution to problem SDU is based: the constraint of the problem changes and so, typically, will its solution. These observations will apply to the analysis of Nordhaus's wrinkle in Section 4.4.5.

4.4.3. Stern versus Nordhaus: The Utility Discount Rate

Stern adopts a utility, or pure-time, discount rate that is based on the survival justification: he adopts $\hat{\delta} = 0.001$, interpreted as the probability that at any given year mankind becomes extinct. In other words, Stern discounts the utility of a future generation only to the extent that the generation may not exist. The (twenty-five year) generational discount rate for Stern is 0.0247.

As argued in the Introduction, Stern's choice of the probability 0.001 per annum is most likely too *large*. It implies that the probability of mankind's not surviving ten years is 0.01, that of not surviving one hundred years is 0.095 and that with probability one-half, the species will not survive another seven hundred years. Of course, the value of the survival probability should be endogenous to the path chosen. We proposed in the Introduction a baseline value of $\delta = \pi = 0.00017$ *per generation* based on the 'back-of-the-envelope' calculation that assumes that the probability that our species has survived 100,000 years was, *ex ante*, one-half.

The approaches of Stern and Nordhaus lead to very different utility discount factors. Stern chooses a value of $\hat{\delta} = 0.001$ per annum according to the probability of extinction of the human species and so his utility discount factor is a little over 0.999 per annum.[22] Nordhaus assumes that $\eta = 2$ and then calculates, via the Ramsey equation, after observing $\hat{r}$ and $\hat{g}$ in today's market data, that $\hat{\delta} = 0.015$, and hence, his utility discount factor is approximately 0.985. It may seem that these two factors are fairly close but they are not. Stern would weight the utility of those living a century from now with a factor of $\left[\frac{1}{1+0.001}\right]^{100} = 0.9049$, while Nordhaus weights their utility with a factor of $\left[\frac{1}{1+0.015}\right]^{100} = 0.2256$. The treatment of those

[22] Stern (2007, 184) computes the discount factor from the continuous-time formula $e^{-\pi}$. For $\pi = 0.001$, this figure is very close to the one obtained from the expression $(1-\pi)$ in Section 1.2.B3, or from the expression $\frac{1}{1+\pi}$.

living a century from now under the two approaches is very different. In particular, the utility discount *rates* of Stern and Nordhaus differ by a factor of 15.[23]

4.4.4. Stern's Consumption Discount Rate and the CBA

As demonstrated, Stern computes the rate of discount of consumption with the help of the Ramsey equation '$\delta + \eta g = r$' but motivated and utilized differently from Nordhaus. Together with $\hat{\delta} = 0.001$, Stern chooses the values $\eta = 1$ and the annual rate of reference consumption growth $\hat{g} = 0.013$, yielding an annual consumption discount rate of 0.014; see Table 4.2. Stern needs the value of $\hat{r}$ in order to perform the CBA: he obtains it from the Ramsey equation $\hat{r} := \hat{\delta} + \eta\hat{g}$ after estimating $\hat{g} = 0.013$ from market data and $\hat{\delta} = 0.001$ from the probability of extinction of mankind and adopting a conjectured value for η. In terms of the two-generation example of Section 4.4.2, Stern uses equation (4.11) to obtain the consumption discount rate that he needs in order to apply the cost-benefit test (4.10).

In contrast, Nordhaus needs the parameters $\hat{\delta}$ and η in order to perform his optimization. In terms of the example of Section 4.4.2, he assumes that the market has solved the optimization problem (4.6), without global-warming constraints, with unknown parameters δ and η. Nordhaus assumes $\eta = 2$, infers δ from market data, via the Ramsey equation, and then applies these parameters to the optimization problem with GHG emissions.

Nordhaus's r is higher than the one estimated by Stern so that, even if they used the same η and g, Nordhaus's analysis is more likely to reject the project 'early GHG reduction' than is Stern's.

The *Stern Review* performs a detailed analysis of the output costs associated with temperature changes (link [4] in Figure 4.1) and with adaptation to climate change (link [6]), as well as the different costs of reduction of emissions (abatement or mitigation, link [5]), based on the *Third Assessment Report* of the IPCC (TAR IPCC, 2001) and on Hope (2006). Assuming a path of growth for the GDP, and starting from a BAU (*laissez-faire*) hypothesis on the path of GHG emissions, it considers alternative policies that reduce emissions in the present and eventually stabilize GHG in the

[23] Nordhaus's generational discount rate (for our twenty-five year generation) is 0.451. This is three orders of magnitude as large as our proposed generational discount rate of 0.00017.

atmosphere. The *Review* recommends "prompt and strong action," arguing that, by using the low consumption discount rate of 0.014, the benefits of strong, early action on climate change outweigh the costs. This recommendation contrasts with the proposals of Nordhaus, which involve strong GHG reductions only in the more-distant future.

Because the *Stern Review* does not solve an optimization program, its recommendations are in principle open to the challenge, voiced by the critics of the *Review*, that the consumption discount rate should reflect the rates of return of the available investment alternatives: even if, using a consumption discount rate of 0.014, carbon-emission reductions pass the cost-benefit test, future generations could conceivably be better off if the current generation avoided incurring the costs of GHG reductions and invested instead in other intergenerational public goods. In defense of the *Review*, Dietz et al. (2007, 137) argue that "it is hard to know why we should be confident that social rates of return would be, say, 3% or 4% into the future. In particular, if there are strong climate change externalities, then social rates of return on investment may be much lower than the observed private returns on capital over the last century, on which suggestions of a benchmark of 3% or 4% appear to be based."

4.4.5. Nordhaus's and Weitzman's Critique of Stern

The commentators of the *Stern Review* suggest higher consumption discount rates than the one adopted by Stern (Arrow 2007; Nordhaus 2007; Weitzman 2007; see the debate in the *Postscripts to the Stern Review* available at http://www.sternreview.org.uk, as well as the issue of *World Economics* 7(4), October–December 2006, and the subsequent Dietz et al. 2007).[24]

The critics' positions share a basic theme: the consumption discount rate adopted by Stern is *too low to agree with the discount rates observed in financial markets.*

For instance, we read in Weitzman (2007, 708–709): "For most economists, a major problem with *Stern's* numbers is that people are not observed to behave as if $\delta \approx 0$ and $\eta \approx 1$."

[24] Arrow (2007) argues that "the present value of the benefits exceeds the present value of the costs—for any social rate of time preference . . . less than 8.5%." He does not propose a particular rate but declares himself convinced by Koopman's 'observed rate' argument against discount rates close to zero, *à la* Stern.

It may well be true that the discount rates observed in financial markets are higher than those obtained by Stern's parameter calibration: this is ultimately an empirical question, although not an easy one, given the need to extrapolate to the long time spans involved and to consider the complications due to risk. The critics, in any event, argue that pretending that this low rate is reflected in markets leads to absurd conclusions. In Weitzman's (2007, 709) words (s is the ratio of saving out of permanent income): "With *Stern's* preferred values . . . $s \approx 100$ percent irrespective of r – a *reductio ad absurdum*." (See also Section 4.4.6 on 'Nordhaus's wrinkle.') *But Stern never pretends that his low rate guides markets.* His analysis is normative: he looks for paths that increase social welfare according to a discounted-utilitarian social-welfare function, and the parameters that he adopts for this function—most notably the utility (or pure-time) discount rate, which he bases on the probability of extinction rather than on the impatience of consumers—result in a low consumption discount rate. His is a *normatively correct*, not a positively observed, discount rate.

Stern's critics reply that the normative discount rate should be based on people's preferences over their own future. In Weitzman's (2007, 707) words: "Concerning the rate of pure time preference, *Stern* . . . selects the lowest conceivable value $\delta \approx 0$ according to the philosophical principle of treating all generations equally irrespective of preferences for present over future utility that people seem to exhibit in their everyday savings and investment behavior."

Weitzman (2007, 709) does concede that "there may be something to Stern's position about the limited relevance of market-based inferences for putting welfare weights on the utilities of one's great-grandchildren," but he finds the parameter choice "unconvincing when super-strong policy advice is so dependent upon nonconventional assumptions that go so strongly against mainstream economics." However, in recent work, Weitzman (2012, 236) sides with the distinguished list of twentieth-century economists who adopt Ramsey's (1928) view that there is no justification for discounting the utility of future generations, in which he writes: "I think that the Ramsey case of zero discounting of future utilities is the appropriate abstraction for a normative analysis of climate change."[25]

[25] Weitzman (2012) lists Ramsey's fellow travelers on this issue as A. Pigou, R. Harrod, T. Koopmans, and R. Solow.

If this statement is to be consistent with his earlier criticisms of Stern, then he must believe the appropriate posture for climate-change economics is positive, rather than normative, in which case his use of the discounted-utilitarian model is of the 'infinitely lived consumer' sort. But perhaps Weitzman has changed his view.

Nordhaus appears to be less accommodating. Nordhaus (2007, 689) writes: "The [*Stern*] *Review* proposes ethical assumptions that produce very low discount rates. Combined with other assumptions, this magnifies impacts in the distant future and rationalizes deep cuts in emissions, and indeed in all consumption, today. If we substitute *more conventional discount rates used in other global-warming analyses, by governments, by consumers or by businesses* [our italics—LRS] the *Review*'s dramatic results disappear."

We do not yet have, however, an argument that these "more conventional discount rates" are the right ones to use. Nordhaus then gives a cogent summary of possible ethical approaches to the problem:

> The *Review* argues that fundamental ethics require intergenerational neutrality as represented by a near-zero time discount rate. The logic behind the *Review*'s social welfare function is not as universal as it would have us believe. It stems from the British utilitarian tradition with all the controversies and baggage that accompany that philosophical stance. Quite another ethical stance would be to hold that each generation should leave at least as much total societal capital (tangible, natural, human and technological) as it inherited. This would admit a wide array of time discount rates. A third alternative would be a Rawlsian perspective that societies should maximize the economic well-being of the poorest generation. The ethical implication of this policy would be that current consumption should *increase* sharply to reflect the projected future improvements in productivity. (692)

We agree with Nordhaus's characterization of Stern's approach as coming from the British utilitarian tradition. Nordhaus then outlines two possible interpretations of a sustainabilitarian ethic. Indeed, his conjecture in the last sentence of this citation turns out not to be correct, for, as we saw in Chapters 2 and 3 above, the *pure-sustainabilitarian* approach leads to *no* future improvements in productivity but rather to a stationary state. Maximization of the utility of the worst-off generation turns out to be inconsistent with future improvements in productivity.

What is Nordhaus's rejoinder to these other possible philosophical approaches that he outlines? "However, none of these approaches touches on the structure of actual intertemporal decision making, in which this generation cannot decide for or tie the hands of future generations. Instead, each generation is in the position of one member of a relay team, handing off the baton of capital to the next generation, and hoping that future generations behave sensibly and avoid catastrophic choices by dropping or destroying the baton" (693).

From this statement and the italicized phrase from the above citation from page 689, it seems that Nordhaus's critique is fundamentally that the philosophical approaches are *unrealistic*, because they "don't use the discount factors employed by consumers, businesses, etc.," and because, as the latest citation explains, we cannot write a plan for future generations. Thus, Nordhaus is not primarily engaged in an ethical inquiry but one that is tempered by the realism of using discount rates that are deduced from observed market behavior. As he writes (2008a, 61): "The assumption behind the DICE model is that the time discount rate should be chosen along with consumption elasticity [here denoted by η—LRS] so that the model generates a path that resembles the actual real interest rate."

We interpret this as meaning that he wishes to constrain his recommendations by realism, and one constraint that realism imposes is that the interest rate, computed via the Ramsey equation, should be more or less what is observed. His approach is an amalgam of a normative and positive inquiry.

4.4.6. Comment on the Nordhaus Wrinkle

Nordhaus intends to show how the high discount factor that Stern uses is ridiculous with a discussion of a 'climate wrinkle.' Here is what he writes in Nordhaus (2008a, 182):

> Suppose that scientists discover a wrinkle in the climate system that will cause damages equal to 0.1 percent of net consumption starting in 2200 and continuing at that rate forever after. How large a one-time investment would be justified today to remove the wrinkle that starts

after two centuries? If we use the methodology of the *Stern Review*, the answer is that we should pay up to 56% of one year's world consumption today to remove the wrinkle. In other words, it is worth a one-time consumption hit of approximately $30 trillion today to fix a tiny problem that begins in 2200.

As noted, Stern's utility discount factor is 0.999 per annum. Stern uses a per-annum utility function of $\tilde{u}(c_t) = \ln c_t$. We can verify Nordhaus's claim in the discrete-time model. The Stern objective function is $\sum_{t=1}^{\infty} 0.999^{t-1} \ln c_t$. The welfare loss induced by the climate wrinkle is

$$\sum_{t=200}^{\infty} 0.999^{t-1} \ln c_t - \sum_{t=200}^{\infty} 0.999^{t-1} \ln(0.999 c_t)$$
$$= -\sum_{t=200}^{\infty} 0.999^{t-1} \ln(0.999) = -\ln(0.999) \times \frac{0.999^{199}}{0.001} = -0.820.$$

This means that social welfare would be identical if the wrinkle were repaired at the cost of reducing the consumption c_1 by a factor r, the solution to:

$$\ln rc_1 - \ln c_1 = -0.820,$$

which implies $\ln r = -0.820$, or $r = 0.44$. Thus follows the claim that to prevent the very small effect of the wrinkle in two hundred years, (Stern's) society should be willing to reduce the first year's consumption by up to 56%.

The main problem with Nordhaus's thought experiment is that the counterfactual that is implicitly envisaged—that the first generation pay the entire cost of repairing the damage to come, two hundred years hence, from the climate wrinkle—is far from the optimal solution to the problem.

Indeed, assuming that the society was on an optimal path before the climate wrinkle is discovered, then there is no feasible way of *entirely* repairing the damage to social welfare from the occurrence of the climate wrinkle. To see this, we must look at the economic model in which the problem is embedded. Let's suppose it is the Ramsey model with Stern's choice of utility function and utility discount factor. Let's write the Ramsey model with an additional positive parameter $\overline{\gamma}$ multiplying the production function from date 200 onward:

$$\max \sum_{t=1}^{\infty} \varphi^{t-1} \ln c_t \quad \text{subject to:}$$
$$F(S_{t-1}) \geq c_t + i_t, \quad t = 1, \ldots, 199,$$
$$\overline{\gamma} F(S_{t-1}) \geq c_t + i_t, \quad t \geq 200,$$
$$S_t \leq (1-d) S_{t-1} + i_t, \quad t = 1, 2, \ldots \tag{4.12}$$

The climate wrinkle, in other words, is created by a fall in the productivity of capital beginning in two hundred years. How large would $\overline{\gamma}$ have to be to engender a decrease in optimal consumption by 0.1%? To answer this, we must first solve program (4.12) for its optimal path when there is no climate wrinkle (i.e., when $\overline{\gamma} = 1$). This is just the Ramsey problem; from Chapter 1, proposition A1.2, the solution at the stationary state is given by:

$$\overline{\gamma} F'(S^*) = d + \delta, \quad i^* = dS^*, \quad c^* = \overline{\gamma} F(S^*) - dS^*.$$

We now implicitly differentiate these equations with respect to $\overline{\gamma}$, viewing c^* and S^* as functions of $\overline{\gamma}$, and we compute that the elasticity of stationary-state consumption with respect to a change in $\overline{\gamma}$ at $\overline{\gamma} = 1$ is given by:

$$\left.\frac{dc^*(\overline{\gamma})}{d\overline{\gamma}}\right|_{\overline{\gamma}=1} \cdot \frac{1}{c^*(1)} = \frac{F(S^*) - \dfrac{F'(S^*)}{F''(S^*)}(F'(S^*) - d)}{F(S^*) - dS^*}.$$

Now let us take the production function $F(S) = S^{\varepsilon}/\varepsilon$. Then this elasticity reduces nicely to:

$$\left.\frac{dc^*(\overline{\gamma})}{d\overline{\gamma}}\right|_{\overline{\gamma}=1} \cdot \frac{1}{c^*(1)} = \frac{1}{1-\varepsilon}.$$

Now we parameterize the model as follows:

$$d = 0.04, \quad \delta = 0.001, \quad \varepsilon = 0.333.$$

(The justification for the choice of ε is that the elasticity of output with respect to capital is about one-third.) A drop in optimal consumption by 0.1%, as in the wrinkle, would thus be induced by a decrease $\Delta\bar{\gamma}$ in $\bar{\gamma}$, satisfying:

$$\frac{0.001}{\Delta\bar{\gamma}/1} = \frac{1}{1-\varepsilon} = 1.5, \quad \text{i.e.,} \ \Delta\bar{\gamma} = 0.00067.$$

In other words, the consumption damages in Nordhaus's wrinkle are induced by a drop in productivity of 0.067% from date 200 on.

The question now becomes: If productivity in two hundred years decreases by a saltus of 0.067%, how much should the optimal path change? Solving that problem may be pretty complicated: we will solve an easier problem—namely, if productivity were to drop *today* by 0.067%, how much should we adjust steady-state consumption? To answer this, we must solve program (4.13):

$$\begin{aligned} &\max \sum_{t=1}^{\infty} \varphi^{t-1} \ln c_t \quad \text{subject to:} \\ &\bar{\gamma} F(S_{t-1}) \geq c_t + i_t, \quad t \geq 1, \\ &S_t \leq (1-d)S_{t-1} + i_t, \quad t \geq 1. \end{aligned} \tag{4.13}$$

Clearly, the disturbance to the optimal path will be worse in (4.13) than in (4.12), since the climate damage hurts *every* generation in (4.12). But we know the answer: since the elasticity of steady-state consumption with respect to α is 1.5, consumption must drop by $1.5 \times 0.067\% = 0.1\%$. Of course, in the actual solution of (4.12), the drop in consumption of *all* generations will be *less than* 0.1%, since, in the actual wrinkle, unlike in (4.13), we do not experience the drop in productive capacity for two hundred years. So the correct response to the Nordhaus wrinkle is: consumption in every year starting now should decrease by something less than 0.1% in order to *respond optimally* to the damage that will occur in two hundred years.

Nordhaus's claim that the present generation should cut its consumption by 56% would never be recommended by a policy maker. Moreover, if a climate wrinkle occurs, it is impossible to find another path that will be socially indifferent to one that was planned before the wrinkle. The value of program (4.12) when $\bar{\gamma}$ is less than 1 is less than its value when $\bar{\gamma} = 1$. It is fruitless to attempt to make society as well off as it would have been, absent the wrinkle.

4.5. Concluding Remarks

We first summarize the differences between our approach and the features common to those of Nordhaus and Stern.

(1) We focus on *intergenerational ethics*, and our analytical time unit is the lifespan of a generation. Nordhaus and Stern, on the contrary, engage in conventional *climate-change economics*, comparing alternative consumption streams defined for relatively short time units, such as decades, years, or even infinitesimally small time periods, more in the spirit of standard macroeconomic models.
(2) Accordingly, both Nordhaus and Stern calibrate the crucial parameters of their models with the help of the Ramsey equation, a staple of standard macroeconomic growth models, whereas the Ramsey equation does not appear or play any role in our model. Of course, our models have their own first-order conditions for optimality, which replace the Ramsey equation.
(3) Our approach to intergenerational ethics is sustainabilitarian, whereas Nordhaus and Stern, to the extent to which they appeal to an intergenerational social-welfare function, are more in line with discounted utilitarianism.
(4) We adopt an 'off the shelf' path for GHG emissions and concentrations proposed by the scientific community and used in the IPCC reports, whereas Nordhaus and Stern endogenously determine the paths of GHG that they recommend.

On the other hand, Nordhaus's analysis differs substantially from Stern's.

(5) Their recommendations widely disagree: Stern advocates strong, early action in the reduction of GHG emissions while Nordhaus postpones drastic reductions until later in the twenty-first century.
(6) Their analytical methods are different: Nordhaus engages in constrained optimization, whereas Stern performs a CBA.
(7) Nordhaus and Stern utilize the Ramsey equation differently. The equation $r = \delta + \eta g$ relates the four magnitudes:

a. the consumption discount rate, denoted r
b. the pure-time discount rate, denoted δ
c. the rate of growth of consumption, denoted g, and
d. the parameter denoted η, variously interpreted as the elasticity of the marginal utility of consumption or as inequality aversion.[26]

Nordhaus's optimization requires calibrating δ and η, which he does by obtaining r and g from market data and applying the Ramsey equation. Stern's CBA requires adding up discounted consumption using the parameter r, which he, too, calibrates from the Ramsey equation but adopts a low value of δ based on the probability of the extinction of the human species.

(8) The different calibration procedures yield substantially higher pure discount rates δ and consumption discount rates r for Nordhaus than for Stern. This, together with somewhat different evaluations of the costs and benefits of GHG abatement (mitigation) and adaptation, underpins their divergent recommendations.
(9) If we interpret Nordhaus's objective function as discounted utilitarian, then the main difference between him and Stern is the discount factor applied to future generations: high in Stern and low in Nordhaus. The verbal justifications for their calibration procedures suggest different underlying views. Stern is philosophically a discounted utilitarian, discounting the utility of each generation by the probability of extinction. Nordhaus in turn believes that 'the market' has solved a Ramsey problem with parameters δ and η, as in Chapter 1 (i.e., without climate change constraints), and utilizes those parameters in his optimization problem with climate-change constraints. Thus, at least implicitly, his approach is that of the long-lived consumer, with preferences as expressed in the market by the current generation. In the argument between Stern, on the one hand, and Nordhaus (and Weitzman), on the other, we side with Stern.

[26] Or, as noted above, as the coefficient of relative risk aversion in models of decision making under risk.

Lastly, we submit the following direct comparisons between our approach and Stern's.

(10) We accept the 'early GHG reduction project' based on the recommendations by the scientific community, without trying to endogenize the GHG path.

(11) As noted in our arguments against utilitarianism in Chapter 1, we agree with Stern in adopting the Ethical-Observer approach, but we substitute a sustainabilitarian Ethical Observer for a utilitarian one.

(12) As we have shown in Llavador et al. (2011, 1616), the discounted-utilitarian program using our utility function of Chapter 3 with the *Stern Review*'s discount factor diverges on the set of feasible paths that we propose. However, the *Stern Review* uses a strictly concave utility function, while our utility function exhibits constant-returns-to-scale, and so the discounted-utilitarian objective with Stern's utility function and discount factor might converge. In any case, Stern only carries out his CBA for a small number of generations.

(13) Our approach is in a sense dual to a CBA. The latter takes as given a path for the economic variables and recommends a path for the environmental variables (based on a cost-benefit criterion in the spirit of discounted utilitarianism). We, on the contrary, take as given a path for the environmental variables and recommend paths for the economic variables based on the human sustainability and human development criteria.

CHAPTER FIVE

Sustainability in a Warming, Two-Region World

5.1. Introduction

This chapter introduces the problem of intragenerational welfare, in addition to the intergenerational issues analyzed in Chapter 3. We study how the budget of total emissions for each generation should be allocated to the regions of the world.

We assume that all countries, developed and underdeveloped, whose gross domestic product (GDP) per capita is sufficiently large must share in the effort to reduce greenhouse gas (GHG) emissions, a view that is gaining generalized acceptance (see, e.g., Aldy and Stavins 2012). Indeed, the 17th Conference of the Parties (COP) (COP-17, Durban, 2011) of the United Nations Framework Convention on Climate Change (UNFCCC) produced a nonbinding agreement, reaffirmed in COP-18 (Doha) and COP-19 (Warsaw), to reach a deal by the COP-21 (Paris) in 2015 that would bring all countries under the same legal regime by 2020.

For the sake of simplicity, we cast our analysis in a world with two regions, North and South, populated by representative households in each region and generation. (Population size is addressed below.) The North is postulated to have the level of economic development of the United States and the South that of China. The reader may consider the model to be one of how the actual nations of the United States and China should allocate emissions rights between them, were they to be the only countries in the world, when the total amount of permissible emissions has already been decided upon, following the RCP2.6 path described in Section 3.4.2. The values for emissions and concentration are presented in Table 5.1.

Indeed, it is probably the case that an agreement between the United States and China concerning how to constrain their emissions is both necessary and sufficient for a global agreement. It is obviously necessary, since these are the two largest emitters of GHGs. It may well be sufficient, since if these two giants can agree, the rest of the world will fall into line (Wagner 2014). In the concluding Section 5.7, we comment on the generalization to a multiregion world.

We maintain the focus on the sustainable growth of human welfare, and we explore the *maximal sustainable-growth rate.* Motivated by egalitarianism, we require long-run equality of welfare in the North and the South and a maximin-based approach to the welfare of the South during transition to the steady state. Finally, we require convergence of North's and South's welfare per capita to occur in seventy-five years, or three generations in our model. We offer some support for this choice in Section 5.2.

More generally, we provide a method to address the *critical issue of identifying the existence of feasible paths that satisfy the above criteria*: convergence in seventy-five years subject to not exceeding the RCP2.6 emissions path. In particular, our method helps discover the degree of growth that is consistent with a successful resolution of the climate-change problem in line with sustainability and egalitarian principles.

A central result of the analysis is that feasible growth paths exist satisfying the conditions above if and only if Northern growth is limited to approximately 1% per year over the next seventy-five years instead of the more conventional expectation of 2%. Correspondingly, the average annual growth rate of the South would be reduced from our projected business-as-usual (BAU) average of 4.5% to 2.5%. Thus, growth expectations in the North and the South must be scaled back substantially for global GHG emissions negotiations to succeed. Politicians who wish to solve the global-warming problem must prepare their polities to accept this reality.

Table 5.1. Our postulated paths for the world annual CO_2 emissions and end-of-generation concentrations, based on RCP2.6. Year 2010 values are from the World Resources Institute (2013). World emissions per capita are constructed from World Total emissions and population data from United Nations (2013).

	World total CO_2 emissions (GtC)	North's total CO_2 emissions (GtC)	South's total CO_2 emissions (GtC)	Concentration of CO_2 in (World) atmosphere (ppm)	World CO_2 emissions per capita (tC)
Year 2010	9.0424	3.8615	5.1809	390.43	1.31
Generation 1	8.1515	endogenous	endogenous	439.21	1.03
Generation 2	3.4146	endogenous	endogenous	445.63	0.34
Generation t, $t \geq 3$	1.4679	endogenous	endogenous	444.56	0.15

5.2. Convergence and Negotiation

Egalitarianism would be inconsistent with an everlasting welfare gap between North and South. Hence, in introducing intragenerational issues, we adopt a convergence criterion: we require the North's and the South's welfare per capita to converge in the future.

How far into the future? We propose that convergence should take place in three generations. Our motivation for this proposal is based on Thomas Schelling's focal-point approach to bargaining (Schelling 1960; Colman 2006): there is a clear focal point in a bargaining problem, and this emerges as the agreement. We propose that 'preserving the date of convergence' may be a focal point in the climate-change bargaining problem.

Suppose that the North and the South engage in comprehensive bargaining on the allocation of GHG emissions and on international economic cooperation. A starting point is provided by the projected BAU growth factors: BAU growth factors here denote those growth factors conforming with commonly held expectations, often enunciated as growth policy targets by governments. Such targets may well be unrealistic, but if held, they imply expectations of convergence, at a certain date, of standards of living across nations.

Our argument is political. Suppose that current GDP per capita in the United States (China) is y^{US} (y^{Ch}), and suppose that annual growth rates of GDP per capita were to average g^{US} and g^{Ch} over the next seventy-five years or so, under BAU assumptions. Then convergence would occur in the number of years T, which solves:

$$\frac{(1+g^{Ch})^T\, y^{Ch}}{(1+g^{US})^T\, y^{US}}=1. \tag{5.1}$$

Taking $y^{US}=\$46{,}179$ and $y^{Ch}=\$8{,}564$ (2010 figures, constant 2010 international dollars PPP) and $(g^{US}, g^{Ch})=(0.02, 0.045)$, equation (5.1) solves to $T^*\approx 70$ years.[1]

[1] Per capita income data from World Development Indicators (World Bank 2013); growth rates roughly coincide with the Asian Development Bank forecasts for the next twenty years.

Now suppose, for the moment, that both the North and the South know the value of T^*, and suppose a proposal were on the table for how China and the United States should share the global emissions budget that entails convergence in one hundred years. The Chinese, we claim, would never accept this proposal: their negotiators would say it was unacceptable to delay the date of convergence by twenty-five years because of the climate-change problem. Similarly, we claim, the US negotiators would veto a proposal that entails convergence in fifty years. These vetoes may well be comprehensible to both sides because of audience costs—the necessity to convince their respective polities to accept the cutbacks entailed in the reduction of GHG emissions.[2] The only agreement that will not be rejected by one side or the other is to allocate emissions so that the growth rates preserve the estimated convergence date.

One might protest that agreeing upon what the date of convergence would have been under BAU is extremely difficult: indeed, negotiators will not know the value of T^*. But one does not have to look that far into the future. If in each five-year period (say), the *ratio of growth factors* $\frac{1+g^{Ch}}{1+g^{US}}$ *is maintained* equal to what it would have been under BAU, then the date of convergence will remain unchanged. To see this, multiply both growth factors by a constant r, and note that the date of convergence, now defined by the equation

$$\frac{(r[1+g^{Ch}])^T y^{Ch}}{(r[1+g^{US}])^T y^{US}} = 1,$$

is exactly the same as in equation (5.1) Therefore, the problem of allocating emissions interregionally can be solved sequentially, with periodic negotiations, without ever having to estimate the putative convergence date. In these periodic negotiations, the two sides would have to agree on what the ratio of growth factors would have been, under BAU, for the next five years. This would surely be a bone of contention but perhaps a relatively simple one to resolve. The problem would be reduced to one about which international teams of economists could haggle.

We do not have proof that *preserving the date of convergence* is a focal point of interregional bargaining. We propose that this may be so. In fact, pro-

[2] We thank Robert Keohane for this point.

posing this may help make it so. Thus, we view this invariance condition not as something that sophisticated negotiators believe is necessary but as a selling point to their polities, to garner their support.

We emphasize the difference between our proposal and many proposals that are currently being discussed. Our proposal ignores history and in particular, the issue of regional responsibility up until the present for the growth in atmospheric carbon concentration. We do not maintain that our proposal is guided by purely ethical considerations—perhaps a more just approach would be to assign responsibility for emissions in the past (say, since 1990) to regions of the world. Our suspicion is that these historically based proposals will not succeed in resolving the bargaining problem. Maintaining the expected date of convergence, on the other hand, may be an offer that no region can refuse. There is an analogy with no-fault insurance, in which responsibility is ignored.

5.3. The North-South Model

We adapt the model for a single representative household constructed in Chapter 3 to a two-region world, namely the North and the South. Generations and regions are indexed by $t \geq 1$ and $\mathcal{J} = N, S$, for North and South, respectively. We postulate a representative household for each generation in each region with identical utility functions as defined in Section 3.2.2, that is,[3]

$$\widehat{u}(c_t^{\mathcal{J}}, x_t^{l\mathcal{J}}, S_t^{n\mathcal{J}}, S_t^m) := (c_t^{\mathcal{J}})^{\alpha_c} (x_t^{l\mathcal{J}})^{\alpha_l} (S_t^{n\mathcal{J}})^{\alpha_n} (\hat{S}^m - S_t^m)^{\alpha_m}. \tag{5.2}$$

The population of Generation t in Region $\mathcal{J}$ is denoted by $N_t^{\mathcal{J}}$, and population projections are exogenous.

Each region's economy is characterized by the same economic constraints as in the one-region model of Section 3.4.1 with the following modifications: first, population appears in the laws of motion of physical capital and knowledge as well as in the education production function; second, as long as the North's stock of knowledge per capita is larger than that of the South's, we let the North's knowledge spill over to the South; and third, there is the possibility of interregional output flows at each date.

[3] Section 3.2.2 provided a justification of our choice for the utility function.

5.3.1. Technology

We postulate that North and South have the same technology but different initial education levels and stocks of knowledge and physical capital. The production function replicates (3.2) in Chapter 3:

$$f(x_t^{cJ}, S_t^{kJ}, S_t^{nJ}, e_t^J, S_t^m) := k_1 (x_t^{cJ})^{\theta_c} (S_t^{kJ})^{\theta_k} (S_t^{nJ})^{\theta_n} (e_t^J)^{\theta_e} (S_t^m)^{\theta_m}, \quad t \geq 1. \quad (5.3)$$

During the transition, we allow for output flows between the countries. Hence, the sum of consumption and investment in either region is not constrained by production in that region; rather, global consumption plus global investment must equal global commodity production.[4] For $t=1, 2$, denote by T_t the number of units of output per capita in the North that the North exports to the South, in net terms. A negative T_t indicates a net flow from the South to the North. Hence, production in the North and the South must satisfy the following constraints:

$$f(x_t^{cN}, S_t^{kN}, S_t^{nN}, e_t^N, S_t^m) \geq c_t^N + i_t^N + T_t, \quad t = 1, 2, \text{for the North.} \quad (5.4)$$

and

$$f(x_t^{cS}, S_t^{kS}, S_t^{nS}, e_t^S, S_t^m) \geq c_t^S + i_t^S - \frac{N_t^N}{N_t^S} T_t, \quad t = 1, 2, \text{for South.} \quad (5.5)$$

Observe that we can rule out net exports by imposing the constraints $T_1 = T_2 = 0$.

5.3.2. Law of Motion of Physical Capital

The law of motion of physical capital in each region is standard, namely

$$(1 - d^k) S_{t-1}^{kJ} \frac{N_{t-1}^J}{N_t^J} + k_2 i_t^J \geq S_t^{kJ}, \quad t \geq 1, \ J = N, S, \quad (5.6)$$

[4] In actuality, net exports from China to the United States are balanced by Chinese claims on US assets. However, the model here recognizes only real (as opposed to financial) variables and so the change in property rights corresponding to the Chinese possession of US treasury bills in exchange for commodities exported from China to the United States is not made explicit.

where, recall, $i_t^J \geq 0$ is the average annual investment in physical capital (units of output per capita) by Generation t in Region J.

5.3.3. Law of Motion of Knowledge and Technological Diffusion

The generational law of motion of the stock of knowledge in the North is

$$(1-d^n)\frac{N_{t-1}^N}{N_t^N}S_{t-1}^{nN} + k_3\, x_t^{nN} \geq S_t^{nN}, \quad t \geq 1. \tag{5.7}$$

In words, a fraction d^n of the $(t-1)^{\text{st}}$ period per capita stock of knowledge becomes obsolete by period t, but it can be increased by investing labor resources.[5]

The law of motion of the stock of knowledge in the South captures the presence of international technological diffusion (Eaton and Kortum 1999; Keller 2004). We make the capacity of knowledge diffusion depend on the knowledge gap between North and South and also on the level of employment of knowledge workers in the South, letting human capital speed the process of diffusion (the so-called Nelson-Phelps technological catch-up hypothesis, Nelson and Phelps 1966; Benhabib and Spiegel 2005).[6] Our formulation starts from a year-to-year equation for knowledge diffusion which, after some manipulation (see Section A5.1 in the Chapter 5 Appendix), yields the generational law of motion of the stock of knowledge in the South

$$S_t^{nS} = (1-d^n)\frac{N_{t-1}^S}{N_t^S}S_{t-1}^{nS} + k_3\, x_t^{nS}, \quad \text{if } S_{t-1}^{nN} - S_{t-1}^{nS} \leq 0, \tag{5.8}$$

$$S_t^{nS} = (1-d^n)\frac{N_{t-1}^S}{N_t^S}S_{t-1}^{nS} + k_3 x_t^{nS} + k_{3d}[S_{t-1}^{nN} - S_{t-1}^{nS}]x_t^{nS}, \quad \text{if } S_{t-1}^{nN} - S_{t-1}^{nS} \geq 0, \tag{5.9}$$

where $k_3 > k_{3d} > 0$, and x_t^{nS} is the average annual efficiency units of labor per capita devoted to the production of knowledge by Generation t in

---

[5] Section A5.1 in the Chapter 5 Appendix derives (5.7) from a year-to-year law of motion.

[6] The catch-up hypothesis was originally proposed by Gerschenkron (1962). Benhabib and Spiegel (1994), Engelbrecht (2002), and Xu and Chiang (2005), among others, provide empirical evidence in favor of the Nelson-Phelps technological catch-up hypothesis.

the South. Of course, for $S_{t-1}^{nN} = S_{t-1}^{nS}$, the law of motion of the stock of knowledge in the South (5.9) coincides with (5.8) and parallels that of the North (5.7).

5.3.4. Education Production Function

The education production function transforms labor-leisure time in efficiency units of labor and leisure. Formally,

$$x_t^{\mathcal{J}} \leq \xi x_{t-1}^{e\mathcal{J}} \frac{N_{t-1}^{\mathcal{J}}}{N_t^{\mathcal{J}}}, \quad t \geq 1, \quad \mathcal{J} = N, S,$$

where $\xi > 0$, and $x_t^{e\mathcal{J}} \geq 0$ (respectively, $x_t^{\mathcal{J}} \geq 0$) is the annual average number of efficiency units of labor per capita devoted to education by Generation t (respectively, per capita efficiency units of labor-leisure available to Generation t) in Region $\mathcal{J}$.

5.4. Optimization Program: Sustainability and Convergence

We implement a version of the sustainable-growth optimization program introduced in Section 3.3 adapted to the two-region world.

The application of the sustainabilitarian approach to a world with two regions is based upon the turnpike theorem, 2.1, and the ray optimization theorem, 3.1. We model the problem of North-South emissions-sharing as one where the Northern and Southern representative households begin with different endowments, and we study the paths of resource use under which both representative agents converge to the same point on the ray $\Gamma(\rho, e^*, S^{m^*})$ in seventy-five years: the assumption is that both economies then enjoy balanced growth at rate ρ from that date on.

The optimization program adopts a long-term growth rate ρ of utility and chooses the feasible path that maximizes the utility of Generation 2 of the South, subject to the constraint that both regions' utilities grow at a rate of at least ρ in the first two generations and that per capita endowments of both regions be identical and lie on the ρ-balanced-growth ray $\Gamma(\rho, e^*, S^{m^*})$ at the end of period 2.[7] It will follow that from period 3 on

[7] As in Chapter 3, the maximin criterion would require the maximization of the utility of the worst-off generation, which is Generation 1 in the South. We choose

(i.e., from 2085), utilities will be equal in the two regions, and each region will grow at the rate ρ henceforth.[8]

The calibration procedures as well as the calibrated values for the parameters and the initial stocks can be found in Appendix A: Calibration.

5.5. Economic Variables along the Transition and in the Steady State

The optimal path is computed using the *NMaximize* routine in *Mathematica*.[9] Recall that among the variables that are endogenous to the solution of the program are the allocations of global emissions to the two regions in each period. After convergence occurs, in Generation 3, emissions *per capita* in the two regions will be equal forever. In addition, investments in knowledge are endogenous, and it is the level of knowledge that determines technological improvements in commodity production. That is to say, both the allocation of emissions to the two regions and technological change are *endogenous* in the program.

▶ **Main result.** *It is possible to sustain a rate of utility growth of* 1% *per year, starting from the* $t = 0$ (*year* 2010) *reference level, with North and South converging in seventy-five years* ($t = 3$), *while keeping global carbon dioxide* (CO_2) *emissions at the levels based on* RCP2.6 *and specified in Section* 3.4.2. *At convergence, North and South reach a common steady state*

---

to maximize, instead, the utility of Generation 2 in the South (the second worst-off generation) because we find by experimentation that doing so yields a large increase in that generation's welfare, with relatively little sacrifice to the utility of Generation 1. In particular, maximizing Generation 1's utility for a sustainable 1% annual growth rate implies a 4.7% increase in the utility of Generation 1 while the utility of Generation 2 falls to 47% of the level attained when maximizing Generation 2's utility. Moreover, this sacrifice of Generation 1 in the South is indispensable: it is not possible to obtain a higher utility for Generation 2 in the South and the required convergence without lowering the utility of Generation 1 in the South. Section A5.3 of the Chapter 5 Appendix reports the transition path for maximizing Generation 1's utility while growing at a sustainable 1% annual rate.

[8] See Section A5.2 in the Chapter 5 Appendix for the detailed optimization program.

[9] See Appendix B: *Mathematica* Code.

Table 5.2. Utility path and generational growth rates for a guaranteed growth rate of at least 1% per year (28.24% per generation).

	Initial	Transition		Steady state	
	$t=0$	$t=1$	$t=2$	$t=3$	$t=4$
North u_t^N	$5.2798=u_0^N$	$6.7710=1.2824\ u_0^N$	$8.6833=1.2824\ u_1^N$	$11.1358=1.2824\ u_2^N$	$14.2808=1.2824\ u_3^N$
South u_t^S	$1.7357=u_0^S$	$2.2259=1.2824\ u_0^S$	$6.3864=2.8691\ u_1^S$	$11.1358=1.7437\ u_2^S$	$14.2808=1.2824\ u_3^S$

where all economic variables grow at a constant rate. In particular, the per capita levels of the stock of knowledge, investment in knowledge, and emissions are then equalized across regions. During the transition, Northern utility grows at 1% *per year and after convergence, both regions grow at that rate forever.*

However, there are no feasible solutions to the program at which both the North and the South grow at sustainable rates much higher than 1.1% *per year.*

To establish the last sentence in the above-stated result, we have run a program that maximizes the growth rate subject to the previous constraints on convergence and sustainability. The highest growth rate that can be sustained for all generations in all regions is 1.112% per year. Higher steady-state growth rates could, in principle, be reached if we allowed for lower growth rates in the North during the transition. Our computations lead to the conclusion that *reaching a convergent steady state with growth rates distinctly higher than* 1% *per year is not possible unless a transition generation in the North or the South grows at less than the target rate.*

Table 5.2 lists the utility values along the optimal path, also illustrated in Figure 5.1; $t=0$ provides the data of the 2010 reference level. The transition generations are $t=1$, 2, and the steady state is reached at $t=3$ and continues forever at the constant growth rate.

As noted, the time paths that we propose have two distinct stages: the *transition* ($t=1$, 2) and the *steady state* ($t \geq 3$). The steady state requires North and South to have the same emissions-to-output ratio and the same emissions per capita, whereas initially ($t=0$, year 2010), the North has a lower emissions-to-output ratio and higher emissions per capita than the South.

The optimal values for the allocation of emissions are presented in Table 5.3 and Figure 5.2. Recall that the postulated path of global emissions decreases to a low value in the steady state, and accordingly, both emissions per capita and the emissions-to-output ratio ('GHG intensity,' in Intergovernmental Panel on Climate Change [IPCC] parlance) must eventually decrease. The initial values show that emissions per capita in the North are 3.4 times as large as those in the South, whereas the emissions-to-output ratio in the South is 1.6 times that of the North. All per capita values are equalized in the steady state, including emissions per capita and emissions-to-output ratios. Of course, these steady-state values are substantially lower than the

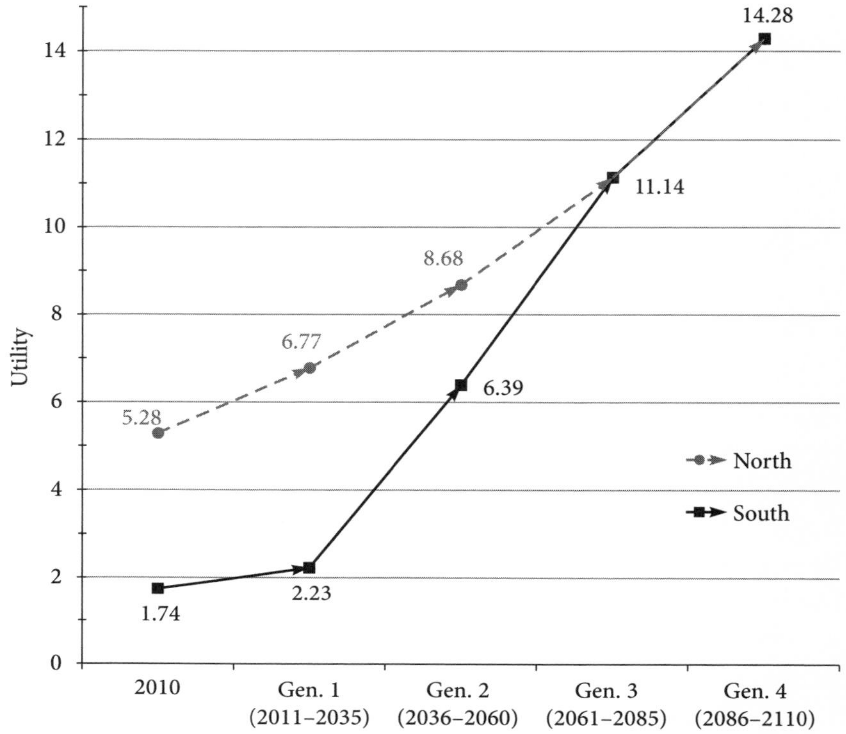

Figure 5.1. Utility path for a guaranteed growth rate of at least 1% per year (28.24% per generation). Simplified and reprinted with kind permission of the publisher from Llavador et al. (2014), fig. 2. Copyright © Springer Science + Business Media Dordrecht 2014.

initial values because we require world steady-state total emissions per year to reduce to 16% of the initial values.

The paths for the economic variables are presented in Tables 5.4 and 5.5. They correspond to a sustainable 1% annual growth rate. Table 5.4 describes the path of stocks (knowledge, physical capital, and human capital) and flows (consumption and investment). Table 5.5 displays the fractions of each period's labor-leisure resource allocated to the various uses. For each region, the rows for $t=0$ and $t=3$ permit the comparison between the steady-state values recommended by our analysis and the initial conditions in 2010.[10]

[10] Recall that the per capita stocks of physical capital, human capital, and knowledge are equalized across the two regions at $t=2$, whereas all stocks and flows of economic variables are equalized at $t=3$. See Section 2.2 for the detailed turnpike analysis of the convergence to the steady state.

Table 5.3. The allocation of CO_2 emissions. The last column is obtained by dividing Total Emissions Region [2] by world emissions (total emissions North plus South).

		Emissions per capita (tC)	Emissions per output ratio (tC/$'000) [1]	Marginal product of emissions θ_e/[1]	Total emissions region (GtC) [2]	Region share in world emissions [2]/E^{World}
North						
Initial	$t=0$	3.112	0.067	1.212	3.861	0.427
Transition	$t=1$	2.743	0.035	2.323	3.506	0.430
	$t=2$	0.242	0.005	15.926	0.313	0.092
Steady state	$t=3$	0.146	0.002	52.618	0.189	0.128
	$t=4$	0.146	0.001	67.969	0.189	0.128
South						
Initial	$t=0$	0.913	0.107	0.754	5.181	0.573
Transition	$t=1$	0.700	0.035	2.323	4.645	0.570
	$t=2$	0.353	0.005	15.926	3.102	0.908
Steady state	$t=3$	0.146	0.002	52.618	1.279	0.872
	$t=4$	0.146	0.001	67.969	1.279	0.872

Table 5.4. The evolution of stocks (physical capital, knowledge, and human capital) and flows (consumption and investment).

		Stock of physical capital S_t^{kJ}	Stock of knowledge S_t^{nJ}	Human capital x_t^{eJ}	Consumption per capita c_t^J	Consumption per capita growth c_t^J/c_0^J	Investment per capita i_t^J
North							
Initial	$t=0$	104.948	26.953	0.072	40.965	1.000	6.854
Transition	$t=1$	294.503	65.562	0.079	53.889	1.315	20.797
	$t=2$	273.867	84.159	0.126	66.925	1.634	16.162
Steady state	$t=3$	353.766	108.712	0.163	72.012	1.758	22.523
	$t=4$	456.975	140.428	0.211	93.021	2.271	29.094
South							
Initial	$t=0$	33.292	0.837	0.028	4.099	1.000	4.130
Transition	$t=1$	75.159	23.821	0.097	15.579	3.801	5.267
	$t=2$	273.867	84.159	0.126	44.167	10.775	19.956
Steady state	$t=3$	353.766	108.712	0.163	72.012	17.568	22.523
	$t=4$	456.975	140.428	0.211	93.021	22.694	29.094

Table 5.5. The allocation of labor-leisure resources, where $X_t := \max\{\text{Net Exports}, 0\}$, and Output = Consumption + Investment + X_t.

		Labor allocation (fraction of total labor-leisure available)							Labor (in efficiency units)		
		Education $\frac{x_t^{eJ}}{x_t^J}$	Knowledge $\frac{x_t^{nJ}}{x_t^J}$	Output $\frac{x_t^{cJ}}{x_t^J}$	Investment $\frac{x_t^{cJ}}{x_t^J}\frac{i_t^J}{\text{output}}$	Consumption $\frac{x_t^{cJ}}{x_t^J}\frac{c_t^J}{\text{output}}$	Net Exports $\frac{x_t^{cJ}}{x_t^J}\frac{X_t}{\text{output}}$	Leisure $\frac{x_t^{lJ}}{x_t^J}$	Education x_t^{eJ}	Knowledge x_t^{nJ}	Leisure x_t^{lJ}
North											
Initial	$t=0$	0.033	0.017	0.283	0.043	0.257	0	0.667	0.072	0.036	1.448
Transition	$t=1$	0.027	0.037	0.307	0.081	0.211	0.016	0.628	0.079	0.107	1.827
	$t=2$	0.039	0.039	0.177	0.034	0.143	0	0.745	0.126	0.126	2.409
Steady state	$t\geq 3$	0.031	0.031	0.286	0.068	0.218	0	0.651	0.163	0.163	3.406
South											
Initial	$t=0$	0.021	0.009	0.320	0.156	0.154	0.010	0.650	0.028	0.012	0.874
Transition	$t=1$	0.096	0.034	0.262	0.066	0.196	0	0.608	0.097	0.034	0.608
	$t=2$	0.042	0.034	0.319	0.092	0.203	0.024	0.606	0.126	0.102	1.830
Steady state	$t\geq 3$	0.031	0.031	0.286	0.068	0.218	0	0.651	0.163	0.163	3.409

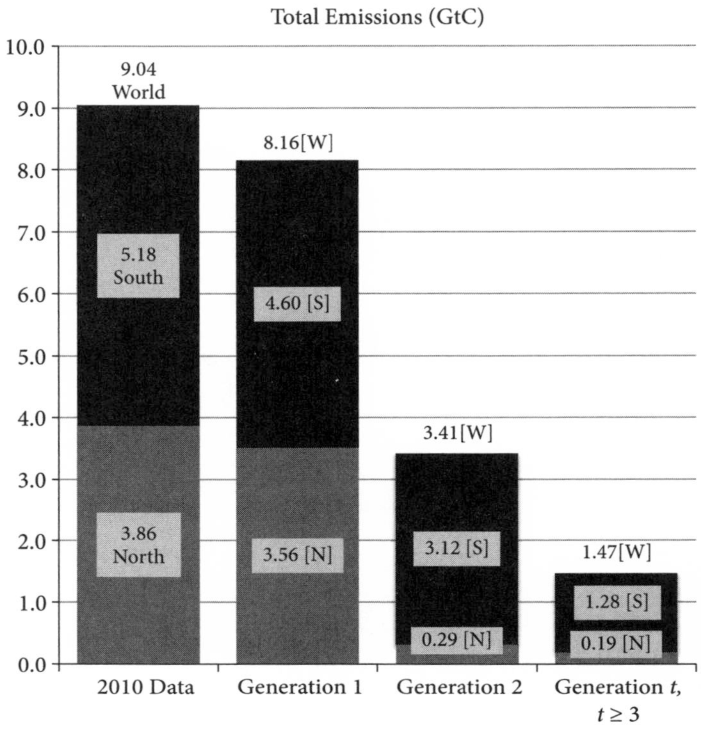
Total Emissions (GtC)
10.0
9.0
8.0
7.0
6.0
5.0
4.0
3.0
2.0
1.0
0.0
9.04
World
5.18
South
3.86
North
8.16[W]
4.60 [S]
3.56 [N]
3.41[W]
3.12 [S]
0.29 [N]
1.47[W]
1.28 [S]
0.19 [N]
2010 Data
Generation 1
Generation 2
Generation t, t ≥ 3

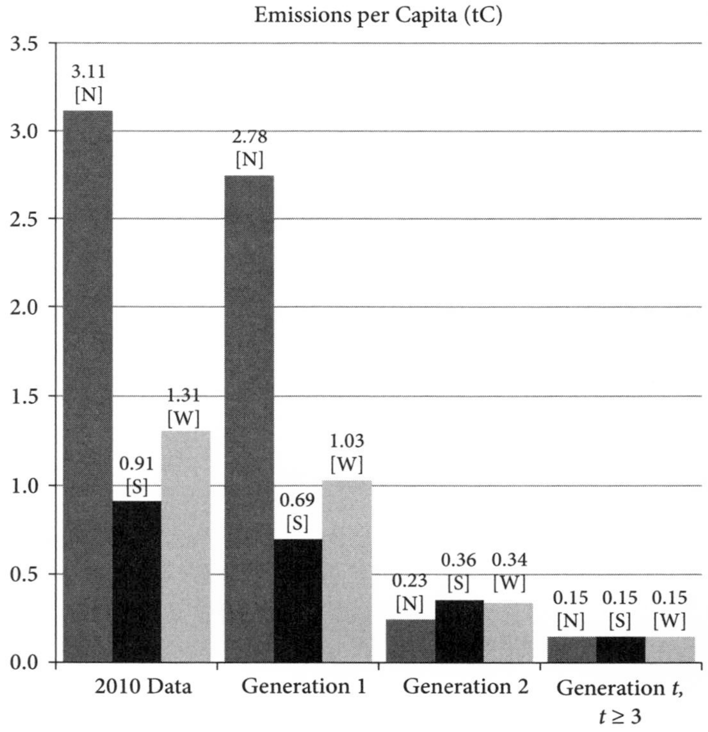
Emissions per Capita (tC)
3.5
3.0
2.5
2.0
1.5
1.0
0.5
0.0
3.11 [N]
0.91 [S]
1.31 [W]
2.78 [N]
0.69 [S]
1.03 [W]
0.23 [N]
0.36 [S]
0.34 [W]
0.15 [N]
0.15 [S]
0.15 [W]
2010 Data
Generation 1
Generation 2
Generation t, t ≥ 3

The steady-state values display the following properties.

(1) Both North and South devote to investment in physical capital 6.8% of their labor-leisure resource, a figure 70% higher than the reference value of 4% in the North but substantially lower than the reference value of 16% in the South.
(2) Both North and South substantially increase the creation of knowledge, and moreover, the South invests heavily in education. More specifically, in the North (respectively the South), the fraction of the labor-leisure resource devoted to knowledge in the steady state is almost twice (respectively three and a half times) that of the reference year. And in the steady state, the South devotes to education a fraction of the labor-leisure resource 48% higher than the reference level.
(3) The fractions of the labor-leisure resource devoted to leisure as well as those devoted to the production of output in either region do not substantially differ from the reference values. The same observation applies to consumption in the North. But the South must devote to consumption, respectively investment, a fraction of its labor-leisure resource 42% higher, respectively 44% lower, than the reference value. This is unsurprising and consistent with the observation, often made, that China is investing too much and consuming too little.

We say that a region exports output, in net terms, if its production is higher than its consumption: the initial 2010 data display net exports from South to North amounting to 3.2% (respectively 2.7%) of the South's (respectively the North's) output. Net exports are zero in the steady state, but during the transition the optimal path entails net exports from North to South at $t=1$ on the order of 3.8% of domestic output in the North or 5.1% of domestic output in the South, and, at $t=2$, the optimal path entails net exports from South to North of about 7.6% of domestic output in

---

Figure 5.2. Total and per capita annual CO_2 emissions (North, South, and World). Year 2010 values from the World Resources Institute (2013). Reprinted with kind permission of the publisher from Llavador et al. (2014), fig. 3. Copyright © Springer Science + Business Media Dordrecht 2014.

the South and around 75% of domestic output in the North. That is, the amount imported by the North is three-fourths of the North's own domestic output. These net output flows could have a financial counterpart by transfers of property rights on regional assets or via trade in emission permits, neither of which appears in the model.[11] But it may well be politically unrealistic to advocate a path that entails that the North import 40% of its consumption from the South in the second transition generation, a point to which we will attend in Section 5.6.

If net exports are indeed allowed, then emissions are allocated efficiently between the regions, which implies that the marginal product of emissions (and hence, under our Cobb-Douglas assumption, the emissions-to-output ratio) is equalized across the two regions not only in the steady state but also during the transition. This requires a relatively small allocation of emissions to the North at $t=2$. The sacrifice by the North is counterbalanced by South-to-North exports in order to satisfy the constraint that the North's utility grow at an annual rate of at least 1% starting from the reference level. The point is that, because output flows are allowed, the problem becomes a completely cooperative one: who produces what goods and how emissions are allocated is decided entirely by optimization, with emissions and the production of output efficiently allocated.

The marginal product of emissions in terms of output implies a shadow price of carbon. For Generation 1, the marginal product of emissions in output is \$2,323 per metric ton of carbon or \$633 per metric ton of CO_2. This is substantially higher than other policy proposals for the United States (see, e. g., table 5-4 in Nordhaus 2008a).

[11] Consider a hypothetical market for emission permits. For instance, suppose that, at t, Region J ($J=N, S$) is allocated the amount ω_t^J of tradable emission permits, emits the amount e_t^J, and exports the amount T_t^J of output. Assume also that Region J has to satisfy a financial balance condition such as the simple one $\tau[e_t^J - \omega_t^J] = T_t^J$ (*value of purchases of permits at t = exports of output at t*), where τ is the price of a permit. The computed optimal values for e_t^J and T_t^J, together with a value of τ equal to the marginal product of emissions at the optimal solution, then determine a value for ω_t^J. Because at the steady state net exports are zero, each region would then receive an amount of permits equal to its steady-state emissions. (Recall that the marginal product of emissions is the rate at which output increases instantaneously as emissions are increased, holding other inputs constant.)

5.6. Optimization under Zero-Exports Constraints

We return to address the issue that, when net exports are unconstrained, the efficient solution of our problem entails large commodity exports from the South to the North in the second transition generation. As an alternative, we have run the optimization program for a 1% annual growth rate with the additional, extreme constraint that net exports between regions be zero at each date. The results are presented in Table 5.6 and Table 5.7.

The steady-state values of the variables (stocks for $t=2$ and all economic variables for $t \geq 3$) do not depend on whether exports are allowed or not, but the values during the transition do. The differences between the 'net-exports-forbidden' and the 'net-exports-allowed' regimes are more noticeable for $t=2$, where net exports, from South to North, are large. As should be expected, when net exports are unconstrained, the net exporter increases the share of labor-leisure resource devoted to the production of output (see Table 5.7) while reducing the fractions devoted to leisure, education, and the investment in knowledge. For instance, Generation 2 in the North increases its labor-leisure resource in the production of output from 18% (when net exports are allowed) to 28% (when they are forbidden). Correspondingly, when net exports are allowed, the North invests 3.9% of its labor-leisure resource in knowledge production at $t=2$, a figure that is reduced to 3.2% when it cannot rely on imports.

Forbidding net exports creates inefficiency: the utility of the South's Generation 2 drops by 5%, while nobody else's utility is increased. But it does not greatly affect sustainable growth rates. The maximum growth that can be sustained falls from an annual 1.112% (31% per generation) in the unconstrained model to an annual 1.110% (28% per generation) when net exports are forbidden.

5.7. Conclusion

This chapter brings together intergenerational and intraregional efficiency and equity in our sustainabilitarian framework. Equity requires that the utility levels of North and South converge in the future. We assume convergence of the North and the South in three generations based

Table 5.6. The path of utility levels, stocks (physical capital, knowledge and human capital), and flows (consumption and investment) for a sustainable 1% annual growth rate when net exports are constrained to be zero. Numbers between parentheses represent the values for the 'net exports allowed' model when they differ from the values in the constrained model.

		Utility u_t^J	Stock of physical capital S_t^{kJ}	Stock of knowledge S_t^{nJ}	Human capital x_t^{eJ}	Consumption per capita c_t^J	Consumption per capita growth c_t^J/c_0^J	Investment per capita i_t^J
North								
Initial	$t=0$	5.280	104.948	26.953	0.072	40.965	1.000	6.854
Transition	$t=1$	6.771	264.620	67.574	0.097	52.105	1.272	18.519
			(294.503)	(65.562)	(0.079)	(53.889)	(1.315)	(20.797)
	$t=2$	8.683	273.867	84.159	0.126	58.228	1.421	16.640
						(66.925)	(1.634)	(16.162)
Steady state	$t=3$	11.136	353.766	108.712	0.163	72.012	1.758	22.523
	$t=4$	14.281	456.975	140.428	0.211	93.021	2.271	29.094
South								
Initial	$t=0$	1.736	33.292	0.837	0.028	4.099	1.000	4.130
Transition	$t=1$	2.226	80.660	24.278	0.090	15.862	3.870	5.687
			(75.159)	(23.821)	(0.097)	(15.579)	(3.801)	(5.267)
	$t=2$	6.175	273.867	84.159	0.126	43.800	10.685	19.889
		(6.386)				(44.167)	(10.775)	(19.956)
Steady state	$t=3$	11.136	353.766	108.712	0.163	72.012	17.568	22.523
	$t=4$	14.281	456.975	140.428	0.211	93.021	22.694	29.094

Table 5.7. The allocation of labor-leisure resources for a sustainable 1% annual growth rate when net exports are constrained to be zero. Numbers between parentheses represent the values for the unconstrained-flows model (Table 5.5) when they differ from the values in the constrained model.

		Labor allocation (fraction of total labor-leisure available)							Labor (in efficiency units)		
		Education	Knowledge	Output	Investment	Consumption	Net exports	Leisure	Education	Knowledge	Leisure
North											
Initial	$t=0$	0.033	0.017	0.283	0.042	0.249	0	0.667	0.072	0.036	1.448
Transition	$t=1$	0.033	0.038	0.290	0.076	0.214	0	0.639	0.097	0.111	1.857
		(0.027)	(0.037)	(0.307)	(0.081)	(0.211)	(0.016)	(0.628)	(0.079)	(0.107)	(1.827)
	$t=2$	0.032	0.032	0.282	0.063	0.219	0	0.654	0.126	0.125	2.582
		(0.039)	(0.039)	(0.177)	(0.034)	(0.143)		(0.745)		(0.126)	(2.409)
Steady state	$t \geq 3$	0.031	0.031	0.286	0.068	0.218	0	0.651	0.163	0.163	3.409
South											
Initial	$t=0$	0.021	0.009	0.320	0.156	0.154	0.047	0.650	0.028	0.012	0.874
Transition	$t=1$	0.090	0.034	0.274	0.072	0.202	0	0.602	0.090	0.034	0.602
		(0.096)	(0.034)	(0.262)	(0.066)	(0.196)		(0.608)	(0.097)	(0.034)	(0.608)
	$t=2$	0.045	0.036	0.301	0.094	0.207	0	0.618	0.126	0.100	1.743
		(0.042)	(0.034)	(0.319)	(0.092)	(0.203)	(0.024)	(0.606)		(0.102)	(1.830)
Steady state	$t \geq 3$	0.031	0.031	0.286	0.068	0.218	0	0.651	0.163	0.163	3.409

on negotiated agreement that preserves the BAU convergence date. This embodies a concept of fairness quite different from the ones where the allocation of emissions is separated from growth considerations (see Aldy and Stavins 2012; Rose et al. 1998; Vaillancourt et al. 2008, pp. 2006, 2011). Ours is a *forward-looking* approach, based upon considerations of political feasibility. We make the analogy with no-fault automobile insurance.

A first recommendation that follows from our analysis is the necessity for both the North and the South honestly to admit the connection between restricting emissions and curbing growth. This admission contrasts with the unwillingness, at least until November 2014, of either United States or China to accept that some of their domestic economic decisions must be on the table during international bargaining over climate policy. It is not very surprising that progress in the COP meetings has been disappointingly slow; we believe it will continue to be so as long as international negotiators do not acknowledge the intimate relationship between emissions control and economic growth and agree simultaneously to address both issues in the bargaining venue.[12]

Indeed, the difficulty that governments have in admitting this relationship may well be due to the audience costs they conjecture they would pay, were the truth of this relationship stated publicly. Perhaps the politically feasible solution would be for the United States and China to make a simultaneous announcement containing two points: first, that successful agreement to curb global emissions can only be achieved if all large countries agree to curb their growth factors to some extent and second, that the fair way to curb growth factors is to do so in a way that preserves the *relative* growth factors of GDP per capita in all regions—thus, in particular, preserving predicted dates of convergence.

To be more precise, we have computed that Northern politicians should prepare their citizens for the necessity of curbing growth to 1% per year, in tandem with an agreement to reduce the growth factor of the South in

[12] In November 2014, and in anticipation of the COP 21 (Paris, 2015), the United States and China made public their compromise to reduce emissions, setting targets for 2025 and 2030. In section A5.4 of the Chapter 5 Appendix we compare the US-China proposal with our optimal path obtained in this chapter. We observe that the US promise does not fall too far from our path.

equal proportion. Similarly, Southern politicians should prepare their citizenries to accept growth rates substantially lower than are currently expressed as targets, in tandem with reductions in the North.

The recommendation to reduce growth is in line with those recently put forth by several other authors (Skidelsky and Skidelsky 2012; Gordon 2012; Rogoff 2012) who call for limiting growth, although they have arrived at the conclusion via different considerations. In fact, Rogoff has called for a target of 1% annual growth as reasonable for the United States.

It also follows from our analysis that both North and South should heavily invest in education and knowledge beyond the current levels, both in the transition and in the more distant future. And finally, the price of carbon should be substantially higher than what has been observed in recent permit markets.

We remind the reader that what is new in our approach is that the regional allocation of emissions emerges as part of the optimal solution of a program based upon egalitarian and sustainabilitarian considerations, rather than being decided upon *a priori* based on historical considerations. We close the model by appending the constraint of convergence in three generations and derive regional emissions as a corollary.

Although we have constrained the analysis to a two-region world, its logic clearly extends to one with more major players. One possibility is that all countries whose GDP per capita is sufficiently large should be included in this agreement: that is, emissions should be allocated so as to preserve the relative growth factors among this set of countries. Very poor countries would be excused from reducing GHG emissions. Or perhaps the criterion for inclusion in the set of countries bound by the agreement should be a level of GHG emissions per capita. India poses a difficult question: its emissions per capita are low, but it has a huge population.

We have not discussed the question of whether implementing GHG emissions reductions should be accomplished by issuing tradable permits to countries or instituting a global carbon tax. Although this issue is obviously important, it is not the most important issue, which is the question of entitlements, which we have addressed here. One might take our recommendation for the regional emissions allocated to the North and the South to set the number of tradable permits that would be allocated to the North and the South in each period.

APPENDIX 5. FORMAL DETAILS

A5.1. Annual and Generational Laws of Motion of Knowledge

Our model is generational, with investment in knowledge written in efficiency units of labor. But our calibration uses yearly data, with investment measured in thousands of 2010 international dollars. The present appendix shows how to obtain the generational laws of motion of knowledge for North and South from annual laws of motion.

Consider a given generation, Generation t, which, it will be recalled, lives for twenty-five years. A double subscript $t\tau$, $\tau = 1, \ldots, 25$, denotes year τ in the life of Generation t. We adopt the following simplifying assumptions. For Region $\mathcal{J}, \mathcal{J} = N, S$: (i) Annual per capita investment in knowledge is constant, written $i_t^{n\mathcal{J}}$ if expressed in monetary units and $x_t^{n\mathcal{J}}$ if expressed in efficiency units of labor; (ii) we take $i_t^{n\mathcal{J}} = \overline{w} x_t^{n\mathcal{J}}$, where $\overline{w}$ denotes the steady-state wage for an efficiency unit of labor; (iii) population remains constant within a generation: $\hat{N}_{t0}^{n\mathcal{J}} = N_{t-1}^{n\mathcal{J}}$ and, for $\tau \geq 1$, $N_{t\tau}^{n\mathcal{J}} = N_t^{n\mathcal{J}}$.

► **North.** Our starting point is the annual law of motion

$$\hat{S}_{t\tau}^{nN} = (1 - \hat{d}^n) \frac{N_{t,\tau-1}^N}{N_{t\tau}^N} \hat{S}_{t,\tau-1}^{nN} + \overline{w} x_t^{nN}, \quad \tau = 1, \ldots, 25, \tag{A5.1}$$

which incorporates simplifying assumptions (i)–(iii), where $\hat{S}_{t\tau}^{nN}$ denotes the per capita stock of knowledge in the North in year τ, with $S_{t-1}^{nN} = \hat{S}_{t0}^{nN}$ and $S_t^{nN} = \hat{S}_{t,25}^{nN}$ (that is, the generational stock is that of the last year of the generation). Recall that we denote with a caret ('hat') variables in annual terms. The iteration of (A5.1) gives

$$\hat{S}_{t1}^{nN} = (1 - \hat{d}^n) \frac{N_{t-1}^N}{N_t^N} S_{t-1}^{nN} + \overline{w} x_t^{nN},$$

$$\begin{aligned} \hat{S}_{t2}^{nN} &= (1 - \hat{d}^n) S_{t1}^{nN} + \overline{w} x_t^{nN} \\ &= (1 - \hat{d}^n)^2 \frac{N_{t-1}^N}{N_t^N} S_{t-1}^{nN} + (1 - \hat{d}^n) \overline{w} x_t^{nN} + \overline{w} x_t^{nN}, \end{aligned}$$

$$\hat{S}^{nN}_{t3} = (1-\hat{d}^n)S^{nN}_{t2} + \overline{w}x^{nN}_t$$
$$= (1-\hat{d}^n)^3 \frac{N^N_{t-1}}{N^N_t} S^{nN}_{t-1} + [(1-\hat{d}^n)^2 + (1-\hat{d}^n) + 1]\overline{w}x^{nN}_t,$$

...

$$\hat{S}^{nN}_{t\tau} = (1-\hat{d}^n)^\tau \frac{N^N_{t-1}}{N^N_t} S^{nN}_{t-1} + \frac{1-(1-\hat{d}^n)^\tau}{\hat{d}^n}\overline{w}x^{nN}_t, \quad \tau = 1, \ldots, 25, \tag{A5.2}$$

and in particular

$$\hat{S}^{nN}_t \equiv \hat{S}^{nN}_{t,25} = (1-\hat{d}^n)^{25} \frac{N^N_{t-1}}{N^N_t} S^{nN}_{t-1} + \frac{1-(1-\hat{d}^n)^{25}}{\hat{d}^n}\overline{w}x^{nN}_t,$$

which is the generational law of motion of the stock of knowledge in the North (5.7) for

$$1-d^n = (1-\hat{d}^n)^{25}, \tag{A5.3}$$

and

$$k_3 = \frac{1-(1-\hat{d}^n)^{25}}{\hat{d}^n}\overline{w} = \frac{d^n}{\hat{d}^n}\overline{w}. \tag{A5.4}$$

▶ **South.** An argument parallel to the preceding one leads to the generational law of motion for the stock of knowledge of the South, which, when $S^{nN}_{t-1} - S^{nS}_{t-1} > 0$, can be written in equality form as

$$S^{nS}_t = (1-d^n)S^{nS}_{t-1}\frac{N^S_{t-1}}{N^S_t} + k_3 x^{nS}_t + k_{3d}(S^{nN}_{t-1} - S^{nS}_{t-1})x^{nS}_t. \tag{A5.5}$$

We start from an annual law of motion of knowledge for the South where knowledge diffusion from the North is a function of both the knowledge gap $S^{nN}_{t-1} - S^{nS}_{t-1}$ inherited from the previous generation and the investment $\overline{w}\hat{x}^{nS}_t$ in knowledge in the South in that year, that is,

$$\hat{S}^{nS}_{t\tau} = (1-\hat{d}^n)\frac{\hat{N}^S_{t,\tau-1}}{\hat{N}^S_{t\tau}}\hat{S}^{nS}_{t,\tau-1} + \overline{w}x^{nS}_t$$
$$+\hat{\lambda}(1-\hat{d}^n)(S^{nN}_{t-1} - S^{nS}_{t-1})\overline{w}x^{nS}_t, \quad \tau = 1, \ldots, 25,$$

where we adopt the simplifying assumptions $\hat{N}_{t0}^{nS} = N_{t-1}^{nS}$ and, for $\tau \geq 1$, $\hat{N}_{t\tau}^{nS} = N_t^{nS}$ and, as before, $\hat{S}_{t0}^{nS} = S_{t-1}^{nS}$, $\hat{S}_{t,25}^{nS} = S_t^{nS}$. The iteration of (A5.5) gives

$$
\begin{aligned}
\hat{S}_{t1}^{nS} &= (1-\hat{d}^n)\frac{N_{t-1}^S}{N_t^S}S_{t-1}^{nS} + \overline{w}x_t^{nS} + \hat{\lambda}(1-\hat{d}^n)(S_{t-1}^{nN} - S_{t-1}^{nS})\overline{w}x_t^{nS};\\
\hat{S}_{t2}^{nS} &= (1-\hat{d}^n)\hat{S}_{t1}^{nS} + \overline{w}x_t^{nS} + \hat{\lambda}(1-\hat{d}^n)(S_{t-1}^{nN} - S_{t-1}^{nS})\overline{w}x_t^{nS}\\
&= (1-\hat{d}^n)\left[(1-\hat{d}^n)\frac{N_{t-1}^S}{N_t^S}S_{t-1}^{nS} + \overline{w}x_t^{nS} + \hat{\lambda}(1-\hat{d}^n)(S_{t-1}^{nN} - S_{t-1}^{nS})\overline{w}x_t^{nS}\right]\\
&\quad + \overline{w}x_t^{nS} + \hat{\lambda}(1-\hat{d}^n)(S_{t-1}^{nN} - S_{t-1}^{nS})\overline{w}x_t^{nS}\\
&= (1-\hat{d}^n)^2\frac{N_{t-1}^S}{N_t^S}S_{t-1}^{nS} + [(1-\hat{d}^n)+1]\overline{w}x_t^{nS} + \hat{\lambda}(1-\hat{d}^n)[(1-\hat{d}^n)+1]\\
&\quad (S_{t-1}^{nN} - S_{t-1}^{nS})\overline{w}x_t^{nS};
\end{aligned}
$$

. . .

$$
\begin{aligned}
\hat{S}_{t\tau}^{nS} &= (1-\hat{d}^n)^\tau\frac{N_{t-1}^S}{N_t^S}S_{t-1}^{nS} + \overline{w}x_t^{nS}\textstyle\sum_{\theta=0}^{\tau-1}(1-\hat{d}^n)^\theta\\
&\quad + \hat{\lambda}(S_{t-1}^{nN} - S_{t-1}^{nS})\overline{w}x_t^{nS}\textstyle\sum_{\theta=0}^{\tau-1}(1-\hat{d}^n)^\theta, \quad \tau = 1, \ldots, 25,
\end{aligned}
$$

. . .

$$
\begin{aligned}
S_t^{nS} \equiv \hat{S}_{t,25}^{nS} &= (1-\hat{d}^n)^{25}\frac{N_{t-1}^S}{N_t^S}S_{t-1}^{nS} + \overline{w}x_t^{nS}\sum_{\theta=0}^{24}(1-\hat{d}^n)^\theta\\
&\quad + \hat{\lambda}(S_{t-1}^{nN} - S_{t-1}^{nS})\overline{w}x_t^{nS}\sum_{\theta=0}^{24}(1-\hat{d}^n)^\theta\\
&= (1-\hat{d}^n)^{25}\frac{N_{t-1}^S}{N_t^S}S_{t-1}^{nS} + \frac{1-(1-\hat{d}^n)^{25}}{\hat{d}^n}\overline{w}x_t^{nS}\\
&\quad + \hat{\lambda}\frac{1-(1-\hat{d}^n)^{25}}{\hat{d}^n}(S_{t-1}^{nN} - S_{t-1}^{nS})\overline{w}x_t^{nS},
\end{aligned}
$$

which is (A5.5) for $1-d^n$ as given by (A5.3), k_3 as given by (A5.4), and for $k_{3d} = \hat{\lambda}k_3$.

A5.2. Optimization Program

Recall from (5.2) that $\hat{u}(c_t^J, x_t^{lJ}, S_t^{nJ}, S_t^m) := (c_t^J)^{\alpha_c}(x_t^{lJ})^{\alpha_l}(S_t^{nJ})^{\alpha_n}(\hat{S}^m - S_t^m)^{\alpha_m}$. Given the growth rate ρ and the emission-concentration path $\{(e_1, S_1^m), (e_2, S_2^m), (e^*, S^{m*})\}$, choose

$$S_1^{kN}, S_1^{kS}, S_2^{k}, S_1^{nN}, S_1^{nS}, S_2^{n}, i_1^N, i_1^S, i_2^N, i_2^S, c_1^N, c_1^S, c_2^N, c_2^S, e_1^N, e_1^S, e_2^N, e_2^S,$$
$$x_1^{lN}, x_1^{cN}, x_1^{eN}, x_1^{nN}, x_2^{lN}, x_2^{cN}, x_2^{nN}, x_2^{e}, x_1^{lS}, x_1^{cS}, x_1^{eS}, x_1^{nS}, x_2^{lS}, x_2^{cS}, x_2^{nS},$$
$$T_1, T_2, c_3, x_3^l \text{ and } S_3^n$$

in order to maximize Λ_2^S subject to:

$$\hat{u}(c_2^S, x_2^{lS}, S_2^n, S_2^m) - \Lambda_2^S \geq 0,$$

$$\left.\begin{aligned}
&\hat{u}(c_1^S, x_1^{lS}, S_1^{nS}, S_1^m) - (1+\rho)u_0^S \geq 0,\\
&\hat{u}(c_1^N, x_1^{lN}, S_1^{nN}, S_1^m) - (1+\rho)u_0^N \geq 0,\\
&\hat{u}(c_2^N, x_2^{lN}, S_2^n, S_2^m) - (1+\rho)\hat{u}(c_1^N, x_1^{lN}, S_1^{nN}, S_1^m) \geq 0,\\
&\hat{u}(c_3, x_3^l, S_3^n, S^{m*}) - (1+\rho)\hat{u}(c_2^N, x_2^{lN}, S_2^n, S_2^m) \geq 0,
\end{aligned}\right\}\text{utility growth,}$$

$$\left.\begin{aligned}
&(1-d^k)S_0^{kN}\frac{N_0^N}{N_1^N} + k_2 i_1^N - S_1^{kN} \geq 0,\\
&(1-d^k)S_1^{kN}\frac{N_1^N}{N_2^N} + k_2 i_2^N - S_2^k \geq 0,\\
&(1-d^k)S_0^{kS}\frac{N_0^S}{N_1^S} + k_2 i_1^S - S_1^{kS} \geq 0,\\
&(1-d^k)S_1^{kS}\frac{N_1^S}{N_2^S} + k_2 i_2^S - S_2^k \geq 0,
\end{aligned}\right\}\text{physical capital accumulation,}$$

$$\left.\begin{aligned}
&(1-d^n)S_0^{nS}\frac{N_0^S}{N_1^S} + k_3 x_1^{nS} + k_{3d}(S_0^{nN} - S_0^{nS})x_1^{nS} - S_1^{nS} \geq 0,\\
&(1-d^n)S_1^{nS}\frac{N_1^S}{N_2^S} + k_3 x_2^{nS} + k_{3d}(S_1^{nN} - S_1^{nS})x_2^{nS} - S_2^{nS} \geq 0,\\
&(1-d^n)S_0^{nN}\frac{N_0^N}{N_1^N} + k_3 x_1^{nN} - S_1^{nN} \geq 0,\\
&(1-d^n)S_1^{nN}\frac{N_1^N}{N_2^N} + k_3 x_2^{nN} - S_2^n \geq 0,
\end{aligned}\right\}\text{knowledge accumulation and diffusion,}$$

$$\left.\begin{array}{l}
\xi x_0^{eN}\dfrac{N_0^N}{N_1^N}-x_1^{lN}-x_1^{cN}-x_1^{eN}-x_1^{nN}\geq 0,\\
\xi x_1^{eN}\dfrac{N_1^N}{N_2^N}-x_2^{lN}-x_2^{cN}-x_2^{e}-x_2^{nN}\geq 0,\\
\xi x_0^{eS}\dfrac{N_0^S}{N_1^S}-x_1^{lS}-x_1^{cS}-x_1^{eS}-x_1^{nS}\geq 0,\\
\xi x_1^{eS}\dfrac{N_1^S}{N_2^S}-x_2^{lS}-x_2^{cS}-x_2^{e}-x_2^{nS}\geq 0,
\end{array}\right\}\text{human capital accumulation,}$$

$$\left.\begin{array}{l}
e_1^{*}-\dfrac{N_1^N}{N_1^N+N_1^S}e_1^N-\dfrac{N_1^S}{N_1^N+N_1^S}e_1^S\geq 0,\\
e_2^{*}-\dfrac{N_2^N}{N_2^N+N_2^S}e_2^N-\dfrac{N_2^S}{N_2^N+N_2^S}e_2^S\geq 0,
\end{array}\right\}\text{emissions,}^{1}$$

$$\left.\begin{array}{l}
-T_1+k_1\left(x_1^{cN}\right)^{\theta_c}\left(S_1^{kN}\right)^{\theta_k}\left(S_1^{nN}\right)^{\theta_n}\left(S_1^{m*}\right)^{\theta_m}\left(e_1^{N}\right)^{\theta_e}-c_1^N-i_1^N\geq 0,\\
-T_2+k_1\left(x_2^{cN}\right)^{\theta_c}\left(S_2^{k}\right)^{\theta_k}\left(S_2^{n}\right)^{\theta_n}\left(S_2^{m*}\right)^{\theta_m}\left(e_2^{N}\right)^{\theta_e}-c_2^N-i_2^N\geq 0,\\
T_1\dfrac{N_1^N}{N_1^S}+k_1\left(x_1^{cS}\right)^{\theta_c}\left(S_1^{kS}\right)^{\theta_k}\left(S_1^{nS}\right)^{\theta_n}\left(S_1^{m*}\right)^{\theta_m}\left(e_1^{S}\right)^{\theta_e}-c_1^S-i_1^S\geq 0,\\
T_2\dfrac{N_2^N}{N_2^S}+k_1\left(x_2^{cS}\right)^{\theta_c}\left(S_2^{k}\right)^{\theta_k}\left(S_2^{n}\right)^{\theta_n}\left(S_2^{m*}\right)^{\theta_m}\left(e_2^{S}\right)^{\theta_e}-c_2^S-i_2^S\geq 0,
\end{array}\right\}\text{output production, and}$$

$$\left.\begin{array}{l}
(x_2^e, S_2^k, S_2^n)\in\Gamma(\rho, e^*, S^{m*}),\\
S_3^n-(1+g)S_2^n\geq 0,\\
c_3-\gamma_1(\rho, e^*, S^{m*})\geq 0,\\
x_3^l-\gamma_2(\rho, e^*, S^{m*})\geq 0,
\end{array}\right\}\text{steady state,}^{2}$$

with initial conditions $(x_0^{eN}, S_0^{kN}, S_0^{nN})$, $(x_0^{eS}, S_0^{kS}, S_0^{nS})$, u_0^N, and u_0^S.

[1] For $t=1,2$, e_t^* denotes the average annual world emissions per capita of carbon dioxide (CO_2).

[2] The rate g is the generational rate of growth of economic variables, satisfying $1+\rho=(1+g)^{1-\alpha_m}$.

Because of the convergence of the economic stocks of North and South at $t=2$ and of flows at $t=3$, we use the notation $S_2^j := S_2^{jN} = S_2^{jS}$, $j=k, n$, $S_3^n := S_3^{nN} = S_3^{nS}$, $x_2^e := x_2^{eN} = x_2^{eS}$, $c_3 := c_3^N = c_3^S$, and $x_3^l := x_3^{lN} = x_3^{lS}$.

The last three inequalities, involving S_3^n, c_3, and x_3^l, require both regions to be in the steady state defined by the ray $\Gamma(\rho, e^*, S^{m^*})$ at the beginning of period three. Functions γ_1 and γ_2 are easily derived from theorem 3.1 and the Chapter 3 Appendix.

For $t=1, 2$, we denote by T_t the number of units of output per capita in the North that the North net exports to the South. A negative T_t indicates a net flow from South to North. We write the optimization program with T_1 and T_2 explicit, which are unconstrained in the exports-allowed regime. But if net exports are ruled out, then the constraints $T_1 = T_2 = 0$ are imposed.

A5.3. Transition Path When Maximizing the Utility of Generation 1 in the South

We have computed the optimal path for the maximization of the utility of Generation 1 in the South, the worst-off generation. Recalling from (5.2) that $\hat{u}(c_t^J, x_t^{lJ}, S_t^{nJ}, S_t^{m^*}) = (c_t^J)^{\alpha_c}(x_t^{lJ})^{\alpha_l}(S_t^{nJ})^{\alpha_n}(\hat{S}^m - S_t^{m^*})^{\alpha_m}$, the program is then:

maximize Λ_1^S subject to:

$$\hat{u}(c_1^S, x_1^{lS}, S_1^{nS}, S_1^{m^*}) \geq \Lambda_1^S,$$

$$\left.\begin{aligned}
&\hat{u}(c_2^S\ x_2^{lS}, S_2^n, S_2^{m^*}) \geq (1+\rho)u_1^S,\\
&\hat{u}(c_1^N, x_1^{lN}, S_1^{nN}, S_1^{m^*}) \geq (1+\rho)u_0^N,\\
&\hat{u}(c_2^N, x_2^{lN}, S_2^n, S_2^{m^*}) \geq (1+\rho)\hat{u}(c_1^N, x_1^{lN}, S_1^{nN}, S_1^{m^*}),\\
&\hat{u}(c_3, x_3^l, S_3^n, S^{m^*}) \geq (1+\rho)\hat{u}(c_2^N, x_2^{lN}, S_2^n, S_2^{m^*}),
\end{aligned}\right\}\text{utility growth,}$$

and the remaining economic and climate constraints in the optimization program of A5.2.

Figure A5.1 and Table A5.1 present the transition path for a 1% annual growth rate and compare it with the one obtained when maximizing the utility of Generation 2 in the South. The convergence of South and North

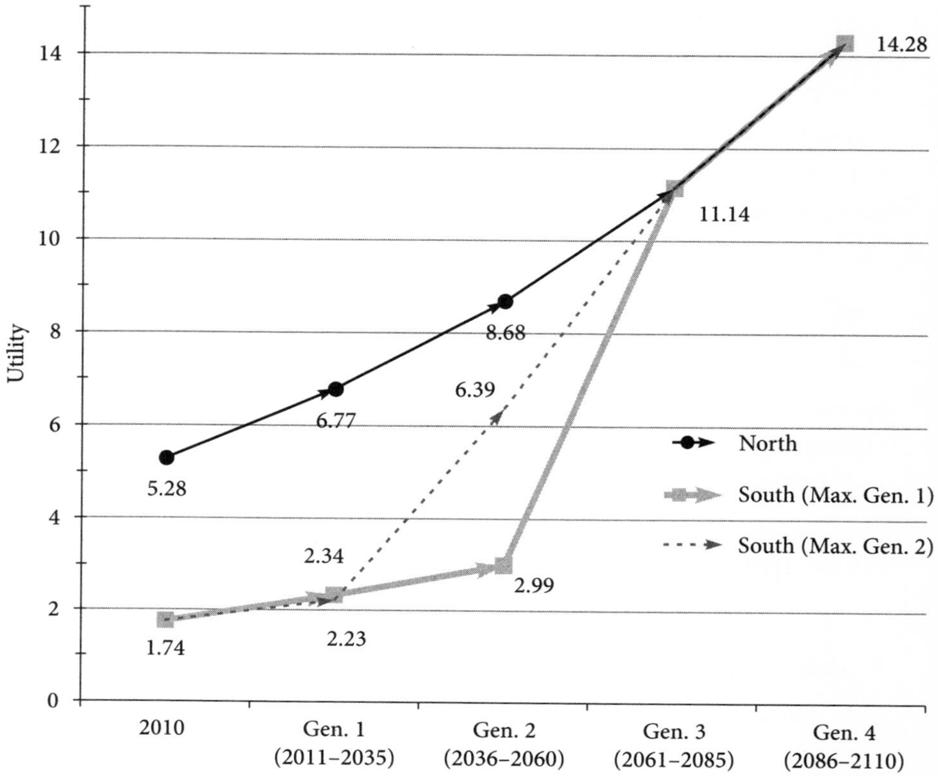

Figure A5.1. Optimal paths for the two optimization programs: maximizing the utility of the first or the second generation in the South. The solid grey line represents the utility of the South when optimizing for the first generation. The dashed line represents the utility of the South when optimizing for the second generation. The solid black line represents the utility of the North, which is the same for both optimization programs. Reprinted with kind permission of the publisher from Llavador et al. (2014), fig. 2. Copyright © Springer Science + Business Media Dordrecht 2014.

in Generation 3 is independent of the maximization program. Maximizing Generation 1's utility for a sustainable 1% annual growth rate implies a relatively small increase in the utility of Generation 1 (less than 5%), especially compared with the fall in the utility of Generation 2 (that is cut to less than one-half). This is the reason why we opted to maximize the utility of Generation 2 in the South, obtaining the smoother transition path, as represented by the dashed line path in Figure A5.1.

Table A5.1. Optimal paths when maximizing the utility of the first or the second generation in the South.

Utility paths for a 1% annual growth rate					
Gen.	$t=0$	$t=1$	$t=2$	$t=3$	$t=4$
Maximizing utility of Gen. 1 in South (MaxGen1)					
u_t^N	5.27979	6.77097	8.68331	11.1358	14.2808
u_t^S	1.73568	2.33513	2.99465	11.1358	14.2808
Maximizing utility of Gen. 2 in South (MaxGen2)					
u_t^N	5.27979	6.77097	8.68331	11.1358	14.2808
u_t^S	1.73568	2.22589	6.38636	11.1358	14.2808
Comparison: % change from MaxGen2 to MaxGen1					
$\frac{\text{MaxGen1} - \text{MaxGen2}}{\text{MaxGen1}}\%$	0.	4.68	−113.26	0.	0.

A5.4. The US–China Joint Announcement of November 2014

In November 2014, the United States and China made a joint announcement where they declared their intention to curb emissions during the coming decades. According to the White House press release, the United States intends "to achieve an economy-wide target of reducing its emissions by 26%–28% below its 2005 level in 2025 and to make best efforts to reduce its emissions by 80%. China intends to achieve the peaking of CO_2 emissions around 2030 and to make best efforts to peak early and to increase the share of non-fossil fuels in primary energy consumption to around 20% by 2030. Both sides intend to continue work to increase ambition over time" (The White House, Office of the Press Secretary, November 11, 2014).

How does our recommended emission path compare to these targets? Table A5.2 reports world emissions from the RCP2.6 path we have adopted and the allocation of these emissions between North and South according to our optimal path in Chapter 5. It also provides their variation with respect to 2005 values. According to our optimal path, the first generation in North (2011–2035) should reduce emissions by 11.2% below its 2005 values.

Table A5.2. CO2 emissions in GtC. The values between parentheses indicate the variation with respect to the 2005 level.

	2005	2010	2011–2035 (Generation 1)	2036–2060 (Generation 2)
World emissions	7.9299	9.042	8.152 (2.8%)	3.415 (−56.9%)
North	3.9490	3.861	3.506 (−11.2%)	0.313 (−92%)
South	3.9809	5.181	4.645 (16%)	3.102 (−22%)

Source for 2005 and 2010 data: World Resource Institute (2013).

This reduction is less than the United States's intended aim of 26–28%, but some qualifications must be mentioned. First, observe that our emissions are generational averages and refer to the entire North, a region in which the United States is a high emitter. Secondly, emissions on our path sharply decrease for the second generation. An earlier and further reduction in the US target, as announced in November 2014, would allow for a smoother transition to the drastic reduction in the second generation that our path requires.

CHAPTER SIX

Modeling Catastrophes: Two Extensions

6.1. Introduction

In Chapters 1, 2, and 4, we have referred to the formulation of catastrophe used in the *Stern Review*. This entails two assumptions: first, that there is a constant and exogenous probability of catastrophe, π, at each date, assuming that the catastrophe has not occurred earlier in history, and second, that catastrophe takes the form of the annihilation of the human species. Recall from Section 1.2 that, under these two assumptions, we were able to derive that a utilitarian von Neumann–Morgenstern (vNM) planner would maximize the discounted sum of generational utilities, where the discount factor is $1-\pi$. Both of these assumptions, however, must be viewed as made for purposes of simplifying the problem. First, for the problem of climate change, it is surely the case that the generational probability of catastrophe, or hazard rate, should depend upon the history of carbon emissions or on the concentration of carbon in the atmosphere.[1] That must be our concern here—not the probability that a meteor destroys

[1] Evidence suggests that Earth's climate system may shift abruptly in response to increasing carbon concentration (Alley et al. 2003; Lenton et al. 2008). Examples of abrupt, irreversible catastrophic events include the collapse of ice sheets (the 'albedo effect'), the death of the rain forest and its induced reduction of carbon capture, and the reinforced feedback by methane release from the tundra in the Arctic.

life on Earth, which might well be taken to be exogenous. Second, the annihilation of the species is a particularly severe form of catastrophe. More likely is that a catastrophe would take the form of reaching a 'tipping point' in atmospheric carbon concentration, above which human life would continue to exist but in a severely deteriorated environment.[2]

Both of these changes in the Stern assumptions on catastrophes—endogenizing the hazard rate and considering catastrophes other than species annihilation—complicate our analysis. It is obvious that the first change does. The second change complicates the analysis because it means we cannot truncate the sequence of utilities, disregarding human life after some finite date, but must continue to consider the welfare of humans after the catastrophe. Either of these changes in the Stern assumptions, for example, will make it the case that a utilitarian vNM planner would no longer maximize a discounted sum of utilities with a constant discount factor. So these more realistic assumptions will nullify the applicability of discounted utilitarianism to the analysis of climate change, even for utilitarians.

Likewise, either of these changes will require us to redo the sustainabilitarian analysis of optimization under uncertainty. This chapter begins such an analysis.

The chapter comprises two substantive sections and a short conclusion. In both sections, we work with the simplified model of Chapter 2, to which we now append equations relating the production of commodities to the probability of catastrophe. In Section 6.2 we compute characteristics of the optimal path of resource allocation using the 'Nehring' objective function that we introduced in Chapter 1, but we now assume that *the probability of catastrophe is endogenous* and depends upon atmospheric carbon concentration. (Section 6.2 maintains the notion that catastrophe entails the annihilation of the species.) The vNM utility function of the Ethical Observer in the Nehring formulation (recall equation (1.24)) is

$$W(u,T) = T \min_{1 \le t \le T} u_t, \tag{6.1}$$

[2] The distinction is relevant. In de Zeeuw and Zemel (2012), a 'doomsday event' (human annihilation) yields different policy implications than a catastrophic regime shift, even as the damage coefficient of the latter goes to infinity.

where $u = (u_1, u_2, \ldots)$ and (u, T) is the event that catastrophe occurs at date T along the chosen path u. The reason we employ the Nehring utility function here is that, when the hazard rate is endogenous, it is important that the Ethical Observer give weight to how long the species will last. With the pure-sustainability objective, this concern is immaterial (see the simplification theorem 2.9). We will expand upon this observation at the end of Section 6.2.

One of the model's ingredients that is necessary when we desire to endogenize the probability of catastrophe—which will depend upon emissions' behavior—is a 'hazard function' that relates that probability to the atmospheric concentration of carbon.[3] We adopt a very simple parametric form for it. The main result of Section 6.2 is that if the hazard rate increases sufficiently rapidly with carbon dioxide (CO_2) concentration, the optimal path requires us to cap concentration at a very low level.

Indeed, the strategy of Section 6.2 is similar to that of Weitzman (2012), who postulates a damage function and deduces the consequences for desirable limits on greenhouse gas (GHG) emissions. The details of our analysis are quite different from Weitzman's, but the conclusion is similar.

In Section 6.3 we alter the meaning of catastrophe: we now assume that catastrophe is of the tipping-point kind, which severely diminishes the quality of life on Earth but does not annihilate the species. For simplicity, we assume that population size is not an issue—the tipping point does not kill off a large section of the population; rather, life on Earth becomes more miserable for everyone (or for the representative household at each date). However, because this change in the model is complicated enough, we maintain the assumption of an exogenous and constant generational hazard rate of catastrophe, π. Clearly, a further step would be to endogenize π as well.

The mathematical complication that is introduced by endogenizing the hazard rates is that the optimization programs are no longer concave

[3] This hazard function is the composition of three component functions: the first relating GHG emissions to atmospheric carbon concentration (link [1] in Figure 4.1), the second relating concentration to climate (link [2]), and the third relating climate to the probability of species annihilation. The second and third functions, especially, are subject to large uncertainties.

programs.[4] Therefore, we are no longer guaranteed that a solution to the Kuhn-Tucker conditions implies optimality. More serious than this, perhaps, is the fact that the turnpike approach no longer works. We will explain this further.

6.2. Endogenizing the Probability of Catastrophe

We now append to the model of Chapter 2 two new equations:

$$S_t^m = (1-b)S_{t-1}^m + qy_t, \tag{6.2}$$

$$\pi_t = \psi(S_t^m), \tag{6.3}$$

where S_t^m is atmospheric carbon concentration at date t; π_t is the probability that catastrophe occurs at date t, if it has not occurred before, here called the *hazard rate at date t*; and y_t is production at date t; that is, $y_t = c_t + i_t$. Equation (6.2) is a simple linear law of motion of carbon concentration, where q is, roughly, the emissions-output ratio.[5] Equation (6.3) is the simplest possible form of hazard function, relating the hazard rate to current atmospheric carbon concentration (de Zeeuw and Zemel 2012).

We assume:

► **Assumption 6.1.** The hazard function ψ is defined as follows:

$$\psi(S^m) = \begin{cases} \pi_*, \text{ if } S^m \in [0, S_*^m] \\ a(S^m - S_*^m)^p + \pi_*, \text{ if } S_*^m \le S^m \le \bar{S}^m, \\ 1, \text{ if } S^m \ge \bar{S}^m \end{cases}$$

where π_* is a small positive number, and the parameters S_*^m and $\bar{S}^m$ satisfy $a(\bar{S}^m - S_*^m)^p = 1 - \pi_*$. We assume that $p > 1$, so ψ is a convex function on the domain where it is strictly increasing.

[4] Recall that a maximization program is concave if its objective function is a concave function and its constraint set is a convex set.

[5] Section A6.5 (resp. A6.6) in the Chapter 6 Appendix discusses the calibration of the parameters b and q (resp. the parameter k_4 in the production function).

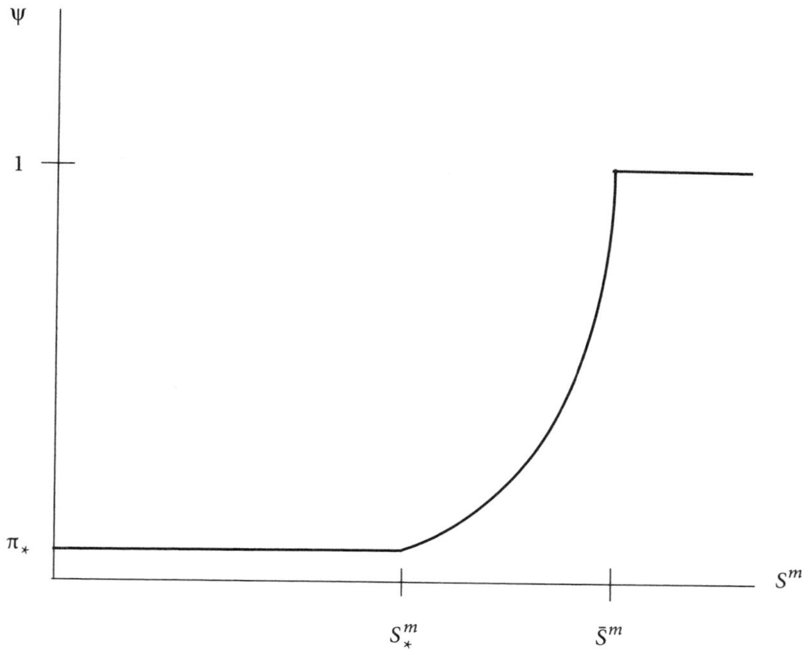

Figure 6.1. The hazard function ψ.

Figure 6.1 presents the graph of the function ψ.[6]

As we said, we call ψ the *hazard function* for this model. The value S^m_* is the atmospheric concentration of carbon below which the hazard rate does not increase above its baseline value of π_*: perhaps $S^m_* = 350$ ppm is a reasonable calibration. Assumption 6.1 says that, if concentration is below S^m_*, then increasing it has no effect on the probability of extinction, but after the critical value S^m_* is reached, the probability increases in an accelerating way with concentration.

Consider a path that generates hazard rates $(\pi_1, \pi_2, \ldots.)$ according to (6.2)—(6.3) where $\pi_t < 1$ for all t, and define the probability that catastrophe occurs at date T on this path as

[6] Van der Ploeg and de Zeeuw (2014) use a linear and a quartic hazard function with a similar structure.

$$R_T = \pi_T \prod_{t=1}^{T-1} (1-\pi_t), \text{ for } T > 1, \text{ where } R_1 = \pi_1.$$

We now write down the program with endogenous probabilities of catastrophe, which is analogous to program (2.5) of Chapter 2 for $\beta = 1$. This is the *Nehring sustainabilitarian program with endogenous probabilities of extinction.*

$$\max \sum_{t=1}^{\infty} R_t t \min\{u_1, \ldots, u_t\}$$

subject to, for all $t \geq 1$:

$$k_4 (S_t^k)^{\theta} (x_t^c)^{1-\theta} \geq c_t + i_t \equiv y_t,$$

$$i_t + (1-d) S_{t-1}^k \geq S_t^k,$$

$$\xi x_{t-1}^e \geq x_t^e + x_t^c + x_t^l,$$

$$c_t^{\alpha} (x_t^l)^{1-\alpha} \geq u_t,$$

$$\pi_t \geq \psi(S_t^m),$$

$$S_t^m \geq (1-b) S_{t-1}^m + q y_t,$$

with initial conditions (x_0^e, S_0^k, S_0^m). (6.4)

Program (6.4) is a simple integrated assessment model (IAM), with endogenous probabilities of catastrophe.

Our first task is to simplify the objective function, which requires:

▶ **Lemma 6.1.** *On any optimal path of program* (6.4), $\{u_t\}$ *is a weakly monotone decreasing sequence.*

▶ **Proof:** Chapter 6 Appendix.

The intuition of the proof is simple. If the path were at any date increasing in utility, it would be possible to transfer back some resources to increase the value of the program.

The lemma allows us to replace (6.4) with program (6.5), which is the analog of program (1.21).

$$\max \sum_{t=1}^{\infty} R_t t u_t$$

subject to, for all $t \geq 1$:

$$k_4 (S_t^k)^{\theta} (x_t^c)^{1-\theta} \geq c_t + i_t \equiv y_t,$$

$$i_t + (1-d) S_{t-1}^k \geq S_t^k,$$

$$\xi x_{t-1}^e \geq x_t^e + x_t^c + x_t^l,$$

$$u_t \geq u_{t+1},$$

$$c_t^{\alpha} (x_t^l)^{1-\alpha} \geq u_t,$$

$$\pi_t \geq \psi(S_t^m),$$

$$S_t^m \geq (1-b) S_{t-1}^m + q y_t,$$

$$\text{with initial conditions } (x_0^e, S_0^k, S_0^m). \tag{6.5}$$

Note the addition of the constraints restricting paths to ones upon which utility is weakly monotone decreasing.

Unfortunately, (6.5) is not a concave program because the functions R_t are not concave functions of the variables π_t, and in addition, ψ is not a convex function on its entire domain. Consequently, we cannot say that a solution of the Kuhn-Tucker conditions gives us the program's optimum. But perhaps more serious is the fact that, for reasonable parameter values and date-zero endowments, there is no optimal path that is a stationary state. This is demonstrated by showing that there is no stationary path that satisfies the Kuhn-Tucker conditions in the case when $S^m > S_*^m$. Consequently, we cannot use the methods that we have employed thus far in the book to calculate optimal paths.

The initial endowment vector of program (6.5) is (x_0^e, S_0^k, S_0^m); it comprises not only a stock of capital and adult teaching labor, as in Chapter 2, but also a stock of atmospheric carbon. We begin by showing a solution to (6.5) exists.

► **Proposition 6.2.** *If assumption* 6.1 *holds, then program* (6.5) *has a solution.*

▶ **Proof:**

1. Since we know that $\{u_t\}$ is a (weakly) decreasing sequence, and because u_1 is bounded above, to show a solution exists, it suffices to show that $\sum_1^\infty tR_t$ is bounded above. (We are assuming that the feasible set is closed in the appropriate topology, so the boundedness of the objective is what's important to guarantee a solution.)
2. We have:

$$\begin{aligned}\sum_1^\infty tR_t &= \pi_1 + 2\pi_2(1-\pi_1) + 3\pi_3(1-\pi_1)(1-\pi_2) + \cdots \\ &\leq \pi_1 + 2\pi_2(1-\pi_*) + 3\pi_3(1-\pi_*)^2 + \cdots \\ &< 1 + 2(1-\pi_*) + 3(1-\pi_*)^2 + \cdots \\ &= \frac{1}{\pi_*} + \frac{1-\pi_*}{\pi_*} + \frac{(1-\pi_*)^2}{\pi_*} + \cdots = \frac{1}{\pi_*^{\;2}}. \blacksquare\end{aligned}$$

The point of proposition 6.2 is that some restriction is needed to force the probabilities not to go to zero too fast or else the program need not have a solution. To see this, suppose we could generate a sequence of probabilities such that for some $\mu > 0$, $R_t = \frac{\mu}{t^2}$; indeed, we can choose μ so that $\sum_1^\infty R_t = 1$, because $\sum_1^\infty \frac{1}{t^2} < \infty$. In this case, we would have:

$$\sum_1^\infty tR_t = \mu \sum_1^\infty \frac{1}{t} = \infty.$$

This shows that some restriction is needed to guarantee boundedness of the program, and assumption 6.1 will do.

As we are unable to characterize the optimal solution to (6.5) analytically, we run simulations. We adopt the parameterization

$$\begin{aligned}&(\xi, \theta, \alpha, d, \delta, q, b, k_4, S_*^m) \\ &\quad = (41, 0.33, 0.33, 0.93, 0.00017, 0.2115, 0.4095, 18, 350)\end{aligned}$$

and we take the initial endowment vector to be $(x_0^e, S_0^k, S_0^m) = (0.072, 102, 390)$, which are realistic values for the US economy (see the calibration

Table 6.1. Values of variables along the approximate optimal path of program (6.5), (truncated at $T=4$) for $p=2$.

t	u	c	x^e	S^m	π
1	5.02869	29.8873	0.0773993	364.852	0.000172757
2	5.02869	29.9381	0.0797006	374.395	0.000177439
3	5.02869	31.0481	0.17934	384.076	0.000184515
4	5.02869	68.4666	2.94668×10^{-6}	1883.500	1.

of k_4, q, and b in the Chapter 6 Appendix). In addition, we parameterize the function ψ as $\psi(S)=\pi_*+a(S-S_*^m)^p$, where the preindustrial hazard rate is $\pi_*=0.00017$ per generation as we argued earlier. We initially let $p=2$ and then choose a so that the hazard would double to $2\pi_*$ if carbon concentration were 700 parts per million (ppm): this gives $a=1.25\times10^{-8}$.

We wish to understand the sensitivity of optimal carbon concentration to the value of p. For the purposes of simulation, we truncate program (6.5) at four generations. In particular, the optimal solution of the truncated program must then have $x_4^e=0$ and $\pi_4=1$. (There is no point in educating the youth in Generation 4, as they will never become adults, and the program should push the hazard rate to one on the last date: Generation 4 goes out in a blaze of glory.) In Table 6.1 we report values along the simulated optimal path for the four-generation problem with these parameter values.

We observe that generational utility is constant, that $x_4^e\approx0$ and that $\pi_4=1$. The most important observation for us is that, before the final date of Armageddon, S^m is in the region of 360 ppm to 380 ppm. The second column reports the computed value of the program. We will see below that the path reported in Table 6.1 is only approximately optimal.

Table 6.2 presents the results, for the variables of Generation 3, of computing optimal paths for the truncated program at $T=4$ for values of p running from 2.0 to 4.0.

In each of these simulations, utility is constant across all four generations, and the value of S^m is approximately constant for the first three generations, spiking at Generation 4. We see that the solutions are only approximate because the (true) value of the program must decrease as p increases, which does not occur in these simulations.[7] In all simulations, $x_4^e\approx0$ and $\pi_4=1$,

[7] Any path that is feasible for parameter value p is feasible for $p'<p$, as long as $S_t^m\geq351.0$, so the value of the program's value must be monotone decreasing in p.

Table 6.2. Changing parameter p: Approximate optimal values of some variables for Generation 3, for program (6.5) truncated at $T=4$

t	p	u	c	x^e	S^m	π	Value
3	2.0	5.02869	31.0481	0.179340	384.076	0.000184515	20.1094
3	2.2	5.02868	31.2148	0.192572	377.348	0.000188120	20.1093
3	2.4	5.02877	30.3222	0.097847	362.898	0.000175783	20.1099
3	2.6	5.02875	31.0472	0.116130	378.114	0.000243132	20.1094
3	2.8	5.02879	30.1024	0.080875	355.739	0.000171666	20.11
3	3.0	5.02879	29.9812	0.078522	353.826	0.000170700	20.11
3	3.2	5.02879	29.9622	0.077476	353.028	0.000170433	20.11
3	3.6	5.02879	29.8925	0.075351	352.109	0.000170183	20.11
3	4.0	5.02879	29.8890	0.075280	351.357	0.000170042	20.11

which are necessary conditions of the optimal path. What coincides with intuition is that the value of S^m on the optimal path, until the last date, is decreasing in p and gets close to 350 ppm. The hazard rate seems quite high at $p=2.6$, but this is probably because the program is not sufficiently near the global optimum in this case.

Despite the simplicity of the model and the first-stage calibration, we believe that the value of ξ is realistic and that the 'true' value of p may well lie in the interval that we have examined. Therefore, we suggest that the optimal value of carbon atmospheric concentration should not be far above 350 ppm when we endogenize the hazard rate. This finding is in line with recent literature showing that introducing uncertainty results in prudent behavior and a substantial reduction of emissions (Cai et al. 2013; de Zeeuw and Zemel 2012; Lemoine and Traeger 2014).

We return to justify why we adopted the Nehring objective function in this investigation rather than the sustainability objectives of Chapters 3 and 5. We indicated earlier that when the hazard rate is endogenous, it is important to use an objective function that gives value to the length of existence of the human species. Had we used the pure-sustainability objective with the associated vNM objective function for the Ethical Observer given by:

$$W^{Sus}(u,T)=\min_{1\le t\le T} u_t,$$

then she would be indifferent between a human species lasting one thousand generations, each enjoying a utility of one, and a species lasting one generation with a utility of one. It seems clear that the Ethical Observer would not care very much about keeping the hazard rate low. This problem does not afflict the pure-sustainability model when the hazard rate is exogenous, because, in that case, the Ethical Observer has no control over the length of species' life.

6.3. Optimal Paths When Catastrophe Does Not Eliminate the Human Species

We now assume that catastrophe, if it occurs, takes the form of severely diminishing production possibilities but does not destroy the species, or indeed, destroy anyone. It simply makes life miserable, brutish, and short. Because this model involves the complexity of introducing this amendment, we do not endogenize the probability of catastrophe but take it to be a constant, π, at each generation. In addition, we assume that catastrophe occurs, at most, once.

We assume that catastrophe takes the form of reducing the production function from $\hat{f}$ to $\lambda\hat{f}$, where λ is some (perhaps small) positive number less than one. After the catastrophe occurs, the new production function is $\lambda\hat{f}$ forever. Thus, if catastrophe occurs at date T, then the sustainabilitarian program to solve beginning at date T is:

$$
\begin{aligned}
&\max \Lambda \\
&\text{subject to:} \\
&(w_t) \quad c_t^{\alpha}(x_t^l)^{1-\alpha} \geq \Lambda, && t \geq T+1, \\
&(a_t) \quad \lambda k_4 (S_t^k)^{\theta}(x_t^c)^{1-\theta} \geq c_t + i_t, && t \geq T+1, \\
&(b_t) \quad (1-d)S_{t-1}^k + i_t \geq S_t^k, && t \geq T+1, \\
&(d_t) \quad \xi x_{t-1}^e \geq x_t^e + x_t^c + x_t^l, && t \geq T+1, \\
&\text{with initial conditions } (S_T^k, x_T^e).
\end{aligned}
\tag{6.6}
$$

We know the solution to this problem (see Chapter 1 and the Chapter 1 Appendix): it is a constant-utility path converging to a stationary state, where the endowments converge to a point on a ray in $\Re_+^2$. Let us denote this constant utility (i.e., the value of program (6.6)) as $Q(S_T^k, x_T^e)$. (Because λ is fixed, we do not write it as an argument of Q.)

In this section, we will study the sustainabilitarian optimization problem under the assumption that the probability of catastrophe at each date is exogenous and equal to π. The problem is, beginning at date zero:

$$
\begin{aligned}
&\max \Lambda \quad \text{subject to:}\\
&(r_1) \quad \pi Q(S_0^k, x_0^e) + (1-\pi)u(c_1, x_1^l) \geq \Lambda,\\
&(r_2) \quad \pi Q(S_0^k, x_0^e) + \pi(1-\pi)Q(S_1^k, x_1^e) + (1-\pi)^2 u(c_2, x_2^l) \geq \Lambda,\\
&\dots\\
&(r_t) \quad \pi Q(S_0^k, x_0^e) + \pi(1-\pi)Q(S_1^k, x_1^e) + \cdots\\
&\qquad + \pi(1-\pi)^{t-1}Q(S_{t-1}^k, x_{t-1}^e) + (1-\pi)^t u(c_t, x_t^l) \geq \Lambda,\\
&\dots\\
&(a_t) \quad k_4(S_t^k)^\theta (x_t^c)^{1-\theta} \geq c_t + i_t, \quad t \geq 1,\\
&(b_t) \quad (1-d)S_{t-1}^k + i_t \geq S_t^k, \quad t \geq 1,\\
&(d_t) \quad \xi x_{t-1}^e \geq x_t^e + x_t^c + x_t^l, \quad t \geq 1,\\
&\text{with initial conditions } (S_0^k, x_0^e).
\end{aligned}
\tag{6.7}
$$

Let us explain the constraints. The r_tth constraint says the expected utility of Generation t should be at least Λ. For instance, the r_1 constraint states that with probability π the catastrophe occurred at date one, in which case the utility of Generation 1 is just its utility on the path that is optimal under the deteriorated technology of program (6.6), and with probability $(1-\pi)$ the catastrophe did not occur, in which case the utility of Generation 1 is $\hat{u}(c_1, x_1^l)$. (We assume the catastrophe, if it occurs, does so at the start of a generation.) The constraint r_2 looks at three possible events: that the catastrophe occurred at date one, that it occurred at date two, or that it did not occur at either date. In the first case, the utility of Generation 2 will be $Q(S_0^k, x_0^e)$ because we know utilities on the optimal path of (6.6) are constant. The rest of the inequality should be clear. Thus, the program says: maximize the value of the *expected utilities* of all generations that can be sustained forever, subject to the laws of motion of capital and education. Note that in the (a_t) constraints, it is the *good* production function $(\hat{f})$ that is used, because we are choosing the path in the case in which the catastrophe has not occurred. We know what the path looks like once the catastrophe occurs.

Program (6.7) is concave, so that to solve it, it suffices to solve the Kuhn-Tucker conditions. We prove:

▶ **Theorem 6.3.** *Given* $(S_0^k, x_0^e) \in \Gamma(0)$. *If* $0 < K(\nu) < 1 - \pi$, *the solution to program* (6.7) *is a path where all variables increase geometrically, given by*

$$(S_t^k, x_t^e, x_t^c, x_t^l, c_t, i_t) = (\nu^t S_0^k, \nu^t x_0^e, \nu^{t-1} x_1^c, \nu^{t-1} x_1^l, \nu^{t-1} c_1, \nu^{t-1} i_1),$$

where $(x_1^c, x_1^l, c_1, i_1, \nu)$ *solves the five equations comprising* (A6.3)–(A6.5), (A6.6), *and* (A6.7). *The value* $Q(S_0^k, x_0^e)$ *is a function of* λ *and the ray* $\Gamma(0)$. *The value of* ν *is greater than* 1 *and is an increasing, convex function of* π.[8]

We will prove the last sentence in the theorem here, while the rest of the proof is found in the Chapter 6 Appendix. As π approaches 0, the value of Λ must approach the utility in the stationary solution when there is no uncertainty. Let $\Lambda(0)$ denote that utility, and suppose that $Q(S_0^k, x_0^e) = \tau\Lambda(0)$, for some $\tau < 1$. Since we know (from the first part of theorem 6.3) that $(S_t^k, x_t^e) = \nu^t (S_0^k, x_0^e)$, it follows that $Q(S_t^k, x_t^e) = \nu^t Q(S_0^k, x_0^e)$. Hence we may write the r_tth constraint of program (6.7) as:

$$\sum_{t=1}^{T} \pi(1-\pi)^{t-1} \nu^{t-1} Q(S_0^k, x_0^e) + (1-\pi)^T \nu^{T-1} u(c_1, x_1^l) = \Lambda. \qquad (6.8)$$

It follows that $(1-\pi)\nu < 1$, for otherwise, the left-hand side of (6.8) would diverge as t becomes large. Therefore, in the limit as $T \to \infty$, the last term on the left-hand side of (6.8) goes to 0 and we have:

$$\sum_{t=1}^{\infty} \pi(1-\pi)^{t-1} \nu^{t-1} Q(S_0^k, x_0^e) = \Lambda,$$

[8] The definition of $K(\cdot)$ and equations (A6.3)–(A6.5), (A6.6), and (A6.7) are provided in the proof (see the Chapter 6 Appendix).

which can be written:

$$\frac{\pi Q(S_0^k, x_0^e)}{1-(1-\pi)\nu} = \Lambda.$$

Finally, define τ by $Q(S_0^k, x_0^e) = \tau\Lambda$; τ is less than 1. Then the last equation becomes:

$$\frac{\pi\tau}{1-(1-\pi)\nu} = 1,$$

from which we have, writing ν as a function of π:

$$\nu(\pi) = \frac{1-\tau\pi}{1-\pi},$$

showing, as claimed, that $\nu > 1$. It immediately follows that ν is an increasing, convex function of π, and that ν is a linear, decreasing function of τ.

These facts make sense and allow us to interpret the optimal path as one on which endowments increase, for as long as the tipping point has not occurred, in order to provide insurance for those who live after the tipping point. For the larger the endowment (S_T^k, x_T^e) when the tipping point occurs at date T, the better off will be the generations who live afterward. The rate (ν) at which the insurance builds up is greater, the larger the hazard rate, and of course, it is also greater, the smaller is λ (because λ and τ move together).

Let us note that were we to attempt to endogenize the hazard rate in this model, we would have to complicate the model further because increasing production geometrically would lead, in the economy of Section 6.2, to very high emissions and hazard rates. That is to say, endogenizing the hazard rate in this model would require also introducing technological change that would reduce the emissions-output ratio over time. It is not clear in the present model (with endogenous hazard rates) that there is an optimal stationary state. How to generalize the present model in that way remains an open question.

6.4. Remarks and Conclusion

We have attempted, in this chapter, to begin a more subtle analysis of catastrophe and its probability in the context of a sustainabilitarian ethic. One of the weak points in much formal climate-change analysis is that the probability of species extinction is taken to be exogenous. Obviously, this is a bit like looking for the lost jewel under the street lamp: taking the hazard rate of species extinction to be exogenous to the emissions process immensely simplifies the analysis, but it deprives it of much of its interest because we are deeply concerned with how our actions affect the probability of catastrophe. In Section 6.2 we endogenized the probability of extinction, making it depend on emissions.

Our hazard function relates the atmospheric carbon concentration to the probability that the human species disappears. We assumed a particular hazard function that is increasing and convex over the relevant interval of atmospheric carbon concentration.

We adopted the Nehring objective function in this analysis because it endows the Ethical Observer with a concern for the length of species' lifetime, as well as for the sustainable level of welfare. We explained why this is important to do in a model in which the hazard rate is endogenous. We showed by simulation that if the hazard function increases rapidly enough, then the optimal path of the model requires that atmospheric carbon concentration be maintained very close to a level at which the hazard rate is insensitive to concentration (S_*^m). We take this to be the main policy-relevant result of this chapter.

In Section 6.2 we assumed that catastrophe means the extinction of the human species. But this is only the most extreme form that catastrophe might take. More likely is the possibility that large carbon concentrations will induce a tipping point, which changes the laws of motion of physical and economic variables in a discontinuous way. In Section 6.3 we chose to model this idea very simply by assuming that catastrophe means a sharp reduction in the production function: inputs that before could produce one unit of the commodity could, post-catastrophe, produce only λ units, for some small positive value of λ. In this section we analyzed the optimization problem only when the hazard rate π is constant and exogenous. We assumed the sustainabilitarian Ethical Observer's objective is to maximize the value of *expected utility* that can be guaranteed to all generations. We showed that the optimal path was one that increased the social endowments of skilled labor and capital geometrically over time, with the rate of increase being an increasing, convex function of the (exogenous) probability of catastrophe. In other words, early generations should save for the future, in effect insuring generations living after the catastrophe occurs. The behavior of this path is to be contrasted with the stationary-state path, which is optimal in the absence of any probability of catastrophe. This result is also relevant for policy, although its relevance is limited by the assumption that the probability of catastrophe is exogenous and fixed.

APPENDIX 6. PROOFS AND CALIBRATION

A6.1. Proof of Lemma 6.1

Suppose the claim were false. Let T be the first date at which $u_T > u_{T-1}$ on an optimal path. Since $u_T > 0$ (because $u_{T-1} \geq 0$) it follows that $x^e_{T-1} > 0$ and $x^l_T > 0$. For if either inequality were false, then $u_T = 0$. We now have two cases:

▶ Case 1

$$u_{T-2} > u_{T-1}$$

The $(T-1)$th and Tth terms of the objective function in question can then be written:

$$R_{T-1}(T-1)u_{T-1} + R_T T u_{T-1}.$$

Now reduce x^e_{T-1} by a small positive amount ε_1, adding this amount to x^l_{T-1}, thus increasing u_{T-1} by a small amount δ_1. We must increase x^e_T by a small amount so that the endowment vector for Generation $T+1$ remains unchanged. The consequence will be to reduce u_T by a small amount δ_2, and this can be done so that $u_T - \delta_2 > u_{T-1} + \delta_1$ and $u_{T-1} + \delta_1 < u_{T-2}$. It follows that the value of the objective function will increase by at least $(R_{T-1}(T-1) + R_T T)\delta_1$, a contradiction to the assumption that the original path was optimal.

▶ Case 2

$$u_{T-2} = u_{T-1}$$

In this case we must reduce both x^e_{T-1} and x^e_{T-2} by small amounts, transferring labor to x^l_{T-1} and x^l_{T-2}, thus increasing u_{T-1} and u_{T-2} by small amounts and decreasing u_T by a small amount. If $u_{T-3} > u_{T-2}$, this will increase the value of the objective function, a contradiction. If $u_{T-3}=u_{T-2}$, then we have to continue iterating this process. By induction, we derive the lemma claim. ■

A6.2. Proof of Theorem 6.3

The dual Kuhn-Tucker conditions for program (6.7) are as follows:

$$(\partial\Lambda) \quad 1=\sum_{1}^{\infty} r_t,$$

$$(\partial c_t) \quad r_t(1-\pi)^t \alpha \frac{u[t]}{c_t}=a_t \quad t\geq 1,$$

$$(\partial i_t) \quad a_t=b_t \quad t\geq 1,$$

$$(\partial S_t) \quad a_t f_1[t]-b_t+(1-d)b_{t+1}+\sum_{j=t+1}^{\infty} r_j \pi(1-\pi)^t Q_1(S_t^k, x_t^e)=0 \quad t\geq 1,$$

$$(\partial x_t^e) \quad \sum_{j=t+1}^{\infty} r_j \pi(1-\pi)^t Q_2(S_t^k, x_t^e)-d_t+\xi d_{t+1}=0 \quad t\geq 1,$$

$$(\partial x_t^c) \quad a_t f_2[t]=d_t \quad t\geq 1,$$

$$(\partial x_t^l) \quad r_t(1-\pi)^t \frac{(1-\alpha)u[t]}{x_t^l}=d_t \quad t\geq 1.$$

(Q_i denotes the ith first-order partial derivative of Q, for $i=1, 2$; f_i is the ith first-order partial derivative of the production function; and $u[t]$ is the utility of Generation t in the case when the catastrophe has not occurred by date t.)

We shall try for a solution of the following sort. We assume that we begin with $(S_0^k, x_0^e)\in\Gamma(0)$: that is, the initial endowment lies on the turnpike for the economy with the good technology, $\hat{f}$. In the solution we conjecture, the endowment grows (or shrinks) by a constant factor, ν, per generation, for as long as the catastrophe does not hit. Thus, we will look for a solution where $(S_t^k, x_t^e)=\nu^t(S_0^k, x_0^e)$ for all $t\geq 1$. Since the program (6.7) with the bad technology enjoys constant returns, we therefore will have $Q(S_t^k, x_t^e)=\nu^t Q(S_0^k, x_0^e)$, and $Q_1(S_t^k, x_t^e)=q_1$ and $Q_2(S_t^k, x_t^e)=q_2$. These derivatives, q_i, are functions of the path $\Gamma(0)$.

We will further conjecture that, at the solution, all the constraints of (6.7) bind. This allows us to solve for $u[t]$ as follows. Consider the r_tth primal constraint. It can be written:

$$Q(S_0^k, x_0^e)(\pi + \pi(1-\pi)\nu + \cdots + \pi(1-\pi)^{t-1}\nu^{t-1}) + (1-\pi)^t u[t] = \Lambda,$$

or:

$$Q[0]\pi\frac{(1-(1-\pi)^t \nu^t)}{1-(1-\pi)\nu} + (1-\pi)^t u[t] = \Lambda. \tag{A6.1}$$

This can hold for all t only if the terms involving $(1-\pi)^t$ annihilate each other; that is, if:

$$u[t] = \frac{\pi Q[0]\nu^t}{1-(1-\pi)\nu},$$

and it further follows from (A6.1) that:

$$\Lambda = \frac{\pi Q[0]}{1-(1-\pi)\nu}.$$

Note that the value of Λ is only defined if $\pi > 0$; if $\pi = 0$, we know the solution to the program is the value of utility on the stationary path associated with the turnpike $\Gamma(0)$. We will use this fact later in the analysis.

Along the path we are searching for, S_t^k grows by the factor ν, and so investment is given by:

$$i_t = \nu^{t-1} S_0^k(\nu - (1-d)),$$

Because x_t^e grows by the factor ν, we have:

$$(\xi - \nu)x_0^e = x_1^c + x_1^l.$$

We will look for a solution where $x_t^c = \nu^{t-1} x_1^c$ and $x_t^l = \nu^{t-1} x_t^l$. The primal constraints (a_t) tell us that

$$c_t + \nu^{t-1} S_0^k(\nu - (1-d)) = \nu^{t-1}\hat{f}(\nu S_0^k, x_1^c),$$

and so $c_t = \nu^{t-1} c_1$. Thus, we can summarize the primal constraints as:

$$i_1 = S_0^k(\nu - 1 + d),$$

$$(\xi - \nu)x_0^e = x_1^c + x_1^l,$$

$$c_1 + i_1 = \hat{f}(\nu S_0^k, x_1^c),$$

plus the fact that all primal variables grow by the factor ν. These equations comprise three equations in five unknowns, so we will need to derive two equations in the primal variables from the dual conditions to solve the problem. Using the (∂c_t), (∂x_t^l), and (∂x_t^c) equations we derive:

$$\frac{1-\alpha}{\alpha} = \frac{x_1^l}{c_1}\hat{f}_2(\nu S_0^k, x_1^c),$$

Using, in addition, the fact that $f_2[t]$ is constant since $\hat{f}$, is homogeneous of degree one. This is one of our two missing equations.

Next, write $R_t = \pi(1-\pi)^t \sum_{j=t+1}^{\infty} r_j$. Then the (∂S_t) and (∂x_t^e) constraints can be written as:

$$R_t q_2 = \hat{f}_2(\nu S_0^k, x_1^c)(b_t - \xi b_{t+1}),$$
$$R_t q_1 = b_t(1 - \hat{f}_1(\nu S_0^k, x_1^c)) - (1-d)b_{t+1},$$

and so, eliminating R_t, we have:

$$b_{t+1} = K(\nu)\, b_t, \text{ where } K(\nu) = \frac{q_2(1-\hat{f}_1(\nu S_0^k, x_1^c)) - q_1 \hat{f}_2(\nu S_0^k, x_1^c)}{q_2(1-d) - q_1 \xi \hat{f}_2(\nu S_0^k, x_1^c)},$$

from which it follows that:

$$b_t = b_1(K(\nu))^{t-1}, \text{ for } t \geq 1. \quad \text{(A6.3)}$$

We note in passing that for the sequence $\{b_t\}$ to be nonnegative, we require:

$$\operatorname{sgn} K(\nu) > 0. \quad \text{(A6.4)}$$

Now from the (∂c_t) and (∂i_t) constraints, we can write:

$$r_t = \frac{b_1 c_1}{\alpha u[1](1-\pi)}\left(\frac{K(\nu)}{1-\pi}\right)^{t-1}; \quad \text{(A6.5)}$$

using the $(\partial\Lambda)$ constraint, we sum (A6.4) over all t, arriving at an equation that can be solved for b_1:

$$1=\frac{b_1 c_1}{\alpha u[1](1-\pi)}\frac{1}{1-\left(\frac{K(\nu)}{1-\pi}\right)}, \tag{A6.6}$$

an infinite summation that holds as long as:

$$K(\nu)<1-\pi.$$

Nonnegative values for all the Lagrangian multipliers now follow immediately from (A6.1). The fifth equation in the unknowns that we need may be taken to be (A6.2), which we write out as:

$$c_1^{\alpha}(x_1^{l})^{1-\alpha}=\frac{\pi Q[0]\nu}{1-(1-\pi)\nu}. \tag{A6.7}$$

We have now proved theorem 6.3, except for that claim that $\nu>1$.

The function Q is difficult to compute because it is difficult to characterize the value of the SUS program when we begin off the stationary-state ray for the economy with technology $\lambda\hat{f}$. This is because the stationary-state ray for the $\lambda\hat{f}$ technology is not the same as the ray for the $\hat{f}$ technology ($\Gamma(0)$). (We do not reproduce the calculation that shows this here.) We could approximate the function Q numerically, using the technique of forcing convergence to the new ray in several periods—that is, by mimicking the computational method we used in Chapter 3.

The proof that ν is an increasing, convex function of π and is greater than one is provided after the statement of the theorem in the text in Section 6.3. ■

A6.3. Calibration of b and q in $S_t^m=(1-b)S_{t-1}^m+qy$

Observe that units and time reference are important.

(1) Estimation of q.

a. Denote by Θ the airborne fraction: the percentage of anthropogenic emissions of carbon dioxide (CO_2) that stays in the atmosphere. $\Theta = 0.45$ (the remaining 55% is taken up within a year by forests and oceans). http://en.wikipedia.org/wiki/Airborne_fraction

b. Denote by $Q = \frac{e_t}{y_t}$ the carbon intensity. Take $Q = 0.47$ tCO_2 per thousand in year 2005 US dollars, as the average 2000–2011 for the United States (US Energy Information Administration).[9] This value is similar for the world economy (0.48) and a bit lower (0.39) for the Organisation for Economic Co-operation and Development (OECD), using purchasing power parity (PPP).

c. Hence, $q = \Theta Q = 0.45 \times 0.47 = 0.2115$ tCO_2 per thousand 2005 US dollars.

(2) Estimation of b.

a. Let $1 - \tilde{b} = 0.81$ (this is ϕ_{11} from DICE-2007, representing the direct decay of CO_2 in the atmosphere after a decade). Because it is measured in decades, $0.81 \equiv 1 - \tilde{b} = (1 - \hat{b})^{10}$, where $\hat{b}$ is the annual rate of regeneration, and so $\hat{b} = 1 - 0.81^{1/10} = 0.02085$.[10] But for us, a generation is twenty-five years, so $1 - b = (1 - \hat{b})^{25} = 0.4095$.

Summarizing:

$q = 0.2115$ tCO_2 per thousand in year 2005 US dollars, and

$b = 0.4095$ represents the generational decay of CO_2 in the atmosphere.

A6.4. Calibration of k_4 in the Production Function $y = k_4 (S^k)^{\theta} (x^c)^{1-\theta}$

Per capita US output in 2010 was $y = 46.179$, in thousand 2010 US dollars. The stock of capital (S^k) was 101.572 thousand 2010 US dollars,

---

[9] http://www.eia.gov/cfapps/ipdbproject/iedindex3.cfm?tid=91&pid=46&aid=31&cid=ww,CG5,&syid=2000&eyid=2011&unit=MTCDPUSD.

[10] In DICE2013, the value of ϕ_{11} is revised to 0.912, which would imply a value of $b = 1 - 0.912^{1/10} = 0.00917$.

and total efficiency units of labor per capita were 2.171 (in 1950 efficiency units). About 18.3% of total labor was not expended in leisure or in the knowledge and education sectors; thus, suppose that total labor in the production sector of the model is $0.183 \times 2.171 = 0.397$. This gives a value of $k_4 \approx 18$.

Conclusion

Our task has been to argue for an application of egalitarian principles to guide our response to climate change induced by greenhouse gas (GHG) emissions. Those principles apply both to an intergenerational human society, in which we seek equality among generations, and to the interregional society, in which we seek equality between regions and nations at a point in time.

Sustainability is the application of the egalitarian principle to intergenerational society: every generation has a right to the highest level of welfare that is feasible for all to enjoy. We extend the unidirectional sustainability of Robert Solow—that each generation should be at least as well off as the previous one—to bidirectionality, that each early generation has a *right* to be as well off as each later one as well. If this right were to be implemented, then there would be no growth, no human development over time. But because humans desire such development, they will not enforce this *right* and will agree to curtail their current welfare, to some extent, in order to permit human development and growth. This gives rise to our advocacy of growth sustainability: to find the feasible path that guarantees (assuming, for the moment, certainty) a given rate of growth of welfare from each generation to the next. The precise value of that rate will be determined by preferences—that is, by how much we desire to sacrifice for the sake of human development.

We contrasted our ethical view with its ubiquitous contender, utilitarianism. Our major objection to utilitarianism is its *inegalitarianism*. Because of the possibility of technological development, an Ethical Observer who wishes to maximize the sum of utilities of all generations will find it attractive to develop great technological prowess in the future through early investment, saving the human species' consumption for later dates when resources will be able, by virtue of that technological prowess, to produce utility very efficiently. The central idea of utilitarianism is to ignore the boundaries between persons; to view the human collectivity as a sink into which one pours as much 'utility' as the sink will hold, without regard to its distribution among the sink's constituent parts (individuals). Technological innovation can turn later generations into 'utility monsters,' who would claim the lion's share of resources under this utilitarian logic.

Utilitarians attempt to overcome this problem in two ways: by discounting future utilities and by adopting strictly concave utility functions of consumption so that the payoff to injecting huge consumptions into future generations has diminishing returns. But these solutions are ad hoc: why not adopt, from the beginning, an ethic that *builds in* equality between individuals, rather than attempting to coax it out through these Rube Goldberg devices?

Indeed, evidently, large numbers of people who are not trained economists find the idea of sustainability entirely natural. It has become the catchword of the environmental movement. We think economics, in this instance, is limited by its history, one in which researchers have relied on discounted-utilitarian models for many years, feel comfortable with them, and have developed techniques for analyzing them. We hope to have shown that it is not so costly to give up these old habits. We can develop a calculus of sustainability.

One great advantage of the mathematics of sustainability, in contrast to the mathematics of utilitarianism, is that maximizing a sustainabilitarian objective function (whether it be of the pure or growth or Nehring variety) always yields a solution. The sustainabilitarian programs never diverge. Because of this, one need not restrict oneself to utility functions that are sufficiently concave that utilitarian programs will converge. In particular, we have used a constant-returns Cobb-Douglas utility function throughout. But with a Cobb-Douglas utility function and production functions enjoying constant or increasing returns to scale, utilitarian programs, unless severely discounted, will diverge.

In one aspect, our aims have been more modest than those of authors of integrated assessment models (IAMs), such as William Nordhaus. A full specification of the optimization problem would require that we optimize over the path of carbon emissions as well as over all other economic variables. Because the quantification of the effects of temperature increases on human welfare is highly uncertain, we have not attempted to endogenize an optimal path for global GHG emissions and concentrations, except for the brief excursion in Section 6.2, when we studied the problem of endogenizing the hazard rate of catastrophe. Instead, we adopted an off-the-shelf low-emissions path prescribed by the RCP2.6, aimed at stabilizing a long-run temperature increase at 2°C. We constrained carbon concentration to follow a path that converges to a concentration of carbon of approximately 450 parts per million (ppm) in seventy-five years (three generations of our model).

On the other hand, our models are more highly articulated in other dimensions than most of the IAM models: we put great stress on education—both for its importance in production and in improving the human condition—and on the creation of new knowledge.

Of course, it is perfectly possible to append to our models a climate module, making them into full IAMs, and we invite other researchers to do so.

The main policy conclusions of our analysis are as follows.

(1) It is feasible, in the sense of satisfying all technological and resource constraints, to indefinitely maintain modest growth rates in human welfare, namely of about 1% per year in the global North and greater in the global South, while keeping the long-run temperature increase at 2°C.
(2) Given these constraints, it is feasible for the significant parts of the global South to attain the standard of living of the global North in three generations.
(3) But there is no politically feasible (global) solution to the climate-change problem unless international negotiators recognize the connection between restricting emissions and curbing growth.

Economic growth and sharing the climate burden must be simultaneously addressed in the international bargaining venues.

(4) Preserving the date at which countries like China will converge to the North in income per capita may provide an effective focal point for reaching a negotiated agreement. This embodies a concept of fairness quite different from the ones in which the allocation of emissions is separated from growth considerations. While we see the eventual convergence of the global South to the North in welfare as a desideratum of egalitarianism, we propose that maintaining the date of convergence may offer the only politically acceptable solution to that bargaining problem.

(5) Investment in education should rise well beyond current levels, both in the transition to convergence and in the more distant future.

(6) A larger fraction of resources should be allocated to the production of knowledge, which directly affects welfare levels in addition to igniting technological progress.

(7) The price of carbon should be substantially higher than what has been observed in recent permit markets.

(8) If the rate at which the probability of catastrophe increases with atmospheric carbon concentration is above a bound that can be calculated, then we should limit that concentration to a low level that also can be calculated.

We close with a remark on the level of abstraction adopted in this book. Our view is that a major weakness in the economics of climate-change analysis has been the insufficient thought that writers have given to the ethical issues. As we have discussed, this has led William Nordhaus, on the one hand, to adopt discount rates for his optimization program that are deduced to be those of contemporary savers and investors, and this has led Nicholas Stern, on the other hand, to adopt a utilitarian objective function. Neither of these moves stands up to our ethical analysis. Despite the bromides that we hear so often in the academy advocating interdisciplinary analysis, the plea has not penetrated this area, critical as it is for the future of our species.

Because our intent has been to focus on the big question, which is how GHG emissions should be allocated across regions of the world and generations of humans, we have ignored a deeper microanalysis entailing the discussion of possibilities for clean energy as well as details of how the allocation of emissions could be implemented regionally through either carbon taxes or cap-and-trade regimes. Naturally, these are critical areas for economic analysis, but they are not the *most* critical, or so we believe. It seems that getting the desired path of GHG emissions right, defined across regions and time, must come first.

Or, perhaps this posture is too dogmatic. Perhaps the momentum that would lead to addressing the problem in an explicit global context will come from initiatives at the local level: in the United States, California is setting an example, despite the gridlock in the US Congress, and there are many examples internationally. After all, China succeeded in extricating hundreds of millions from poverty not with a grand plan, but by "crossing the river while feeling for stones."[1] We remain open-minded.

[1] Deng Xiaoping.

Appendix A: Calibration

Appendix B: *Mathematica* Code

References

Index

APPENDIX A

Calibration

A.1. Data and Calibration Procedures

This appendix provides the information for the calibration of the models in Chapters 3 and 5. We interpret that generations live for twenty-five years. For the calibration, flow variables are typically defined as per-year averages, and it is understood that stocks are located in the last year of life of a generation.

Chapter 3 depicts a one-region world, calibrated to US data. Chapter 5 partitions the world into two regions, North and South, following the United Nations classification of 'more developed regions' (Europe, Northern America, Australia/New Zealand, and Japan) and 'less developed regions' (Africa, Asia [excluding Japan], Latin America and the Caribbean plus Melanesia, Micronesia, and Polynesia). The North is calibrated after the United States and the South after China. Hence, the North and the one-region world share the parameters for the utility function, for the output and education production functions, and for the law of motion for physical capital and knowledge, as well as the per capita values of the economic stocks and flows for the benchmark 2010 year.

A.2. Values

The precise definitions of parameters and initial values are provided in Sections A.3 and A.4 following. Details for the calibration and source

Table A.1. Calibrated parameter values.

Parameter	Value	Parameter	Value
α_c	0.318	ξ	41.434
α_l	0.636	d^k	0.787
α_n	0.017	d^n	0.787
α_m	0.028	$\hat{S}^m$	1,249.090
k_1	15.992	θ_c	0.670
k_2	13.118	θ_k	0.284
k_3	558.309	θ_n	0.046
k_{3d}	5.583	θ_e	0.081
$\hat{\lambda}$	0.010	θ_m	−0.036

Table A.2. Initial values of stocks in the reference year (2010).

Stocks	Value	Units
S_0^{kN}	104.948	thousands of 2010 international dollars per capita
S_0^{kS}	33.292	thousands of 2010 international dollars per capita
S_0^{nN}	26.953	thousands of 2010 international dollars per capita
S_0^{nS}	0.837	thousands of 2010 international dollars per capita
S_0^m	390.430	ppm
x_0^{eN}	0.072	US 1950 efficiency units per capita
x_0^{eS}	0.028	US 1950 efficiency units per capita

Table A.3. Initial values of the flows in the reference year (2010).

Flows	Value	Units
c_0^N	40.965	thousands of 2010 international dollars per capita
c_0^S	4.280	thousands of 2010 international dollars per capita
i_0^N	6.854	thousands of 2010 international dollars per capita
i_0^S	4.280	thousands of 2010 international dollars per capita
e_0^N	3.112	tC per capita
e_0^S	0.913	tC per capita

of the parameter values in Table A.1 and the initial values of the stocks and flows for the reference year (2010) in tables A.2–A.5 are in Sections A.6–A.13.

The calibrated values of the utility arguments yield the initial utility levels u_0^N and u_0^S.

Table A.4. Labor allocation in the reference year (2010).

Variable	Value	Units
x_0^N	2.171	1950 US efficiency units per capita
x_0^S	1.340	1950 US efficiency units per capita
x_0^{lN}	1.448	1950 US efficiency units per capita
x_0^{lS}	0.871	1950 US efficiency units per capita
x_0^{cN}	0.615	1950 US efficiency units per capita
x_0^{cS}	0.429	1950 US efficiency units per capita
x_0^{eN}	0.072	1950 US efficiency units per capita
x_0^{eS}	0.028	1950 US efficiency units per capita
x_0^{nN}	0.036	1950 US efficiency units per capita
x_0^{nS}	0.012	1950 US efficiency units per capita

Table A.5. Population and emissions, United States and China, in the reference year (2010).

Variable	Value	Units
N_0^{USA}	312,247	thousands
N_0^{China}	1,367,406	thousands
e_0^{USA}	4.952	tC per capita
e_0^{China}	1.774	tC per capita

A.3. Variables

S_t^{kJ} = capital stock available to Generation t in Region J (in thousands of international dollars per capita).

S_t^{nJ} = stock of knowledge available to Generation t in Region J (in thousands of international dollars per capita).

S_t^m = carbon dioxide (CO_2) concentration in the atmosphere at the end of Generation t's life (in parts per million [ppm]).

x_t^J = average annual efficiency units of time (labor and leisure) available to Generation t in Region J (in efficiency units per capita).

x_t^{eJ} = average annual labor devoted to education by Generation t in Region J (in efficiency units per capita).

x_t^{cJ} = average annual labor devoted to the production of output by Generation t in Region J (in efficiency units per capita).

x_t^{lJ} = annual average leisure by Generation t in Region J (in efficiency units per capita).

x_t^{nJ} = average annual labor devoted to the production of knowledge by Generation t in Region J (in efficiency units per capita).

c_t^J = annual average consumption by Generation t in Region J (in thousands of international dollars per capita).

i_t^J = average annual investment by Generation t in Region J (in thousands of international dollars per capita).

e_t^J = average annual emissions per capita of CO_2 from energy (fuel and cement) by Generation t in Region J (in tC per capita).

A.4. Parameters

α_j = exponents of the utility function for $j \in \{c$ (consumption), l (leisure), n (stock of knowledge), and m (CO_2 concentration)$\}$.

k_1 = parameter of the production function f.

k_2 = parameter of the law of motion of capital.

k_3 = parameter of the law of motion of the stock of knowledge.

k_{3d} = parameter of the law of motion of the stock of knowledge with technological diffusion from North to South.

ξ = parameter of the education production function.

$\hat{\lambda}$ = annual rate of technological transfer from North to South.

θ_j = exponents of the inputs in the production function f for $j \in \{c$ (labor), k (stock of capital), n (stock of knowledge), e (emissions of CO_2), m (atmospheric carbon concentration)$\}$.

d^k = depreciation rate of the stock of capital (per generation).

d^n = depreciation rate of the stock of knowledge (per generation).

e_t^* = average annual world emissions per capita of CO_2 from fuel and cement by Generation t (in tC per capita).

S_t^m = carbon dioxide concentration in the atmosphere at the end of Generation t (in ppm).

$\hat{S}^m$ = catastrophic level of carbon dioxide concentration in the atmosphere (in ppm).

$\hat{\rho}$=annual rate of growth of utility.

ρ=generational rate of growth of utility ($\rho = (1+\hat{\rho})^{25}$).

A.5. Functions

Utility function: $(c_t^J)^{\alpha_c}(x_t^{lJ})^{\alpha_l}(S_t^{nJ})^{\alpha_n}(\hat{S}^m - S_t^m)^{\alpha_m}$.

Production function: $f(x_t^{cJ}, S_t^{kJ}, S_t^{nJ}, e_t^J, S_t^m)$
$\equiv k_1(x_t^{cJ})^{\theta_c}(S_t^{kJ})^{\theta_k}(S_t^{nJ})^{\theta_n}(e_t^J)^{\theta_e}(S_t^m)^{\theta_m}$, $\theta_c+\theta_k+\theta_n=1$.

Law of motion of physical capital: $S_t^{kJ} \leq (1-d^k)\dfrac{N_{t-1}^J}{N_t^J}S_{t-1}^{kJ} + k_2 i_t^J$.

Law of motion of the stock of knowledge without technological diffusion:
$S_t^{nJ} \leq (1-d^n)S_{t-1}^{nJ} + k_3 x_t^{nJ}$.

Law of motion of the stock of knowledge with technological diffusion from North to South: $S_t^{nS} = (1-d^n)S_{t-1}^{nS}\dfrac{N_{t-1}^S}{N_t^S} + k_3 x_t^{nS} + k_{3d}(S_{t-1}^{nN} - S_{t-1}^{nS})x_t^{nS}$.

Education production function: $x_t^J \leq \xi\dfrac{N_{t-1}^J}{N_t^J}x_{t-1}^{eJ}$.

A.6. Population

We follow the United Nations (2013) population forecast. We assign the average forecasted population for 2011–2035 to Generation 1 and the average forecasted population for 2036–2100 to Generation 2. World population is 6.9 billion people in 2010, increases to 7.9 billion people for Generation 1, and stabilizes at 10 billion people from Generation 2 and on. Table A.6 reports the specific population paths for the world, North, South, and the United States.

A.7. The Calibration of the Utility Function

For the exponent of leisure, we choose $\alpha_l = 2\alpha_c$ in line with the conventional observation in the literature that, on average, households devote to work one-third of their time endowment (see, e.g., Cooley and Hansen 1992).

We calibrate $\alpha_n/\alpha_c = 0.055$ as the average ratio of expenditure in knowledge (research and development [R&D] expenditure plus investment in

Table A.6. World population paths.

	North		South		United States	World
	Total population (thousands of people)	Percentage of world population	Total population (thousands of people)	Percentage of world population	Total population (thousands of people)	Total population (thousands of people)
Year 2010	1,240,935	17.9%	5,675,249	82.1%	312,247	6,916,183
Generation 1	1,278,338	16.2%	6,635,766	83.8%	345,122	7,914,104
Generation 2	1,295,940	12.8%	8,790,833	87.2%	426,333	10,086,772

computer components and software) over expenditure in consumption during the period 1996–2009.[1]

The utility function has two parameters that concern the stock of CO_2, namely the catastrophic level $\hat{S}^m$ and the exponent α_m.

Because CO_2 concentration affects utility through temperature changes, here and in what follows we adopt the conventional functional form for the relation between temperature and greenhouse gases (GHG)

$$\Delta T = \sigma \frac{\ln(S^e/S^m_{1850})}{\ln 2}, \qquad \text{(A.1)}$$

where S^e is the concentration of GHG measured in ppm of CO_2 equivalent, S^m_{1850} is the preindustrial level of GHG in the atmosphere, ΔT is the *warming effect* defined as the average surface temperature increase in °C since preindustrial times, and the parameter σ is called the *climate sensitivity*.[2] Expression (A.1) can be inverted to yield $\widehat{S}^e(\Delta T) = S^m_{1850} \times 2^{\Delta T/\sigma}$. Because our variable S^m only considers the CO_2 concentration, which accounts for 84% of all GHG, we can write S^m as the function of ΔT:

$$\widehat{S}^m(\Delta T) = \frac{S^m_{1850}}{1.16} 2^{\Delta T/\sigma}. \qquad \text{(A.2)}$$

We take $S^m_{1850} = 280$ ppm and adopt the common best guess for the climate sensitivity of $\sigma = 3$.[3]

We consider that an increase in temperature of 6°–8°C (relative to preindustrial level) would have catastrophic impacts.[4] From (A.2) an increase

[1] Expenditures on R&D are from the National Science Foundation (2013), and those of investment in computer components and software are from the Bureau of Economic Analysis (BEA) (2013). Since the BEA only provides aggregate data for equipment and software, we take the share of private software on private software and equipment to construct public investment in software.

[2] In words, the climate sensitivity σ is the increase in global average surface temperature over that of year 1850 caused by doubling the preindustrial amount of GHG.

[3] Higher values of the climate sensitivity parameter reduce the level of welfare attainable, but the effects are small.

[4] The *Stern Review* consistently associates catastrophic consequences to temperature increases of 6–8°C, like, for example, sea-level rise threatening major world cities (including London, Shanghai, New York, Tokyo, and Hong Kong);

of 6°C (resp. 8°C) is associated with a S^m value of 965.52 ppm (resp. 1532.66). We calibrate $\hat{S}^m$ by the mean of these two values as $\hat{S}^m = 1249.09$ ppm.

We calibrate the exponent α_m by published information on nonmarket impacts, which include health and environmental degradation. In particular, we calibrate the ratio α_m/α_c by the *Stern Review* estimate that a 5°C increase in the global temperature over the preindustrial level would imply a nonmarket impact equivalent to a 6% loss of global gross domestic product (GDP) (Stern 2007, 186; see also page x in the executive summary, Stern 2006). Again from (A.2) a 5°C temperature increase corresponds to an S^m value of $766.33 \equiv \tilde{S}^m$. Accordingly, we consider a 6% decrease in consumption equivalent to suffering an atmospheric CO_2 concentration of $\tilde{S}^m$ instead of the preindustrial level S^m_{1850}, that is,

$$(0.94c)^{\alpha_c}(x^l)^{\alpha_l}(S^n)^{\alpha_n}(\hat{S}^m - S^m_{1850})^{\alpha_m} = (c)^{\alpha_c}(x^l)^{\alpha_l}(S^n)^{\alpha_n}(\hat{S}^m - \tilde{S}^m)^{\alpha_m},$$

which yields

$$(0.94)^{\alpha_c}(\hat{S}^m - S^m_{1850})^{\alpha_m} = (\hat{S}^m - \tilde{S}^m)^{\alpha_m},$$

or

$$\alpha_c \ln 0.94 = \alpha_m[\ln(\hat{S}^m - \tilde{S}^m) - \ln(\hat{S}^m - S^m_{1850})].$$

It follows that $\dfrac{\alpha_m}{\alpha_c} = \dfrac{\ln 0.94}{\ln(\hat{S}^m - \tilde{S}^m) - \ln(\hat{S}^m - S^m_{1850})}$. That is,

$$\frac{\alpha_m}{\alpha_c} = \frac{\ln 0.94}{\ln(1249.09 - 766.33) - \ln(1249.09 - 280)} = 0.0888.$$

Finally, we normalize $\alpha_c + \alpha_l + \alpha_m + \alpha_n = 1$ to yield the values reported in Section A.2.

---

entire regions experiencing major declines in crop yields and high risk of abrupt, large-scale shifts in the climate system (Stern 2006, fig. 2, p. v); and catastrophic major disruptions and large-scale movements of population (Stern 2007, table 3.1, pp. 66–67). Also based on the *Stern Review*, Acemoglu, Aghion et al. (2012, 155) define a disaster as an increase in temperature equal to 6°C.

A.8. The Calibration of the Production Function

We calibrate the production function

$$f(x_t^c, S_t^k, S_t^n, e_t, S_t^m) \equiv k_1 (x_t^c)^{\theta_c} (S_t^k)^{\theta_k} (S_t^n)^{\theta_n} (e_t)^{\theta_e} (S_t^m)^{\theta_m}$$

in the following inputs: the usual labor, physical capital, and knowledge, to which we add the environmental emissions and stock.

We assume constant returns to scale in the first three inputs, that is, $\theta_c + \theta_k + \theta_n = 1$.

Following standard growth literature, we take labor income share equal to two-thirds (Kaldor 1961; Kongsamut, Rebelo, and Xie 2001; Valentinyi and Herrendorf 2008). We construct time series for the stocks of physical capital and knowledge (see Sections A.9 and A.10), and we compute their average shares in the total stock of capital for the period 1960–2010, corresponding to 0.86 and 0.14, respectively. Hence, $\theta_c = 0.670$, $\theta_k = 0.284$, and $\theta_n = 0.046$, representing the income share of each input.

We take $\theta_e = 0.081$ as the average of the elasticity of output with respect to carbon services reported in Popp (2006).[5]

We calibrate θ_m, the elasticity of output to the CO_2 concentration in the atmosphere, by published information on market or economic damages. The composition of the production function and (A.2) yields

$$\widehat{f}(x_t^c, S_t^k, S_t^n, e_t, \Delta T) = \left(\frac{280}{1.16} 2^{\Delta T/3} \right)^{\theta_m} \widehat{a}(\cdot),$$
$$\text{where } \widehat{a}(\cdot) \equiv k_1 (x_t^c)^{\theta_c} (S_t^k)^{\theta_k} (S_t^n)^{\theta_n} (e_t)^{\theta_e}.$$

We assume, following Nordhaus (2010, 11723), that a 3.4°C increase in temperature implies a 2.8% loss of GDP; that is, $\left(\frac{280}{1.16} 2^{3.4/3} \right)^{\theta_m} \widehat{a}(\cdot) = 0.972 \left(\frac{280}{1.16} 2^{0/3} \right)^{\theta_m} \widehat{a}(\cdot)$, or $2^{1.13 \times \theta_m} = 0.972$, that is, $\theta_m = \frac{\ln 0.972}{1.13 \ln 2} = -0.036$.

[5] An earlier estimation is found in Nordhaus and Boyer (2000), who also incorporate emissions as an input in the production function and use an elasticity of 0.091 (191).

Finally, we compute k_1 from the US economy calibrated to year 2010 values:[6]

$$k_1 = \frac{y_{2010}^{USA}}{(x_{2010}^{c,USA})^{\theta_c}(S_{2010}^{k,USA})^{\theta_k}(S_{2010}^{n,USA})^{\theta_n}(e_{2010}^{USA})^{\theta_e}(S_{2010}^{m})^{\theta_m}}$$
$$= \frac{46.18}{0.61^{0.670}\,104.95^{0.284}\,26.95^{0.046}\,4.95^{0.081}\,390.43^{-0.036}} = 15.99.$$

Observe that, although we adopt the same production function for North and South, the endowments of knowledge, the levels of skill, the stock of capital, and the emissions are very different in the two regions. Therefore, the productivity of labor and capital, as well as the total factor productivity, will also be very different. More specifically, we can rewrite the production function as a more conventional capital-labor production function (with emissions and climate damages):

$$q_t = \tilde{k}_t (L_t^c)^{\theta_c}(S_t^k)^{\theta_k}(e_t)^{\theta_e}(S_t^m)^{\theta_m}$$

where q_t is total output, L_t represents working hours in the production of the commodity good, and $\tilde{k}_t = k_1(\tilde{x}_t^c/L_t)^{\theta_c}(S_t^n)^{\theta_n}$ is the total factor productivity (TFP) (with $\tilde{x}_t^c/L_t$ representing the human capital per unit of labor), which increases with knowledge and education. (Observe that TFP ($\tilde{k}_t$) will be different for the North and the South not only for the initial period but also along the path until they converge).

We can compute the marginal productivity of capital, labor, and emissions as:

$$\frac{df}{dL} = \theta_c \frac{q}{L}, \quad \frac{df}{dK} = \theta_k \frac{q}{K}, \quad \frac{df}{de} = \theta_e \frac{q}{e}.$$

We use the 2010 values for North and South: initial values are reported in Section S.3.1. For working hours in the production of output, we normalize

[6] GDP is denoted in thousands of constant 2010 dollars per capita from the World Development Indicator (WDI) (World Bank 2013). US emissions are obtained from the World Resources Institute (2013). See Sections A.9–A.13 for the values of the other stocks and flows in the year 2010.

total labor-leisure time in both regions to one and then use the fraction of labor-leisure time in working hours and the fraction of working hours in the production of output (see S.3.2.11).

Table A.7 presents the results, confirming that North and South have very different productivities in the initial reference year.

A.9. The Stock of Physical Capital

The generational *law of motion of physical capital* in each region is standard:

$$(1-d^k)S_{t-1}^{kJ}\frac{N_{t-1}^J}{N_t^J}+k_2 i_t^J \geq S_t^{kJ}.$$

We take $\hat{d}^k = 0.06$ as the annual rate of depreciation (Cooley and Prescott 1995). In generational terms, $d^k = 1-(1-\hat{d}^k)^{25} = 0.787$.

To approximate the year-to-year discounting, we take i as the average investment in physical capital per year of a given generation and compute that, at the end of the generation's life, the accumulated investment amounts are

$$i + i\times(1-\hat{d}^k) + i\times(1-\hat{d}^k)^2 + \cdots + i\times(1-\hat{d}^k)^{24} = \frac{1-(1-\hat{d}^k)^{25}}{1-(1-\hat{d}^k)}i.$$

Thus, since $1-\hat{d}^k = 0.94$, the parameter $k_2 = \dfrac{1-(1-\hat{d}^k)^{25}}{1-(1-\hat{d}^k)} = 13.118.$

Initial Stock of Physical Capital for the North

We assign the North the stock of physical capital per capita in the United States. The time series of the stock of physical capital is constructed by

Table A.7. Total factor productivity and marginal productivities of labor, capital, and emissions for North and South in the reference year (2010).

	North	South	North/South
Total factor productivity $\tilde{k}_o$	31.321	16.296	1.92
Marginal productivity of labor	3443.1	227.3	15.15
Marginal productivity of capital	3.93	1.19	3.3
Marginal productivity of emissions	106.9	12.4	8.62

the perpetual inventory method (PIM), using US gross capital formation data adjusted for imports and exports for the period 1960–2010 (World Bank 2013) and taking 1960 as the initial year. For the initial value, $S_{1960}^{kN} = i_{1960}^{kN}/(\hat{d}^k + g^{kN}) = 27.62$ thousands of constant 2010 dollars per capita, where i^{kN} represents gross capital formation, and g^{kN} represents the average yearly growth rate of investment between 1960 and 1970 (computed at 4.33%). The value for the stock of physical capital in the year 2010 is $S_0^{kN} = 104.95$ thousands of 2010 international dollars per capita. (We use deflators information from the WDI to convert to 2010 international dollars.)

Initial Stock of Physical Capital for the South

We assign the South the stock of physical capital per capita in China. We start from Albala-Bertrand and Feng (2007), who provide a figure of 11,243.3 billion 1952 yuan for the capital stock in 2005, or 14.74 thousands of constant 2005 international dollars per capita (once dividing by population and using Consumer Price Index (CPI) data from Officer and Williamson (2008) and PPP data from the World Bank). Then we update the value to 2010 by the PIM, using gross capital formation in China from the WDI (World Bank 2013), and obtain $S_0^{kS} = 33.29$ thousands of 2010 international dollars per capita.[7]

A.10. The Stock of Knowledge

Law of Motion of the Stock of Knowledge

We calibrate the law of motion of the stock of knowledge with technological diffusion from North to South

$$S_t^{nS} = (1 - d^n) S_{t-1}^{nS} \frac{N_{t-1}^S}{N_t^S} + k_3 x_t^{nS} + k_{3d}(S_{t-1}^{nN} - S_{t-1}^{nS}) x_t^{nS}, \tag{A.3}$$

where

[7] We follow Bai et al. (2006) in considering gross capital formation as an accurate measure of the change in China's reproducible capital stock.

$$k_3 = \frac{d^n}{\hat{d}^n}\overline{w}, \; k_{3d} = \hat{\lambda} k_3, \tag{A.4}$$

$\overline{w}$ is the average wage of an efficiency unit of labor, and $\hat{\lambda}$ is the rate of annual technological diffusion. The derivation of these expressions from a year-to-year law of motion can be found in Section A5.1.

In the absence of technological diffusion, $k_{3d}=0$, and the South's law of motion becomes the same as the North's. Therefore, the calibration of the laws of motion of the stock of knowledge only requires the estimation of three values: the annual depreciation rate of knowledge ($\hat{d}^n$) the average wage of an efficiency unit of labor ($\overline{w}$), and the diffusion rate of knowledge from North to South per year ($\hat{\lambda}$).

The yearly depreciation rate commonly used for knowledge is much higher than the one used for capital (e.g., the Bank of Spain uses 15%, which would mean that knowledge dissipates almost entirely in one generation). We believe that the discount factor should be higher because of the intergenerational-public-good character of knowledge. A dollar invested in R&D by a firm may well generate no returns to the firm twenty-five years later, yet its impact to the accumulation of social knowledge capital may be substantial.[8] Thus, as an approximation we take the depreciation rate of the stock of knowledge to be the same as that of physical capital; that is, $\hat{d}^n = \hat{d}^k = 0.06$, and in generational terms, $d^n=0.787$.

We approximate the wage of an efficiency unit of labor by $\overline{w} = i_t^n / x_t^n$, where i_t^n is the average annual expenditure per capita in knowledge, and x_t^n is the share of labor devoted to the production of knowledge. We use the average US values of expenditures and labor in knowledge for the last generation (1976–2000) to obtain $\overline{w} = i^n_{1970-2010}/x^n_{1970-2010} = 42.56$ of 2010 dollars (expenditure in knowledge from the National Science Foundation (2003) and the Bureau of Economic Analysis [BEA, 2013], labor allocation from the Bureau of Labor Statistics [BLS, 2012], and CPI from the WDI).

---

[8] See, e.g., Jones and Williams (1998) for a discussion of the 'standing on the shoulders of giants' effect.

The calibration of $\hat{\lambda}$ is more problematic.[9] We choose a conservative value of $\hat{\lambda} = 0.01$.[10]

Using a depreciation rate of $\hat{d}^n = 0.06$, an annual diffusion rate of $\hat{\lambda} = 0.01$, and an estimation of $\bar{w} = 42.56$, we compute $k_3 = 5.583$ and $k_{3d} = 5.583$, in accordance with (A.4).

Initial Stock of Knowledge for the North

The time series of the stock of knowledge in the North is constructed by the PIM, using US data for 1960–2005 and taking 1960 as the initial year. For the stock of knowledge in 1960, we take $S_{1960}^{nN} = i_{1960}^{nN}/(\hat{d}^n + g^{nN}) = 0.396/(0.06+0.049) = 3.624$ thousands of constant 2010 dollars per capita, where i^{nN} represents total expenditure per capita in R&D plus public and private investment in software, and g^{nN} represents the average yearly growth rate between 1960 and 1970. The value for the stock of knowledge in the year 2010 is $S_0^{nN} = 26.950$ (in thousands of 2010 international dollars per capita).

Initial Stock of Knowledge for the South

We assign to the South the per capita stock of China. The time series of the stock of knowledge in China is constructed by the PIM, using the annual knowledge equation with technology diffusion given in (A.3). We take one-third of the GDP per capita in 1980 (i.e., 222 international dollars per capita) as the initial value for the stock of knowledge in China.[11] The date is unusually recent for applying the PIM, but it can be justified by the particular circumstances of China.[12] Year 1980 roughly coincides with the new

[9] The recent literature on technological diffusion estimates a twenty-five-year adoption lag (Comin and Hobijn 2010). This implies an annual technological diffusion rate of 4%.

[10] We have run a sensitivity analysis for a range of values of $\hat{\lambda}$ above and below 0.01 (from 0.005 to 0.04), obtaining that the optimal path moves smoothly, with higher diffusion rates associated with higher utility for the second generation in the South. We have also computed the optimal path for $\hat{\lambda} = 0$, showing that technological diffusion is not a necessary condition for finding a convergent path to a sustained 1% annual growth.

[11] Currency is always in constant 2010 PPP international dollars.

[12] The choice of the initial value has a moderate effect for the stock in 2010. Choosing as initial value R&D investment in 1980 would decrease the year 2010 stock around

development path set by Deng Xiaoping after the failure of the Great Leap experiment.[13] As Song (2008, 236) argues, "For the first time in China's history, science and technology were viewed as driving force behind economic development [*sic*]." The reform also initiated the flow of many students to the West for further scientific education, which also justifies the use of a rate of diffusion starting in 1980.[14] For the time series of investment in knowledge, we use data on R&D investment from Gao and Jefferson (2007), the *China Statistical Data Book* (Ministry of Science and Technology in China, MOST 2000), and the *China Statistical Yearbook on Science and Technology* (National Bureau of Statistics of China 2012).[15] The PIM with a 6% annual depreciation rate and a diffusion rate $\hat{\lambda} = 0.01$ yields a value for the stock of knowledge in the year 2010 of $S_0^{nS} = 0.837$ thousands of 2010 international dollars per capita.

A.11. The Calibration of the Education Production Function

We assume that both regions have access to the same production function of education:

$$x_t^{\mathcal{J}} \leq \xi \, x_{t-1}^{e\mathcal{J}} \frac{N_{t-1}^{\mathcal{J}}}{N_t^{\mathcal{J}}}, \quad t \geq 1, \quad \mathcal{J} = N, S, \tag{A.5}$$

which we calibrate with US data. The parameter ξ, capturing the productivity of education, plays an important role in the model. By definition,

$30 per capita. But this figure most likely underestimates the real value (see notes in the Organisation for Economic Co-operation and Development [OECD] statistics). On the other hand, choosing total GDP would increase year 2010 stock to less than $30 per capita.

[13] Deng Xiaoping reforms started in 1978. We choose 1980 instead since this is the first year for which we have a PPP conversion factor.

[14] By 2006, 1.67 million Chinese students had enrolled in universities in more than 108 countries. "This confirms that the policy of free access to overseas education is and will continue to be instrumental in China's drive toward modernization" (Song 2008, 236).

[15] Since data is only available from 1986, we take investment in R&D constant at 0.5% of GDP for the decade of the 1980s (the value for the years where we have information).

$\xi = N_t^J x_t^J / N_{t-1}^J x_{t-1}^e$, where both the numerator and the denominator are measured in efficiency units. We can transform efficiency units into hours by the equality

$$\frac{N_t^J x_t^J}{N_{t-1}^J x_{t-1}^{eJ}} = \frac{(1+s)^{\bar{t}}\,\hat{x}_t}{(1+s)^{\bar{t}-1}\hat{x}_{t-1}^e} = (1+s)\frac{\hat{x}_t}{\hat{x}_{t-1}^e},$$

for some given $\bar{t}$, which plays no role; $(1+s)$ is the growth factor of human capital per generation; and where the 'hats' represent the data in total annual hours. Hence, the calibration of ξ is based on two rates: s and the share $\hat{x}_{t-1}^e/\hat{x}_t$ of time devoted to education out of total time. Note that ξ is increasing in s and decreasing in the share $\hat{x}_{t-1}^e/\hat{x}_t$.

We take the value $\hat{s} = 1.3\%$ for the average yearly growth rate of the human capital stock, which yields the per-generation factor $(1+s) = (1+\hat{s})^{25} = 1.381$. This figure is based on the 1950–2010 average provided by Barro and Lee (2013) and supported by other recent findings (see, e.g., Christian 2010; Wei 2008; Gu and Wong 2010).[16]

The rate $\hat{x}_{t-1}^e/\hat{x}_t$ is the product of the rate of education in labor and the rate of labor in total time. We assume that 10% of total labor is devoted to education (a figure roughly constant since 1990; BLS 2013), and that labor accounts for one-third of total time. It follows that

$$\xi = (1.013)^{25}\left(\frac{1}{3}\times 0.1\right) = 41.434. \tag{A.6}$$

This figure is conservative in the sense that higher growth rates of human capital, lower labor rates, and population growth would yield a larger value for ξ.

A.12. Initial Values for Total Labor and Labor Allocation

We construct the US human capital stock (in efficiency units) by normalizing year 1950 equal to 1 and taking the average yearly growth rate

[16] Looking at a twelve-year period in US data, Christian (2010, 34) finds an average growth in the human capital stock of 1.1%. The Australian Bureau of Statistics finds an average growth rate of 1.3% over a twenty-year period (Wei 2008, 8). Gu and Wong (2010) find a growth rate of 1.7% in Canada over a twenty-seven-year period.

of human capital stock equal to 1.3% (Barro and Lee 2013). Hence, $x_t^N = 1.013^{t-1950}$ in 1950 US efficiency units, and therefore $x_0^N = 1.013^{60} = 2.17$. We take the standard assumption of 33% of time devoted to working hours. We allocate total working hours among education, knowledge, and production in the North according to their average proportions in the United States, namely 10% in education, 5% in knowledge, and the remaining 85% in the production of output (Standard Occupation Classification [SOC] of the BLS 2012, 2013).

For the estimation of human capital in the South, we use the ratio of years of education between China and the United States. We obtain from Barro and Lee (2013) the average years of school of the total population aged 15 and over for the United States and China: 13.09 and 8.11 years, respectively.[17] Therefore, $x_0^S = 2.17 \times (8.11/13.09) = 1.34$, in 1950 US efficiency units. Based on the study by Li and Zax (2003), we take Chinese workers to devote 65% of their time to leisure. For the allocation of working time, we take the 2005–2010 averages from the *China Statistical Yearbook* (National Bureau of Statistics of China 2012): 6% in education, 2.5% in knowledge, and the remaining 91.5% in the production of output.[18]

A.13. Initial Values for Consumption and Investment

The values for consumption and investment in the benchmark year for the North and the South are presented in Table A.3. We use the values for the United States and China, respectively (World Bank 2013). For consumption and investment we use 'final consumption expenditure' and 'gross capital formation' as percentages of GDP. Output per capita is defined as the sum of consumption, investment, and net exports, all in per capita terms.

---

[17] More sophisticated analyses, like those of Wang and Yao (2003) and Perkins and Rawski (2008) find similar values for China.

[18] For labor in knowledge we compute employed persons in urban units in 'Scientific Research, Technical Services, and Geological Prospecting,' 'Information Transmission, Computer Service and Software,' 'Management of Water Conservancy, Environment and Public Facilities,' and 'Culture, Sports and Entertainment.' For education we compute employed persons in 'Education' in urban areas plus 1.5% of employed persons in rural areas.

Mathematica Code

This appendix presents a short version of the *Mathematica* code used to run the optimization programs in chapters 3 and 5.[1] Each section represents a different file. Section B.1 describes the main file with the different environments and its options and directs the program to the appropriate subroutines, described in sections B.2–B.5. In order to facilitate the reader's understanding of the program, the output only displays the utility paths, and other simplifications have been adopted. The data are described in the Calibration Appendix and we do not provide the code here.

B.1. Main program

Instructions.

- It is recommended to *Quit* the kernel prior to any computation and when switching models.
- Keep all *Mathematica* subroutines in the same directory as this notebook.
- The cells with a □ can [ENTER] directly.

[1] A complete version of the program can be found in http://econ.upf.edu/~llavador/Llavador/SfWP.html

- The cells with a ✪ contain options and require information prior to [ENTER].
- Default options are <u>underlined</u>.
- When the user enters one of the three programs below, the data are uploaded, all calculations are performed, and output is printed. To understand the logic of the program, please read the subroutines that are called.

One-Region World (Chapter 3)

Options

—Annual Growth Rate (ρannum or $\hat{\rho}$). The book reports the outcomes for values 0.00, 0.01, and 0.02.

—Scenarios

- **scenario=1.** US share of total emissions is maintained constant at its 2010 value: $E_t^{USA} = \text{USShare} \times E_t^W$.
- **scenario=2.** US per capita emissions equal World per capita emissions: $e_t^{USA} = e_t^W$.

```
✪ {scenario,ρannum}={1, 0.00};
Date[]
FileNameJoin[{NotebookDirectory[],"DataValues.m"}]//Get
FileNameJoin[{NotebookDirectory[],"DataGenerated.m"}]//Get
FileNameJoin[{NotebookDirectory[],"OneRegionWorld.m"}]//Get
Print["{ρ̂, ρ}=",{ρannum,ρ}/.output]
Print["Scenario=",scenario]
Show[{upathline,u0line}]
```

One-Region World: Consumption-Only Maximization (Section 3.9)

NOTE: This program only works for a zero-growth rate.

```
□ Date[]
FileNameJoin[{NotebookDirectory[],"DataValues.m"}]//Get
FileNameJoin[{NotebookDirectory[],"DataGenerated.m"}]//Get
FileNameJoin[{NotebookDirectory[],"ConsumptionOneRegionWorld.m"}]
    //Get
Print["Consumption-only maximization"]
Show[{upathlineC0,u0line}]
```

Two-Region World (Chapter 5)

Options

—Annual Growth Rate ρannum ($\hat{\rho}$). The book reports the outcome for 0.01.

—Objective

- **objective=1.** Maximizing the utility of GENERATION 1 in the South. (Reported in Section A5.3 in the Appendix for Chapter 5.)
- **objective=2.** Maximizing the utility of GENERATION 2 in the South.

—Commodity Flows:

- **CFlows=1.** The commodity good CAN flow between regions.
- **CFlows=0.** The commodity good CANNOT flow between regions.

```
✪ {objective,ρannum,CFlows}={1,0.01,1};
Date[]
FileNameJoin[{NotebookDirectory[],"DataValues.m"}]//Get
FileNameJoin[{NotebookDirectory[],"DataGenerated.m"}]//Get
Which[objective==1,Get[FileNameJoin[{NotebookDirectory[],"TwoRegion
      World1.m"}]],
   objective==2,Get[FileNameJoin[{NotebookDirectory[],"TwoRegion
      World2.m"}]],
   True,Print["Please,choose objective ∈{1, 2}"];Quit[]]
Print["{ρ̂, ρ}=",{ρannum,ρ}/.output]
Show[upathline]
```

B.2. Subroutine *OneRegionWorld.m*

Emissions

```
Which[
   scenario==1,USshare=Round[100*EUSA0/EW0]/100.;{eUSA1,eUSA2,eUSA
      star}=USshare*{EW1/NUSA1,EW2/NUSA2,EWstar/NUSA2}*10^6,
   scenario==2,{eUSA1,eUSA2,eUSAstar}={eW1,eW2,eWstar},
   True,Print["Please,choose \!\(\* StyleBox[\"scenario\",\nFontSlant->\"Italic
      \"]\)=1 or \!\(\* StyleBox[\"scenario\",\nFontSlant->\"Italic\"]\)=2"];
      Quit[]];
estar=eUSAstar;
```

Growth Factors

```
ρ=(1+ρannum)^25–1;ρρ=1+ρ;
g=(1+ρ)^(1/(αc+αl+αn))–1;gg=1+g;
```

Steady-State Ray

```
RayParam={
vn=(g+δn)/k3,
pi=(g+δk)/k2,
pc=(1–(1–δk)/k4)*((1+g)/(k2*θk))–pi,
vl=(1–(1–δn)/k4)*(αl/k3)*(pc/(αc*θn*(pc+pi)+αn*pc))*(1+g),
vc=(1–(1–δn)/k4)*((αc*θc)/k3)*((pc+pi)/(αc*θn*(pc+pi)+αn*pc))*(1+g),
qn=(k4–(1+g))/(vl+vn+vc),
qk=((k1*vc^θc)/(pc+pi))^(1/(θc+θn))(1+g)^((θk+θn)/(θc+θn))*qn*estar^
    (θe/(θn+θc))*Smstar^(θm/(θn+θc))};
```

Constraints

```
c1a=c1^αc*xl1^αl*Sn1^αn*(Smhat–Sm1)^αm–Λ;
c1b=c2^αc*xl2^αl*Sn2^αn*(Smhat–Sm2)^αm–ρρ*Λ;
c2a=(1–δk)*SkUSA0+k2*i1–Sk1;
c2b=(1–δk)*Sk1+k2*i2–Sk2;
c3a=(1–δn)*SnUSA0+k3*xn1–Sn1;
c3b=(1–δn)*Sn1+k3*xn2–Sn2;
c4a=ξ*xeUSA0–xe1–xn1–xc1–xl1;
c4b=ξ*xe1–xe2–xn2–xc2–xl2;
c5a=k1*xc1^θc*Sk1^θk*Sn1^θn*eUSA1^θe*Sm1^θm–c1–i1;
c5b=k1*xc2^θc*Sk2^θk*Sn2^θn*eUSA2^θe*Sm2^θm–c2–i2;
c6a=qk*xe2–Sk2;
c6b=qn*xe2–Sn2;
c7a=c3^αc*xl3^αl*Sn3^αn*(Smhat–Smstar)^αm–ρρ^2*Λ;
c7b=(1+g)*qn*xe2–Sn3;
c7c=pc*qk*xe2–c3;
c7d=vl*qn*xe2–xl3;
```

Optimization Program

```
output=Part[NMaximize[{Λ,
c1a>=0&&c1b>=0&&
c2a>=0&&c2b>=0&&
c3a>=0&&c3b>=0&&
c4a>=0&&c4b>=0&&
c5a>=0&&c5b>=0&&
c6a==0&&c6b==0&&
```

```
    c7a==0&&c7b==0&&c7c==0&&c7d==0,
    Sk1>0&&Sk2>0&&Sn1>0&&Sn2>0&&i1>0&&i2>0&&c1>0&&c2>0&&xl1>
       0&&xc1>0&&xe1>0&&xn1>0&&xl2>0&&xc2>0&&xe2>0&&xn2>0&&Λ
       >0&&c3>0&&xl3>0&&Sn3>0},
    {Sk1,Sk2,Sn1,Sn2,i1,i2,c1,c2,xl1,xc1,xe1,xn1,xl2,xc2,xe2,xn2,Λ,c3,xl3,Sn3},
Method->{"SimulatedAnnealing","Tolerance"->10^(-6),"Perturbation
       Scale"->0.05},MaxIterations->10000],2];
Module[{tx1=(xc1+xl1+xn1+xe1)/.output,tx2=(xc2+xl2+xn2+xe2)/.output,
       txc3=vc*qn*xe2/.output,txn3=vn*qn*xe2/.output,txe3=(1+g)*xe2/.
       output,tSk3=(1+g)qk*xe2/.output,ti3=pi*Sk2/.output,txl3=xl3/.outp
       ut},output=Flatten[Append[output,{xc3->txc3,xn3->txn3,xe3->txe3,
       Sk3->tSk3,i3->ti3,x1->tx1,x2->tx2,x3->txl3+txc3+txn3+txe3}]]];
```

Tests

```
Print["TESTS"];Print["Constraints evaluated at the solution"];
primalconst=Round[(({{c1a,c1b},{c2a,c2b},{c3a,c3b},{c4a,c4b},{c5a,c5b},
       {c6a,c6b},{c7a,c7b,c7c,c7d}}/.output)*10^5]/10.^5;
tempfunc[x_,y_]:=Flatten[{x,y}]; Print[MapThread[tempfunc,{{"(1):", "(2):",
       "(3):", "(4):", "(5):", "(6):", "(7):"}, primalconst}]//TableForm];
       ClearAll[tempfunc];
```

Utility Path

```
u1=fu[c1,xl1,Sn1,Sm1]/.output;
u2=fu[c2,xl2,Sn2,Sm2]/.output;
u3=fu[c3,xl3,Sn3,Smstar]/.output;
upathline=ListLinePlot[{1,u1/uUSA0,u2/uUSA0,u3/uUSA0,ρρ*u3/uUSA0,
       ρρ^2*u3/uUSA0},AxesLabel->{"t","\!\(\*SubscriptBox[\(u\),\(t\)]\)/\!
       \(\*SubscriptBox[\(u\),\(0\)]\)"},AxesStyle->Directive[20],PlotRange->
       {0,Ceiling[ρρ^2*u3/uUSA0]},DataRange->{0,5},PlotMarkers->
       {Automatic,12},AxesOrigin->{0,0},PlotStyle->{AbsoluteThickness[2]},
       AspectRatio->0.5];
u0line=Graphics[{Black,Dashing[Tiny],Line[{{0,1},{5,1}}],Text["year 2010=1",
       {4.65,1.1}]}];
```

B.3. Subroutine *ConsumptionOneRegionWorld.m*

Emissions

```
   USshare=Round[100*EUSA0/EW0]/100.;{eUSA1,eUSA2,eUSAstar}=USs
       hare*{EW1/NUSA1,EW2/NUSA2,EWstar/NUSA2}*10^6;
estar=eUSAstar;
```

Growth Factors

```
ρannum=0.00;ρ=(1+ρannum)^25−1;ρρ=1+ρ;
g=(1+ρ)^(1/(αc+αl+αn))−1;gg=1+g;
```

Steady-State Ray

```
RayParamC={
vn=δn/k3,
pi=δk/k2,
pc=(k4(1−δk*θk)−(1−δk))/(k2*k4*θk),
vc=(k4−(1−δn))/(k4*k3)*θc/θn,
qn=(k3*(k4−1))/(k3*vc+δn),
qk=((k2*k4*θk)/(k4−(1−δk))*k1*vc^θc)^(1/(1−θk))*qn};
```

Constraints

```
{propxl1,propxl2,propxl3}={0.6459896271234655,0.6644002463858095,
      0.6605645757646765};(* The fraction of time devoted to leisure
      equals the values obtained in Scenario 1 under no growth *)
c1a=c1−ΛC;
c1b=c2−ΛC;
c2a=(1−δk)*SkUSA0+k2*i1−Sk1;
c2b=(1−δk)*Sk1+k2*i2−Sk2;
c3a=(1−δn)*SnUSA0+k3*xn1−Sn1;
c3b=(1−δn)*Sn1+k3*xn2−Sn2;
c4a=(1−propxl1)*ξ*xeUSA0−xe1−xn1−xc1;
c4b=(1−propxl2)*ξ*xe1−xe2−xn2−xc2;
c5a=k1 xc1^θc* Sk1^θk*Sn1^θn*eUSA1^θe*Sm1^θm−c1−i1;
c5b=k1 xc2^θc* Sk2^θk*Sn2^θn*eUSA2^θe*Sm2^θm−c2−i2;
c6a=qk* xe2−Sk2;
c6b=qn* xe2−Sn2;
c7a=c3−ΛC;
c7b=qn*xe2−Sn3;
c7c=pc*qk*xe2−c3;
```

Optimization Program

```
outputC0=Part[NMaximize[{ΛC,
   c1a==0&&c1b>=0&&
   c2a>=0&&c2b>=0&&
   c3a>=0&&c3b>=0&&
   c4a>=0&&c4b>=0&&
   c5a>=0&&c5b>=0&&
   c6a==0&&c6b==0&&
```

```
c7a==0&&c7b==0&&c7c==0,
Sk1>0&&Sk2>0&&Sn1>0&&Sn2>0&&i1>0&&i2>0&&c1>0&&c2>0&&xc1>
   0&&xe1>0&&xn1>0&&xc2>0&&xe2>0&&xn2>0&&ΛC>0&& c3>0
   &&Sn3>0},
{Sk1,Sk2,Sn1,Sn2,i1,i2,c1,c2,xc1,xe1,xn1,xc2,xe2,xn2,ΛC,c3,Sn3},
Method->{"SimulatedAnnealing","Tolerance"->10^(-6),"Perturbation
   Scale"->0.05},MaxIterations->2000],2];
Module[{txc3=vc*qn*xe2/.outputC0,txn3=vn*qn*xe2/.outputC0,
   txe3=xe2/.outputC0,tSk3=qk*xe2/.outputC0,ti3=pi*Sk2/.outputC0,
   tx1=ξ*xeUSA0/.outputC0,tx2=ξ*xe1/.outputC0,tx3=ξ*xe2/.output
   C0},outputC0=Flatten[Append[outputC0,{xl1-> propxl1*tx1,xl2->
   propxl2*tx2,xl3-> propxl3*tx3,xc3-> txc3,xn3-> txn3,xe3-> txe3,
   Sk3-> tSk3,i3-> ti3,x1-> tx1,x2-> tx2,x3-> tx3}]]];
```

Tests

```
Print["TESTS"];Print["Constraints evaluated at the solution"];
primalconstC0=Round[({{c1a,c1b},{c2a,c2b},{c3a,c3b},{c4a,c4b},{c5a,c5b},
   {c6a,c6b},{c7a,c7b,c7c}}/.outputC0)*10^5]/10.^5;
tempfunc[x_,y_]:=Flatten[{x,y}];Print[MapThread[tempfunc,{{"(1):","(2):",
   "(3):","(4):","(5):","(6):","(7):"},primalconstC0}]//TableForm];Clear
   All[tempfunc]
```

Utility Path

```
u1C0=fu[c1,xl1,Sn1,Sm2]/.outputC0;
u2C0=fu[c2,xl2,Sn2,Sm2]/.outputC0;
u3C0=fu[c3,xl3,Sn3,Smstar]/.outputC0;
u4C0=u3C0;
upathlineC0=ListLinePlot[{1,u1C0/uUSA0,u2C0/uUSA0,u3C0/uUSA0,u4C0/
   uUSA0,u4C0/uUSA0},AxesLabel-> {"t","\!\(\*SubscriptBox[\(u\), \(t\)]
   \)/\!\(\*SubscriptBox[\(u\), \(0\)]\)"},AxesStyle->Directive[20],DataRange
   ->{0,5},PlotMarkers->{Automatic,12},AxesOrigin->{0,0},PlotStyle->
   {AbsoluteThickness[2]},AspectRatio-> 0.5];
u0line=Graphics[{Black,Dashing[Tiny],Line[{{0,1},{5,1}}],Text["year 2010=1",
   {4.65,1.1}]}];
```

B.4. Subroutine *TwoRegionWorld1.m*

Growth Factors

```
ρ=(1+ρannum)^25−1;ρρ=1+ρ;
g=(1+ρ)^(1/(αc+αl+αn))−1;gg=1+g;
```

Steady-State Ray

```
RayParam={
vn=(g+δn)/k3,
pi=(g+δk)/k2,
pc=(1–(1–δk)/k4)*((1+g)/(k2*θk))–pi,
vl=(1–(1–δn)/k4)*(αl/k3)*(pc/(αc*θn*(pc+pi)+αn*pc))*(1+g),
vc=(1–(1–δn)/k4)*((αc*θc)/k3)*((pc+pi)/(αc*θn*(pc+pi)+αn*pc))*(1+g),
qn=(k4–(1+g))/(vl+vn+vc),
qk=((k1*vc^θc)/(pc+pi))^(1/(θc+θn))(1+g)^((θk+θn)/(θc+θn))*qn*eWstar^
    (θe/(θn+θc))*Smstar^(θm/(θn+θc))};
```

Constraints

```
Which[
   CFlows==0,T1=T2=0,
   CFlows==1,ClearAll[T1,T2],
   True,Print["Please choose CFlows∈{0,1}"];Quit[]];
c1a=(1–δk)*SkN0*NN0/NN1+k2*iN1–SkN1;
c1b=(1–δk)*SkN1*NN1/NN2+k2*iN2–Sk2;
c1c=(1–δk)*SkS0*NS0/NS1+k2*iS1–SkS1;
c1d=(1–δk)*SkS1*NS1/NS2+k2*iS2–Sk2;
c2a=(1–δn)*SnS0*NS0/NS1+k3*xnS1+k3d*(SnN0–SnS0)*xnS1–SnS1;
c2b=(1–δn)*SnS1*NS1/NS2+k3*xnS2+k3d*(SnN1–SnS1)*xnS2–Sn2;
c2c=(1–δn)*SnN0*NN0/NN1+k3*xnN1–SnN1;
c2d=(1–δn)*SnN1*NN1/NN2+k3*xnN2–Sn2;
c3a=ξ*xeN0*NN0/NN1–xlN1–xcN1–xeN1–xnN1;
c3b=ξ*xeN1*NN1/NN2–xlN2–xcN2–xe2–xnN2;
c3c=ξ*xeS0*NS0/NS1–xlS1–xcS1–xeS1–xnS1;
c3d=ξ*xeS1*NS1/NS2–xlS2–xcS2–xe2–xnS2;
c4a=e1–NN1/(NN1+NS1)*eN1–NS1/(NN1+NS1)*eS1;
c4b=e2–NN2/(NN2+NS2)*eN2–NS2/(NN2+NS2)*eS2;
c5a=–T1+k1*xcN1^θc*SkN1^θk*SnN1^θn*eN1^θe*Sm1^θm–cN1–iN1;
c5b=–T2+k1*xcN2^θc*Sk2^θk*Sn2^θn*eN2^θe*Sm2^θm–cN2–iN2;
c5c=T1*NN1/NS1+k1*xcS1^θc*SkS1^θk*SnS1^θn*eS1^θe*Sm1^θm–cS1–iS1;
c5d=T2*NN2/NS2+k1*xcS2^θc*Sk2^θk*Sn2^θn*eS2^θe*Sm2^θm–cS2–iS2;
c6a=cN1^αc*xlN1^αl*SnN1^αn*(Smhat–Sm1)^αm–(1+ρ)*uN0;
c6b=cN2^αc*xlN2^αl*Sn2^αn*(Smhat–Sm2)^αm*(1+ρ)*cN1^αc*xlN1^αl*
    SnN1^αn*(Smhat–Sm1)^αm;
c6c=cS1^αc*xlS1^αl*SnS1^αn*(Smhat–Sm1)^αm–ΛS1;
c6d=cS2^αc*xlS2^αl*Sn2^αn*(Smhat–Sm2)^αm*(1+ρ)*cS1^αc*xlS1^αl*Sn
    S1^αn*(Smhat–Sm1)^αm;
c6e=c3^αc*xl3^αl*Sn3^αn*(Smhat–Smstar)^αm*(1+ρ)*cN2^αc*xlN2^αl*S
    n2^αn*(Smhat–Sm2)^αm;
c7a=Sk2–qk*xe2;
```

```
c7b=Sn2–qn*xe2;
c7c=Sn3–gg*qn*xe2;
c8a=c3–pc*qk*xe2;
c8b=xl3–vl*qn*xe2;
```

Optimization Program

```
output=Part[NMaximize[{ΛS1,
   c1a>=0&&c1b>=0&&c1c>=0&&c1d>=0&&
   c2a>=0&&c2b>=0&&c2c>=0&&c2d>=0&&
   c3a>=0&&c3b>=0&&c3c>=0&&c3d>=0&&
   c4a>=0&&c4b>=0&&
   c5a>=0&&c5b>=0&&c5c>=0&&c5d>=0&&
   c6a>=0&&c6b>=0&&c6c>=0&&c6d>=0&&c6e>=0&&
   c7a==0&&c7b==0&&c7c==0&&
   c8a==0&&c8b==0&&
   SkN1>0&&SkS1>0&&Sk2>0&&SnN1>0&&SnS1>0&&Sn2>0&&iN1>0&&iS1>
      0&&iN2>0&&iS2>0&&cN1>0&&cS1>0&&cN2>0&&cS2>0&&eN1>0&&e
      S1>0&&eN2>0&&eS2>0&&xlN1>0&&xcN1>0&&xeN1>0&&xnN1>0&&
      xlS1>0&&xcS1>0&&xeS1>0&&xnS1>0&&xlN2>0&&xcN2>0&&xe2>0&
      &xnN2>0&&xlS2>0&&xcS2>0&&xnS2>0&&ΛS1>0&&c3>0&&xl3>0
      &&Sn3>0},
   {SkN1,SkS1,Sk2,SnN1,SnS1,Sn2,iN1,iS1,iN2,iS2,cN1,cS1,cN2,cS2,eN1,eS1,e
      N2,eS2,xlN1,xcN1,xeN1,xnN1,xlS1,xcS1,xeS1,xnS1,xlN2,xcN2,xe2,xnN2,
      xlS2,xcS2,xnS2,T1,T2,ΛS1,c3,xl3,Sn3},
Method–>{"SimulatedAnnealing","Tolerance"–>10^(–6),"Perturbation
      Scale"–>0.05},MaxIterations–>500],2];
Module[{txc3=vc*qn*xe2/.output,txn3=vn*qn*xe2/.output,txe3=(1+g)*
      xe2/.output,tSk3=(1+g)*qk*xe2/.output,ti3=piSk2/.output,txl3=xl3/.
      output},output=Flatten[Append[output,{xc3–>txc3,xn3–>txn3,
      xe3–>txe3,Sk3–>tSk3,i3–>ti3,x3–>txl3+txc3+txn3+txe3}]]];
```

Tests

```
Print["TESTS"];Print["Constraints evaluated at the solution"];
primalconst=Round[(({{c1a,c1b,c1c,c1d},{c2a,c2b,c2c,c2d},{c3a,c3b,c3c,c3d},
      {c4a,c4b},{c5a,c5b,c5c,c5d},{c6a,c6b,c6c,c6d,c6e},{c7a,c7b,c7c},{c8a
      ,c8b}}/.output)*10^5]/10.^5;
tempfunc[x_,y_]:=Flatten[{x,y}];Print[MapThread[tempfunc,{{"(1):","(2):",
      "(3):","(4):","(5):","(6):","(7):","(8):"},primalconst}]//TableForm];
      ClearAll[tempfunc];Print["\!\(\*SubsuperscriptBox[\(u\),\(1\),\(S\)]\)>=
      (1+ρ)\!\(\*SubsuperscriptBox[\(u\),\(0\),\(S\)]\)\[DoubleLongLeftArrow]",
      (ΛS1–(1+ρ)*uS0>=0)/.output];
```

Sustainable, Convergent Path

```
uN1=fu[cN1,xlN1,SnN1,Sm2]/.output;
uN2=fu[cN2,xlN2,Sn2,Sm2]/.output;
uN3=fu[c3,xl3,Sn3,Smstar]/.output;
uN4=ρρ*uN3;
uS1=fu[cS1,xlS1,SnS1,Sm2]/.output;
uS2=fu[cS2,xlS2,Sn2,Sm2]/.output;
uS3=fu[c3,xl3,Sn3,Smstar]/.output;
uS4=ρρ*uS3;
upathline=ListLinePlot[{{{0,uN0},{1,uN1},{2,uN2},{3,uN3},{4,uN4}},{{0,uS0},
      {1,uS1},{2,uS2},{3,uS3},{4,uS4}}},AxesLabel->{"\!\(\*StyleBox[\"Genera
      tions\",\nFontSize->14,\nFontSlant->\"Italic\"]\)","\!\(\*StyleBox
      [\"Utility\",\nFontSize->14]\)"},Mesh->All,PlotStyle->{Directive[Thick
      ness[.004],Gray], {AbsoluteThickness[2]}},PlotMarkers->{"\!\(\*Style
      Box[\"N\",\nFontSize->14,\nFontWeight->\"Bold\"]\)","\!\(\*Style
      Box[\"S\",\nFontSize->14,\nFontWeight->\"Bold\"]\)"}];
```

B.5. Subroutine *TwoRegionWorld2.m*

Growth Factors

```
ρ=(1+ρannum)^25−1;ρρ=1+ρ;
g=(1+ρ)^(1/(αc+αl+αn))−1;gg=1+g;
```

Steady-State Ray

```
RayParam={
   vn=(g+δn)/k3,
   pi=(g+δk)/k2,
   pc=(1−(1−δk)/k4)*((1+g)/(k2*θk))−pi,
   vl=(1−(1−δn)/k4)*(αl/k3)*(pc/(αc*θn*(pc+pi)+αn*pc))*(1+g),
   vc=(1−(1−δn)/k4)*((αc*θc)/k3)*((pc+pi)/(αc*θn*(pc+pi)+αn*pc))*(1+g),
   qn=(k4−(1+g))/(vl+vn+vc),
   qk=((k1*vc^θc)/(pc+pi))^(1/(θc+θn))(1+g)^((θk+θn)/(θc+θn))*qn*eWstar
      ^(θe/(θn+θc))*Smstar^(θm/(θn+θc))};
```

Constraints

```
Which[CFlows==0,T1=T2=0,
   CFlows==1,ClearAll[T1,T2],
   True, Print["Please choose CFlows∈{0,1}"];Quit[ ]];
c1a=(1− δk)*SkN0*NN0/NN1+k2*iN1−SkN1;
c1b=(1−δk)*SkN1*NN1/NN2+k2*iN2−Sk2;
```

```
c1c=(1–δk)*SkS0*NS0/NS1+k2*iS1–SkS1;
c1d=(1–δk)*SkS1*NS1/NS2+k2*iS2–Sk2;
c2a=(1–δn)*SnS0*NS0/NS1+k3*xnS1+k3d*(SnN0–SnS0)*xnS1–SnS1;
c2b=(1–δn)*SnS1*NS1/NS2+k3*xnS2+k3d*(SnN1–SnS1)*xnS2–Sn2;
c2c=(1–δn)*SnN0*NN0/NN1+k3*xnN1–SnN1;
c2d=(1–δn)*SnN1*NN1/NN2+k3*xnN2–Sn2;
c3a=ξ*xeN0*NN0/NN1–xlN1–xcN1–xeN1–xnN1;
c3b=ξ*xeN1*NN1/NN2–xlN2–xcN2–xe2–xnN2;
c3c=ξ*xeS0*NS0/NS1–xlS1–xcS1–xeS1–xnS1;
c3d=ξ*xeS1*NS1/NS2–xlS2–xcS2–xe2–xnS2;
c4a=e1–NN1/(NN1+NS1)*eN1–NS1/(NN1+NS1)*eS1;
c4b=e2–NN2/(NN2+NS2)*eN2–NS2/(NN2+NS2)*eS2;
c5a=–T1+k1*xcN1^θc*SkN1^θk*SnN1^θn*eN1^θe*Sm1^θm–cN1–iN1;
c5b=–T2+k1*xcN2^θc*Sk2^θk*Sn2^θn*eN2^θe*Sm2^θm–cN2–iN2;
c5c=T1*NN1/NS1+k1*xcS1^θc*SkS1^θk*SnS1^θn*eS1^θe*Sm
      1^θm–cS1–iS1;
c5d=T2*NN2/NS2+k1*xcS2^θc*Sk2^θk*Sn2^θn*eS2^θe*Sm2^θm–cS2–iS2;
c6a=cN1^αc*xlN1^αl*SnN1^αn*(Smhat–Sm1)^αm–(1+ρ)*uN0;
c6b=cN2^αc*xlN2^αl*Sn2^αn*(Smhat–Sm2)^αm–(1+ρ)*cN1^αc*xlN1^αl*
      SnN1^αn*(Smhat–Sm1)^αm;
c6c=cS1^αc*xlS1^αl*SnS1^αn*(Smhat–Sm1)^αm–(1+ρ)*uS0;
c6d=cS2^αc*xlS2^αl*Sn2^αn*(Smhat–Sm2)^αm–ΛS2;
c6e=c3^αc*xl3^αl*Sn3^αn*(Smhat–Smstar)^αm–(1+ρ)*cN2^αc*xlN2^αl*
      Sn2^αn*(Smhat–Sm2)^αm;
c7a=Sk2–qk*xe2;
c7b=Sn2–qn*xe2;
c7c=Sn3–gg*qn*xe2;
c8a=c3–pc*qk*xe2;
c8b=xl3–vl*qn*xe2;
```

Optimization Program

```
output=Part[NMaximize[{ΛS2,
  c1a>=0&&c1b>=0&&c1c>=0&& c1d>=0&&
  c2a>=0&&c2b>=0&&c2c>=0&&c2d>=0&&
  c3a>=0 && c3b>=0 && c3c>=0 && c3d>=0 &&
  c4a>=0 && c4b>=0 &&
  c5a>=0 && c5b>=0 && c5c>=0 && c5d>=0 &&
  c6a>=0 && c6b>=0 && c6c>=0 && c6d>=0 && c6e>=0 &&
  c7a==0 && c7b==0 && c7c==0 &&
  c8a==0 && c8b==0 &&
  SkN1>0&&SkS1>0&&Sk2>0&&SnN1>0&&SnS1>0&&Sn2>0&&iN1>0&&iS1
     >0&&iN2>0&&iS2>0&&cN1>0&&cS1>0&&cN2>0&&cS2>0&&eN1>0&&
     eS1>0&&eN2>0&&eS2>0&&xlN1>0&&xcN1>0&&xeN1>0&&xnN1>0&
     &xlS1>0&&xcS1>0&&xeS1>0&&xnS1>0&&xlN2>0&&xcN2>0&&xe2>0
```

```
&&xnN2>0&&xlS2>0&&xcS2>0&&xnS2>0&&ΛS2>0&& c3>0 && xl3>0
    && Sn3>0},
  {SkN1, SkS1, Sk2, SnN1, SnS1, Sn2,iN1, iS1, iN2, iS2, cN1, cS1, cN2, cS2,eN1,
    eS1, eN2, eS2, xlN1, xcN1, xeN1, xnN1, xlS1, xcS1, xeS1, xnS1, xlN2,
    xcN2, xe2, xnN2, xlS2, xcS2, xnS2, T1, T2,ΛS2,c3,xl3,Sn3},
Method->{"SimulatedAnnealing","Tolerance"->10^(-6),"Perturbation
    Scale"->0.05},MaxIterations->500],2];
Module[{txc3=vc*qn*xe2/.output,txn3=vn*qn*xe2/.output,txe3=(1+g)
    *xe2/.output,tSk3=(1+g)*qk*xe2/.output,ti3=pi*Sk2/.output,txl3=
    xl3/.output}, output=Flatten[Append[output,{xc3-> txc3,xn3->
    txn3,xe3-> txe3,Sk3-> tSk3,i3-> ti3,x3-> txl3+txc3+txn3+txe3}]]]];
```

Tests

```
Print["TESTS"];Print["Constraints evaluated at the solution"];
primalconst=Round[({{c1a,c1b,c1c,c1d},{c2a,c2b,c2c,c2d},{c3a,c3b,c3c,c3d},
    {c4a,c4b},{c5a,c5b,c5c,c5d},{c6a,c6b,c6c,c6d,c6e},{c7a,c7b,c7c},{c8a
    ,c8b}}/.output)*10^5]/10.^5;
tempfunc[x_,y_]:=Flatten[{x,y}];Print[MapThread[tempfunc,{{"(1):","(2):",
    "(3):","(4):","(5):","(6):","(7):","(8):"},primalconst}]//TableForm];
    ClearAll[tempfunc];Print["\!\(\*SubsuperscriptBox[\(u\),\(2\), \(S\)]\)>=
    (1+ρ)\!\(\*SubsuperscriptBox[\(u\), \(1\), \(S\)]\) \[DoubleLongLeft
    Arrow]",(ΛS2-(1+ρ)*uS1>=0)/.output];
```

Sustainable, Convergent Path

```
uN1=fu[cN1,xlN1,SnN1,Sm2]/.output;
uN2=fu[cN2,xlN2,Sn2,Sm2]/.output;
uN3=fu[c3,xl3,Sn3,Smstar]/.output;
uN4=ρρ*uN3;
uS1=fu[cS1,xlS1,SnS1,Sm2]/.output;
uS2=fu[cS2,xlS2,Sn2,Sm2]/.output;
uS3=fu[c3,xl3,Sn3,Smstar]/.output;
uS4=ρρ*uS3;
upathline=ListLinePlot[{{{0,uN0},{1,uN1},{2,uN2},{3,uN3},{4,uN4}},{{0,uS0},
    {1,uS1},{2,uS2},{3,uS3},{4,uS4}}},AxesLabel->{"\!\(\*StyleBox[\"Genera
    tions\", \nFontSize->14,\nFontSlant->\"Italic\"]\)","\!\(\*StyleBox
    [\"Utility\", \nFontSize->14]\)"},Mesh-> All,PlotStyle->{Directive[Thi
    ckness[.004],Gray], {AbsoluteThickness[2]}}, PlotMarkers->{"\!\(\*Style
    Box[\"N\",\nFontSize->14,\nFontWeight->\"Bold\"]\)","\!\(\*StyleBox
    [\"S\",\nFontSize->14,\nFontWeight->\"Bold\"]\)"}];
```

References

Acemoglu, Daron, Philippe Aghion, Leonardo Bursztyn, and David Hemons. 2012. "The environment and directed technological change." *American Economic Review* 102(1): 131–166.

Ackerman, Frank, Stephen J. DeCanio, Richard B. Howarth, and Kristen Sheeran. 2009. "Limitations of integrated assessment models of climate change." *Climate Change* 95: 297–315.

Albala-Bertrand, Jose Miguel, and Hao Feng. 2007. "Net capital stock and capital productivity for China and regions: 1960–2005. An optimal consistency method." London: Department of Economics Working Paper 610. Queen Mary University.

Aldy, Joseph, and Robert Stavins. 2012. "Climate negotiators create an opportunity for scholars." *Science* 337: 1043–1044.

Alley, R. B., J. Marotzke, W. D. Nordhaus, J. T. Overpeck, D. M. Peteet, R. A. Pielke Jr., R. T. Pierrehumbert, P. B. Rhines, T. F. Stocker, L. D. Talley et al. 2003. "Abrupt climate change." *Science* 299: 2005–2010.

Arneson, Richard. 1989. "Equality and equality of opportunity for welfare." *Philosophical Studies* 56: 77–93.

Arrow, Kenneth J. 2007. "Global climate change: A challenge to policy." *Economists' Voice*. Berkeley Electronic Press, http://www.bepress.com/ev, June 1–5.

Bai, Chong-En, Chang-Tai Hsieh, and Yingyi Qian. 2006. "The return to capital in China." *Brookings Papers on Economic Activity* 2: 61–101.

Barrett, Scott. 1992. "Economic growth and environmental preservation." *Journal of Environmental Economics and Management* 23(3): 289–300.

Barro, Robert J., and Jong-Wha Lee. 2013. "A new data set of educational attainment in the world, 1950–2010." *Journal of Development Economics*.

Barro, Robert J., and Xavier Sala-i-Martin. 1999. *Economic Growth*. Cambridge, MA: MIT Press.

Basu, Kaushik, and Tapan Mitra. 2007. "Utilitarianism for infinite utility streams: A new welfare criterion and its axiomatic characterization." *Journal of Economic Theory* 133: 350–373.

Benhabib, Jess, and Mark Spiegel. 2005. "Human capital and technology diffusion." In Philippe Aghion and Steven N. Durlauf, eds., *Handbook of Economic Growth* 1A. Amsterdam: North-Holland Elsevier.

Blackorby, Charles, Walter Bossert, and David Donaldson. 2005. *Population Issues in Social Choice Theory, Welfare Economics, and Ethics*. New York: Cambridge University Press.

Blackorby, Charles, and David Donaldson. 1984. "Social criteria for evaluating population change." *Journal of Public Economics* 25: 13–33.

Bureau of Economic Analysis (BEA). 2013. "National Economic Accounts." http://www.bea.gov/national/. Accessed July 31, 2013.

Bureau of Labor Statistics (BLS). 2012. "Occupational Employment Statistics." http://www.bls.gov/oes/tables.htm.

———. 2013. "Current Employment Statistics (CES) 1990–2011." http://www.bls.gov/ces/.

Cabeza Gutés, Maite. 1996. "The concept of weak sustainability." *Ecological Economics* 17(3): 147–156.

Cai, Yongyang, Kenneth L. Judd, and Thomas S. Lontzek. 2013. "The social cost of stochastic and irreversible climate change." National Bureau of Economic Research Working Paper Series no. 18704.

Christian, Michael S. 2010. "Human capital accounting in the United States, 1994–2006." *Survey of Current Business* 90(5): 31–36.

Clark, Colin W. 1990. *Mathematical Bioeconomics*. 2nd ed. New York: John Wiley & Sons.

Cohen, Gerald A. 1989. "On the currency of egalitarian justice." *Ethics* 99: 906–944.

Colman, Andrew M. 2006. "Thomas C. Schelling's psychological decision theory: Introduction to a special issue." *Journal of Economic Psychology* 27: 603–608.

Comin, Diego, and Bart Hobijn. 2010. "An exploration of technology diffusion." *American Economic Review* 100(5): 2031–2059.

Cooley, Thomas F., and Gary D. Hansen. 1992. "Tax distortions in a neoclassical monetary economy." *Journal of Economic Theory* 58(2): 290–316.

Cooley, Thomas F., and Edward C. Prescott. 1995. "Economic growth and business cycles." In *Frontiers of Business Cycle Research*. Princeton, NJ: Princeton University Press.

Dasgupta, Partha. 2005. "Three conceptions of intergenerational justice." In H. Lillehammer and D. H. Mellor, eds., *Ramsey's Legacy*. Oxford: Oxford University Press.

———. 2008. "Discounting climate change." *Journal of Risk & Uncertainty* 37: 141–169.

d'Aspremont, Claude, and Louis Gevers. 1977. "Equity and the informational basis of collective choice." *The Review of Economic Studies* 44: 199–209.

de Zeeuw, Aart, and Amos Zemel. 2012. "Regime shifts and uncertainty in pollution control." *Journal of Economic Dynamics and Control* 36(7): 939–950.

Diamond, Peter. 1965. "The evaluation of infinite utility streams." *Econometrica* 33: 170–177.

Dietz, Simon, Chris Hope, Nicholas Stern, and Dimitri Zenghelis. 2007. "Reflections on the *Stern Review* (1): A robust case for strong action to reduce the risks of climate change." *World Economics* 8(1): 121–168.

Dworkin, Ronald. 1981. "What is equality? Part 1: Equality of welfare." *Philosophy & Public Affairs* 10: 185–246.

Dyson, Freeman. 2008. "The question of global warming." *New York Review of Books*, June 12.

Eaton, Jonathan, and Samuel Kortum. 1999. "International technology diffusion: Theory and measurement." *International Economic Review* 40: 537–570.

Engelbrecht, Hans-Jurgen. 2002. "Human capital and international knowledge spillovers in TFP growth of a sample of developing countries: An exploration of alternative approaches." *Applied Economics* 34(7): 831–841.

Fisher, Anthony C., John V. Krutilla, and Charles J. Cicchetti. 1972. "The economics of environmental preservation: A theoretical and empirical analysis." *American Economic Review* 62(4): 605–619.

Fleurbaey, Marc. 2009. "Beyond the GDP: The quest for a measure of social welfare." *Journal of Economic Literature* 47(4): 1029–1075.

Fleurbaey, Marc, and Didier Blanchet. 2013. *Beyond GDP: Measuring Welfare and Assessing Sustainability*. Oxford: Oxford University Press.

Freeman, Richard B. 1986. "Demand for education." In Orley Ashenfelter and Richard Layard, eds., *Handbook of Labor Economics*, vol. 1. Amsterdam: North-Holland.

Friedlingstein, Pierre, and Susan Solomon. 2005. "Contributions of past and present human generations to committed warming caused by carbon dioxide." *Proceedings of the National Academy of Sciences* (PNAS) 102(31): 10832–10836.

Gao, Jian, and Gary H. Jefferson. 2007. "Science and technology take-off in China? Sources of rising R&D intensity." *Asia Pacific Business Review* 13(3): 357–371.

Gerlagh, Reyer, and Bob van der Zwaan. 2002. "Long-term substitutability between environmental and man-made goods." *Journal of Environmental Economics and Management* 44: 329–345.

Gerschenkron, Alexander. 1962. *Economic Backwardness in Historical Perspective: A Book of Essays*. Cambridge, MA: Belknap Press of Harvard University Press.

Goldin, Claudia, and Lawrence F. Katz. 2008. *The Race between Education and Technology*. Cambridge, MA: Harvard University Press.

Gordon, H. Scott. 1954. "The economic theory of a common property resource: The fishery." *Journal of Political Economy* 62: 124–142.

Gordon, Robert J. 2012. "Is US economic growth over? Faltering innovation confronts the six headwinds." NBER Working Paper 18315.

Gronau, Reuben. 1986. "Home production: A survey." In Orley Ashenfelter and Richard Layard, eds., *Handbook of Labor Economics*, vol. 1. Amsterdam: North-Holland.

Gu, Wulong, and Ambrose Wong. 2010. "Estimates of human capital in Canada: The lifetime income approach." Economic Analysis Research Paper Series 62. Statistics Canada.

Hall, Robert E., and Charles I. Jones. 2007. "The value of life and the rise in health spending." *Quarterly Journal of Economics* 102(1): 39–72.

Hansen, James, Inez Fung, Andrew Lacis, David Rind, Sergej Lebedeff, Reto Ruedy, Gary Russell, and Peter Stone. 1988. "Global climate changes as forecast by Goddard Institute for Space Studies three-dimensional model." *Journal of Geophysical Research* 93: 9341–9364.

Hartman, Richard. 1976. "The harvesting decision when a standing forest has value." *Economic Inquiry* 14(1): 52–58.

Hartwick, John M. 1977. "Intergenerational equity and the investment of rents from exhaustible resources." *American Economic Review* 67(5): 972–974.

Heckman, James J. 1976. "A life-cycle model of economics, learning and consumption." *Journal of Political Economy* 84: S11–S44.

Hope, Chris. 2006. "The marginal impact of CO_2 from PAGE2002: An integrated assessment model incorporating the IPCC's five reasons for concerns." *Integrated Assessment Journal* 6(1): 19–56.

Johnson, D. Gale. 2000. "Population, food, and knowledge." *American Economic Review* 90(1): 1–14.

Jones, Charles I., and Peter J. Klenow. 2010. "Beyond GDP? Welfare across countries and time." NBER Working Paper no. 16352.

Jones, Charles I., and John Williams. 1998. "Measuring the social return to R&D." *Quarterly Journal of Economics* 113: 1119–1135.

Kaldor, Nicholas. 1961. "Capital accumulation and economic growth." In F. A. Lutz and D. C. Hague, eds., *The Theory of Capital*. New York: St. Martin's Press.

Karp, Larry S. 2013. "Provision of a public good with altruistic overlapping generations and many tribes." Available at SSRN: http://dx.doi.org/10.2139/ssrn.2298180.

Keeler, Emmett, Michael Spence, and Richard Zeckhauser. 1972. "The optimal control of pollution." *Journal of Economic Theory* 4(1): 19–34.

Keller, Wolfgang. 2004. "International technology diffusion." *Journal of Economic Literature* 42: 752–782.

Keynes, John M. 1930. "Economic possibilities for our grandchildren." Part I, *The Nation and Athenaeum* 48(2): 36–37; Part II, *The Nation and Athenaeum* 48(3): 96–98. Reprinted in John M. Keynes. 1931. *Essays in Persuasion*. London: Macmillan.

Kongsamut, Piyabha, Sergio Rebelo, and Danyang Xie. 2001. "Beyond balanced growth." *Review of Economic Studies* 68(4): 869–882.

Koopmans, Tjalling C. 1960. "Stationary ordinal utility and impatience." *Econometrica* 28: 287–309.

Leibowitz, Arleen. 1975. "Education and the allocation of women's time." In F. Thomas Juster ed., *Education, Income, and Human Behavior*. New York: McGraw-Hill, NBER Books.

Lemoine, Derek, and Christian Traeger. 2014. "Watch your step: Optimal policy in a tipping climate." *American Economic Journal: Economic Policy* 6(1): 137–166.

Lenton, Timothy M., Hermann Held, Elmar Kriegler, Jim W. Hall, Wolfgang Lucht, Stefan Rahmstorf, and Hans Joachim Schellnhuber. 2008. "Tipping elements in the Earth's climate system." *Proceedings of the National Academy of Sciences* 105(6): 1786–1793.

Li, Haizheng, and Jeffrey S. Zax. 2003. "Labor supply in urban China." *Journal of Comparative Economics* 31(4): 795–817.

Llavador, Humberto, John E. Roemer, and Joaquim Silvestre. 2010. "Intergenerational justice when future worlds are uncertain." *Journal of Mathematical Economics* 46: 728–761.

———. 2011. "A dynamic analysis of human welfare in a warming planet." *Journal of Public Economics* 95: 1607–1620.

———. 2013. "Should we sustain? And if so, sustain what? Consumption or quality of life?" In Roger Fouquet, ed., *Handbook of Energy and Climate Change*, 639–665. London: Palgrave.

———. 2014. "North-South convergence and the allocation of CO_2 emissions." *Climatic Change*, August. DOI: 10.1007/s10584-014-1227-8.

Lucas, Robert E. Jr. 1988. "On the mechanics of economic development." *Journal of Monetary Economics* 22: 3–42.

Maskin, Eric. 1978. "A theorem on utilitarianism." *The Review of Economic Studies* 45: 93–96.

Meadows, Donella H., Dennis L. Meadows, Jørgen Randers, and William W. Behrens III. 1972. *The Limits to Growth: A Report for the Club of Rome's Project on the Predicament of Mankind*. London: Earth Island Press.

Meinshausen, Malte, S. J. Smith, K. Calvin, J. S. Daniel, M. L. T. Kainuma, J. F. Lamarque, K. Matsumoto et al. 2011. "The RCP greenhouse gas concentrations and their extensions from 1765 to 2300." *Climatic Change* 109(1–2) (November 1): 213–241.

Michael, Robert T. 1972. "The effect of education on efficiency in consumption." NBER Occasional Paper 116, New York: Columbia University Press.

———. 1973. "Education in nonmarket production." *Journal of Political Economy* 81(2, part 1): 306–327.

Ministry of Science and Technology (MOST). 2000. "China Science and Technology Statistics Data Book (1998–2000)." http://www.most.gov.cn/eng/statistics/.

Mirrlees, James. 1967. "Optimum growth when technology is changing." *Review of Economic Studies* 67: 95–124.

National Bureau of Statistics of China. 2012. *China Statistical Yearbook 2012*.

National Science Foundation. 2003. "Division of Science Resources Statistics." Arlington, VA. http://www.nsf.gov.

———. 2013. "National Patterns of R&D Resources: 2010–11 Data Update." NSF 13-318. Detailed Statistical Tables. National Center for Science and Engineering Statistics. http://www.nsf.gov/statistics/nsf13318/pdf/nsf13318.pdf.

Nelson, Richard R., and Edmund S. Phelps. 1966. "Investment in humans, technological diffusion, and economic growth." *American Economic Review* 56(1/2): 69–75.

Neumayer, Eric. 1999. "Global warming: Discounting is not the issue, but substitutability is." *Energy Policy* 27: 33–43.

———. 2001. "The human development index and sustainability: A constructive proposal." *Ecological Economics* 39: 101–114.

———. 2010. *Weak versus Strong Sustainability: Exploring the Limits of Two Opposing Paradigms* (3rd ed.). Cheltenham, UK: Edward Elgar.

Nordhaus, William D. 1976. "Economic growth and climate: The problem of carbon dioxide." Cowles Foundation for Research in Economics Discussion Paper no. 435. New Haven, CT: Yale University.

———. 1977. "Strategies for the control of carbon dioxide." Cowles Foundation for Research in Economics Discussion Paper no. 443. New Haven, CT: Yale University.

———. 1991. "To slow or not to slow: The economics of the greenhouse effect." *Economic Journal* 101: 920–937.

———. 1994. *Managing the Global Commons: The Economics of Climate Change.* Cambridge, UK: Cambridge University Press.

———. 2007. "A review of the *Stern Review on the economics of climate change.*" *Journal of Economic Literature* 45: 686–702.

———. 2008a. *A Question of Balance.* New Haven, CT: Yale University Press.

———. 2008b. *The DICE Model.* http://www.econ.yale.edu/~nordhaus/homepage/DICE2007.htm.

———. 2010. "Economic aspects of global warming in a post-Copenhagen environment." *Proceedings of the National Academy of Sciences* 107(26): 11721–11726.

———. 2013. *The Climate Casino.* New Haven, CT: Yale University Press.

Nordhaus, William D., and Joseph Boyer. 2000. *Warming the World.* Cambridge, MA: MIT Press.

Nordhaus, William D., and Paul Sztorc. 2013. *DICE 2013R: Introduction and User's Manual,* online publication. http://www.econ.yale.edu/~nordhaus/homepage/documents/DICE_Manual_100413r1.pdf.

Nordhaus, William D., and James Tobin. 1972. "Is growth obsolete?" In *Economic Growth,* National Bureau of Economic Research. New York: Columbia University Press.

Nozick, Robert. 1974. *Anarchy, State, and Utopia.* New York: Basic Books.

Oeppen, Jim, and James W. Vaupel. 2002. "Broken limits to life expectancy." *Science* 296: 1029–1031.

Officer, Lawrence, and Samuel H. Williamson. 2008. "Measures of Worth." *MeasuringWorth.* http://www.measuringworth.org.

Oreopoulos, Philip, and Kjell G. Salvanes. 2011. "Priceless: The nonpecuniary benefits of schooling." *Journal of Economic Perspectives* 25(1): 159–184.

Ortigueira, Salvador. 1999. "A dynamic analysis of an endogenous growth model with leisure." *Economic Theory* 16: 43–62.

Page, Edward A. 2006. *Climate Change, Justice and Future Generations.* Cheltenham, UK: Edward Elgar.

———. 2011. "Climatic justice and the fair distribution of atmospheric burdens." *Monist* 94: 412–432.

Parfit, Derek. 1984. *Reasons and Persons.* Oxford: Oxford University Press.

Perkins, Dwight H., and Thomas G. Rawski. 2008. "Forecasting China's economic growth to 2025." In Loren Brandt and Thomas G. Rawski, eds., *China's Great Economic Transformation*, ch. 20. Cambridge, UK: Cambridge University Press.

Phelps, Edmund. 1961. "The golden rule of capital accumulation: A fable for growthmen." *American Economic Review* 51(4): 638–643.

Piketty, Thomas. 2014. *Capital in the Twenty-First Century.* Cambridge, MA: Belknap Press of Harvard University Press.

Popp, David. 2004. "ENTICE: Endogenous backstop technology in the DICE model of global warming." *Journal of Environmental Economics and Management* 48(1): 742–768.

———. 2006. "ENTICE-BR: The effects of backstop technology R&D on climate policy models." *Energy Economics* 28: 188–222.

Ramsey, Frank. 1928. "A mathematical theory of saving." *Economic Journal* 38: 543–559.

Rawls, John. 1971. *A Theory of Justice.* Cambridge, MA: Harvard University Press.

Rebelo, Sergio. 1991. "Long-run policy analysis and long-run growth." *Journal of Political Economy* 99: 500–521.

Roemer, John E. 1996. *Theories of Distributive Justice.* Cambridge, MA: Harvard University Press.

———. 2009. "Equality: Its justification, nature, and domain." In Wiemer Salverda, Brian Noland, and Timothy M. Smeeding, eds., *The Oxford Handbook of Economic Inequality.* Oxford: Oxford University Press.

———. 2011. "The ethics of intertemporal distribution in a warming planet." *Environmental and Resource Economics* 48: 363–390.

Rogoff, Kenneth. 2012. "Rethinking the growth imperative." *Project Syndicate.* http://www.project-syndicate.org/commentary/rethinking-the-growth-imperative.

Rose, Adam, Brandt Stevens, Jae Edmonds, and Marshall Wise. 1998. "International equity and differentiation in global warming policy." *Environmental and Resource Economics* 12: 25–51.

Sarofim, Marcus C., Chris E. Forest, David M. Reiner, and John M. Reilly. 2005. "Stabilization and global climate policy." *Global and Planetary Change* 47: 266–272.

Schelling, Thomas. 1960. *The Strategy of Conflict.* Cambridge, MA: Harvard University Press.

Schneider, Maik T., Christian P. Traeger, and Ralph Winkler. 2012. "Trading off generations: Equity, discounting, and climate change." *European Economic Review* 56: 1621–1644.

Scott, Anthony D. 1955. "The fishery: The objectives of sole ownership." *Journal of Political Economy* 63(2): 116–124.

Sidgwick, Henry. 1907. *The Methods of Ethics*. London: Macmillan.

Silvestre, Joaquim. 2002. "Progress and conservation under Rawls's maximin principle." *Social Choice & Welfare* 19: 21–27.

Skidelsky, Robert, and Edward Skidelsky. 2012. *How Much Is Enough?* New York: Other Press.

Solow, Robert M. 1956. "A contribution to the theory of economic growth." *Quarterly Journal of Economics* 70: 65–94.

———. 1974. "Intergenerational equity and exhaustible resources." *Review of Economic Studies, Symposium on the Economics of Exhaustible Resources* 41: 29–45.

———. 1993. "An almost practical step toward sustainability." *Resources Policy* 19: 162–172.

Song, Jian. 2008. "Awakening: Evolution of China's science and technology policies." *Technology in Society* 30(3–4): 235–41.

Stern, Nicholas. 2006. *Stern Review on the Economics of Climate Change (Pre-Publication Edition). Executive summary*. London: HM Treasury.

———. 2007. *The Economics of Climate Change: The Stern Review*. Cambridge, UK: Cambridge University Press.

———. 2008. "The economics of climate change." *American Economic Review: Papers & Proceedings* 98(2): 1–37.

Stiglitz, Joseph E., Amartya Sen, and Jean-Paul Fitoussi. 2009. "Sarkozy report." *Report by the Commission on the Measurement of Economic Performance and Social Progress (CMEPSP)*. http://www.stiglitz-sen-fitoussi.fr/en/documents.htm.

Swan, Trevor W. 1956. "Economic growth and capital accumulation." *Economic Record* 32: 334–361.

United Nations. 2013. "World Population Prospects: The 2012 Revision." Population Division of the Department of Economic and Social Affairs. http://esa.un.org/unpd/wpp/index.htm. Accessed August 8, 2013.

United Nations Development Programme (UNDP). 1990. *Human Development Report 1990*. http://hdr.undp.org/en/reports/global/hdr1990/.

———. 2010. *Human Development Report 2010*. New York: Palgrave Macmillan.

———. 2013. *Human Development Report 2013*. New York: Palgrave Macmillan.

United Nations Environment Program (UNEP). 2011. *Bridging the emissions gap*. United Nations Environment Programme.

Uzawa, Hirofumi. 1965. "Optimal technical change in an aggregative model of economic growth." *International Economic Review* 6: 18–31.

Vaillancourt, Kathleen, Richard Loulou, and Amit Kanudia. 2008. "The role of abatement costs in GHG permit allocations: A global stabilization scenario analysis." *Environmental Modeling and Assessment* 13: 169–179.

Valentinyi, Akos, and Berthold Herrendorf. 2008. "Measuring factor income shares at the sector level." *Review of Economic Dynamics* 11(4): 820–835.

van der Ploeg, Frederick, Aart de Zeeuw. 2014. "Climate tipping and economic growth: Precautionary saving and the social cost of carbon." OXCarre Research Paper 118.

van Vuuren, Detlef P., Jae Edmonds, Mikiko Kainuma, Keywan Riahi, Allison Thomson, Kathy Hibbard, George C. Hurtt et al. 2011. "The Representative Concentration Pathways: An overview." *Climatic Change* 109(1–2) (November 1): 5–31.

van Vuuren, Detlef P., Michel G. J. den Elzen, Paul L. Lucas, Bas Eickhout, Bart J. Strengers, Bas van Ruijven, Steven Wonink, Roy van Houdt. 2007. "Stabilizing greenhouse gas concentrations at low levels: An assessment of reduction strategies and costs." *Climatic Change* 81: 119–159.

van Vuuren, Detlef P., Elke Stehfest, Michel G. J. den Elzen, Tom Kram, Jasper van Vliet, Sebastiaan Deetman, Morna Isaac et al. 2011. "RCP2.6: Exploring the possibility to keep global mean temperature increase below 2°C." *Climatic Change* 109(1–2): 95–116.

Wagner, Ulrich J. 2014. "Estimating a Strategic Model of Treaty Formation: The Case of the Montreal Protocol." Available at SSRN: http://dx.doi.org/10.2139/ssrn.1730183.

Wang, Yan, and Yudong Yao. 2003. "Sources of China's economic growth, 1952–1999: Incorporating human capital accumulation." *China Economic Review* 14(1): 32–52.

Wei, Hui. 2008. "Developments in the estimation of the value of human capital in Australia." Australian Bureau of Statistics.

Weitzman, Martin L. 2007. "A review of the *Stern Review on the economics of climate change*." *Journal of Economic Literature* 45: 703–724.

———. 2012. "GHG targets as insurance against catastrophic climate damages." *Journal of Public Economic Theory* 14: 221–244.

Wolf, Martin. 2007. "Education is a worthwhile end in itself." *The Financial Times*, February 1.

World Bank. 2013. "World Development Indicators." World Bank Group. http://databank.worldbank.org. Accessed August 8, 2013.

World Commission on Environment and Development. 1987. "Our Common Future." *The Brundtland Report*. Oxford: Oxford University Press.

World Resources Institute. 2013. "Climate Analysis Indicators Tool (CAIT 2.0)." http://cait2.wri.org/wri. Accessed August 8, 2013.

Xu, Bin, and Eric P. Chiang. 2005. "Trade, patents and international technology diffusion." *Journal of International Trade and Economic Development* 14(1): 115–135.

Index

DATE DUE
